A
Advances
N
in Nursing
S
Science Series

D1523683

Developing Substance
Mid-Range Theory in Nursing

Peggy L. Chinn, RN, PhD, FAAN

Editor, *Advances in Nursing Science*
Associate Dean for Academics
Faculty Associate,
Center for Human Caring
University of Colorado School of Nursing
Denver, Colorado

An Aspen Publication®
Aspen Publishers, Inc.
Gaithersburg, Maryland
1994

Library of Congress Cataloging-in-Publication Data

Developing substance : mid-range theory in nursing / [edited by] Peggy
L. Chinn.
p.   cm. — (Advances in nursing science series)
Articles reprinted from Advances in nursing science.
Includes bibliographical references and index.
ISBN 0-8342-0578-5
1. Nursing models. 2. Nursing--Philosophy.
I. Chinn, Peggy L. II. Advances in nursing science. III. Series.
[DNLM: 1. Nursing Theory—collected works.
WY 86 D4898 1994]
RT84.5.D49   1994
610.73′01—dc20
DNLM/DLC
for Library of Congress
94-7364
CIP

Aspen Publishers, Inc. grants permission for photocopying for limited personal or internal use.
This consent does not extend to other kinds of copying, such as copying for
general distribution, for advertising or promotional purposes, for creating new collective
works, or for resale. For information, address Aspen Publishers, Inc.,
Permissions Department, 200 Orchard Ridge Drive, Suite 200,
Gaithersburg, Maryland 20878.

Editorial Resources: Ruth Bloom

Library of Congress Catalog Card Number: 94-7364
ISBN: 0-8342-0578-5
Series ISBN: 0-8342-0576-9

Printed in the United States of America

1   2   3   4   5

Table of Contents

Preface

There are numerous collections of broad nursing theories, and books that contain writings of nurse theorists that are foundational to the discipline of nursing. Mid-range theories that focus on specific nursing phenomena have not yet appeared in nursing texts, but rather as isolated journal articles that reflect various stages of development of substantive theory.

In 1987, Meleis (1987) called for a shift toward the development of mid-range theories that focus on specific, rather than general nursing phenomena. Mid-range theories are closely linked to practice, reflect the practice values and knowledge of the discipline, and form the basis for challenging and developing substantive knowledge that can form the basis for practice. Mid-range theories do not provide prescriptions for practice, nor do they provide specific practice guidelines. Rather, this type of theory provides a specific conceptual focus and mental image built on foundational concepts and values of the discipline. The focus of mid-range theory is viewed through the lens of the foundational concepts and values of the discipline, but shifts away from the broad concepts to more specific, practice-oriented processes and phenomena.

The articles selected for inclusion in this volume have been published in *Advances in Nursing Science* since 1980, and illustrate the range of conceptual focus around which mid-range theory is emerging in the discipline. The foundational concepts and values found in the emerging body of mid-range theory published in *Advances in Nursing Science* include health and wholeness, social and cultural context, growth and development, caring and relationship, diversity and complexity. The phenomena of theoretical focus include such things as crisis, stress, protection, social support, life-style change, and self-transcendence. Often the theory is also focused on a specific population, such as the elderly, adolescents, women, or people with a specific type of health problem.

The articles included in this volume represent a wide range of method and stage of development in the theory-building process. Some of these articles focus on critique of existing theories, often found in other disciplines, viewed through the lens of nursing's perspective. In this type of article, the article includes suggested directions for development of mid-range theory in nursing. Other articles present evidence from practice or research from which a theory or model for nursing practice is derived. The articles in this volume are presented not as a definitive set of nursing's mid-range theories, but rather as a collection illustrative of the emerging possibilities for developing mid-range theory in nursing. This volume is an important contribution toward the re-visions with which Meleis has challenged the profession. Many more volumes are needed to meet this challenge.

—*Peggy L. Chinn, RN, PhD, FAAN*
Editor, Advances in Nursing Science

REFERENCE

Meleis, AI. ReVisions in knowledge development: A passion for substance. *Scholarly Inquiry for Nursing Practice.* 1987; 1 (1), 5–19.

Crisis Theory and Intervention: A Critique of the Medical Model and Proposal of a Holistic Nursing Model

Suzanne M. Narayan, RN, MSN
Instructor
School of Nursing
Wright State University
Consultant
Crisis Services
Eastway Community Mental Health Center

Daniel J. Joslin, RN, MS
Coordinator
Crisis Team
Eastway Community Mental Health Center
Mental Health Consultant
Miami Valley Hospital
Dayton, Ohio

THE THEORETICAL framework of crisis intervention has evolved over the past decades. Numerous writers, including Lindemann, Caplan, Parad and Rapaport, have contributed to the development of crisis theory.[1-4] Despite the abundance of literature on crisis, crisis theory and crisis intervention continue to be poorly understood techniques without common meaning for the mental health professions as a whole.

As Korchin noted, "At this point crisis intervention is more an orientation and a way of thinking than a systematic body of theory, knowledge and practice."[5(p509)] One result of the lack of solid theory base has been several efforts to align crisis with other theoretical schemes. Taplin gives two examples of this: linkage of the concept of crisis first with the notion of homeostasis and then with psychoanalytic theory.[6] A third conceptual influence on crisis theory has been the medical model as focused on the concept of mental illness. Each approach, however, has decided shortcomings.

Adv Nurs Sci 1980;2(4):27–39

There is one other, possibly viable alternative: alignment of crisis theory with a nursing model. Such an approach could overcome many of the shortcomings of contemporary modes of crisis intervention. It would emphasize the growth-producing aspects of crisis, rather than dwell on its pathogenic quality. Adoption of a nursing model in crisis intervention could, in fact, be a significant step toward realization of the concept of holistic health.

HISTORICAL PERSPECTIVE: CRISIS THEORY AND THE MEDICAL MODEL

Erikson's Model

The concept of crisis grew out of psychoanalytic theory and its foundations were laid by the egopsychologists, among them Allport, Maslow and Erikson.[7–9] Erikson in particular developed an eight-stage model of social growth and development based on the notion that psychosocial development proceeds in a series of crisis or critical periods and that a person's degree of success in passing through one stage will influence his or her ability to move to the next.[9] Erikson's theory is significant because it explains the individual's psychosocial development on the basis of encounters with the social environment. An additional, relevant aspect is Erikson's exposition of the healthy rather than the pathological development of human interactions. His work has been used by crisis theorists in formulating the concept of maturational crises and has served as a springboard for those who followed and continue to delineate situational crises. It is worth noting that many of Erikson's ideas are being seriously challenged by feminist scholars. Several of his statements have had a profound effect on the thinking of others in regard to women's psychological development and on the therapies provided for women undergoing conflicts in relation to their psychosocial development. Among his ideas is the notion that a woman's identity crisis is and ought to be tied to two factors: the search for the man by whom she wishes to be chosen, and a "biological, psychological and ethical commitment to take care of human infancy."[10(p586)]

Lindemann's Theories

Erich Lindemann is widely regarded as one of the pioneers of crisis theory. His classic paper on grief explored bereavement as an example of emotional crisis and provided a description of the course and resolution of grief reactions and some guidelines regarding how professionals could assist the bereaved in working through the stages of grief.[1] He believed that the type of intervention used in grief resolution could also be applied to other life crises, both situational and developmental, and that mental disorders could be prevented through the use of such interventions. In short, Lindemann believed that the importance of crisis intervention was its potential usefulness for prevention of mental illnesses, hence its medical model influence.

Lindemann also proposed that the prevention of mental disorder could be achieved on a community-wide basis by using a public health model. A preventive approach based on a public health model would seek to reduce the rate of new cases of mental illness in a population over a specified time period by counteracting harmful circumstances before they had a chance to produce illness. Writing from the perspective of a physician and a psychiatrist, Lindemann never questioned such issues as the definition of mental illness, how one would define a "new case," what harmful circumstances produce mental illness, and the conflicts implicit in one group choosing to "prevent" mental illness in a community as a whole.

Caplan's Findings

Gerald Caplan, through his work with Lindemann and through other studies, further evolved the concept of crisis periods in the development of individuals and groups.[2,11]

Among his critical observations were the following:

1. The individual is seen as living in a state of emotional equilibrium with the goal always to return to or maintain that state.
2. Life can be viewed as a succession of crisis events that occur within the life span of each individual and these crises upset the equilibrium of the individual.
3. Crisis is a transitional point in a person's life that is marked by cognitive and emotional upset. While not in itself a sign of mental disorder, crisis seems to be a manifestation of adjustment and adaptation in the face of a temporarily insoluble problem.
4. Crisis is precipitated by identifiable antecedents, usually of a situational or interpersonal nature. Examples include bereavement, marriage, the birth of a child, a job loss or promotion.
5. Crisis has a definite course in time and is self-limiting, lasting from four to six weeks and consisting of four phases.
6. Crisis is more accessible to intervention at its peak and may be resolved adaptively or maladaptively.
7. Crisis can be seen as a turning point toward or away from mental disorder. Histories of unsuccessful crisis resolution increase the probability of unsuccessful crisis resolution in the future. In fact, Caplan views mental disorder as the end product of a pattern of nonreality-based solutions of life problems.
8. Crisis intervention is an important part of primary prevention of mental disorders as a whole.

Limitations of Caplan's Findings

Caplan's propositions warrant a more detailed examination. In further delineating his crisis model, Caplan borrowed the concept of homeostasis from the field of physiology, adding an aura of "medical respectability" to his endeavor.[6] His application of the concept is weak in that the analogy between physiological processes such as correction of an imbalance by secretion of a hormone is only superficially similar to resolving a problem through the use of new coping strategies.

Limited applicability of homeostasis

The homeostasis model is limited in the range of human behavior and mental life that it explains. According to this model, behavior consists of drive reduction, gratification of biological needs, relaxation of tension, adjustment, reestablishment of psychological, social, physiological balance, and so on.[12] The theoretical core of homeostasis does not account for processes of increasing order such as learning, growth, change, actualization. Indeed, women and men are constantly seeking out psychological disruptions, creatively exploring alternatives in living, thinking and feeling. The evolution of humankind would not have occurred if homeostasis ruled psychological functioning.

In relation to crisis, homeostatic notions shed no light on concepts associated with psychological functioning such as feelings, relationships, perceptions and skills. As Taplin noted, homeostasis is essentially content free.[6] An additional problem is that homeostasis cannot in itself differentiate between adaptive and maladaptive imbalances. In essence, the homeostasis model adds little to the theoretical structure of crisis.

Deviation from homeostasis as an index of functioning is commonly associated with a physiological view of health. To date, most medically oriented crisis theorists have outlined ways to prevent maladaptive reactions to stress or to return to "normal" individuals who have already strayed from the norm. No theorist has addressed a process by which the ongoing health level of the individual can be buttressed or the manner in which crises can be utilized to improve beyond the norm, the general level of functioning of the individual. At best this aspect of crisis intervention has received minimal attention.

Problems in defining mental illness

A second major criticism of Caplan's exposition of the crisis model is the linkage of crisis with the concept of mental illness. This alignment was implicit in Lindemann's studies, but Caplan makes it explicit.[11] Although he stops short of stating that crisis is a sign of mental illness, mental illness is the pivotal concept upon which crisis is based. For Caplan, crisis is a way station on the road toward or away from mental illness, with emphasis given to its pathogenic quality. From this standpoint crisis can be viewed as a precursor of mental illness. Neither Lindemann nor Caplan clearly delineated what he meant by "mental illness," although the assumed existence of the condition is crucial and there is no single unitary concept of what mental illness is. This is aptly demonstrated by Kessler and Albee's description of mental illnesses as "conditions which are not clearly defined, which vary in rate enormously as a function of community tolerance for deviance, which change frequencies with changing social conditions, and which may not even exist as identifiable individual defects."[13(p560)]

Ambiguous applications

It seems reasonable to expect that one might find an operational definition of mental illness in the literature of the epidemiology of mental illness—the branch of knowledge that studies the prevalence and incidence, distribution and determinants of mental illness states in populations. Most studies have defined cases, the basic units of epidemiologic study, in terms of admission to psychiatric treatment. Although this is operationally a clear definition, in practice the implications are ambiguous. Treatment rates vary with the availability of facilities and with public attitudes toward their use. As a result, practical and reliable case-finding techniques do not exist.[14] The original problem of defining mental illness remains.

A flawed analogy?

Several writers, including Szasz, Chesler, Laing and Scheff, have questioned the usefulness of the concept of mental illness.[15-18] Szasz points out that much of the support for the concept of mental illness derives from an analogy with physical illness.[15] According to this analogy, while physical illnesses affecting various organ systems (such as the heart, kidneys, lungs) manifest symptoms attributable to those body parts, those mental illnesses that affect the brain manifest themselves through mental symptoms. These mental symptoms are typically statements of belief such as the idea that one's behavior is being directed by the voices of demons or that one's bodily organs are decaying. Unlike physical symptoms these mental symptoms cannot be ascribed to a particular brain lesion. Moreover, none of the other components of the medical model including cause, uniform and invariate symptoms, and treatment of choice has been reliably demonstrated for any of the major mental illnesses.

Inapplicable norms

A second area of conflict in comparing physical and mental illness occurs in the type of standard or norm against which the pathological state is measured. While Szasz's argument has certain weaknesses, which will become more apparent when holistic health is discussed, it does highlight some of the problems associated with the physical illness analogy as applied to mental illness.

In physical disease, the norm that is typically applied is the structural and physiological integrity of the body. Although one can view health as a value (and in this sense it is an ethical proposition), physical health can also be described objectively in terms of physiology and anatomy. On the other hand, the norm or standard by which mental illness is judged is open to many interpretations. Whatever the norm or standard it is often phrased in subjective terms using ethical, legal or psychosocial concepts. Some examples will serve to clarify this statement.

The notion that promiscuity, chronic anger and lying are signs of mental illness demonstrates the use of ethical norms to define mental illness (implied are the desirability of marital fidelity or monogamy, love toward others, and truth). An example of a legal norm would be the proposition that only a mentally ill person would commit rape. Concepts such as "an overactive superego" or "motivation by an unconscious death wish" typify the use of psychological concepts as standards of mental health or illness. Thus the norm from which mental illness is the deviation is an ethical, legal or psychological standard. Yet, following the illness analogy, the corrective approach that is applied is a medical one. The conflict between the nature of the problem and the proposed remedy has powerful and dangerous significance.

Who defines norms and standards?

A major question raised by the application of a medical approach is, who defines what the norms and standards are and, by inference, their deviations? In some instances it is the individual client who determines that she or he deviates from a norm. For example, a novelist may determine that she or he has writer's block and may seek help for her- or himself from a psychotherapist. In other cases it is some other person who determines that the individual is deviant—for example a family member, friend, physician, law officer, member of the clergy or other societal agent. A psychiatrist or other therapist may then be selected by someone other than the client to "deal" with the problem and "correct" the deviant behavior. The latter situation not uncommonly leads to involuntary commitment to a psychiatric institution.

What is the relevance of these arguments to the exposition of the concept of crisis? Owing to the lack of consensus regarding the meaning of mental illness, the linkage of crisis with mental illness fails to clarify what crisis is. At best, such an alignment endows crisis with all the confusion and variability associated with the concept of mental illness. At worst, it imbues crisis and its treatment with all the negative features associated with the medical model and its disease-oriented approach.

The Community Mental Health Movement

Various forces have served to create the community mental health movement, many of them based in a medically oriented context. Among these has been the psychiatric community's growing recognition since World War II that "mental illness" is a major public health problem. Coupled with this was the development of new tranquilizing drugs which proved more effective than prior treatments in decreasing the anxieties and bizarre behaviors of clients, so that they could be returned to the community setting. Use of these pharmacologic agents facilitated the emptying of state hospitals and raised hopes that indeed "mental illnesses" were treatable. The geographical decentralization of the large state hospitals served to bring hospital personnel into closer contact with professionals in the community and triggered piecemeal growth of the numbers of community-based mental health agencies.

The increasing involvement of the federal government in funding and policymaking decisions about mental health care accelerated the movement toward more community-based care. Three particular governmental acts spearheaded the development of community mental health programs: the 1961 Report of the Joint Commission on Mental Illness and Health, President Kennedy's 1963 message on mental illness, and the consequent 1963 passage of the Community Mental Health Centers Construction Act. It is clear from the wording of the pronouncements and enabling legislation that community mental health was to be under the ideological guidance of proponents of the medical model.

Crisis Intervention

One of the newly emerging mental health technologies that was viewed as having value both as a preventive and as a treatment approach was crisis intervention.

Proponents of community mental health latched on to crisis intervention as a therapeutic approach for a number of reasons. First was their acceptance of Caplan's proposition that the client is more receptive to clinical intervention during a crisis. Along with this was the attractiveness of a time-limited treatment approach which would reach a larger number of clients without a concomitant increase in demand for additional staff. In addition there were the preventive implications of crisis intervention. This line of thinking followed directly from Lindemann's belief that crisis intervention techniques, utilized within a public health framework, could reduce the subsequent incidence of mental illness. To a greater extent than the other two reasons for interest in crisis intervention, this rationale arose from a commitment to a medical model view of mental health problems. Here again is the analogy with physical illness, the need to find a causative agent and to eliminate it from the environment. The variables that have been identified as contributing to "psychopathology" include such factors as poverty, slums and lower social class. The important thing to note here is that reactions to these stressors are laid to psychopathology rather than to a less medically oriented formulation.

Social tampering

Application of medical solutions to these problems, such as the removal of causative agents, raises major questions as to the "right" of community health professionals to tamper, on a large scale, with social conditions of such magnitude. It is worthy of note that, in actual practice, the financial priority given to the preventive aspects of crisis intervention has been low in comparison with the funding of the treatment component, a fact quite consistent with a medical model perspective.

Rationales

The clinical literature on crisis intervention documents the medical orientation of the writers and the impact of the medical model on client care. Some examples will illustrate the trend. Jacobson et al., in describing a crisis intervention program at Benjamin Rush Center in Los Angeles, offer the following rationale for the use of crisis intervention: "Early intervention provides the occasion and the instrumentality for preventive psychiatric treatment in much the same way that acute physical disease is served by medical care brought to bear soon after the physical disease is disclosed."[19(p138)] The authors' acceptance of the medical model with its emphasis on disease and symptom treatment is quite evident .

Normand and associates describe a similar walk-in crisis intervention program and discuss the goals of crisis treatment in that setting.[20] They view the goals of crisis intervention not as cure but as symptom amelioration and reestablishment of the previous more effective state of psychological equilibrium. They place little emphasis on addressing the root causes of the problems resulting in crisis and, in fact, anticipated a pattern of repeated intervention. They see the treatment approach as comparable to the way in which persons use a medical clinic or physicians. Treatment is aimed at the presenting problem and often is nonspecific. The "patient" feels better and stops coming. The "illness" may recur and the "patient" can return for further treatment, or exacerbations in the course of a chronic illness can be handled as they appear. This type of health care approach is very narrow in focus and seems geared primarily toward illness maintenance.

A review of literature on clinical applications of crisis intervention documented a definite trend toward the offering of crisis intervention primarily to lower socioeconomic clients.[20–28] This is consistent with the aim of community mental health to provide services to the entire community, including the frequently neglected segments.

Proponents of the use of crisis intervention as the treatment of choice with lower socioeconomic clients offer a rationale based on the following characteristics:

1. The lower socioeconomic client's time perspective is more limited than that required for a formal treatment regimen.
2. For such a person there is difficulty in appreciating the value of treatment if its rewards are delayed for a lengthy period.
3. The cultural and social values of the lower socioeconomic client do not include consideration of psychotherapeutic contracts in which the main elements are "talk" about the self and one's life experiences.
4. There are language deficits that clearly inhibit comprehension and pursuit of the goals of traditional therapy.

These characteristics are felt to render the lower socioeconomic client a poor candidate for most traditional therapies, while crisis intervention is seen as an ideal fit for the lower socioeconomic client owing to its short duration and here-and-now orientation.

A caste system

The foregoing discussion reflects the well-ordered caste system of medical practice, with the "doctor" or "expert" on top and the patient in the subordinate position, powerless and acted upon by the "wiser" intervener. In this system, the client is viewed as the passive recipient of diagnoses, prescriptions and treatment. Additionally, lower socioeconomic clients, by virtue of their limiting characteristics, are seen as most suitable for only certain types of therapy.

A fundamental goal of crisis intervention is the restoration of the individual to a precrisis level of functioning. How appropriate is a crisis intervention approach with a lower socioeconomic client or family with multiple medical, socioeconomic, psychological and cultural problems? To establish a brief therapeutic relationship and identify the one or two most pressing problems as the focus of that therapy and then rapidly return the client to a severely deprived and depriving environment can hardly be deemed in the best interests of the client. Clearly there is need for a concept of crisis that accounts for its unique characteristics and advantages but at the same time overcomes the disadvantages of previous theoretical alignments.

A NURSING MODEL OF CRISIS AND HOLISTIC CARE

In recent years, nursing has become disenchanted with traditional approaches to health and illness care. This disenchantment has led to a reexamination of the concept of health and the role of the nurse in providing health care to clients. Increasingly nursing has begun to align itself with the concepts of health and wellness in contrast to medicine's traditional alignment with illness and disease states.

This alignment is reflected in the growing nursing literature devoted to elaboration of concepts such as high-level wellness, maximum health potential and holistic health.[29-31]

Components of Holistic Health

These concepts of health share certain things in common. First is that health is more than the absence of disease or symptoms. It implies the unity of all aspects of the individual: mind, body and spirit. No one aspect can be separated from the others. Such a view of health incorporates the genetic makeup of the individual, developmental patterns, the interaction of person and environment and processes such as learning and self-actualization.

Second, humans are open systems and subsystems of other systems such as the family and other groups. Within this open system the individual continually strives toward greater order, complexity and self differentiation. From this one can infer that humans are capable of learning, acquiring knowledge, building cognitive maps or schema and designing and choosing strategies for coping with life events. One can also infer that the healthy individual must have a clear sense of "who I am" and "where I am going," an organizing sense of self and life purpose.

A third aspect is that one's attitudes, values, perceptions and beliefs affect one's health and can lead to alterations in one's health status.

Fourth, maximum health requires the allocation of various resources or supplies from within and without the individual. These comprise matter, energy and information.[32]

Fifth, health can be conceived as existing on a continuum with the maximum state of health on one end and death on the other. This view allows for a healthy set of attitudes toward death and for a healthy living style even in the face of imminent death.[33] Such a view of health implies that change in health states is possible and that the individual can be at different states at different times as the result of a variety of factors. If one accepts the premise that maximum health requires allocation of sufficient resources, then it is logical that movement away from a maximum health state would involve the expenditure and eventual exhaustion of these resources.

A sixth aspect of this view of health is that the focus of health and healing exists within the individual. The nurse can act as catalyst or facilitator for healing, but change in the health state can come only from within the individual. Thus the responsibility for one's health rests with the individual.

The final notion is that states of health that are not maximal can be opportunities for growth and learning if adequately utilized by the individual. In keeping with this view, the symptoms are not the focus; rather, the interruption in balance among the mind-body-spirit aspects is the focus.

Nursing Model of Crisis

With respect to the model of health as described above, the concept of crisis would seem to best fit the state of depleted health potential. This health state occurs when there is an "alteration in the dynamic pattern of functioning whereby there is an inability to interact with internal and external forces as the result of a temporary or permanent loss of necessary resources."[34 (p137)] Depleted health potential can be viewed as part of the health continuum. At its extreme, depleted health would lead to disorganization, entropy and, finally, death of the individual.

A useful nursing model should incorporate and explain the observations of crisis and crisis behavior, and overcome the deficits of the medical model alignment. A preliminary outline of such a model utilizing the concept of depleted health and incorporating the components of crisis is developed below.

In accordance with the components of health listed earlier, the individual is conceived as a purposeful, thinking, problem-solving being who from time to time during the life span will encounter obstacles to life goals. Such obstacles may be in the form of precipitating events of a sudden, unexpected nature or those that are of gradual onset but occur during a period of developmental transition. In either case these precipitating events involve a threat to the sense of self and life purpose often in the form of a real or perceived loss. The individual responds to the obstacle by utilizing past knowledge and coping strategies in attempts to remove the obstacle. The person's perceptions, attitudes and values affect how the obstacle is viewed and the types of strategies used to remove it. In addition, the individual's resources—both inner and outer sources of strength and support—are mobilized to provide assistance in the situation. If these attempts are abortive, the individual will begin to experience increased tension and anxiety and eventually, if the threat is not relieved, or the perceptions of the situation are not altered, or the resources are inadequate to deal with the obstacle, disorganization and depletion of the individual's health state will occur.

Evidence from research into cognitive processes supports the existence of a phenomenon that Olson and Lubach term *floundering,* the point at which there is too much conflicting information entering for processing to enable the individual to carry out normally the usual planning and implementation functions.[35] One might anticipate that this would occur at the peak of crisis. At this time, the individual could be characterized as more sensitive to proffered assistance than after the peak point has passed. This floundering state is a temporary one. It is so energy-depleting that either some type of resolution, whether healthy and growth-enhancing or unhealthy and growth-restricting, occurs or eventually exhaustion and death ensue.

Implications for Holistic Care

In keeping with the notion that minimal health states can provide opportunities for growth and learning, one can view crisis as a situation in which perceptions of self and life purpose are open to question, when old patterns of behavior have proved ineffective, when, in essence, the person is at a turning point. The nursing model, as opposed to the medical model of crisis, emphasizes the potential growth enhancement that crisis offers rather than its pathogenic quality. Thus the nurse assists the individual in moving beyond the baseline functioning manifested prior to crisis. Deviation from the norm is not seen necessarily as rooted in pathology and therefore moving the client back within the bounds of "normative functioning" is not the expressed goal of holistic nursing care.

Nursing is in agreement with the traditional crisis tenet that past successes in resolving crisis tend to increase the likelihood of future successes in crisis resolution. However, within the nursing model major emphasis is given to the growth-producing aspects of crisis while the medical model of crisis gives these scant attention.

Table 1 illustrates a comparison between the medical and the holistic nursing models of crisis. In contrast to the medical model of crisis, which views the physician as the expert who utilizes crisis intervention to alleviate symptoms and restore the individual to psychological equilibrium, the nursing model sees the nurse as a facilitator who helps generate within the client the potential for achieving self growth and a more creative, healthy life pattern. The ultimate responsibility for health, however, remains with the client. Accordingly, nurse and client would work together to monitor the client's health status. Within this context, the client's perceptions and values in regard to how well he or she is functioning and the need for, desirability of and direction of change are of paramount importance. Change

Table 1. A Comparison of the Medical and Holistic Nursing Models of Crisis

	Medical Model	**Holistic Nursing Model**
View of behavioral deviation	Crisis is viewed as a precursor of mental illness.	Crisis is viewed as a potential opportunity for growth and self-enhancement.
Aim/goal of therapy	Restoration of level of functioning prior to crisis.	Promotion and growth of client through learning about self in relation to the crisis.
Activity of therapist	Physician assesses and gives a prescriptive response to a passive patient.	Nurse facilitates client's potential for self-growth.
Role of client and therapist	Patient complies with prescribed regimen. Patient's values are not a significant part of therapeutic considerations. A dependent relationship is encouraged.	Client collaborates with nurse in assessing, developing plan and evaluating care. Client's values and perceptions are a vital therapeutic consideration. Reciprocity and self-care are encouraged.

would be aimed at achieving a more harmonious integration of the mind, body and spirit of the client. That is the essence of holistic nursing care.

REFERENCES

1. Lindemann E. Symptomatology and Management of Acute Grief. *Amer J Psychiatry.* 1944; 101 (4): p. 141–148.
2. Caplan G. *Principles of Preventive Psychiatry.* New York: Basic Books, 1964.
3. Parad H. *Crisis Intervention: Selected Readings.* New York: Family Service Association of America, 1965.
4. Rapaport L. The State of Crisis: Some Theoretical Considerations. In Parad, H. J, ed. *Crisis Intervention: Selected Readings.* New York: Family Service Association of America 1965.
5. Korchin, S. *Modern Clinical Psychology: Principles of Intervention in the Clinic and Community.* New York: Basic Books, 1956.
6. Taplin JR. Crisis Theory: Critique and Reformulation. *Community Ment Health J.*1971; 7 (1): 13–23.
7. Allport GW. *Pattern and Growth in Personality.* New York: Holt, Rinehart, and Winston, 1961.
8. Maslow A. *Motivation and Personality* 2nd ed. New York: Harper & Row, 1970.
9. Erikson EH. *Childhood and Society* 2nd ed. New York: W. W. Norton and Co., 1963.
10. Erikson EH. Inner and Outer Space: Reflections on Womanhood. *Daedalus.* 1964; 93 (2):582–606.
11. Caplan G. *An Approach to Community Mental Health.* New York: Grune and Stratton, 1961.
12. Von Bertalanffy L. General Systems Theory and Psychiatry–An Overview. In Gray W, Duhl FJ, and Rizzo, ND, eds. *General Systems Theory and Psychiatry.* Boston: Little, Brown and Co., 1969, p. 33–46.

13. Kessler M, Albee GW. Primary Prevention. *Annu Rev Psychol.* 1975; 26: 557–591.
14. Dohrenwend BP. Psychiatric Epidemiology as a Knowledge Base for Primary Prevention in Community Psychiatry and Community Mental Health. In Serban G, ed. *New Trends of Psychiatry in the Community.* Cambridge, Mass: Ballinger Publishing Co., 1977.
15. Szasz T. *Ideology and Insanity.* New York: Anchor Books, 1970.
16. Chesler P. *Women and Madness.* New York: Doubleday, 1972.
17. Laing RD, Esterson A. *Sanity, Madness and the Family.* London: Tavistock Publication, 1964.
18. Scheff TJ. *Labeling Madness.* Englewood Cliffs, NJ: Prentice-Hall, 1975.
19. Jacobson GF et al. The Scope and Practice of an Early-Access Brief Treatment Psychiatric Center. In Barten HH, ed. *Brief Therapies.* New York: Behavioral Publications, Inc., 1971.
20. Normand WC, Gensterheim H, Schrenzel S. A Systematic Approach to Brief Therapy for Patients from a Low Socioeconomic Community. In Barten HH, ed. *Brief Therapies.* New York: Behavioral Publications Inc., 1971.
21. Allgeyer J. The Crisis Group–Its Unique Usefulness to the Disadvantaged. *Int J Group Psychother.* 1970; 20 (2):235–240.
22. Block S. An Open-ended Crisis-oriented Group for the Poor Who Are Sick. *Arch Gen Psychiatry.* 1968; 19 (2): 178–185.
23. Jacobson FG. Crisis Theory and Treatment Strategy: Some Sociocultural and Psychodynamic Considerations. *J Nerv Ment Dis.* 1965; 141 (2):209–218.
24. Lazare A. et al. The Walk-in Patient as a Customer: A Key Dimension in Evaluation and Treatment. *Am J Orthopsychiatry.* 1972; 42 (5):872–883.
25. Morley W, Brown V. The Crisis Intervention Group: A Natural Mating or a Marriage of Convenience? *Psychotherapy: Theory, Research, and Practice.* 1969; 6 (1):30–36.
26. Morales HM. Bronx Mental Health Center. *New York State Division Bronx Bulletin.* 1971; 13 (8): 6.
27. Rabiner EL, Wells CF, Yager J. A Model for the Brief Hospital Treatment of the Disadvantaged Psychiatrically Ill. *Am J Orthopsychiatry.* 1973; 43 (5):774–782.
28. Seward G. *Psychotherapy and Cultural Conflict.* New York: Ronald Press, 1972.
29. Bermost LS, Porter SE. *Women's Health and Human Wholeness.* New York: Appleton-Century-Crofts, 1979.
30. Dunn HL. *High-Level Wellness.* Arlington, Va: Beatty, 1973.
31. "Salk: Holistic Health Approach Inevitable in 'Epoch B.' " *Brain-Mind Bulletin: Frontiers of Research, Theory and Practice 2* (September 19, 1977) p. 3.
32. Hart SK, Herriott PR. Components of Practice: A Systems Approach. In Hall J, Weaver B, eds. *Distributive Nursing Practice: A Systems Approach to Community Health.* Philadelphia: J. B. Lippincott Co., 1977.
33. Simonton C. et al. *Getting Well Again.* Los Angeles: J. P. Tarcher, Inc., 1978.
34. "Glossary of Terms" Self-Evaluation Report Submitted to the National League for Nursing September, 1979, Wright State University, Dayton, Ohio.
35. Olson B, Lubach JE. Innovation in the Nursing Role in a Psychiatric Program. *Am J Nurs.* 1966; 66 (2):314–318.

A Stress-Coping Model

Diane W. Scott, RN, PhD
Nurse Scientist

Marilyn T. Oberst, RN, EdD
Director

Mary Jo Dropkin, RN, MSN
Research Associate
Department of Nursing Research
Memorial Sloan-Kettering Cancer Center
New York, New York

A MODEL or scientific paradigm, according to Thomas Kuhn,[1] is a set of interrelated assumptions about classes of phenomena. Models have a heuristic value, in that they have a closely linked protocol or set of procedures for observing and analyzing the phenomena. For an applied discipline such as nursing, models can be useful because they combine theoretical assumptions, research-based knowledge, diagnostic problem-solving, and clinical intervention. A model is a link between concept and action, and can function as a tool to coordinate the structure and process of a research program designed to improve the effectiveness and therapeutic value of nursing practice.

Development of a stress-coping framework or model for nursing research has been attempted by Goosen and Bush,[2] and Roy.[3] Numerous other frameworks with possible utility for nursing exist.[4,5-22] However, as Wild and Hanes[21] indicate, framework development is incomplete given the lack of continuity of basic theoretical and operational constructs. Few attempts have been made to develop a dynamic model—one which maps the entire adjustive process and recognizes the complete interaction between individual and environment.

One stress-coping model, described later, has been developed as a conceptual framework for a department of nursing research in an acute care cancer center and will be used as a theoretical foundation for studies the department undertakes.

BACKGROUND

Stress

Stress arises from a transaction between individual and environment when the individual construes stimuli as damaging, threatening, or challenging. In general, stress situations involve awareness of demands that tax or exceed available re-

Adv Nurs Sci 1980;3(1):9–23

sources as appraised by the individual. Demands can be of several types: social, cultural, psychological, and physiological, but basically each represents a change in balance between the demand and the resources to deal with it. Stressors, or stimuli that produce stress, differ in quality and intensity for each individual, and they may act together to augment, intensify, or reduce the total effect. Stress threshold and tolerance levels differ with each person, and depend on genetic and constitutional make-up, past experience, self-concept and other factors. Stress is particularly important in health because it has the potential to impair human functioning.[23]

Beginning with the work of Hans Selye,[24] researchers have sought, over the past three decades, to describe and analyze the effects of stress. Selye and others found that the demands imposed on a person by internal and external environments can cause difficulty, fatigue, exhaustion, and even death, if not counterbalanced by forces that contribute to maintaining his or her integrity. How the human organism maintains integrity was the subject of further research in the 1970s. From that work a science of stress, coping, and adaptation has evolved.

A substantial branch of stress research has addressed itself to the physical and physiological manifestations of stress. In the initial phase of stress exploration, Selye[24] proposed and demonstrated a general syndrome arising from the application of specific physical stresses to animals. His *general adaptation syndrome* and its characteristic physiology dominated the experimental domain until recently. Mason et al[25] proposed more specific responses based on the type of stressor and the associated functioning of specific hormonal axes and their many related substrates.

The trend in stress analysis research is heavily in favor of a cognitively based theory.[26–30] Stress is a generic entity involving many variables working in concert rather than any one specific negative emotion, stimulus, or response. This idea has moved stress research from an emotion or arousal context to one in which the individual's interpretation and evaluation of a stimulus-filled environment becomes the basis for a response to the stress experience, and in which emotions and physiological responses are viewed as by-products of cognition.

The cognitive branch of stress research is based on Piaget's developmental psychology, according to which innate schemata are the underlying basis for growth and life. Piaget described the interaction between person and environment as an assimilation-accommodation process whereby people assimilate the environment and accommodate their own structure to learn and survive.[31] Using this framework, other cognitive psychologists suggest that a mental operation underlies and affects the physiological level of response.

Some researchers using a cognitive approach identify levels of awareness or consciousness and their variations over time and experience in humans in the normal course of living. Levels of consciousness, information, representation (imagery, conceptualization and language), and the chemical and structural bases of memory are basic components of the cognitive process.[32] Proponents of the cognitive interpretation of stress such as Averill and Opton,[33] Lazarus,[4,23] Monat and Lazarus[34] and others have outlined an appraisal process whereby the individual continuously scans the environment for stimuli and then operates upon it through a careful and continual evaluation of threat to system survival.

The essential point of the cognitive approach is that in the critical progression of events occurring after stressor-person impact, cognitive functioning occurs which encompasses all neurological levels of system control, autonomic regulation, elicitation of feeling states, sensory selection processes, and individual and species preservation; and the cortical structure contributions of memory and mental operation. The latter two functions, taken together, form a basis for thought and evaluation.

Coping

Study of the dynamics of adaptation has focused on the natural counterpart to stress, known as coping. The multiplicity of coping strategies utilized to bring about change and growth is seen as the linkage between stressor impact and adaptation. Lazarus,[23] in his systematic model of the stress-coping process, identifies two elements of coping: (1) problem-solving and (2) regulation of emotion. He emphasizes that cognitive appraisal of the stress situation occurs as a primary condition, and that emotional and other response categories follow the appraisal.

A constellation of coping strategies, rather than any single one, ultimately brings about adaptation and growth—the maintenance of integrity. Initial direction of the process is controlled by cognition, but the total coping response is comprised of cognitive activity, emotions, and physiological response *in interaction*. Therefore, in the development of a model, literature will be reviewed in terms of cognitive, emotional, and physiological responses to stressor impact and the known options within each.

LITERATURE REVIEW

Cognitive Response to Stress

Although information about the environment is largely processed at the level of the cerebral cortex, subcortical areas of the brain contain important structures through which information processing and arousal are mediated. The cerebral cortex handles memory, symbolic representation, and thinking and reasoning. Several subcortical structures direct sensation to the cortex and are source structures for generalized arousal, certain specific emotions, and visceral regulation for somatic survival. These structures receive feedback through chemical signals from the pituitary gland and autonomic nervous system via the hypothalamus, and some information from the internal and external environment directly.[18] The role of the subcortical nervous system structures as sources of arousal, certain emotions, and somatic integrity has been demonstrated.[35–41] The concept of cognition, then, is expanded to incorporate the broader context of neural control, rather than solely cortical control of emotion and physiological responses. However, coping responses are governed principally by cortical level integration.

Posner[42] has identified two major components of thinking and reasoning ability: (1) mental structure and (2) mental operations. The structure of thinking and reasoning ability includes long- and short-term memory systems and their codes, and the capacity for abstraction and concept formation. Memory has three qualitative codes: (1) imagery, the internal representation of sensory experience; (2) enactive, the learning, reproduction, and preservation of motor skills and movement; and (3) symbolic, the representation of language and other characters that represent reality in another form. Memory is organized so that input can be selected, organized, changed, and retrieved with varying amounts of effort. Abstraction and concept formation allow people to move from the immediate sensation of form, color, and size to identification of patterns and their differences.

Mental operations are considered the dynamic components of thinking and reasoning and include:

1. Tools of symbolic logic: deduction, inference, evaluation, interpretation, and understanding the unstated assumptions with which people operate on perceived stimuli.

2. Levels of consciousness: facilitating both sensory and motor systems and implied by the degree of alertness or changes in performance and brain activity. Generally the more reflexive mental operations are preserved as consciousness decreases. Thatcher and John[32] have identified six levels of information input and processing that correlate with the extent of cortical activity and progressively higher levels of consciousness or awareness: (1) sensation, or reflex response; (2) perception, or interaction between sensation and memory; (3) reorganization of basic processes; (4) processing of multisensory perception as experience; (5) sequential or long-term memory; and (6) symbolic representation and critical thinking. Diurnal patterns, pharmacologic depressants and stimulants, and internal and external environmental conditions, such as amount and rate of stimulus input, age, and physical condition may affect level of cognitive functioning. To comprehend an individual's cognitive coping pattern, understanding of his or her position on the awareness scale described above is essential.

3. Problem solving: the global process by which a person moves from problem identification to solution and evaluation. The objective of problem solving is to achieve new representations through the performance of mental operations.[42] The process includes identifying the problem or initial representation, collecting information or using search strategies, operating on the information or incubation, and determining a solution or termination. Neisser[43] summarizes the process well when he defines cognition as the way in which sensory inputs are "transformed, reduced, elaborated, stored, reconciled and used."

Lazarus[23] has outlined the cognitive process during primary appraisal of the stress situation. The individual's initial evaluation of the stress situation in terms of his or her well-being produces one of three possible appraisals of the stressor: (1) irrelevant; (2) benign, resulting in positively toned emotions; or (3) stressful, resulting in negatively toned emotions. If the stimuli are appraised as stressful, further differentiation occurs and includes: (1) harm or loss, injury or damage already done; (2) threat, anticipated trauma has not yet occurred, assuming a hostile and dangerous environment with the self as lacking in resources to master it; or (3) challenge, opportunity for growth, mastery, or gain, assuming the demands are difficult but not impossible, using existing or acquirable skills. The cognitive phase of the primary appraisal determines the intensity and quality of emotional response to any transaction.

Emotional Response to Stress

The literature reflects considerable disagreement among researchers regarding concepts of emotion. While there is agreement that different emotions exist and are initiated by cognitive processes, many different interpretations of the fundamental dynamics of emotions exist. Researchers also disagree about the exact relationship between outward expressions and their underlying emotions. No consensus exists on whether emotion is a symptom secondary to cognition or an independent entity,[44] but there is growing recognition that affect and cognition are closely linked.

Plutchik et al[45] have developed a systematic model of emotion, identifying four pairs of basic bipolar emotions: (1) fear-anger, (2) joy-sadness, (3) acceptance-distrust, and (4) expectancy-surprise. A constellation of defense mechanisms, diagnostic categories, and behaviors is associated with each bipolar pair. Although Plutchik et al are psychoanalytically oriented, their model does imply that thinking and judgment go into the choice of emotion, and that the specific emotion felt is a product of some objective on the part of the individual.

For the purposes of the present stress-coping model, the defense mechanisms that Plutchik et al associate with specific emotions will be considered general labels for the behavioral response as shown in Table 1.

The model of Plutchik et al differentiates the eight specific emotions qualitatively from anxiety. Anxiety is regarded as general energy arousal that, over time and experience, is refined into specific dominant emotions.

Emotions can vary in both duration and intensity. When an emotion is prolonged over time, according to Weisman,[46] it becomes a *mood*; when prolonged over an even longer period of time, to the extent that the emotional state becomes almost a trait fixed in the personality, it becomes an *attitude*. Arieti[47] has devised a similar classification, but calls the groupings *first-*, *second-*, and *third-order* emotions. Intensity might be defined as complexity or a tightly woven set of emotions that present themselves as a syndrome. Conflict and guilt are examples of the

Table 1. Emotion, Defense, and Behavior

Emotion	Defense	Behavior
Joy	Reaction formation	Hyperactivity
Sadness	Compensation	Attempts to regain loss
		Takes on characteristics of loss
Acceptance	Denial	Overlooks or ignores
Distrust	Projection	Uses blame
Surprise	Regression	Crying
	Fantasy	Daydreaming
	Acting out	Impulse-activity
Anticipation	Intellectualization	Redefines, recategorizes
	Rationalization	Makes excuses
	Undoing	Cancels out
	Sublimation	Transforms direction of energy
Fear	Repression	Forgetting, loss of memory
	Introjection	Nonadmission
	Isolation	Lack of feelings
Anger	Displacement	Attack-like
		Aggressive

Source: Adapted from Plutchik R, Kellerman H, Conte HR: A structural theory of ego defenses and emotions, in Izard CE (ed): *Emotions in Personality and Psychopathology.* New York, Plenum Press, 1979, pp 227–260.

complex interaction of several emotions and represent another dimension of the nature of emotion.

Current understanding of emotion, then, suggests that (1) emotion occurs as a consequence of the person's evaluation of the environment; (2) emotion is a feeling state with physiologic parameters; (3) emotion is experienced initially in global form and later refined into specific basic emotions; (4) emotions may be classified according to type, duration, and intensity—characteristics that change over time and events.

Following the cognitive evaluation of a stressor, a person determines the degree of threat and the resources available to meet the demand. Almost simultaneously, a fluctuation in general anxiety takes place, followed by a refinement of the energy into one or more specific emotions. The resultant response is a translation of the emotion into a behavior. Over time and many reappraisals an emotional response may become increasingly fixed and trait like within the personality, and may play an important role in determining the ultimate adaptation. For the purpose of this model, emotion will be considered an intervening variable having a powerful and direct effect on behavioral response.

Physiological Response to Stress

The literature identifies three major physiologic transmitters of stress reaction: (1) hormonal stimulation, (2) sympathetic activation, and (3) end-organ response. All three are interrelated and interdependent.

The early work of Cannon,[48] later extended by Euler,[49] laid the groundwork for understanding the sympathetic-adrenal-medullary system and its responsiveness to emotion.[26,50] Recent work by Frankenhauser,[51] Levi,[52] and Mason[53] has explored the role of physiology in adaptation to stress in more detail. The sympathetic nervous system provides for neural activation and neurotransmission of chemical substrates through multiple pathways and many levels of integration that assure, by convergence and redundancy, appropriate functional responses when the organism is thrown off balance.[54]

Mason[53,55] has identified a number of neuroendocrine axes, each responding to different emotions and different stressors. The multiple endocrine secretory changes involve growth hormone, prolactin, ACTH and cortisol, luteinizing and follicle-stimulating hormones (androgens, estrogens), thyroid-stimulating hormone and thyroxine, vasopressin, oxytocin, epinephrine and norepinephrine, and insulin. To determine the effect of each axis, Mason used tests of 17-OHCS, epinephrine, norepinephrine, butanol-extractable iodine (thyroid index), growth hormone, insulin, testosterone, ERIO (androgen metabolite), estrone, and urinary volume. Variances in levels of each of these substances in relation to one another have begun to produce certain predictive patterns in response to certain stressors and emotions. In carefully controlled studies, Mason stressed primates with four discrete stressors (heat, cold, hunger, and exercise) and found different patterns or profiles of hormonal excretion in response to each. This finding is important evidence to support a theory of *specific* adaptational response in opposition to Selye's notion of a general arousal response common to all emotion and stress situations. Although Mason and associates have also documented unique hormonal profiles in studies with parents of leukemic children and in army recruits undergoing basic training,[56,57] much more research is needed in this area.

Neural activation by hormonal secretion and sympathetic passage terminates in end-organ response. The classic end-organ reactions are cardiac changes, dilation of coronary vessels, vasodilation in voluntary muscles, vasoconstriction in the intestinal tract, decreased peristalsis, and metabolic actions that mobilize glucose and fat metabolism.[54] In the stress-coping model, neurotransmission occurs simultaneously with emotional response. End-organ changes are considered to be behavioral outcomes of the process.

STRESS-COPING MODEL

A stress-coping model has been developed by the authors to provide theoretical direction for a department of nursing research and as a foundation for generating research proposals. This model represents what Kuhn calls a "class of phenomena" with its set of interrelated assumptions, including those of structure and process.[1]

Structure of the Model

The structure of the stress-coping model is represented by a set of definitions of model components.

Stress: A situation in which environmental demands, internal demands, or both tax or exceed the adaptive resources of an individual, social, or tissue system.[34]

Coping: A process characterized by continuous use of goal-directed strategies that are initiated and maintained over time and across encounters by means of cognitive appraisal and regulation of emotion and physiologic response.[23] Modes of coping include motor and expressive behaviors aimed at neutralizing the stressor(s), and regulation of emotional and physiologic response aimed at preservation of integrity.

Appraisal: The total comprehension of stress including related coping strategies, neurocognitive activity, affective and physiologic responses, and behavioral outcomes. Primary appraisal focuses on evaluation of the stressor array; secondary appraisal and later reappraisals concentrate on effectiveness of coping responses and changes in stress configuration.

Neurocognitive activation: Evaluation of a stimulus array at any given moment in time utilizing the neurocognitive apparatus for stress interpretation.

Affective response: Arousal of a feeling state as a consequence of neurocognitive activation. Characteristics include type, intensity, and duration with close linkage to simultaneously occurring biochemical and physiologic changes. Primary appraisal involves a generalized global anxiety reaction. Secondary appraisal refines the general response into more specific emotions associated with the stress situation. Later reappraisals and ultimate adaptation may reflect mood states and attitudinal development.

Physiological response: Changes in secretion of substances and activation of sympathetic nervous system pathways in response to the cognitive "fight," "flight," or "freeze" command. The pattern of activation generally coordinates with affective response and occurs as a function of neurocognitive evaluation. Primary appraisal reflects a generalized response where pituitary-adrenal axis activity predominates. Secondary appraisal and subsequent reappraisals reflect interaction patterns of multineuroendocrine axes secretion. Ultimate adaptation may reflect cellular, tissue, organ, and system effects of physiologic response over time. Immediate results are measured directly or indirectly through end-organ response.

Behavioral response: All neurocognitive, affective, and physiologic responses to the stress situation may be measured by direct observation of expressive and motor actions, self-report indices, or end-organ response levels. Primary appraisal includes behaviors in response to the stressor impact. Secondary appraisal and subsequent appraisals focus behavior on initial coping strategies and their effectiveness in neutralizing the stress situation.

Adaptation: The result of coping efforts to maintain integrity by establishing balance between demands and the power to deal with them.[23] Desirable outcomes include minimum impairment of human functioning; economical balance among demands, power or resources, and cost; strengthening of assimilation and accommodation modes within the system; growth and learning; achievement of acceptable goals.

The Stress-Coping Process

The process of stress-coping is depicted in the model as a flow of events occurring over time and across encounters. Coping with stress represents a gradual movement toward specified goals and is a necessary characteristic of growth. Coping strategies consist of the neurocognitive, affective, and physiologic responses to a stress situation and may be observed in the behavioral response dimension.

Figs 1 to 3 depict the stress-coping process in increasingly specific terms. Fig 1 shows the process in its broadest, most general form.

The first phase of coping includes a primary appraisal consisting of a neurocognitive evaluation of the stress configuration, the initial affective response, the corresponding physiologic response, and the resultant composite cop-

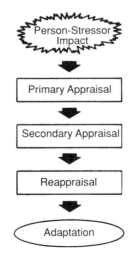

Fig 1. Stress-coping process (over time and events).

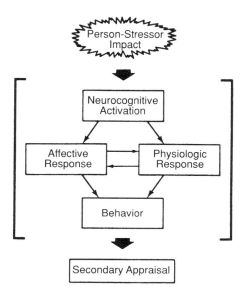

Fig 2. Primary appraisal.

ing behaviors that occur as precursors to the secondary appraisal or second neuro-cognitive evaluation.

Fig 2 demonstrates the connections among cognitive appraisal as defined by Lazarus,[23] the affective response based on the work of Izard,[44] Plutchik et al,[45] Weisman,[46] and others, and the physiologic response from the findings of Frankenhauser,[51] Mason,[53] and Sigg.[54]

Fig 3 amplifies the major components of primary appraisal.

Fig 4 depicts the next phase of coping where a secondary appraisal occurs using the same operational sequence as the primary appraisal, but with a different focus. Here attention is focused on the effectiveness of the coping strategies that occurred during the primary appraisal and on subsequent changes in the stress configuration. The model suggests that following the initial stressor-person impact and its related cognitive interpretation, there are three dependent variables: (1) fluctuation of emotion, (2) fluctuation of endocrine profile, and (3) behavioral response. As a rule, all responses tend to move from general to specific in character. Following the primary appraisal, a secondary appraisal or reappraisal occurs, which uses feedback from the initial transaction to reappraise the relevance and meaning of the stressor; evaluate coping options, resources, and the effect of those used initially; and change the primary appraisal of the event. Reappraisal continues repeatedly until adaptation or neutralization of the stressor occurs. The ulti-

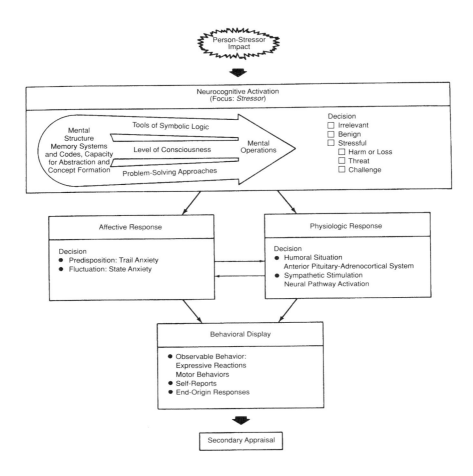

Fig 3. Coping phase 1: primary appraisal.

mate adaptation is unique for each individual and occurs within a range of effectiveness from maintenance of ideal integrity to death.

It should be noted that the time required for the entire process varies with each person and each event. The process, from primary appraisal to adaptation, is continuous in nature, and can be represented by a helical, multidimensional figure (Fig 5).

Model Utilization and Evaluation

Thomas Kuhn defined paradigms or models as "universally recognized scientific achievements that for a time provide model problems and solutions to a com-

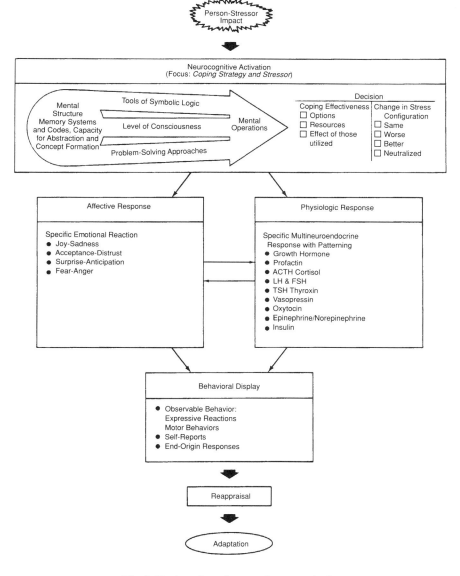

Fig 4. Coping phase 2: secondary appraisal.

munity of practitioners."[1(pviii)] He proposed the use of paradigms or models as a way to connect the several distinct views of nature—all or most of which have scientific, observational, or pragmatic merit—held by youthful sciences.

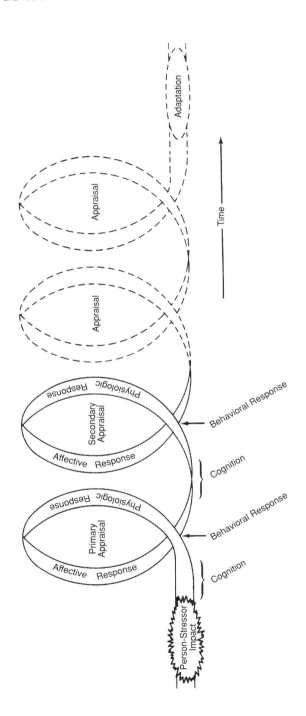

Fig 5. Helical process of coping and adaptation over time.

Modeling orders questions relating to fundamental entities and their interaction, seeks answers in logical and sometimes predictive sequence, and then allows for further discovery, expansion, growth, and validation of the model.

A model is a class of interrelated assumptions closely linked to a set of methods or procedures for measuring observations and analyzing data. The proposed model offers a description of response to stress and the process by which one grows and survives. The assumptions are deliberately broad and general, thus inviting further specification. Further specification is accomplished by entering the model at one or more points and raising questions. This process allows for generation of research problems and questions and guidance in the analysis of data.

The proposed model can be entered at a number of points, singly or simultaneously, including:

- Nature of the stressor,
- Exploration of the entire coping response or parts thereof,
- Exploration of a mediating variable or its relationship to another (regulation of emotion, physiological response),
- Identification of adaptive outcomes,
- Multiple determinants of the stress-coping process,
- Tool or instrument development,
- Exploration of one or more variables in the behavioral response dimension and the patterning of those responses,
- Outcome of primary appraisal,
- Further definition of secondary appraisal, and
- Exploration of modes of coding: information-seeking, direct action, inhibition of action, intrapsychic.

Regular, periodic evaluation of the model, with further specification through research, will generate new knowledge and provide new direction for nursing diagnoses and intervention. The knowledge and insights generated and reinvested in the model will allow for further specification of component parts and continuous expansion of the entire form. The original idea of the model is dynamic in that it becomes increasingly complex, generating an extension of knowledge that allows for further problem identification, and, more importantly, solutions that may be applied in practice.

REFERENCES

1. Kuhn T. *The Structure of Scientific Revolutions.* Chicago: University of Chicago Press, 1970.
2. Goosen GM, Bush HA. Adaptation: A feedback process. *Adv Nurs Sci.* 1979; 1:51–65.
3. Roy C. The Roy adaptation model: Testing the adaptational model in practice. *Nurs Outlook.* 1976; 24:682–691.
4. Lazarus RS. *Psychological Stress and the Coping Process.* New York: McGraw-Hill, 1966.
5. Appley MH, Trumbell R. *Psychological Stress.* New York; Appleton-Century-Crofts, 1967.

6. Bandura A. Self-efficacy: Toward a unifying theory of behavioral change. *Psychol Rev.* 1977; 84:191–215.
7. Beck H. Minimal requirements for a biobehavioral paradigm. *Behav Sci.* 1971; 16:442–455.
8. Becker BJ. A holistic approach to anxiety and stress. *Am J Psychoanal.* 1976; 36:139–146.
9. Bern DO. Psychological adaptation and development under acculturative stress: Toward a general model. *Soc Sci Med.* 1970; 3:529–547.
10. Cox T. *Stress.* Baltimore: University Park Press, 1978.
11. Ashby WR. *Design for a Brain.* London: Science Paperbacks, 1960.
12. Hermann MG. Testing a model of psychological stress. *J Pers.* 1966; 34:381–396.
13. Hesketh JL. Development of a normative model of performance and satisfaction in individual decision making: An empirical test of initiative, need for power, self-esteem, intelligence, decisiveness, need for achievement and grade point average as predictive factors. *Diss Abstr Int.* 1975; 35:4242.
14. Kagan A. Epidemiology, disease and emotion. In Levi L, ed. *Emotions: Their Parameters and Measurement.* New York: Raven Press, 1975.
15. Lazare A. Hidden conceptual models in clinical psychiatry. *N Engl J Med.* 1973; 288:345–351.
16. Levine S, Scotch NA. *Social Stress.* Chicago: Aldine, 1970.
17. McGrath JE. *Social and Psychological Factors in Stress.* New York: Holt Rinehart & Winston, 1970.
18. Mechanic D. Illness behavior, social adaptation and the management of illness: A comparison of educational and medical models. *J Nerv Ment Dis.* 1977; 165:79–87.
19. Schor AG. Acute grief in adulthood: Toward a cognitive model of normal and pathological mourning. *Diss Abstr Int.* 1974; 35:2447.
20. Vogel W, et al. A model for the integration of hormonal behavior, EEG and pharmacological data in psychopathology. In Landahn G, Herrman WH, eds. *Psychotropic Action of Hormones.* New York: Spectrum 1976; 121-134.
21. Wild BS, Hanes C. A dynamic conceptual framework of generalized adaptation to stressful stimuli. *Psychol Rep.* 1976; 38:319–334.
22. Yusin AS. Analysis of crises using a stress-motivation-response model. *Am J Psychother.* 1974; 28:409–417.
23. Lazarus RS. The stress and coping paradigm. Paper presented at the conference on the critical evaluation for behavioral paradigms for psychiatric science, University of Washington, Seattle, November 1978.
24. Selye H. *The Story of the Adaptation Syndrome.* Montreal: Acta, 1952.
25. Mason JW. A re-evaluation of the concept of non-specificity in stress theory. *J Psychol Res.* 1971; 8:323–333.
26. Von Euler US, et al. Cortical and medullary adrenal activity in emotional stress. *Acta Endocrinol.* 1959; 30:567–573.
27. Beck AT. Cognition, affect and psychopathology. *Arch Gen Psychiatry.* 1971; 24:495–500.
28. Dember WN. Motivation and the cognitive revolution. *Am Psychol.* 1974; 29:161–168.
29. Mandler G. *Mind and Emotion.* New York: John Wiley & Sons, 1975.
30. Weiner B, ed. *Cognitive Views of Human Emotion.* New York: Academic Press, 1974.
31. Piaget J, Inhelder B. *The Psychology of the Child.* New York: Basic Books, 1969.
32. Thatcher RW, John ER. *Foundations of Cognitive Processes.* New York: John Wiley & Sons, 1977.
33. Averill JR, Opton EM, Jr. Psychophysiological assessment: Rationale and problems. In McReynolds P, ed. *Advances in Psychological Assessment.* Palo Alto, Calif: Science & Behavior Books, 1968.
34. Monat A, Lazarus RS, eds. *Stress and Coping: An Anthology.* New York: Columbia University, 1977.

35. Gellhorn E, Loofbourrow GN. *Emotion and Emotional Disorders: A Neuro-Physiological Study.* New York: Harper & Row, 1963.
36. Gray J. *The Psychology of Fear and Stress.* London: Werdenfild & Nicolson, 1971.
37. Hebb DO. Drives and the conceptual nervous system. *Psychol Rev.* 1955; 62:243.
38. Hess WR. *The Functional Organization of the Diencephalon.* New York: Grune & Stratton, 1957.
39. Lindsley DB. Psychological phenomena and the electroencephalogram. *Electroencephalogr Clin Neurophysiol.* 1952; 4:443.
40. MacLean PD. The limbic system in relation to psychoses. In Black P, ed. *Physiological Correlates of Emotion.* New York: Academic Press, 1970.
41. Moruzzi G, Magoun HW. Brainstem reticular formation and activation of the EEG. *Electroencephalogr Clin Neurophysiol.* 1949; 1:455.
42. Posner MI. *Cognition: An Introduction,* Glenview, Ill: Scott, Foresman, 1973.
43. Neisser U. *Cognitive Psychology.* New York: Appleton-Century-Crofts, 1967.
44. Izard CE. Emotions in personality and psychopathology: An introduction. In Izard CE, ed. *Emotions in Personality and Psychopathology.* New York: Plenum Press, 1979.
45. Plutchik R, Kellerman H, Conte HR. A structural theory of ego defenses and emotions. In Izard CE, ed. *Emotions in Personality and Psychopathology.* New York: Plenum Press, 1979.
46. Weisman AD. *Coping with Cancer.* New York: McGraw-Hill, 1979.
47. Arieti S. Cognition and feeling. In Arnold MB, ed. *Feelings and Emotions.* New York: Academic Press, 1970.
48. Cannon WB. New evidence for sympathetic control of some internal secretions. *Am J Psychiatry.* 1922; 2:15–30.
49. Von Euler US. *Noradrenalin: Chemistry, Physiology, Pharmacology, and Clinical Aspects.* Springfield, Ill: Charles C Thomas, 1956.
50. Von Euler US, Lundberg U. Effects of flying on the epinephrine excretion in air force personnel. *J Appl Physiol.* 1954; 6:551–555.
51. Frankenhauser M. Experimental approaches to the study of catecholamines and emotion. In Levi L, ed. *Emotions–Their Parameters and Measurement.* New York: Raven Press, 1975.
52. Levi L, ed. *Emotions–Their Parameters and Measurement.* New York: Raven Press, 1975.
53. Mason JW. Endocrine parameters and emotion. In Levi L, ed. *Emotions–Their Parameters and Measurement.* New York: Raven Press, 1975.
54. Sigg EB. The organization and functions of the central sympathetic nervous system. In Levi L, ed. *Emotions–Their Parameters and Measurements.* New York: Raven Press, 1975.
55. Mason JW. The scope of psychoendocrine research. *Psychosom Med.* 1968; 30(pt 3):565–808.
56. Friedman SB, Chodoff P, Mason JW, et al. Behavioral observations on parents anticipating the death of a child. *Pediatrics.* 1963; 32(pt 1):610–625.
57. Mason JW, et al. Pre-illness hormonal changes in army recruits with acute respiratory infections. *Psychosom Med.* 1967; 29:545.

Congruence between Existing Theories of Family Functioning and Nursing Theories

Ann L. Whall, RN, PhD, FAAN
Associate Professor of Nursing
Wayne State University
Detroit, Michigan

FAMILY THEORIES have largely been accepted "as is" by nursing practitioners and researchers. The implications regarding the use of these existing theories need to be evaluated both in terms of the syntax of the discipline and the future courses that wholesale adoption may dictate. This discussion examines the relationship between specific family theories and the nursing theories of King, Peplau, and Rogers.[1-3]

RELATIONSHIPS AMONG THEORIES

According to Schwab, the knowledge base of a discipline may be divided into substantive and syntactical structures.[4] The substantive knowledge of a discipline is mostly concerned with the proper subject of inquiry, and the syntactical knowledge is concerned with determining the acceptability of that subject base and the way in which the substantive knowledge is used.

Schwab further describes the long-term syntax of a discipline as the way in which the discipline synthesizes and examines the substantive knowledge. Thus, syntactically a discipline examines the subject area for adequacy of concepts, for identification of weaknesses, and for devising reformulations. Existing theories of family functioning have been developed primarily within the disciplines of sociology and psychology. These family theories are mostly midrange in level (more specific than grand theory but not to the level of specificity of microlevel theory, which is situation-prescribing and -producing). This is especially the case in sociology; the psychological theories of family function tend, in contrast, to be midrange to micro-level in nature.

Adv Nurs Sci 1980;3(1):59–67
© 1980 Aspen Publishers, Inc.

Within these disciplines, family theories form a substantive knowledge base that is viewed from the context of each discipline. The discipline of nursing has largely adopted the existing theories of family functioning from sociology and psychology. The use of this theoretical base takes place across clinical areas of nursing.[5–7] In general, these theories have not been viewed from the syntax of nursing theory.

This discussion is premised on the assumption that the discipline of nursing considers family functioning a proper subject of inquiry or a substantive knowledge base for nursing. Nursing conceptual frameworks, or theories, with their broad level of applicability, can be used as the theoretical umbrella or syntax by which existing theories of family functioning may be examined for adequacy as well as weakness, for the purposes of reformulation and revision. The consideration of existing theories from a discipline other than nursing in light of nursing knowledge is supported by nursing theorists.

According to Fawcett, for an existing theoretical structure to be viewed as a nursing theory, that theory must first be evaluated and reformulated in terms of congruence and consistency with the central concepts of nursing theory (person, environment, health, and nursing).[8] This is consistent with Hardy's position that because nursing draws upon biopsychosocial knowledge, it is free to draw upon knowledge developed by these disciplines; but nursing has an obligation to alter theories it draws upon to fit the problems associated with nursing.[9] Ellis also addressed this issue when she discussed theories of, in, and for nursing.[10] Existing theories used in nursing are to be examined in light of current nursing knowledge. Fawcett also makes the point that once reformulation of the major concepts of an existing theory has occurred, along with evaluation of the relational statements, the resultant formulations can be designated as nursing theory.[8]

The major nursing theories are mostly at the conceptual framework level in terms of theory development; nursing theories are not, therefore, generally situation-producing or -prescriptive. According to Fawcett, it is crucial that prescriptive theories borrowed from other fields be carefully scrutinized in terms of the basic concepts of nursing theory. The discussion here attempts to address this issue and move forward the scrutiny of borrowed family theory .

FAMILY FUNCTIONING THEORY

Theories of family functioning from the discipline of psychology appear to have the most applicability to nursing practice. Most sociological theories are deductive and midrange; in contrast, some psychological theories of family functioning are inductive and situation-prescribing. Psychological theories of family functioning thus tend to be more useful to nursing practice. Rather than discussing what is, psychological theories tend to prescribe what will be of assistance to a particular family. Because nursing as a discipline is concerned with caring, helping, and nurturing, lack of specificity in many a priori midrange sociological formulations leads to delay or impasse in utilization. Duffey and Muhlenkamp point out that the usefulness of theoretical structures is of prime importance in the evaluation of theories.[11] The psychologically based theories referred to here are those of the family theorists considered somewhat psychoanalytic in approach, such as Framo[12] and Boszormenyi-Nagy;[13] those considered communicationist in approach, such as Haley,[14] Satir,[15] and Jackson;[16] and those using a systems approach, such as Napier and Whitaker,[17] and Minuchin et al.[18] These theorists discuss specific approaches, interventions, and goals in dealing with family functioning.

NURSING THEORY

All nursing theories deal somewhat with four central concepts: person, environment, health, and nursing. Because nursing theories are generally at the broad conceptual framework level of theory development, for the purposes of this discussion nursing theory is considered to be the syntax of nursing.[8,9] The nursing theories referred to are those of King, Peplau, and Rogers.[1-3]

The syntax of nursing theory indicates the way to handle the four central concepts; the existing theory or substantive knowledge area can thus be viewed in terms of congruence and consistency with person, environment, health, and nursing. Given that existing theories do not discuss nursing as such, aspects of the nursing process which are addressed, such as goal and mode of intervention, can also be evaluated. It is important to note that the nursing theories vary in the way in which the central concepts are handled.

Most nursing theories define *person* in some holistic fashion. However, the way in which the term *holistic* is interpreted by nursing theorists varies; some believe that aspects of a person may be addressed separately, while others insist upon terms that handle only the whole person. Nursing theorists also consider environment in various held-figure arrangements, either as separate, as a unified entity with person, or as a somewhat unified entity.

The term *health* is also discussed in different ways by the nursing theorists. Some describe the health-illness continuum; others discuss health in more holistic terms, such as optimum well-being. Both linear and holistic approaches to family health are represented in the existing theories of family functioning. Likewise, the concepts of person and environment are primarily handled in either a linear or holistic manner. The congruence between nursing theory and existing theories of family functioning forms the basis of the following discussion.

HOLISM AND LINEARITY

Maslow states that if one is to perceive holistically, then it is necessary to assess holistically or in some manner that considers the total and not the parts.[19] In a discussion of reductionist tendencies, he says that "good knowers," or those who know not only through cognitive operations but also through the senses, do not split mind from body, but attempt to perceive the whole person.[19] Once the Cartesian position that mind and body may be considered separately is accepted, it follows that the parts may be assessed separately. Maslow explains that the latter approach leads to reductionism, or the belief that a sum of the parts equals the whole.

Linear conceptualizations place person, health, or environment on a plane. The health-illness continuum is a familiar linear conceptualization. If the person is seen as progressing through time and space in such a fashion that past problems may be returned to and addressed, then the whole of the person is not perceived. Obviously, because no one gets younger, all persons progress through time and space. For this linear conceptualization to remain consistent, the person is perceived separately from the environment of time and space Therefore, the separatism of many linear models does not handle the concepts of person and environment as a whole.

When the conceptualization is such that problems may be returned to, addressed, and corrected, then for a while the time and space environment is ignored. The person is thus viewed as independent from the environmental field, and it is then possible to discuss the person adapting in a time-lag sequence to the environment. Problems of the environment can be addressed as separate from the person and vice versa.

The helper, who can be viewed as separate from the field, may "fix-up" the environment or the client separately, without joining the field. From this linear field-independent perspective, active participation of client with helper becomes questionable. In the world of strict linear formulations, the helper may be separate from the client, the client separate from the environment, and all on a continuum in which progression and retrogression are possible. This approach appears antithetical to Maslow's holistic approach. Because the whole person is generally considered the proper subject matter for nursing,[1–3, 20] it is important to consider the implications of the use of linear concepts.

CONGRUENCE OF FAMILY FUNCTIONING AND NURSING THEORIES

Existing theories of family functioning primarily use holistic or linear approaches, view environment as separate or as a whole with person, and address health as a linear continuum or as part of the whole of time and space. Minuchin et al classify theories of family functioning as primarily holistic or linear. Theories of family functioning are divided into three general types: psychoanalytic, communicationist, and systems.[18] The Minuchin et al classification system is used to organize the following discussion.

Psychoanalytic Approach

In the commonly held psychoanalytic view, each of the family architects, the parents, brings into the present family unit needs formulated via the heritage of their early life experiences.[12] The parents, as individuals, are thus the prime unit of consideration. Early events in the lives of the parents are of prime importance; these early events must be addressed for there to be a change in the present family unit. This view considers personhood as deterministically foretold by prior events.

The type and magnitude of past events can determine the type of mate selected, the career chosen, and even the selection of friends. The psychoanalytic view is thus primarily a linear approach in which energy may be stopped (fixated), progress (be worked through), or even go backward (regression). The marriage partners are mostly seen as separate, in terms of influence from the present environmental field. The present family is clearly not the prime focus of intervention because resolution of present difficulties lies in the working through of past problems.

As in the classical psychoanalytic approach, theories of family functioning using this theory base consider the therapeutic relationship to be of prime importance. Because much of the problem is unconscious and therefore unavailable to the client, the client depends upon the helper to discover and work through past problems.

In this view the family is an aggregate of individuals with complementary needs. The question is not one of whole family unit versus individual interventions, but one of preeminence and a working out of symptoms of the most needy individual through the rest of the family members. Theories of family functioning that demonstrate this view begin with a working through of the "tension states" or underlying problems of the marital partners. Once these tensions are resolved, the family unit is expected to function well. Health is thus viewed as a working through of past difficulties so that it is no longer necessary to attempt to repetitively work through the past problems in to the present.

Nursing theory

Nursing theories congruent with the psychoanalytic view would consider person, environment, and health in some composite fashion—person as a biopsychosocial being with the psychological portion preeminent. Health is seen as a continuum with the possibility of assisting the client back to health through the interpersonal relationship. Because of past experiences, the client is unable to clearly discern problems and thus depends upon the nurse for clarification; the client is therefore less active. The helper assists each client to work through present problems that reflect past deficits. The goal and focus of the intervention is insight developed via the interpersonal relationship.

Although there are some inconsistencies, Peplau's approach to nursing theory is generally congruent with the psychoanalytic approach to family functioning.[2] Peplau defines *person* as an organism that strives to reduce tension generated by needs and defines *nursing* as a significant interpersonal process. The person is viewed as a biopsychosocial being with emphasis upon the psychological aspects. This composite view of person is compatible with a linear view of tension reduction. The client responds to the nursing intervention, primarily the interpersonal relationship, with a reduction in tension. The tension is generated primarily from past needs. A notable incongruence between Peplau's approach and the psycho-analytic approach is that Peplau insists upon participation of the client in such things as mutual goal setting and action. The family is not addressed as a specific unit. This is considered consistent with Peplau's discussion of person as an individual striving to work through individual needs.

Communicationist Approach

Minuchin et al identify a second group of family theorists as com-municationists, including Haley,[14] Bateson,[21] and Satir.[15] Due to the theorizing of Harry Stack Sullivan, a shift in thinking took place with interest focusing upon the pattern of signals by which information is transferred within dyads and triads.[18] The communicationists emphasize present communication patterns in terms of pattern, sequence, and hierarchy, rather than the past nature of people.[13] The person is perceived as actively involved in the present, not the past and the cause-effect influence of early relationships. The communicationists stress the ways in which the person interacts, not only in terms of parts but also the whole. The field within which the person functions becomes highlighted. The helper and client influence and become influenced by one another; the split between action and reaction becomes less with the concept that actions and reactions occur together in the same field. Persons interact with the environment in terms of patterns and cues. The unit of intervention thus changes from helper and individual client to helper uniting with the field, and in particular, the dyadic and triadic relationships in which the client is involved.[15]

The communicationist approach is viewed as an extension of the prior psycho-analytic view, from individual to interactional patterns among people. Double bind communication patterns, scapegoating processes, pseudomutualities and silencing strategies within the dyads or triads of the family are of prime importance. The locus of difficulty lies in transmission processes. Homeostasis considerations prevail as equilibrium concepts imply that equality of relationships is health. The goal becomes clarification of relationships among all people within the dyadic and triadic patterns. The helpers' authority is subject to challenge, for as part of the field, the helper is an active participant in the communication sequences. The communicationist approach, emphasizing mutual action and reaction among people, may imply a time lag, thus suggesting linearity. However, the linearity is much less clear than in the psychoanalytic approach. The held is emphasized and field and person are treated as one.

Nursing theory

King's theory, which focuses on transactions within the dyad of nurse and client, is most consistent with the approach of the communicationists. King states that person (*man* in her terminology) is a reacting being with awareness of the environment.[1] The response or reaction is a comprehensive response of mind and body; the nurse and client work together toward a mutually acceptable goal. Health implies continuous adaptation to internal and external stresses. The relationship between nurse and client is prime. Although the environment is discussed as one with the individual, families are not specifically addressed. The therapeutic relationship is central and the person and nurse are viewed as part of the same field. Although King sometimes uses linear terms such as reaction and adaptation, the linearity of person is less clear than in psychoanalytic conceptualizations. As with the communicationists, King's model implies field dependence. The interpersonal orientation implies that the client and nurse are of the same field.

Systems Approach

The systems theories of family functioning emerged in the late 1950s and are considered extensions of the communicationist approach. The unit of intervention in systems theory is a dramatic departure from previous theory. Not only is the family unit perceived holistically, but it must be analyzed and approached holistically, not reductively. No longer are subsystem dyads considered primary and sometimes seen alternatively. In the pure systems approach, the family is always seen together. Sometimes three and four generations are included in the approach, and all problems are handled in total family sessions. According to a systems framework, the family is a type of unitary living organism.[18] The family is a living system relating to the systems of community, country, and universe. Just as one organ of the body relates to and is influenced by every other organ, the family system is influenced by internal subsystems as well as the larger community system. The family grows and changes, giving birth to new and different forms, just as an organism grows, changes, and reproduces. The family is a system in that it is a series of interrelated parts. Family rules govern the system and the individual's margin of choice. An important point is that family systems theorists generally imply a closed system perspective. Dysfunction or illness is defined as the closing down of the family system in much the same way as the closing down of the body's circulatory system is dysfunctional for the whole body. In terms of mode of intervention, the helper works with the system and becomes part of the system. By changing a key element of the system, not always the most negative portion, the total system changes and hopefully dysfunctions are alleviated.

Nursing theory

In terms of a nursing conceptual framework, Rogers is perhaps closest to the family systems approach.[3] The greatest departure perhaps is that Rogers considers the person from an open rather than a closed systems perspective. The person is always open or in mutual, simultaneous interaction with the environment. As do family systems theorists, Rogers sees boundaries as more perceptual than real, everything is connected to everything else. According to both Rogers and the family systems theorists, pattern and organization characterize the system. Change in one portion of the system affects changes in the whole, and these changes create reverberations in the system in wavelike fashion.

The unit of intervention for both Rogers and family system theorists is the total *family system*. Both consider the fields of nurse and family environments as coextensive and infinite energy fields. There is also congruence between the approaches of Rogers and family systems theory in terms of working within the system as opposed to external manipulation in a psychoanalytic sense. Health in Rogers's terms is a value judgment, because disease conditions are not entities by themselves but manifestations of the total pattern of the family system. The goal of nursing is to promote a symphonic interaction between persons (subsystems of the family), the family system, and the environment. The focus is thus redirection of patterns and organization within the family.[22]

Behaviorist Approach

The behaviorist approach to family is not discussed at length here because it is not well developed. However, compatible positions might be found between the behaviorist approaches to family and nursing theorists such as Roy who discuss adaptation.[19] According to Minuchin et al, the behaviorist views the family as a unit to decondition individual behavior, producing certain signals that organize the patient's behavior. The person is considered as somewhat separate, not one with the field.[18] Thus the unit of intervention is the individual. The behaviorist helper appears separate from the system. The view is one of person interacting with the environment to bring about an adopted state on the health-illness continuum. The linear causality focus of the behaviorist does not appear compatible with the communications or systems theorists who view person as part of total system or field.

IMPORTANCE OF THEORY REFORMULATION

Reformulation of the theories of family functioning so as to achieve consistency with nursing approaches is important. With some of the theories of family functioning, such as the systems approach, reformulation in terms of nursing theory may be readily achieved. The perspective, however, would be changed from a closed to an open systems perspective. In the case of the psychoanalytic approach, reformulation in terms of the nursing theory that requires client independence may not be as readily achieved. If nursing is to follow a holistic approach to person, environment, and health—and the major nursing theories would lead one to believe this is the direction with the most support—then linear conceptualizations in both existing theories and nursing theories need to be evaluated. Newman states the true holistic approach is not to be confused with the summing of many facts, but with factors reflective of the whole.[22] Reformulation of linear aspects may be necessary.

The important point is that the existing theory is to be examined for reformulation in terms of the nursing theory. In the past, the nursing approach was often reformulated for congruence with existing theories from other disciplines.

REFERENCES

1. King I. *Toward a Theory of Nursing: General Concepts of Human Behavior.* New York: John Wiley & Sons, 1971.
2. Peplau H. *Interpersonal Relations in Nursing.* New York: Putnam, 1952.
3. Rogers M. *The Theoretical Basis of Nursing.* Philadelphia: FA Davis, 1970.
4. Schwab J. Structure of the disciplines: Meanings and significances. In Ford G, ed. *The Structure of Knowledge and the Curriculum.* Chicago: Rand McNally & Co, 1964.
5. Miller J, Janosik E. *Family Focused Care.* New York: McGraw-Hill, 1980.
6. Hymovich D, Barnard M. *Family Health Care.* New York: McGraw-Hill, 1979.
7. Smoyak S. *The Psychiatric Nurse as a Family Therapist.* New York: John Wiley & Sons, 1975.
8. Fawcett J. The what of theory development. In *What, Why and How of Theory Development.* New York: National League for Nursing, 1978.
9. Hardy M. Evaluating nursing theory. In *What, Why and How of Theory Development.* New York: National League for Nursing, 1978.
10. Ellis R. Characteristics of significant theories. *Nurs Res.* May–June 1968; 17:217–222.
11. Duffey M, Muhlenkamp A. A framework for theory analysis. *Nurs Outlook.* 1974; 22:570–574.
12. Framo J. Rationale and techniques of intensive family therapy. In Boszormenyi-Nagy I, Framo J, eds. *Intensive Family Therapy: Theoretical and Practical Aspects.* New York: Harper & Row, 1965.
13. Boszormenyi-Nagy I. Intensive family therapy as process. In Boszormenyi-Nagy I, Framo J, eds. *Intensive Family Therapy: Theoretical and Practical Aspects.* New York: Harper & Row, 1965.
14. Haley J. *Problem Solving Therapy.* San Francisco: Jossey-Bass, 1978.
15. Satir V. *Conjoint Family Therapy.* Palo Alto, Calif: Science & Behavior Books, 1967.
16. Jackson D. The question of family homeostasis. *Psychiatr Q Suppl.* 1957; 31:79–90.
17. Napier A, Whitaker C. *The Family Crucible.* New York: Harper & Row, 1978.
18. Minuchin S, Rosman B, Baker L. *Psychosomatic Families.* Cambridge, Mass: Harvard University Press, 1978.
19. Maslow A. *The Psychology of Science.* South Bend, Ind: Gateway, 1966.
20. Roy C. *Introduction to Nursing: An Adaptation Model.* Englewood Cliffs, NJ: Prentice-Hall, 1976.
21. Bateson G. The birth of a matrix or double bind and epistemology. In Berger M, ed. *Beyond the Double Bind.* New York: Brunner/Mazel, 1978.
22. Newman M. *Theory Development in Nursing.* Philadelphia: FA Davis, 1979.

Evaluation of Health Care Professionals in Facilitating Self-Care: Review of the Literature and a Conceptual Model

Betty L. Chang, RN, DNSc
Assistant Professor
School of Nursing
University of California
Los Angeles, California

A HOLISTIC APPROACH to health behavior begins with a focus on individuals, their interactions with the environment, and how the environment affects their health and well-being. This approach is geared toward those persons who have assumed a considerable amount of responsibility for their own health care such as recognition of symptoms and management of selected health conditions. It is often referred to as "self-care," which is described as "a process whereby a layperson functions on his/her own behalf in health promotion and prevention and in disease detection and treatment at the level of the primary health resource in the health care system."[1(p11)] Roles in self-care include health maintenance, disease prevention, self-diagnosis, self-medication, self-treatment, and patient participation in use of professional services.

The nurse practitioner is in a strategic position to assist individuals in self-care programs since self-care practices are particularly prominent at the level of primary care. Literature reviewed by Levin, Katz and Holst indicated that practitioners believed that self-care could have been substituted for 25% of the illness episodes seen in general practice (excluding some conditions such as trauma and cancer), and 15% to 18% of those listed illnesses could have had a better outcome if supplemented by self-care.[1]

With few exceptions, health care professionals have focused on the patient as a passive recipient of care. In the past, much of professional concern regarding the public has focused on the extent to which patients accept physicians' advice and

The author gratefully acknowledges the helpful contributions of Mrs. Gwen C. Uman, R.N., N.P., in early discussions of this article.

Adv Nurs Sci 1980;3(1):43–58

the extent to which patients use the care system. More recent emphasis on the patient as an active participant has resulted in the encouragement of social accountability of health care professionals. A need exists for the evaluation of health professionals in facilitating self-care. Such an evaluation must take into account laypersons' judgments regarding the health care received. A conceptual framework is needed for the evaluation of the role of health professionals in facilitating self-care.

COMPONENTS OF A FRAMEWORK

One of the most well-established frameworks in self-care was articulated by Orem in *Nursing: Concepts of Practice*.[2] Orem delineates two kinds of self-care: universal and health deviation. Universal self-care includes all demands necessary for the activities of daily living such as air, fluids, food, elimination, rest, activity, solitude, interaction with others, and protection from hazards. Health deviation care demands derive from illness, injury, or disease. Many nurses currently use this framework as a basis for their practice.

The framework suggested by the author for the evaluation of health professionals is in part derived from Orem's work, and in part from other literature related to the evaluation of quality of care. Three major dimensions are considered in the framework: (1) patient or layperson characteristics, (2) health care professional characteristics, and (3) patient outcomes. As shown in Fig 1, each dimension consists of two or more components. The last dimension, patient outcomes, is influenced by the preceding two.

Characteristics of Individual Laypersons or Patients

To assist patients in the promotion of health and the prevention, detection, and treatment of illnesses, Orem suggests that individual characteristics of the patients must be considered.[2] These factors have been found to influence individuals' needs and perceptions and include (1) age (and developmental stage), sex, level of education, occupation, and marital status, and (2) individual beliefs, expectations, and attitudes. These characteristics are represented by the first circle in Fig 1.

Individual responses to illness, health care, and treatment are influenced by the individual's development stage, sex, and supportive network such as spouse or family members. In addition, any health care or potential self-care activities are evaluated by individuals in relation to their own value systems, beliefs, expectations, and attitudes. Research indicates that patient characteristics are associated with both patient satisfaction[3–13] and patient adherence.[14–20] Therefore any assessment of individual patient health status and evaluation of patient outcomes must consider the above patient characteristics. The characteristics can be established in research through the use of demographic variables and selected measures of expectations, attitudes, and beliefs regarding health care.

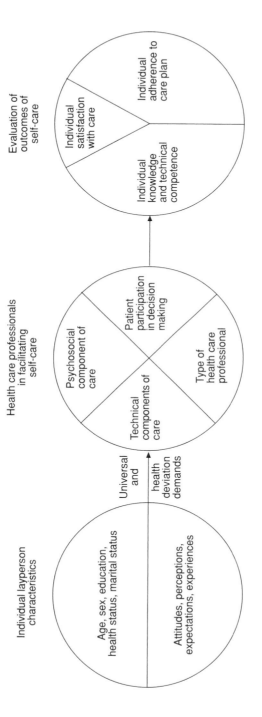

Fig 1. Framework for evaluation of health care professionals in self-care.

Characteristics of Health Care Professionals

The second dimension relates to characteristics of the health care professional in facilitating self-care and is represented by the middle circle in Fig 1. Its components include (1) medical-technical component of care, (2) psychosocial component of care, (3) patient participation in care, and (4) type of health care professional (eg, physician, nurse).

Medical-technical component

The medical-technical aspect of care refers to the practitioners' understanding and application of medical science and technology in recognizing interruptions in health that arise from stress, illness, or injury, or that arise from medical treatments. Technical quality of care has been one of the important components in studies of factors contributing to patient satisfaction.[21] Most studies of medical-technical quality (eg, history taking, physical examinations, counseling) of nurses in ambulatory settings have compared patient evaluations of nurse practitioners and physicians.[22–26] In research terms, this component can be expressed as the number of relevant history and physical examination items included by a heath care professional in an assessment for a selected health problem.

Psychosocial component

A second component of care is the psychosocial aspect, which includes attention to patients' feelings and responses to their health, treatment, and other factors in the environment. Psychosocial factors are important in nursing. Roy,[27] Johnson,[28] and other nursing theorists have included various psychosocial factors in their conceptual models for nursing care. Research on patient satisfaction indicates that patients were more satisfied when health care providers gave information[29] and showed a personal interest in the patients.[30]

For purposes of research, the psychosocial component can be seen in data obtained regarding patients' feelings about their health status (or illness, symptoms) and how the illness affects their views of themselves, interactions with others, and their daily activities (work, rest). The data may include information elicited by direct questions or by following up patient cues in a selected problem for study.

Patient participation

The third component, patient participation in health care, requires that the nurse assist laypersons in participating in their own care. This involves interaction between the layperson and health care professional in which the layperson takes an active part in decision making. The layperson participates in identifying goals, seeking clarification of data, evaluating options, selecting an option, and implementing the course of action selected. This is a key component of self-care that health care professionals must address. Research indicates that the quality of interactions between patients and health care providers influences patient satisfaction,[4,9,10,13] adherence, and compliance.[14,20] However, the amount of patient participation was not addressed in these studies. Involving patients in decision making about the use of medications in the home has been studied. In this model the patient and the nurse jointly identify goals for a given interaction. Goal delineation reflects knowledge and values and is followed by a clarification of data relevant to decision and goal attainment. In this phase the nurse and patient impart knowledge to each other and share values. For example, the patient may reveal that he or she abhors the idea of taking pills for fear of side effects. The nurse can relate to this important concern by sharing information on the drug in question and discussing other ways of managing the problem. This leads directly to identification and evaluation of options and their consequences. Finally, the two parties agree on the selection of one course of action, and the patient is provided with the tools for implementation. Implementation is in the hands of the client. The evaluation of the patient's action in terms of the goal is a joint effort between the nurse and the patient.[31]

The above decision-making approach can also be used in other areas of self-care, such as the identification of signs and symptoms, the meaning of positive signs, and the options available for the treatment of conditions identified by the patient (eg, self-medication, self-management by diet, exercise, change in lifestyle, or using professional services). Ability and skills necessary for meeting universal and health deviation needs can be assessed and facilitated through this approach. Implementing patient participation in health care will involve the delineation of selected content for interaction, as well as the steps in the decision-making process to be followed.

Type of health care professional

The type of health care professional involved in assisting individuals in self-care may influence patient evaluations of health care. Studies of patient satisfaction indicate that nurse practitioners compare well with physicians.[22,23,32] The acceptance of nurse practitioners, however, may vary. Graham found that satisfaction was significantly greater among parents whose children were treated by nurse practitioners than those who were treated by physicians; however, one third stated they preferred a physician to a nurse practitioner.[22] Further studies have found that experience with nurse practitioners may increase patients' preference for them in performing physical examinations and other procedures.[24]

Evaluation of Outcomes

The evaluation of outcomes is represented by the circle to the far right in Fig 1. The framework proposes an examination of three components in terms of individual layperson or patient outcomes. The first component is an evaluation of the layperson's competence in meeting universal and health deviation needs.

Patient competence

This component of evaluation would include knowledge and skills obtained by laypersons in order to maintain wellness and recognize signs and symptoms of health deviation. It would also include behavior or action to be taken in instituting appropriate care. This component constitutes an indirect measure of the health care professional in assisting individual patients in self-care. It is recognized that factors other than the quality of the health care professional's care influence this component of outcome. Certainly the individual's preexisting characteristics such as developmental and educational levels, and beliefs, attitudes, and expectations play a role. However, a health care professional should have taken these character-istics into consideration in assisting a patient in self-care. The evaluation of lay-persons' competence may be done by the individuals themselves or with the assistance of the health care provider. In practice, such evaluations may be found in teaching diabetics, patient teaching following a myocardial infarction, and in other persons with illnesses requiring long-term care by the patient or family. This component may be evaluated by means of specific written or oral tests of knowl-edge, a checklist of critical elements in a demonstration of a skill, and the observa-tion of actual patient behaviors in action-taking situations. Patient behaviors in relation to action taking may also be obtained through the use of simulated situa-tions.

Research in the association of knowledge and skill with other types of behavior (such as adherence) has been inconclusive. Although reviews of literature indicate that an increase in knowledge does not necessarily lead to an increase in adher-ence,[33] it is a prerequisite in terms of helping the patient assume responsibility for self-care.

Patient satisfaction

The second component is the evaluation of patient satisfaction with care re-ceived. There is increased recognition that patient satisfaction constitutes a legiti-mate measure of quality of care. National standards of practice in nursing empha-size accountability, thus making patient evaluation of health care a key factor. Patient satisfaction as part of the evaluation of quality of care has been observed in the care provided by nurses in hospital settings,[34,35] nurse practitioners[22,32,36] and other health care professionals.[37]

Satisfaction with care provided by health care professionals may be obtained as a global rating by the patient as well as a specific rating for each component of care: medical-technical, psychosocial, patient participation in planning care, and the type of health care professional. Evaluating each component of care may be particularly helpful to health care professionals so that information may be ob-tained to determine which of the components are most highly associated with pa-tient satisfaction. In measuring patient satisfaction, as with other outcomes, it is important to take into consideration the patient's preexisting characteristics that influence evaluations.

Adherence to care plan

The third component in the evaluation of health care professionals in facilitating self-care is the patient's adherence to the self-care plan. The extent to which the physician's orders are followed by the patient (compliance) has been a key factor in the physician's evaluation of the quality of medical practice. However, compliance implies that the physician is the decision maker and the patient is the person to follow orders or comply. In self-care the individual layperson or patient participates in the decision-making process. Thus individuals need to be informed as to their health status, the meaning of signs and symptoms, and kinds of treatment or options available, each with its own set of consequences. The patient then selects a plan and implements or adheres to the plan selected. Thus adherence includes a wide range of patient behaviors that may include compliance as well as the decision to enter into a treatment program, to terminate a program, or to implement a mutually agreed on plan of care.

Information on adherence is doubling approximately every five years,[38] a fact that is believed to be in part due to an increased awareness of patients' rights, a decline in professional paternalism, and to scientific advances.

Reports of compliance and adherence behaviors show wide variations from 4% to 100%.[38] It is misleading, however, to compare compliance rates from different studies because of the wide variations in operational definitions of compliance among investigators. There has also been a lack of truly objective measures. For example, some techniques have used self-reports, pill counts, detection of drug levels in body fluids and estimates given by physicians, family, and others. Research on adherence to a care plan needs to be highly specific. Rather than observing actual behavior (which is often difficult when studying changes in life-style), two common sources of data are used, each with its own pitfalls: (1) a patient's intent to adhere to highly specific aspects of the plan and (2) an actual log of the patient's activities relating to the plan. Nevertheless, the measurement of adherence remains problematic in research studies.

REVIEW OF LITERATURE

A review of literature describes the self-care approach and various components and characteristics associated with an individual's evaluation of care. The research cited provides further support for the factors included in the framework for the evaluation of health care professionals.

Self-Care

Self-care is an approach that is derived from patients' perceived needs and preferences regardless of whether such needs and preferences conform to professional perceptions of patients' needs.[39] Patients determine the desired outcome in accordance with their decisions as to which risks they choose to contend with or avoid.

While this does not preclude the patients from obtaining relevant information and prescriptions from health care professionals such as a physician or nurse, it does shift the decision-making responsibility to the patients. The responsibility is based on patients' perceptions of the risks involved in the illness, treatment, or various activities (rest, exercise, diet), which many believe to be lay decisions rather than professional ones.

Patients' choices may not always conform to professional values. In medical and nursing literature patients whose choices do not coincide with professional values are said to be noncompliant. A more neutral term may be "adherence" to the health care plan, which may or may not involve patient decision making in the formulation of the plan.

Nurses and self-care

Self-care, with its goal of promoting health and preventing disease, and its emphasis on patients as active participants and decision makers, requires that nurses assist patients in arriving at informed decisions and in developing behaviors to improve health. An example of the relevance of self-care to nursing is found in the care of elderly patients with stable chronic diseases. Much of this care must be performed by the patients themselves. It is particularly important, therefore, that nurses develop methods of assisting patients to care for themselves to forestall progression of chronic illnesses, prevent complications, and maintain health at the highest possible level. A care plan that the patient will implement at home must take into consideration patient characteristics such as developmental level, life experiences, and attitudes and beliefs. These characteristics will influence the perceived need for care and the satisfaction with care received, as reflected in the literature cited in the following sections.

Patient competence

Technical competence of the patient is essential in self-care and includes recognition of symptoms of health and illness and action to be taken. The knowledge and skills necessary for self-care of an older chronically ill adult may include recognition of symptoms of shortness of breath, angina pain, or taking of the individual's own pulse, blood pressure, and medications. The individual may draw on primary health care providers such as nurse practitioners as resource persons. The health professional may facilitate individuals' self-care abilities by examining the individuals and by assisting them in gaining the necessary knowledge and skills. Recent consumer literature on self-care may also be useful.[40]

For the most part, the self-care movement has emphasized the teaching of skills and has placed little emphasis on evaluating the competence of the individual.[41] Accuracy of laypersons in the recognition of symptoms and the adequate management of their problems should also be included. Evaluations of this aspect should include individual knowledge and skills acquired by laypersons as well as their behavior in obtaining professional help when warranted by their conditions. There should be an evaluation of the patients' techniques to recognize and verify symptoms and to solve problems. Since the self-care approach allows for varying decisions in some situations, follow-up investigation would help to verify that the most helpful options were considered. When laypersons take such responsibilities, professional reevaluation and guidance are essential. Nurses have a responsibility to assist in the evaluation of self-care situations and to offer feedback and suggestions when necessary.

Patient Satisfaction

As mentioned, there has been an increase in recognition that patient satisfaction constitutes a measure of quality of care. Ware et al found over 100 articles and reports on patient satisfaction published in the last 25 years, attesting to the importance of this concept in evaluation of quality of care.[21]

Patient characteristics

A number of studies have reported on the association of patient characteristics with satisfaction with health care.[3–13] Most of these were based on demographic data.

In a study of emergency room patients, Apostle and Oder found no correlation between age and satisfaction.[3] However, in a more recent study, Hulka et al found elderly individuals less satisfied with access to care and financial aspects of health care.[6] Satisfaction with the health care professional in general was seen to decrease with age in men only.[3] Kirscht et al found that older patients had less favorable opinions regarding efficacy of diagnosis and preventive practices.[8] However, there are a number of studies showing that elderly persons are more satisfied than younger persons with their private physicians[3,10,11] and that they are more satisfied with medical services in general.[11] Ware et al found that in homogeneous populations, older people are more satisfied with medical care than younger people and that the elderly rate technical quality less important than the art of care.[13]

None of the work on satisfaction differentiated the elderly (over age 60) into age subgroups. Gerontologists have shown that the elderly cannot be considered a homogeneous group. Important differences exist between "young" old age (65–75) and "old" old age (over 75). For example, there is more physical disability in the latter group,[42,43] a higher incidence of widowhood and living alone, and a higher incidence of mental decline.[44] It is possible that the greater incidence and degree of illness in the older old-age group might make their perceptions of health care different from those of the younger old-age group.

Most studies of patient satisfaction reviewed by Ware et al revealed that educational level, socioeconomic status, and occupational level were all positively correlated with patient satisfaction,[13] both globally,[11,45] and in relation to specific components of art and technical quality.[4,5,7,8,12,13,45] The only study to show no correlation between education or social class and satisfaction was done by Korsch et al.[9] Hulka et al found no correlation between age and satisfaction with the technical quality, art of care, or access to services.[7]

Quality of care

Art and technical quality. In a study examining the measurement of patient satisfaction, Ware et al extrapolated eight dimensions of care addressed by research over the years: (1) technical quality, (2) art of care, (3) accessibility and convenience, (4) finances, (5) physical environment, (6) availability, (7) continuity and (8) efficacy and outcome.[21] Hulka et al[46] and Ware and Snyder[47] suggested that the art of care and technical quality could be distinguished but were highly interrelated. Art was defined as behavior that enabled physicians to deal effectively with patients in order to develop rapport and gain trust, such as calling the patient by name and informing him or her of a procedure before performing it. Technical quality was defined as the number of pertinent items elicited in the history and physical examination.

Studies have alluded to the art of care. Patients indicated that the nurse practitioner was warm and friendly, able to answer patients' questions, and made patients comfortable.[22,32] Technical quality of nurse practitioners has been compared to that of physicians and found comparable in specific patient populations and settings.[22-26] Henriques et al found that annual physical examinations performed by nurse practitioners and physician assistants were well accepted by 30,000 healthy and worried patients in a health maintenance organization over a 37-month period.[48] Physician-nurse practitioner teams were studied by Gardner and Ouimette.[23] In their study, patients were satisfied with history taking, physical examination, and counseling by the nurse practitioner. Team care was rated better than care by the physician only by 51% of the patients; 42% rated team care as equal to physician care. Only 7% of the patients rated team care as worse than physician care.[23]

Psychosocial component. Studies indicated that patients are sensitive to psychosocial aspects of care, although this aspect may not have been specifically delineated. Patients tended to be more satisfied when health care providers gave more information,[29] when counseled by a physician,[10] and when health care providers showed a personal interest.[30] The amount of time spent with patients, the amount of time in clinics,[10] and the nature of communication[9] have also been related to satisfaction.

Orem recognized that potential self-care activities are evaluated by patients in relation to their personal value systems and beliefs. Individual differences in established patterns of responding to stimuli and feelings about health status will affect decisions and self-care actions.[2] Thus before care can be planned, relevant beliefs and feelings of patients about reactions to illness or treatment, how illness may affect interactions with others, and patients' activities in rest, sleep, work, or play should be considered.

The health care professional's interactions with patients in soliciting such information is delineated as a psychosocial component. The emphasis on psychosocial aspects of care is also evident in various frameworks for nursing[27,49] as well as specific literature on nursing care of the aged.[6,50,51] Stewart and Buck noted that studies of health care increasingly have included measures of psychosocial elements of care.[52]

Patient participation. The amount of patient participation in planning of care has not been studied in relation to satisfaction. Correlational studies suggest that patient satisfaction is sensitive to differences in patient and health care provider interaction.[4,9,10,13,29,30,52]

Principles of education indicate that for behavioral change to take place the learner must take an active part in the learning process to determine the desired outcomes and the best methods to employ in order to achieve the outcomes.[53,54]

In contracting with the patients as a method of planning care, the nurse and patient determine the behavior the patient will agree to exhibit. Kuhn, taking a systems approach to the study of social behavior, identifies three functions (intrasystems or psychological level) within the individual: (1) knowing (knowledge base), (2) wanting (values), and (3) doing (effecting behavior). When two or more individuals are working together (intersystem or social level), communication of knowledge and transfer of values held by each takes place and results in some action by one or more parties (organization of behavior). The plans developed to deal with an ambulatory patient's health problem require that the patient follow through with some action on his or her own behalf. Kuhn's social systems theory suggests that the knowledge and values of both parties (patient and health care professional) be explicated to allow the most appropriate organization of behavior for solution of the given problem.[55] Hallburg's decision-making model,[31] discussed previously, has also been useful in studies of patient participation in decision making.

Type of provider. Studies comparing nurse practitioners and physicians provide some insight into the importance of the health care provider as an issue separate from the quality of care. Studies of patient satisfaction indicate that patients generally express satisfaction with care provided by a nurse practitioner as compared to that provided by a physician.[22–24,26,32,48,56,57] In an early study, Spitzer et al reported that there have been only a few instances of rejection of nurse practitioners' services by patients even when patients have previously expressed negative attitudes.[25] Linn, in a study of family nurse practitioners from the University of California at Los Angeles, reported that from the patient's perspective, the family nurse practitioner is as acceptable as, if not more acceptable than, a physician or a registered nurse.[56]

Despite significantly greater satisfaction among parents whose children were cared for by nurse practitioners, rather than by physicians, when a global question was asked as to preference for physician or pediatric nurse practitioner, fully one third of the respondents preferred physician care because of the physician's perceived extensive preparation.[22] Chenoy et al, in a household survey of a medically underserved rural population in Ontario, found that nurses were acceptable for health maintenance, sickness surveillance, and for home visits if a physician was not available. A physician was preferred in worry-inducing situations. The population studied had not been exposed to nurse practitioner care.[58]

McGlone and Schultz surveyed 300 elderly patients to determine their attitudes toward various health care innovations.[26] Almost all indicated a willingness to accept a nurse as an intermediary in delivery of care. Graduate nurse practitioner students cared for elderly patients in nursing homes and couples in the community, and they were well accepted. Experience with nurse practitioners was seen as influential in their acceptance by patients.[26] Lewis and Resnik studied a control group of 33 patients assigned to regular care in a university medical center and an experimental group of 33 patients assigned to a nurse clinic. All 66 patients had chronic diseases, and there were no intergroup differences prior to the study. After one year there was no change in the attitudes of the control group, but the experimental group had a decrease in frequency of complaints, a decreased tendency to seek physician care for minor complaints, and an increased preference for nurses to perform various procedures (eg, physical examination, laboratory interpretation).[24]

Patient satisfaction may be seen as an end in itself or as one factor in the longer range perspective of patient adherence to treatment regimen, or increased level of wellness. Becker and Maiman's review indicates that positive correlations have been found between patient satisfaction (with the therapist, visit, or clinic) and compliance.[14]

Factors Influencing Patient Adherence to Regimen

For this discussion, *patient adherence* will be used in preference to *patient compliance* because of the broader variety of behaviors the former encompasses. However, literature on patient compliance will be included as compliance and is viewed as one aspect of patient adherence.

Blackwell noted that despite the wealth of literature, adherence is an inadequately studied subject. Two of the major problems have been the poor study designs in published studies and the lack of definition of compliance. He cited a report that evaluated 185 studies, and identified over 200 variables that had been measured, but results from various studies often contradicted each other.[38] Thus a marked lack of consensus exists, and studies have been designed in such a way that measurements in one study are not comparable to measurements in another.

Demographic characteristics

In a review of the literature, Marston indicated that the results of most investigations have led to the conclusion that age is probably not significantly related to compliance.[33] However, some studies have found that younger patients were less likely to follow their medical regimens than were older patients.[15–17] The comparison for the most part included children and adults under the age of 65 years. Becker and Maiman, however, pointed out that noncompliance and medication errors were associated with extremes of age, perhaps because the very young were more resistant to ingesting bad-tasting medicine, and geriatric patients experienced forgetfulness or self-neglect.[14]

Contradictory findings have been reported regarding the relationship of educational level and compliance. Some investigators[18] have found that increasing levels of education were associated with compliance, while others[19] found that increasing levels of education were associated with noncompliance. Marston's review indicated that socioeconomic status, marital status, and race have not been found to be related to compliance.[33] Kasl noted that demographic variables are related to adherence in fairly specific ways that represent interaction with other variables.[20]

Attitudes and beliefs

A number of studies cite attitudes and beliefs as influencing factors in adherence, such as attitudes and beliefs toward perceived susceptibility to[59–61] and severity of the illness.[19,61–63] Heinzelmann found that among college students with a history of rheumatic fever, continued penicillin prophylaxis was related to subjective estimates of the likelihood of having another attack.[64] Elling et al reported significant positive associations between a mother's belief in the possibility of recurrence of rheumatic fever in her child and compliance in administering the penicillin and visiting a clinic.[65] Christensen's review of the literature on drug compliance noted that diminished compliance was observed in children whose mothers' expectations were not in relation to the cause and nature of the illness.[66] Thus patients' expectations regarding an illness influence compliance.

In a review of the literature, Becker and Maiman concluded that perceived severity of an illness was a factor in compliance.[14] However, they found that for the asymptomatic individual, very low levels of perceived severity were not sufficiently motivating, while very high levels of perceived seriousness (including fear) were inhibiting. Both extremes were found to be associated with low likelihood of taking preventive action. Heinzelmann found the patient's view of the seriousness of rheumatic fever, both in an absolute sense and when compared with other diseases, was predictive of compliance with prophylaxis.[64] Charney et al found that a mother's perception of severity of the illness at onset was significantly related to likelihood of giving the medication. Patients' perceptions of the severity of illness were also predictive of compliance with the prescribed regimen in some preventive and all sick-role conditions studied.[67]

Studies have shown that individual beliefs influence adherence to regimen.[33] Patients who believed that their disease was due to supernatural causes were less

likely to continue their treatment than patients who believed that there are measures individuals may take to avoid health hazards.

Characteristics of regimen

Characteristics of medication regimen have been found to be fairly reliable predictors of adherence. Multiple recommendations or restrictions lead to greater
noncompliance than single recommendations; multiple drugs or multiple doses of
one drug tend to have a higher rate of default. Also, patients who have been on a
long medication regimen tend to default more. However, such information is of
limited value if the patient suffers from a chronic condition that requires adherence to a regimen for a prolonged period of time. Similarly, the physician's choice
of single or multiple recommendations is based on his or her judgment of what is
the best treatment for the patient. A more fruitful area of investigation is the relationship between the patient and the health care provider and patient participation
in decision making about the regimen.[20,68]

Patient and health care provider interactions

The nature of the patient and health care provider relationship may influence
individual adherence to medication regimen. In an early study, Davis tape-
recorded patient-physician interactions and categorized them according to Bales's
Interaction Process Analysis. He then examined the relationship between the types
of interactions and patient compliance. Patterns of communication (formality, rejection of the patient) that deviate from a normative physician-patient relationship
were associated with noncompliance. Behaviors that allowed for tension release,
patient agreement with physician, and provision of orientation to physician were
associated with compliance.[68] Becker and Maiman[14] found that studies reported
greater compliance when the physician is perceived as friendly and understanding
of the patient's complaint. Noncompliance was more likely with less reciprocal
interaction between the patient and physician and the physician's failure to communicate the purpose of the treatment.[14] Similarly, Kasl noted that possessing correct information about the disease and medication regimen was, at best, weakly
related to adherence; the crucial element was probably the nature of the patient's
role expectations.[20] However, a more recent study that examined physician-patient
interactions reported that compliance was higher in situations where patients were
given more information about their drugs.[69] Numerous studies have suggested that
unfulfilled patient expectations led to dissatisfaction and poor compliance.[20]

CONCLUSION

A model based on the framework presented can be used to identify components
of health care or patient and health care professional interactions that contribute
most to measurable outcomes such as patient competence (in health maintenance,

disease prevention, self-diagnosis, self-treatment, and use of professional services), and patient evaluations of satisfaction and adherence to a health care plan.

Information from an investigation based on the model can contribute to the practice of nursing in two ways. First, the findings regarding components of care and satisfaction can be applied by nurses to systematically increase patient competence and patient satisfaction. Second, the study may specify patient profiles that interact with different components of care to yield high levels of patient satisfaction and adherence to formulated care plans. The knowledge regarding patient profiles and components of care can be effectively used by nurses to tailor their care to different patients.

Nurses can systematically evaluate their effectiveness in facilitating self-care where patients are given a considerable amount of responsibility for their own health care. Such evaluations will contribute to nursing's professional accountability in assisting individuals in self-care and in taking a holistic approach to health care.

REFERENCES

1. Levin LS, Katz AH, Holst E. *Self-Care: Lay Initiatives in Health.* New York: Prodist, 1979.
2. Orem D. *Nursing: Concepts of Practice.* New York. McGraw-Hill, 1971.
3. Apostle D, Oder F. Factors that influence the public's view of medical care. *JAMA.* 1967; 202:140-146.
4. Bashshur RL, Metzner CA, Worden C. Consumer satisfaction with group practice: The CHA case. *Am J Public Health.* 1967; 57:1991-1999.
5. Enterline PE, Salter V, McDonald AD, McDonald JC. The distribution of medical care services before and after free medical care: The Quebec experience. *N Engl J Med.* 1973; 289:1174-1178.
6. Hulka B, Kupper L, Daly M, et al. Correlates of satisfaction and dissatisfaction with medical care: a community perspective. *Medical Care.* 1975; 13:648–658.
7. Hulka B, Zyzanski S, Cassel J, Thompson SJ. Satisfaction with medical care in a low-income population. *J Chron Dis.* 1971; 24:661–673.
8. Kirscht JP, Haefner DP, Kegels DP, et al. A national study of health beliefs. *Health Hum Behav.* 1966; 7:248–254.
9. Korsch GM, Gozzi EK, Francis V. Gaps in doctor-patient communication. *Pediatrics.* 1968; 42: 855–869.
10. Linn LS. Factors associated with patient evaluation of health care. *Milbank Mem Fund Q.* 1975; 53:531–548.
11. Rojek DG, Clemente F, Summers CF. Community satisfaction. A study of contentment with local services. *Rural Sociol.* 1975; 40:77–192.
12. Suchman EA. Social patterns of illness and medical care. *J Health Hum Behav* 6:2–16, 1965.
13. Ware JE, Snyder MK, Wright WR. *Development and Validation of Scales to Measure Patient Satisfaction with Health Care Services. Vol 1. Final Report: Part A—Review of Literature, Overview of Methods, and Results Regarding Construction of Scales.* Carbondale, Ill: Southern Illinois University School of Medicine, 1976.
14. Becker MH, Maiman LA. Sociobehavioral determinants of compliance with health and medical care recommendations. *Medical Care.* 1975; 13:10–24.
15. Bergman AB, Werner RJ: Failure of children to receive penicillin by mouth. *N Engl J Med.* 1963; 268:1334–1338.

16. Luntz GRWN, Austin R. New stick test for PAS in urine: Report on use of Phenistix and problems of long-term chemotherapy for tuberculosis. *Br Med J.* 1960; 1:1679–1684.

17. Morrow R, Rabin DL. Reliability in self-medication with Isoniazid. *Clin Res.* 1966; 14:362.

18. Cobb B, et al. Patient-responsible delay of treatment in cancer: A social psychological study. *Cancer.* 1954; 7:920-925.

19. Davis MS, Eichhorn RL. Compliance with medical regimens: A panel study. *J Health Hum Behav.* 1963; 4:240–249.

20. Kasl SV. Issues in patient adherence to health care regimens. *J Hum Stress.* 1975; 1:5–17.

21. Ware JE, Davies-Avery A, Stewart AL. The measurement and meaning of patient satisfaction: a review of the literature. *Health Med Care Serv Rev.* 1978; 1:1015.

22. Graham N. A quality of care assessment: Pediatricians and pediatric nurse practitioners. *Image.* 1978; 2:41-48.

23. Gardner HH, Ouimette R. A nurse-physician team approach in a private internal medicine practice. *Arch Intern Med.* 1974; 134: 956–959.

24. Lewis C, Resnik B. Nurse clinics and progressive ambulatory patient care. *N Engl J Med.* 1967; 227:1236–1241.

25. Spitzer WO, Sackett DL, Sibley JC, et al. Burlington randomized trial of the nurse practitioner. *N Engl J Med.* 1974; 290:251–256.

26. McGlone F, Schultz P. Problems in geriatric health care delivery. *J Am Geriatr Soc.* 1973; 21:533–537.

27. Roy Sr C. *Introduction to Nursing: An Adaptation Model.* Englewood Cliffs, NJ: Prentice-Hall, 1976.

28. Johnson D, as described by Auger JR. *Behavioral Systems and Nursing.* Englewood Cliffs, NJ: Prentice-Hall, 1976.

29. Houston CS, Pasanen WE. Patients' perceptions of hospital care. *Hospitals.* 1972; 46:70–74.

30. King SH, Goldman B. Variables in patient satisfaction with medical care. *J Am Coll Health Assoc.* 1975; 24:100–105.

31. Hallburg JC. *A Decision-Making Approach as a Teaching-Learning Strategy for Preparing Patients for Self-Care,* thesis. University of California: Berkeley, 1969.

32. Levine JI, Orr ST, Sheatsley DN, et al. The nurse practitioner: Role, physician utilization, patient acceptance. *Nurs Res.* 1978; 27:245–254.

33. Marston MV. Compliance with medical regimens: A review of the literature. *Nurs Res.* 1970; 19:312–323.

34. Holloway J. The association of nursing activities with mental status outcomes of elderly hip-fractured patients at three points during hospitalization. Paper presented at the 11th Annual Communicating Nursing Research Conference, Western Society for Research in Nursing, Portland, Ore, May 1978.

35. Lum J. Nursing care of oncology patients receiving chemotherapy. Paper presented at the 11th Annual Communicating Nursing Research Conference, Western Society for Research in Nursing, Portland, Ore, May 1978.

36. Day LR, Egli R, Silvers HK. Acceptance of nurse practitioners. *Am J Dis Child.* 1970; 119:204–208.

37. Donabedian A. *A Guide to Medical Care Administration. Vol 2. Medical Care Appraisal Quality and Utilization.* New York: American Public Health Association, 1969.

38. Blackwell B. Treatment adherence. *Br J Psychiatr.* 1976; 129:513–531.

39. Levin LS. Patient education and self-care: How do they differ? *Nurs Outlook.* 1978; 26:170–175.

40. Vickery DM, Fries JF. *Take Care of Yourself: A Consumer's Guide to Medical Care.* Menlo Park, Calif: Addison-Wesley, 1978.

41. HEW National Center for Health Services Research. *Consumer Self-Care in Health.* DHEW Publ. No. (HRA) 77–3181. Government Printing Office, August 1977.

42. Busse E, Pfeiffer E, eds. *Behavior and Adaptation to Late Life,* ed. 2. Boston: Little Brown & Co, 1977.
43. Butler RN, Lewis M. *Aging and Mental Health.* St. Louis: The CV Mosby Co, 1973.
44. Spengler JJ. The Aged and Public Policy. In Busse E, Pfeiffer E, eds. *Behavior and Adaptation to Late Life,* ed. 2. Boston: Little Brown & Co, 1977.
45. Suchman EA. Sociomedical variations among ethnic groups. *Am J Sociol.* 1964; 70:319–331.
46. Hulka BS, Zyzanski SJ, Cassel JC, Thompson SJ. Scale for the measurement of attitudes toward physicians and primary medical care. *Medical Care.* 1970; 8:429-436.
47. Ware JE, Synder MK. Dimensions of patient attitudes regarding doctors and medical care services. *Medical Care.* 1975; 13:669–682.
48. Henriques CC, Virgadamo VG, Kahane MD. Performance of adult health appraisal examinations utilizing nurse practitioner-physician teams and paramedical personnel. *Am J Public Health.* 1974; 64:47–53.
49. Auger JR. *Behavioral Systems and Nursing.* Englewood Cliffs, NJ: Prentice-Hall, 1976.
50. Burnside IM, ed. *Psychosocial Nursing Care of the Aged.* New York: McGraw-Hill, 1973.
51. Burnside IM, ed. *Nursing and the Aged.* New York: McGraw-Hill, 1976.
52. Stewart MA, Buck CW. Physicians' knowledge of and response to patients' problems. *Medical Care.* 1977; 15:578–585.
53. Bruner J. *Toward a Theory of Learning.* Cambridge, Mass: Harvard University Press, 1966.
54. deTornyay R. *Strategies for Teaching Nursing.* New York: John Wiley & Sons, 1971.
55. Kuhn A. *The Logic of Social Systems.* San Francisco: Jossey-Bass, 1974.
56. Linn L. *Patient Acceptance of the Family Nurse Practitioner,* research memorandum. Family Practitioner Program, UCLA Extension Division and School of Medicine, March 8, 1976.
57. Spitzer WO, et al. Nurse practitioners in primary care. Pt 3. The southern randomized trial. *Can Med Assoc J.* 1973; 108:1005.
58. Chenoy NC, Spitzer WO, Anderson GD. Nurse practitioners in primary care. Pt 2. Prior attitudes of a rural population. *Can Med Assoc J.* 1973; 108:998–1003.
59. Kegeles SS. Some motives for seeking preventive dental care. *J Am Dent Assoc.* 1963; 67:90.
60. Kegeles SS. Why people seek dental care: A test of a conceptual formulation. *J Health Hum Behav.* 1963; 4:166.
61. Bonnar J, Goldberg A, Smith JA. Do pregnant women take their iron? *Lancet.* 1969; 1:457.
62. MacDonald ME, Hagberg KL, Grossman BJ. Social factors in relation to participation in follow-up care of rheumatic fever. *J Pediatr.* 1963; 62:503.
63. Pragoff H. Adjustment of tuberculosis patients one year after hospital discharge. *Public Health Rep.* 1962; 77:671–679.
64. Heinzelmann F. Factors in prophylaxis behavior in treating rheumatic fever: An exploratory study. *J Health Hum Behav.* 1962; 3:73.
65. Elling R, Whittemore R, Green M. Patient participation in a pediatric program. *J Health Hum Behav.* 1960; 1:183.
66. Christensen DR. Drug taking compliance: A review and synthesis. *Health Serv Res.* 1978; 13:171–187.
67. Charney E, et al. How well do patients take oral penicillin? A collaborative study in private practice. *Pediatrics.* 1967; 40:188.
68. Davis MS. Variations in patients' compliance with doctors' advice: An empirical analysis of patterns of communication. *Am J Public Health.* 1968; 58:247.
69. Hulka BS, Cassel JC, Kupper LL, Burdette JA. Communication, compliance, and concordance between physicians and patients with prescribed medications. *Am J Public Health.* 1976; 66:847.

Social Support: A Model for Clinical Research and Application

Jane S. Norbeck. RN, DNSc
Assistant Professor
Department of Mental Health and Community Nursing
University of California
San Francisco, California

THE CONCEPT of attachment has recently been extended from a concern unique to infancy to a life-span concept.[1-5] In this context, attachments acquired in infancy are seen as prototypes and precursors of supportive interactions in adulthood. Just as the well-adjusted, attached infant is considered to have a secure base from which to explore, interact, and discover the world,[6] Kahn and Antonucci[7] proposed that adults with a strong supportive relationship are able to cope better with the stresses of their environment. Kalish and Knudtson[2] further developed the theme that attachment is related to feelings of competency across the life span. According to Kalish and Knudtson, self-initiated attachment behaviors produce feedback from the attachment object that provides a sense of mastery, thereby reducing feelings of vulnerability and helplessness. The security that arises from this mastery can be a basis for creativity, generativity, and risk taking.

Supportive interactions in adulthood have been studied in relation to a variety of outcomes. "Social support" is currently used by behavioral and health scientists to denote variously defined supportive interactions. In the statement of Research Priorities for the 1980s, the American Nurses' Association (ANA) Commission on Nursing Research[8] included social support networks as an example of personal and environmental determinants of wellness and health functioning in individuals and families that needs further study.

THE EFFECT OF SOCIAL SUPPORT ON HEALTH AND ILLNESS

Prior to incorporating social support into nursing practice, how it relates to health outcomes must be made clear. To date, numerous studies have been reported in which significant relations have been found between social support and a variety of outcomes. Review articles outline the historical context and scope of research in this field.

Adv Nurs Sci 1981;3(4):43–59
© 1981 Aspen Publishers, Inc.

From an epidemiological perspective, Cassel[9] wondered if there were social-environmental factors that can change human resistance to environmental disease agents. After reviewing animal and human studies, he concluded that changes in the social environment act as predisposing factors that enhance the host's susceptibility to disease. The particular mechanism postulated for the increased susceptibility of the organism was that changes in the social environment lead to alterations in the neuroendocrine balance.

The common social environment found in several studies reviewed by Cassel was a marginal status in society for individuals who developed tuberculosis, schizophrenia, alcoholism, and other conditions. Cassel speculated that by being deprived of meaningful social contact, individuals do not receive adequate feedback that their actions are leading to anticipated consequences. In contrast, adequate social supports provide a protective function that buffers or cushions the individual from the physiological and psychological consequences of exposure to the stressor situation.

The studies that Cassel reviewed did not study social support directly, but they did deal with related variables or concepts. None of the studies alone provided convincing evidence for his thesis, but taken together, an impressive array of findings points to the importance of social support.

Cobb[10] organized his review of social support around major transitions and crises of the life cycle. He suggested that social support functions as a moderating variable that facilitates coping with crisis and adaptation to change. As in the Cassel review, Cobb reinterpreted studies in which social support had not been explicitly studied but was implied. The areas included pregnancy, birth, and early life; transitions to adulthood; hospitalization; recovery from illness; life stress; employment termination; bereavement; aging and retirement; and threat of death. Although the relation of social support to the various outcomes studied tended to be substantiated, there were negative findings among the studies reported.

Kaplan, Cassel, and Gore[11] argued that social support is likely to be protective only in the presence of stressful circumstances and that conflicting findings among studies may have resulted from the failure of certain investigators to study social support in the context of stressors. The studies they reviewed were organized into three areas: support defined as the gratification of basic social needs; support defined by the presence or absence of support from significant others (eg, support loss through death, institutionalization, etc); and support defined in terms of person-environment fit (eg, personal need for support in relation to the level of support available). Kaplan et al emphasized inadequacies of conceptualization and measurement in social support research and outlined elements from social network theory that could be used to provide greater conceptual clarity in the field.

In addition to reviewing representative findings in social support research, Dean and Lin[12] identified key empirical, theoretical, and methodological problems. They proposed a shift from case-control designs to cohort studies, studies with normal populations, and longitudinal studies in a path-analytic model to test cause-effect relationships. Further refinements recommended include the possibility that social support may buffer different categories of life events differentially and only within certain limits.

Heller[13] reviewed the evidence for the social support hypothesis and concluded that there is an abundance of naturalistic and correlational research supporting the beneficial effects of social support. He called for going beyond that simple truism to an examination of the conditions and mechanisms by which support operates optimally. A rival hypothesis identified for the results from naturalistic and correlational studies of social support was social competence: Competent persons may be more immune to the adverse effects of stress and more likely to have well-developed social networks. Because of the limitations of research designs, Heller identified the need for laboratory studies to investigate the parameters of support and field studies in which support programs are tested in controlled demonstration projects.

Walker, MacBride, and Vachon[14] reviewed social support in relation to bereavement; Cochran and Brassard[15] developed a theoretical framework to discuss the effects of the social network on child development; and Mueller[16] presented a comprehensive review of the literature on social support and psychiatric disorders.

In summary, the link between social support and various outcomes has been established, but there is a need for refinement and replication to gain knowledge with the precision required to guide clinical application. Specifically, there is a need for consensus on the conceptual definitions of social support and on its measurement. Longitudinal studies are needed to establish causal relationships; more focused questions must be asked; and tighter designs are required to determine specific properties of persons, situations, types of support, and other variables that influence outcome.

MODEL TO INCORPORATE SOCIAL SUPPORT INTO NURSING PRACTICE

The bulk of the social support research has explored relations between social support and health or other adjustment outcomes. Although these relations imply that interventions for persons with inadequate social support might reduce their risk for certain negative outcomes, serious gaps in knowledge exist that must be studied to provide a scientific basis for intervention. Figure 1 is a model of the elements and relationships that must be studied to incorporate social support into nursing practice. The four components that comprise most existing nursing practice theories—person, environment, health-illness, and nursing actions[17]—are included in the model, as well as the elements of assessment, planning, intervention, and evaluation of the nursing process. Particular emphasis is placed on developing the component of environment, the component that Flaskerud and Halloran[17] specify as the least developed in nursing theories and nursing curricula.

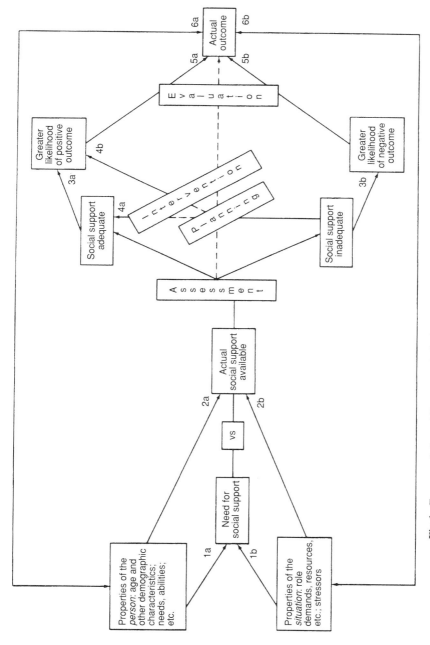

Fig 1. Framework for guiding research for incorporating social support into clinical practice.

Beginning with concepts proposed by Kahn and Antonucci,[7] properties of the *person* and properties of the *situation* jointly determine the *need for social support*, as well as the actual support available (arrows 1a, 1b, 2a, and 2b). The situation can produce both stressors and stress-buffering elements.

An *assessment* involves weighing the need for social support versus the actual social support available to determine whether the level of social support is *adequate* or *inadequate* and to provide a basis for *planning*.

Because empirical evidence for the social support hypothesis is presented for groups rather than individuals, the relation in an individual case must be stated as a *greater likelihood of positive* (or negative) *outcome* (arrows 3a and 3b). The *actual outcome* is determined through *evaluation* (arrows 5a and 5b). Additional, but as yet unknown, influences from the person, the situation, or other sources may affect the actual outcome (arrows 6a and 6b).

When social support is determined to be inadequate, *planning* and *intervention* are done to influence the probable outcome. Two major types of intervention are possible—(1) interventions that focus on changing an inadequate level of social support to an adequate level through influencing the structure, functioning, or use of the person's social support network, and (2) interventions that provide direct support or other help to the person during a specified period of time (or crisis) rather than attempting to influence the adequacy of social support through the indigenous network.

Persons with adequate social support or those who have benefited from successful intervention have a greater likelihood of a positive outcome (arrows 3a, 4a, and 4b). Persons with inadequate social support without effective intervention have a greater likelihood of a negative outcome (arrow 3b).

For each of the arrows indicating a relation between concepts in the model, a number of questions must be addressed. These questions provide a basis for planning the research that is needed for implementing findings about social support to specific clinical populations.

Properties of the Person

Demographic variables, such as age, sex, marital status, religion, and culture, influence how much social support may be needed by a person, as well as how much might be available to them. Similarly, individual differences in needs, abilities, and orientations are likely to influence the need for, availability, and use of social support. The extent to which these variables influence social support is not known, but evidence in a variety of areas is emerging.

Person influences on the need for social support

Age influences the amount and type of social support required for optimal functioning. During infancy almost constant support from one or a few primary caretakers is required. With maturation the frequency of supportive interactions decreases and the number of persons who can provide support is expanded to include other family members, relatives, other adults, and finally peers. The relative importance of peers increases in middle childhood and reaches a high level in adolescence. In adulthood role-related support is sought from work associates, other parents, etc. As roles are relinquished in later adulthood, support needs shift to accommodate a variety of losses. Research that explores age-related requirements for social support has focused mainly on studies on attachment in infancy and early childhood and studies on aging.

Sex differences in need for support are implied in several studies that indicate that females receive more social support than males. Female adolescents not only reported having more social support available from peers but also more life stress than males.[18] Female college students reported spending more time interacting with their social network, but there was no difference in satisfaction with social or emotional support between males and females.[19] Elderly women are more likely to report having a confidant than elderly men, despite a greater incidence of widowhood among women.[20] Whether females actually need more social support than males, rather than simply obtain more, is not clear from these studies.

Individual differences also influence the amount of social support that an individual requires. A person's need for affiliation is an important dimension that has not been studied in relation to social support; however, Heller[13] clearly indicated the need for study in this area. Lowenthal and Haven[20] point out that the late-life adaptation of some lifelong isolates is not influenced by the availability of social resources. Another study of older women living in single room hotels in Seattle found that these women were voluntary isolates who highly valued individualism, independence, and self-sufficiency.[21] Their restrictive social networks were not a result of social pathology but represented a natural life history progression instead. Conversely, persons with a high need for affiliation would be expected to need more social support than persons with a moderate or low need for affiliation.

Additional research is needed to further clarify the age, sex, and personality differences that influence the differential need for social support among individuals. Differences in coping styles and cultural differences are other important areas that have not been studied in relation to social support requirements.

Person influences on the availability of social support

Just as persons differ in the amount of social support they need, they differ in the amount of social support that is available to or used by them. The amount of social support available to individuals at different ages has not been widely studied. A preliminary study with adult subjects indicated that the size of the social support network (convoy) increased during the years of young adulthood and was stable during the years from 35 to 55.[22] With aging, losses in role and interaction are likely to decrease the opportunities for social support, and losses of network members through death increase.

The sex differences reported earlier clearly indicate that females receive more social support or have larger social networks than males. Patterns of support also appear to differ; for example, female adolescents are more likely than males to name same-sex peers as helpers, and males are more likely than females to name fathers as helpers.[18] Among older, married adults, men are more likely to list their spouse as their confidant, and women are more likely to name an adult child, another relative, or friends as their confidant.[20]

Other demographic variables appear to influence the amount of social support available. Middle-class wives of heart attack victims were found to have more diverse sources of social support than working class wives, who tended to be limited to support from families of origin.[23] Among older adults, marital status was related to whether or not the person reported having a confidant: Married persons were more likely to have a confidant than widowed, widowed more than divorced or separated, and divorced or separated more than single persons.[20] Family income was significantly related to the level of social support available to postmastectomy women.[24] The use of support groups, such as lay postpartum support groups or Parents Without Partners, is determined by a self-selection process in which more educated and affluent middle-class women tend to be the sole participants;[25,26] however, self-help groups that focus on behavior change, like Alcoholics Anonymous, contain working class individuals, including men.[27] Crosscultural differences in social support have not been studied.

The ability of the person to attract and maintain a social support network may be influenced by their social competence. Although the cause and effect relationship between limited support and mental illness cannot be determined because longitudinal studies have not been done, it is known that mentally ill patients have smaller, more restrictive social networks; receive less support; and have experienced more network disruption than the general population.[16] When hospitalized, they receive fewer visitors than a medical population[28] and they demonstrate a negative orientation toward drawing on their network resources for support.[29]

In the general population there may be other individual differences that influence how much social support is available to a person, such as self-esteem, physical attractiveness, range of interests, and social competence. The importance of study in this area is related to intervention: If a person is basically unable to attract, maintain, or use a social support network, then interventions aimed at enhancing their indigenous sources of social support will fall short. However, when specific factors are isolated through research, intervention strategies can be tailored to particular deficits.

Properties of the Situation

Situational variables that influence the amount of social support that is needed and available are important for nursing research, particularly to determine factors that arise from different health and illness situations.

Situational influences on the need for social support

Situational determinants of the need for social support are of specific relevance to health care providers who have contact with people in a variety of maturational and situational crises, including changes along the health-illness continuum. Table 1 presents a theoretical grid for predicting the intensity and duration of support required for different situational demands and stressors. Studies in which outcome measures of functioning or adaptation for specific groups of patients contribute to the data base for this grid.

Theorists in social support hold that individuals need support on a day-to-day basis to promote individual well-being and adequate performance in their major social roles.[22] A study of functioning in the single parent role found that network support was significantly related to day-care staff ratings of parenting adequacy and the preschool child's emotional development and behavior.[30] Extensive support did not seem to be required, since neither current or past use of counseling nor ongoing help with parenting or household responsibilities was related to functioning. However, having friends or relatives to confide in and the availability of

Table 1. Grid for predicting the intensity and duration of support required for situational demands and stressors

Duration of support required	Intensity of support required		
	Low	Medium	High
Short-term			Support needed for acute stressors or illnesses
Intermediate		Support needed for managing life changes and transitions and for facilitating rehabilitation from major illnesses or surgery	
Long-term or continuous	Support needed for day-to-day living for individual well-being and performance in the major social roles	Support needed to cope with chronic stressors or illnesses	

people to call on for practical help discriminated between the adequate and inadequate functioning groups of single parents (see Table 1, column 1).

In a situation of great stress, such as life changes and transitions, more intense support is required but for a shorter duration (see Table 1, column 2). Outcome studies of bereavement lend support to this claim. For example, in a retrospective study of widows 13 months after the deaths of their husbands, outcome was determined by self-reports of physical and mental health. Widows with bad outcomes were compared with widows with good outcomes. Those with good outcomes had been assisted with resolution of their grief by their social networks. In contrast, for those with bad outcomes, network members had discouraged the expression of affect and review of the past, had pressed the widows toward present and future orientations, and had been deficient in the provision of concomitant needs.[31]

Support of medium intensity is also required to cope with chronic stressors or illnesses, but this support must be long term or continuous. For example, mothers of children with chronic illnesses reported that they were not receiving many forms of assistance, particularly sympathetic listeners, to help them cope with their children's chronic conditions.[32] Although not specifically testing propositions related to the intensity and duration of support required, a study of the functioning of formerly hospitalized schizophrenics revealed that inadequate functioning was associated with a low level of social support in terms of the amount of recent interaction with associates and a less restrictive support network (ie, support from both within and outside the home).[33]

Support is often extended during certain acute crises, but in the transition from acute to rehabilitation or chronic status, support resources do not tend to persist. For example, immediately after their husbands had suffered a myocardial infarction, wives reported extensive offers of help. During the course of the following year, however, significant differences appeared between the favorable and unfavorable outcome groups.[23] Likewise, family and friends were initially interested and concerned about a woman after a mastectomy, but they soon expected her to return to normal—often before even the physical healing was complete, let alone the psychological adjustment.[34]

Although high levels of support are often mobilized during an acute illness or for acute stressors, this is not always the case. Helmrath and Steinitz[35] reported a small study of seven middle-class couples who experienced the death of an infant under three weeks of age. Despite good network resources, these couples found that their family and friends actively avoided mentioning the infant or the death and did not seem to understand that a grief process was warranted. Evidence for the need for high-intensity support for a brief duration is found in a study of crisis intervention for car accident victims who were hospitalized. The most effective aspect of the intervention was to mobilize genuine concern and to reduce hostility and misunderstanding from people in the patient's social network. The patients who did not receive this intervention were as disturbed as typical psychiatric outpatients at follow-up, whereas the intervention group had returned to normal functioning at three to four months.[36,37]

The studies that have been presented as evidence for the amount of support required for different situations are preliminary; several need replication or refinement in methodology. Nonetheless, these studies point to differential needs for support in patterns reflecting the properties of the situations.

Situational influences on the availability of social support

The type of support that a situation demands may influence the availability of support that individuals receive from their network. Pregnancy and parenthood are maturational crises that evoke a great deal of spontaneous support from friends, relatives, and even strangers. In contrast, support for grief work is not easy for network members to provide. Quint[34] suggested that taboo subjects such as disfigurement and the threat of death from cancer are difficult for network members and professionals to deal with; thus they fail to offer needed support to post-mastectomy patients.

Support in anticipation of a stressful event appears to be difficult to provide. College students reported satisfaction with the support they received during or after final exams but not before exams.[19] Likewise, mastectomy patients reported that the period of time after discovering the breast lump and before the biopsy was done was very stressful, but most women received little opportunity to talk about their feelings at this time.[38]

Societal expectations of role demands also may influence the amount of support received. Anecdotal evidence indicates that single fathers receive practical support from friends and neighbors, but single mothers are regarded as simply doing their job (albeit alone) and not requiring assistance, despite their dual roles of provider and parent.

The loss of social roles influences potential sources of support. If a major source of support for an individual were through work-related associates, then retirement or changing jobs might significantly reduce the avenues for obtaining support relationships. The social roles of spouse or parent are subject to loss through death or emancipation from the home.

Thus a beginning has been made in exploring the support needs and resources in certain crisis or illness situations; yet many important areas remain unexplored. Ultimately, research that combines person and situation variables in single studies will provide the clearest findings for clinical knowledge and application.

Assessment

An individual's need for social support and the actual support that is available have been shown to be jointly determined by properties of the person and properties of the situation. Assessment procedures should determine relevant factors from each of these areas as a basis to weigh need versus availability of social support to judge whether the existing support is adequate or inadequate. Details contributing to this judgment will also be useful in planning intervention.

To date, reliable and valid instruments to measure social support for clinical assessment have not been developed, but two useful approaches have been described. Murawski, Penman, and Schmitt[39] proposed that until further research is able to more narrowly define the critical elements of social support, the following elements should be included in current clinical assessment of social support: an inventory of the individual's interpersonal support system and some measure of the nature, strength, and availability of this support; a definition of the individual's social obligations (roles); an indication of the amount of support available to meet these role obligations during illness; a measure of the individual's patterns of social affiliation; and a measure of the individual's need for social affiliation. With this assessment guide, Murawski et al recommend a focus on those individuals with low social support and high need and in health care situations in which the structure of the treatment alters the individual's social support negatively.

Rich[40] described the use of a sociogram for depicting social support and illustrating change over time. Through a series of concentric circles, the immediate family, extended family, more distant relatives, nonfamily persons, and institutional sources of support are represented. This scheme is similar in concept to Kahn and Antonucci's[7] method for depicting the person's convoy of network members who provide support, but their emphasis is on the roles that the network members hold in relation to the individual.

Research findings, supplemented with clinical judgment, can guide the practitioner in determining whether the level of social support is adequate or inadequate for a given person. The question of how much or what types of social support are needed for adequate or optimal functioning has not been answered. Empirical results suggest that different constellations may be crucial for different stressors or life events. For example, family cohesiveness, family expressiveness, and spouse support were significant sources of support for the dialysis patient, but the presence of a confidant was not.[41] The presence of a confidant for older adults enhanced adaptation to retirement and bereavement but did not buffer the impact of serious or long-term illness.[20] Network stability was found to be an important quality of the support, whereas loss of a confidant was associated with depressed morale. Maintaining a confidant was very helpful, but *gaining* a confidant was only mildly helpful.[20]

Hirsch[19,42] studied two dimensions of network structure and found that low density, multidimensional support systems were preferable for college students, recent young widows, and mature women returning to college. Because high-density networks provide more effective support in certain situations,[43] Hirsch speculated that high-density networks may enhance adaptation under stress and that low-density networks may be more adaptive under conditions of change or personal growth.[19]

Litwak and Szelenyi[44] contributed theoretical insights and empirical data from the United States and Hungary which suggest that different functions are best carried out by specific primary groups. Because of proximity, neighbors are often best suited to assisting in emergencies. The permanence of relationships in the kinship system provides a basis for extending support for long-term commitments. Friends are freely chosen on the basis of mutual affectivity rather than territorial proximity or family relationships. For this reason, friends can offer support in matters involving continuous fluctuation, such as changing values that may not be understood similarly across generations.

Research in which person-related and situational variables are studied as joint influences on the need for social support and on the amount of support that is available is necessary for a sound basis of assessment. With that knowledge, a clinician may ask if a given network can provide support long enough and strong enough for a particular situation that fits the requirements of a specific individual.

Planning

In cases in which an individual's social support is inadequate, several questions must be addressed to determine what interventions are possible:
1. What is the capacity of the network to change?
    A. Network structure: Are there persons who can be brought into (or back into) the network?
    B. Network functioning: Can existing network members be assisted to provide the kind of support that is needed (eg, allow talk about the pregnancy or about a loss)?
    C. Network disruption: Can policies be changed or resources employed to minimize network disruption (eg, due to hospitalization at a distant tertiary care facility)?
2. Does the individual have the interpersonal skills and attitudes required to establish and maintain contact with network members?
3. Is the individual receptive to using existing self-help or support groups or to having contact with a person who has coped with a similar experience?
4. If help from the indigenous social support system cannot be made available or acceptable, exactly what support does this individual require to cope with the current stressors or illness?
5. What long-term help would be required to assist the individual to establish and maintain an adequate social support network?

Intervention

Just as research is needed to determine which factors are associated with adequate support for individuals in specific situations, research is needed to evaluate the effectiveness of intervention strategies. In particular, it must be determined whether interference with natural support systems produces undesirable consequences.

An issue central to intervention is to distinguish social support from the professional helping process. Although social support may involve talking with a confidant about personal concerns, the essential qualities of social support appear to be tied more to interactions about day-to-day living. Consistent with Kahn's[22] definition, social support could be experienced through expressions of positive affect, through having people to call on for assistance, and through discussing the events of the day. Above all, a social support relationship is reciprocal in nature: Each member is giving and receiving,[22,45,46] and network members feel part of a network of communication and mutual obligation.[10]

In the context of attachment theory, social support reflects the human need for comfort through social bonds.[47] Mechanic states that "social support systems are responsive to the need to affiliate under stress, a need that seems to be acquired very early in life and that may have a biological basis."[48(p85)]

Gottlieb[49] cautions against the potentially damaging effects of consultation or training with existing informal helpers that might inadvertently suppress their natural repertoire of effective helping behaviors. For example, hairdressers were found to see approximately 55 customers a week, and about one-third of their talking time concerned clients' moderate to serious personal problems.[50] Although a small pilot study demonstrated that hairdressers could be taught a new response strategy— reflection of feelings—this appeared to be at the expense of presenting alternatives, whereas advice giving was unchanged.[51]

A general guideline for intervention is to produce minimal disruption or alteration in the natural support system—unless it is a pathological system—while enhancing the capacity of that system to provide support. Also, care should be taken to avoid making recommendations that the person is unlikely to be able to carry out: Persons who lack the interpersonal skills to enhance their social support network will probably feel even more incompetent and discouraged if they are told to go out and find more friends or support persons.

Enhancing the social support system

For carefully planned interventions within the capacity of the individual or network, the point of entry is a useful concept for organizing a discussion of options. The individual with an inadequate social support system may be the point of entry for enhancing the adequacy of social support. As mentioned earlier, the person may need assistance to develop, maintain, or use their network. The individual might be assisted to consider persons for support who are not presently in their network, particularly persons who were once a part of the social support system. During pregnancy, for example, women often experience a reawakening or deepening of the bond between themselves and their mothers or sisters. If an unresolved conflict prevents this from occurring, the woman might need assistance to work through the conflict, or perhaps just encouragement to initiate contact once again.

A key network member may be the point of entry for enhancing the functioning of the network. Ervin[52] developed an approach with the husbands of mastectomy patients in which he discussed the emotional responses and needs of women after mastectomy with the husbands and gave specific guidance for how the husbands could provide support in the immediate postoperative period. The effectiveness of this approach needs to be studied using a control group. Network therapy involves a significant portion of the entire network as the point of entry.[53]

When the individual's needs for support cannot be met by the network, supplementary sources of support through mutual help or support groups may be effective. Self-help groups are a focus of professional interest and research, although professional involvement in self-help groups is often limited by the autonomy of these groups. Caplan and Killilea's[54] book deals with many types of mutual help, and other studies have resulted in a classification of self-help groups,[55] a report of the member's perspective,[27] and the perceptions of mental health professionals.[56] Little is known about the actual effectiveness of these groups, however, because no follow-up has been done for those who drop out of the groups. Nonetheless, the reports of satisfied participants clearly indicate that these groups provide needed support to certain individuals.

Successful involvement of professionals in facilitating mutual help was reported by Budman.[57] "Psychoeducational" groups were created by the agency around common life transitions or situational problems. These groups formed the basis for continuing mutual help in the participant's informal networks following official termination of the groups. In fact, one of the main purposes of the groups had been to link people in similar circumstances and to provide them with opportunities to share resources.

Other clinical approaches to promote help giving through lay helpers have been seen in attempts to arrange for contact with persons who have successfully experienced the same event or illness. Offering a couple whose infant has died the opportunity to meet with another couple who had gone through the same experience[35] is one example. Weiss[26] differentiates between the veteran (an individual who has been through the experience and who can demonstrate that recovery is possible) and the fellow participant (an individual who can offer the immediate understanding that comes from being in the same boat). For situations that are essentially "new" to the experience of the network, these kinds of outside help may be far more effective in providing support and guidance to individuals currently trying to navigate the transition, crisis, or illness.

Providing direct support

The use of self-help groups or arranging for contact with an experienced lay person are interventions that supplement support from the indigenous network. Support that is provided directly by the professional is aimed at decreasing the likelihood for a negative outcome, but this help is not social support because the giving of support is usually unidirectional rather than reciprocal, the helper is not a part of the client's network, and the helping process is usually limited to only certain types of interpersonal transactions. Nonetheless, certain support needs for the individual can be met, particularly during major transitions, crises, or when changes are occurring in the person's social support network. After facilitating coping with the immediate situation, the goal of direct support is to enable the person to create and maintain his or her own social support system if possible.

For situations that require long-term or continuous support at a more intense level than is usually provided for day-to-day functioning (see Table 1), the network may become exhausted over time. A family coping with the chronic illness of a child is an example of such a situation.

Pless and Satterwhite[32] described a successful intervention program that employed empathic paraprofessionals to provide talking and action-oriented help. This assistance was designed to help families understand their child's illness and needs and make use of available resources. At the end of one year, 60% of the children in the intervention group showed an improvement in psychological status compared to 40.5% of the untreated comparison group. Interestingly, the low-risk families showed greater improvement than high-risk families, suggesting that this kind of supportive intervention was not adequate for "hard core," multiproblem situations. Nonetheless, the program was a cost-effective approach to providing needed support to these families. The feasibility and effectiveness of similar programs for many other areas of chronic care need to be studied.

Although programs of direct support have been studied, research on the effectiveness of interventions aimed at enhancing the natural support system has not been done. Clinical research in nursing can contribute to the needed field studies in which controlled demonstration projects are tested to determine the most appropriate intervention for particular clinical populations.

Evaluation

The final component in the model (see Fig 1) is evaluation to determine the actual outcome. The dotted arrow from intervention to evaluation indicates that the intervention itself must be evaluated. If the intervention was not successful in altering inadequate social support, then the predicted likelihood of a negative outcome would remain (arrow 3b).

Through evaluation, additional data to support the link between social support and outcome can be gained (arrows 3a and 3b). When the actual outcome is not the predicted outcome, other variables related to person (arrow 6a) or situation (arrow 6b) may be discovered. In addition, the nature of the relationships in the model can be refined through evaluation.

CONCLUSION

Nursing has a long tradition of concern for the environment of the patient as an important factor in healing and in promoting optimal health and functioning. Support, too, has been a concept of foremost importance in clinical nursing. Systematic ways to assess the influences of the environment or the support the patient may need or receive have been lacking. The model developed here can be used as a guide for building a body of knowledge about the patient's social environment for clinical practice. Research that incorporates person and situation variables, as well as other elements in the model, will lead to an accumulation of knowledge toward answering the question: "What types of social networks are most useful for which individuals in terms of what particular issues under what environmental conditions?"[58(p28)]

REFERENCES

1. Antonucci T. Attachment. A life-span concept. *Hum Dev.* 1976; 19:135–142.
2. Kalish RA, Knudtson FW. Attachment versus disengagement: A life-span conceptualization. *Hum Dev.* 1976; 19:171–181.
3. Knudtson FW. Life-span attachment: Complexities, questions, considerations. *Hum Dev.* 1976; 19:182–196.
4. Lerner RM, Ryff CD. Implementation of the life-span view of human development: The sample case of attachment. In Baltes PB, ed. *Life-span Development and Behavior.* New York: Academic Press, 1978.
5. Troll LE, Smith J. Attachment through the life-span: Some questions about dyadic bonds among adults. *Hum Dev.* 1976; 19:156–170.
6. Ainsworth MDS. The development of infant-mother attachment. In Caldwell BM, Ricciuti HN, eds. *Review of Child Development Research.* Chicago: University of Chicago Press, 1973.
7. Kahn RL, Antonucci TC. Convoys over the life course: Attachment, roles, and social support. In Baltes PB, Brim O, eds. *Life-Span Development and Behavior.* New York: Academic Press, in press, vol 3.
8. ANA Commission on Nursing Research. Generating a scientific basis for nursing practice: Research priorities for the 1980s. *Nurs Res.* 1980; 29:219.
9. Cassel J. The contribution of the social environment to host resistance. *Am J Epidemiol.* 1976; 104:107–123.
10. Cobb S. Social support as a moderator of life stress. *Psychosom Med.* 1976; 38:300–314.
11. Kaplan BH, Cassel JC, Gore S. Social support and health. *Med Care.* 1977; 15(5):47–58 (suppl).
12. Dean A, Lin N. The stress-buffering role of social support: Problems and prospects for systematic investigation. *J Nerv Ment Dis.* 1977; 165:403–417.
13. Heller K. The effects of social support: Prevention and treatment implications. In Goldstein AP, Kanfer FH, eds. *Maximizing Treatment Gains: Transfer Enhancement in Psychotherapy.* New York: Academic Press, 1979.
14. Walker KN, MacBride A, Vachon MLS. Social support networks and the crisis of bereavement. *Soc Sci Med.* 1977; 11:35–41.
15. Cochran M, Brassard JA. Child development and personal social networks. *Child Dev.* 1979; 50:601–616.
16. Mueller DP. Social networks: A promising direction for research on the relationship of the social environment to psychiatric disorder. *Soc Sci Med.* 1980; 14A:147–161.
17. Flaskerud JH, Halloran EJ. Areas of agreement in nursing theory development. *Adv Nurs Sci.* 1980; 3(1):1–7.
18. Burke RJ, Weir T. Sex differences in adolescent life stress, social support, and well-being. *J Psychol.* 1978; 98:277–288.
19. Hirsch BJ. Psychological dimensions of social networks: A multimethod analysis. *Am J Community Psychol.* 1979; 7:263–277.

20. Lowenthal MF, Haven C. Interaction and adaptation: Intimacy as a critical variable. *Am Sociol Rev.* 1968; 33:20–30.
21. Lally M, Black E, Thornock M, Hawkins JD. Older women in single room occupant (SRO) hotels: A Seattle profile. *Gerontologist.* 1979; 19:67–73.
22. Kahn RL. *Aging and social support.* Paper presented at the meeting of the American Association for the Advancement of Science, Washington, DC, February 1978.
23. Finlayson A. Social networks as coping resources: Lay help and consultation patterns used by women in husbands' post-infarction career. *Soc Sci Med.* 1976; 10:97–103.
24. Woods NF, Earp JAL. Women with cured breast cancer: A study of mastectomy patients in North Carolina. *Nurs Res.* 1978; 27:279–285.
25. Cronenwett LR. Elements and outcomes of a post-partum support group program. *Res Nurs Health.* 1980; 3:33–41.
26. Weiss RS. The contributions of an organization of single parents to the well-being of its members. In Caplan G, Kellilea M, eds. *Support Systems and Mutual Help: Multidisciplinary Explorations.* New York: Grune & Stratton, 1976.
27. Knight B, Wollert RW, Levy LH, et al. Self-help groups: The members' perspectives. *Am J Community Psychol.* 1980; 8:53–65.
28. Bernstein RA, Manchester RA, Weaver LA. The effect of visiting on psychiatric patients in a general hospital. *Community Ment Health J.* 1980; 16:235–240.
29. Tolsdorf CC. Social networks, support, and coping: An exploratory study. *Fam Process.* 1976; 15:407–417.
30. Norbeck JS, Sheiner M. Sources of social support related to single parent functioning. *Res Nurs Health.* In press.
31. Maddison D, Walker WL. Factors affecting the outcome of conjugal bereavement. *Br J Psychiatry.* 1967; 113:1057–1067.
32. Pless IB, Satterwhite B. Chronic illness in childhood: Selection, activities and evaluation of nonprofessional family counselors. *Clin Pediatr.* 1972; 11:403–410.
33. Turner SL. Disability among schizophrenics in a rural community: Services and social support. *Res Nurs Health.* 1979; 2:151–161.
34. Quint JC. The impact of mastectomy. *Am J Nurs.* 1963; 63(11):88–92.
35. Helmrath TA, Steinitz EM. Death of an infant: Parental grieving and the failure of social support. *J Fam Pract.* 1978; 6:787–790.
36. Bordow S. Porritt D. An experimental evaluation of crisis intervention. *Soc Sci Med.* 1979; 13A:251–256.
37. Porritt D. Social support in crisis: Quantity or quality? *Soc Sci Med.* 1979; 13A:715–721.
38. Jamison KR, Wellisch DK, Pasnau RO. Psychosocial aspects of mastectomy: I. The woman's perspective. *Am J Psychiatry.* 1978; 135:432–436.
39. Murawski BJ, Penman D, Schmitt M. Social support in health and illness: The concept and its measurement. *Cancer Nurs.* 1978; 1:356–371.
40. Rich OJ. The sociogram: A tool for depicting support in pregnancy. *Matern Child Nurs J.* 1978; 7:1–9.
41. Dimond M. Social support and adaptation to chronic illness: The case of maintenance hemodialysis. *Res Nurs Health.* 1979; 2:101–108.
42. Hirsch BJ. Natural support systems and coping with major life changes. *Am J Community Psychol.* 1980; 8:159–171.
43. Hammer M. Influence of small social networks as factors on mental hospital admission. *Hum Org.* 1963–1964; 22:243-251.
44. Litwak E, Szelenyi I. Primary group structures and their functions: Kin, neighbors and friends. *Am Sociol Rev.* 1969; 34:465–481.
45. Caplan G. Introduction and overview. In Caplan G, Killilea M, eds. *Support Systems and Mutual Help: Multidisciplinary Explorations.* New York: Grune & Stratton, 1976.

46. Erickson GD. The concept of personal network in clinical practice. *Fam Process.* 1975; 14:487–498.

47. Henderson S. The social network, support and neurosis: The function of attachment in adult life. *Br J Psychiatry.* 1977; 131:185–191.

48. Mechanic D. Illness behavior, social adaptation, and the management of illness: A comparison of educational and medical models. *J Nerv Ment Dis.* 1977; 165(2):79–87.

49. Gottlieb BH: The primary group as supportive milieu: Applications to community psychology. *Am J Community Psychol.* 1979;7:469–480.

50. Cowen EL, Gesten EL, Boike M, Norton P, Wilson AB, DeStefano MA. Hairdressers as caregivers. I. A descriptive profile of interpersonal help-giving involvements. *Am J Community Psychol.* 1979; 7:633–648.

51. Wiesenfeld AR, Weis HM. Hairdressers and helping: Influencing the behavior of informal caregivers. *Prof Psychol.* 1979; 10:786-792.

52. Ervin CV Jr. Psychological adjustment to mastectomy. *Med Aspects Hum Sexuality.* 1973; 7:42–65.

53. Speck R, Rueveni U. Network therapy—A developing concept. *Fam Process.* 1969; 8;182–192.

54. Caplan G, Killilea M, eds. *Support Systems and Mutual Help: Multidisciplinary Explorations.* New York: Grune & Stratton, 1976.

55. Levy LH. Self-help groups: Types and psychological processes. *J Appl Behav Sci.* 1976; 12:310–322.

56. Levy LH. Self-help groups viewed by mental health professionals: A survey and comments. *Am J Community Psychol.* 1978; 6:305–313.

57. Budman SH. A strategy for preventive mental health intervention. *Prof Psychol.* 1975; 6:394–398.

58. Mitchell RE, Trickett EJ. Social networks as mediators of social support: An analysis of the effects and determinants of social networks. *Community Ment Health J.* 1980; 16:27–44.

The Health Belief Model: A Review and Critical Evaluation of the Model, Research, and Practice

Blanche Mikhail
Boston University
School of Nursing
Boston, Massachusetts

INTEREST in human behavior has existed from the early years of humankind. What is new in the 20th century is the belief that behavior can be understood and controlled through science.[1(p92)]

Concern with health behavior developed in the early 1950s when low levels of public participation in preventive health programs were observed, despite the services being provided free of charge or at low cost.[2,3] Behavioral scientists and health workers see increasing need to understand why and under what conditions people take action to prevent, detect, and treat diseases.

The health belief model (HBM) is a psychosocial formulation developed to explain health-related behavior at the level of individual decision making. It was originated in the early 1950s by G.M. Hochbaum, S.S. Kegeles, H. Leventhal, and I.M. Rosenstock.[3] They were concerned with such issues as, Why do some people use health services but others do not? Why is there a high rate of noncompliance with health and medical care recommendations? What are the factors that prevent or interfere with people's following of health care recommendations? How can health-related behavior be changed when necessary?

The term health-related behavior (HRB) is used to refer to a group of behaviors, namely health behavior, illness behavior, sick role behavior, chronic illness behavior, and at-risk behavior, unless otherwise specified. As defined by Kasl and Cobb,[4] health behavior is "an activity undertaken by a person believing himself to be healthy, for the purpose of preventing disease or detecting it in an asymptomatic stage."[4(p246)] Illness behavior is "an activity undertaken by a person who feels ill, to define the state of his health and to discover a suitable remedy."[4(p246)] Sick role behavior is "the activity undertaken by those who consider themselves ill, for the purpose of getting well."[4(p246)] Chronic illness behav-

Adv Nurs Sci 1981;4(1):65–82

74

iors are described by Kasl[5] as those behaviors undertaken by persons with chronic diseases to reduce risk and maintain health. According to Baric, people at risk are "those who are engaged in certain activities which increase their risk to a much higher degree than the rest of the population."[6(p27)] For example, middle-aged men who are obese, smoke cigarettes, and have a raised blood pressure would belong to this group.

AN OVERVIEW OF THE HEALTH BELIEF MODEL

Lewin's Theory

Before examining the HBM, it is important to consider briefly some aspects of the social psychological theory of Kurt Lewin from which the model variables are drawn and adapted.

In Lewinian tradition, the individual is thought to exist in a life space composed of regions. Some of these are positively valued, others are negatively valued, and still others are relatively neutral.[7,8] A positively valued region contains a goal object and will reduce tension for the person entering it. On the other hand, a negatively valued region does not contain a goal object and will increase tension for the person entering it. Diseases were conceived to be regions of negative valence. They could be expected to exert a force moving the person away from that region unless doing so would require entering a region of even greater negative valence.[3(pp2,3)]

The origin of the HBM is attributed to a special case of Lewin's theory, goal setting in the level-of-aspiration situation.[9] Level of aspiration was defined as "the degree of difficulty of attainment of the goal toward which the person is striving."[10(pp453,454)] In this situation the choice between different levels of difficulty is made on the basis of the relative valences of these levels for success or failure and the subjective probability of success at each level.

Success that is highly improbable will not be chosen over reasonably probable success even though the improbable success is much more highly valued.[11] Most people tend to aspire to levels that are close to or slightly higher than their performance level in the past. However, the valence of any level is culturally as well as personally determined. Lewin then hypothesized that behavior depends mainly on two variables: (1) the value of an outcome to an individual and (2) the individual's estimate of the probability that a given action will result in that outcome.[12]

Subjective Emphasis

The HBM, originally formulated to explain preventive health behavior, extended the use of Lewin's theory to fulfill this purpose. The model has a phenomenological orientation. It assumes that the subjective world of the perceiver determines behavior rather than the objective environment, except as the objective environment comes to be represented in the mind of the behaving individual.[9]

People can only act on what they believe to exist, even though this may not match professional viewpoints. The model is more concerned with the current subjective state of the individual than with history or experience.[3]

According to Rosenstock,[3,19,13] the HBM proposes that the likelihood that a person will take action relative to a health condition is determined both by the individual's psychological state of readiness to take that action and by the perceived benefit of the action weighed against the perceived cost or barriers involved in the proposed action. The individual's psychological state of readiness to take action is determined by both perceived susceptibility to the particular health condition and the perceived severity of the consequences of contracting the condition. Action will not occur unless the individual believes in both personal susceptibility and the serious repercussion of illness, should it occur.

A perceived benefit of taking action is the individual's evaluation of the advocated action in terms of its feasibility and efficacy in reducing the threat (perceived susceptibility to and/or severity of the condition). The perceived benefit of an action is weighed against the perceived psychological, physical, financial, and other cost or barriers of taking action. Becker and Maiman[14] have shown that even if an individual is ready to act, the likelihood of taking action will depend on beliefs about the probable effectiveness of the action in reducing the health threat and about the difficulties that must be encountered if such action is taken.

In addition, it is proposed that a stimulus (or cue to action) must occur to trigger the appropriate behavior. This cue might be internal, like perception of bodily states, or external, like interpersonal interactions and the impact of communications media. The intensity of a cue that is required to instigate action is presumed to vary with the level of psychological readiness to act. Relatively low psychological readiness will require intense stimuli, whereas a relatively high level of readiness will only require slight stimuli.

A group of modifying and enabling factors serves to condition the individual's perceptions of susceptibility, severity, and benefits of taking action.[14-16] These modifying factors are (1) demographic variables; (2) structural variables, such as complexity and side effects of the regimen; (3) attitudinal variables, such as satisfaction with clinic staff and procedures; (4) interaction variables such as quality and type of patient-provider relationships; and (5) enabling variables, such as source of advice and social pressure.

Motivation

Health motivation, thought to influence HRB, was introduced into the model by Becker and associates[17] on the assumption that motives selectively determine an individual's perception of the environment. Health motivation refers to an individual's degree of interest in and concern about health matters. The desire to attain or maintain a positive state of health and to avoid a state of illness is a dimension of health motivation. The major dimensions of the model that have been developed to explain motivation are perceived susceptibility, perceived severity, perceived benefits, perceived barriers or costs, and cues to action.

Although the model was formulated originally to explain preventive health behavior, several investigators have expanded its use to explain other kinds of HRB. For example, with respect to taking action for the early detection of a disease, Hochbaum[18] and Rosenstock[3] noted that the same foregoing variables of the HBM are deemed necessary, with the additional requirement that the individual believe the disease could exist even in the absence of symptoms. In attempting to apply the model to illness behavior, Kirscht[19] drew attention to the importance of symptoms, as they may represent a threat to the individual and may arouse health motivation or act as a cue to taking action.

Special Situations

Additional expansion of the HBM was done by Becker et al[17] to explain sick role behavior. They modified the concept of personal susceptibility, since in this case some diagnosis of illness has already occurred. Here susceptibility means the probability of progressive effects or recurrence .

Kasl[5] called for some reformulation of the model so that it can help in explaining behavior in chronic diseases. Such behavior can be distinguished from sick role behavior in acute or short-term illnesses and thus requires special consideration. Chronic illness behavior requires the person to (1) stay in treatment and comply with the regimen although not feeling sick, (2) take medication although no changes in health status are taking place, (3) follow treatment indefinitely, and (4) do this in a setting that has minimal social and institutional support.

Kasl[5] and Rosenstock and Kirscht[20] suggested that the HBM be used to study the at-risk role as delineated by Baric.[6] Baric pointed out that the at-risk role differs from the sick role in that (1) the person in the sick role has certain rights and duties or obligations, whereas in the at-risk role the person has only duties and no overt rights (such as exemption from social responsibilities), (2) the at-risk role is not institutionalized and thus is not formally recognized by society, (3) the at-risk role has no time limit, and the person is expected to follow the required behavior continuously, (4) the at-risk role is not constantly reinforced by either the medical profession or the social environment, and (5) the person in the at-risk role is held responsible for the role taken on, whereas in the sick role the person is not held responsible for it.[6(pp32,33)]

EVALUATION OF THE HEALTH BELIEF MODEL

Scientists have proposed a variety of criteria for evaluating theories.[21–24] The criteria for evaluation should depend on the purpose of the theory being evaluated. Since the HBM was formulated for the purpose of understanding HRB, and since nursing is mainly interested in theories that will guide and improve practice, it seems appropriate that the criteria of empirical adequacy, contribution to understanding, and usefulness be used here to evaluate the HBM.

Empirical Adequacy

Empirical adequacy refers to the degree of agreement between theoretical claims and empirical outcomes.[25,26] To assess empirical support for a theory, one must identify and review the studies that address it. The next step is to determine that the hypotheses of the study are clearly deduced from the theory; otherwise the research is not testing that theory. In reviewing these studies, one has to assess the empirical support each study gives to the hypotheses being tested and to the theory itself.[25] A theory cannot be part of the scientific body of knowledge or be used as a basis for action unless its empirical support has been assessed.

Perceived susceptibility

The individual's perception of personal susceptibility to a disease has been found to be positively related to the taking of a wide variety of preventive health actions such as immunization,[27-30] making prophylactic dental visits,[31,32] and obtaining screening for health problems such as tuberculosis,[2,18,33] Tay-Sachs disease,[34] and cancer.[35,36]

Adherence to therapeutic regimens was also found to be positively correlated with perception of susceptibility or resusceptibility to illness. For example, parents who have relatively high perceptions of their children's susceptibility or resusceptibility to disease are more likely to comply with their children's medication regimen for asthma,[37] with a diet regimen for obese children,[38] and with physician visits and clinic use.[39,40] Kirscht and Rosenstock[41] demonstrated a similar relationship between perception of susceptibility and compliance with an antihypertension drug regimen. This variable is more supported by empirical studies than any other variable in the HBM.

Perceived severity

The positive association between perceived severity of a health condition and HRB has received increasing support from research studies on a variety of behaviors. A relatively high degree of perceived seriousness of incurring a health condition was found to be related to receiving influenza immunization,[27,29,42] making preventive dental visits,[31,43] and making regular check-up or well-child clinic visits.[33,39]

Additional evidence comes from studies of sick role behavior and chronic illness behavior. For example, many researchers[17,38,40,44-46] found that perceived severity is positively associated with compliance with medication or other recommended regimens and with keeping follow-up clinic appointments. Studies done on hypertensive patients also demonstrated positive association between perceived severity and HRB.[41,47]

Inducing a high perceived severity through fear communication is effective in influencing HRB when the individual is provided with specific instructions on how to cope with the threat or reduce the danger. On the other hand, if perceived severity is high and ways to cope with the danger are not available or not known to the individual, defense mechanisms such as denial might be used to restore emotional balance, rather than taking the appropriate health action.[48,49]

Perceived benefits

Studies have revealed that people are more likely to comply with health recommendations of various sorts when they believe that the recommended action is effective in preventing, detecting, or treating the disease and thus reduce its threat to them.[28,30,33,39,50–53]

Perceived costs

Evidence for the effect of barriers to action on HRB is also accumulating. Monetary cost of service was found to be negatively associated with obtaining the service.[28,37] If the action is seen as painful, inaccessible, or inconvenient, the person is less likely to take it.[32,39,41] Noncompliance was found to be common among people who doubt the safety of the regimen or believe it has some side effects[29,38,41,47] and whose regimen is relatively complex and long in duration.[33,54] More data are needed on what constitutes barriers and how they influence HRB.

Health motivation

Concern or worry about health matters in general, as a measure of health motivation, was found to be positively correlate with preventive health behavior[55,56] and with adherence to medical regimens.[38,46,51] Other studies have measured health motivation in terms of intention to comply or willingness to accept medical advice and have shown that more compliers than noncompliers initially intend to do so or are willing to accept and follow medical recommendations.[17,27] Belief in personal control over health matters has been employed in a number of studies as one of the measures of health motivation, and it has been positively correlated with compliance behavior.[34,37]

On the other hand, there are studies that showed no relationship between compliance behavior and general concern with health, willingness to seek and accept medical advice,[29,34] or belief in personal control over health matters as a measure of health motivation.[17]

The reason for these inconsistent findings may lie in the fact that the concept of health motivation is hard to operationalize, and adequate measures for it are not available. Moreover, as stated by Rosenstock and Kirscht,[20] a variety of behaviors that may affect health are probably undertaken for reasons unrelated to health. For example, adhering to a diet regimen for weight loss may occur not because of concern for one's own health but rather because of peer pressure and social desirability. Further investigations are needed to provide more evidence for the role of this variable in influencing HRB.

Cues to action

Specifically what constitutes the cues to action and how they affect behavior are still in need of intensive study. Some investigations have shown that the use of mass media or exposure to information from health workers has been influential in urging people to take a recommended health action.[2,34,42] The use of postcard reminders was found to increase compliance with recommended action.[28] Moreover, other studies indicated that the presence of symptoms stimulated action and acted as a cue to seeking care.[40,54]

Because the studies done on one or more of the factors included under the category of modifying variables have not tested their role in modifying health beliefs (as postulated in the HBM), they will not be discussed here. However, it is impractical and probably impossible to test the HBM as a whole with all of the modifying variables taken into consideration.

Although investigators regard health beliefs as having a joint influence on the likelihood of taking action, few attempts have been made to study the combined effect of health beliefs and their interactions. For example, Becker et al[38] found that the combination of health beliefs accounted for approximately 49% of the variance in weight change in the first follow-up visit. Rundall and Wheeler[29] showed that they accounted for 34% of the variance in the use of vaccine.

Perceptions of susceptibility to and severity of an illness have been found in several studies to be positively correlated with one another and with compliance behavior.[28,33,57] Other studies have revealed that perceptions of susceptibility to a disease and benefits or efficacy of an action interact and exert a joint influence on HRB.[2,18,29,32,40] Another interesting finding is the moderate negative relationship shown by Cummings et al[58] between perceived susceptibility and perceived barriers. They interpreted this as reflecting either the subjects' effort at achieving cognitive balance or inability of the measures to adequately discriminate between the two variables. More consideration should be given to the study of interactions between health beliefs and the influence of different combinations of beliefs on HRB.

The reader is referred to the appendix for an overview of research studies that dealt with one or more of the HBM variables.

Contribution to Understanding

A sense of understanding is an individual matter that may vary from one scientist to another. However, scientists generally see understanding as involving clarity of meaning of concepts and statements, full description of the relationship between variables, and new ideas and ways of looking at phenomena.[23,26,59]

The HBM gives some insight into why people behave in certain ways with regard to health matters and what affects their decision-making process. It relates various variables to the individual's HRB and accounts for some variations in behaviors in groups of individuals studied in a variety of settings. It provides a new way of explaining health actions not only in the area of preventive behaviors but in sick role behaviors and chronic illness behaviors as well. Moreover, it seems promising for understanding HRB of the at-risk individual.

Concerning clarity of meaning, although the HBM has provided theoretical definitions for the major constructs or variables included, agreement on the meaning of these constructs is not yet achieved and difficulties in operationalizing some of them are still encountered. For instance, Becker et al[39] used "worry about child's health" as one of the measures of perceived severity, whereas the same phrase is used in other studies as a measure of health motivation.[37,38]

A sense of understanding is provided only when the relationships between variables are fully described.[26] In this sense, the HBM does not provide a complete understanding of HRB. Although it states that certain variables are related, the description of these relationships is by no means complete. The nature of the relationships for some variables, how much influence the independent variables have on the dependent variable (HRB), and what kind and how much interaction there is between independent variables are not completely understood.

For example, although the modifying variables are thought to influence the individual's perceptions and beliefs, the nature and form of this influence as well as the conditions under which the modifying variables act on behavior are not yet clear. This may be due to the fact that the inclusion of all modifying variables in the HBM makes the model hard to test. Thus empirical evidence for their proposed role could not be obtained, and understanding of HRB would not be enhanced.

The HBM has made some progress toward understanding why people do or do not follow health and medical care recommendations. Rosenstock and Kirscht suggested that "the HBM is a partially developed theory, many of whose hypotheses have been tested and found useful in explaining behavior."[60(p143)] They added that the model is not considered complete, but is well enough established as the beginning of a scientific base to understand HRB. Further development of the model is needed to increase its contribution to an understanding of the phenomenon.

Usefulness

The usefulness of a theory may be measured by its ability to provide clear directions and guidance for practice and research.[61] A useful theory should enable the practitioner to exert control over the phenomena of interest by manipulating or influencing the major variables that are part of the theory.[25] To be useful for research, the theory should be able to stimulate thinking and provide guidelines for the ongoing process of scientific research.[62]

The usefulness of the HBM for practice lies in whether the health beliefs can be activated or changed in the right direction so that appropriate health behavior becomes more likely. Ability to alter any of the other variables in the model or a combination of them may increase the usefulness of the model. Health beliefs are potentially modifiable, and some empirical researchers have supported this issue.[33,38,63]

Variables in the model other than beliefs can be manipulated so as to produce the desired outcome. For example, barriers to action can be minimized by reducing the financial cost of service; action may be triggered by the use of cues such as postcard reminders or informative brochures. The HBM does not suggest a specific approach for intervention to be used by the practitioner. Different strategies are considered pertinent, depending on the needs of the individual or group and the requirements of the situation. This flexibility of the model enables the practitioner to choose the intervention that best suits the specific clients and considers differences between individuals.

The usefulness of the model is enhanced by its potential for application to a wide variety of health-related actions in the preventive, therapeutic, and rehabilitative domains. However, more studies are needed to throw light on the usefulness of the model for people from different age groups and different cultural backgrounds.

As for usefulness of the HBM for research and theory building, the model helps in unifying the unrelated findings from previous investigations, provides a clearer presentation of ideas, and demonstrates some of the relationships between variables. It also serves as a framework of variables and concepts that can direct future research in a fruitful way.

The model itself provides new questions to be answered and new topics to be studied. Such questions include: What is the role of cues? How do the modifying factors work? What are the interrelations between beliefs? Are beliefs stable or changing over time? The model helps to stimulate thinking and serves as an important base and guide for future investigations and theories. Kaplan[62] pointed out that the value of a theory lies not only in the answers it gives but also in the new questions it raises. More research is needed to refine the model. Nurses can have an active role in improving the model through clinical observations and nursing studies.

MODIFICATION OF HEALTH BELIEFS

Several experimental efforts have been made to change health beliefs and determine their influence on behavior. Such endeavors were done mostly by using fear communications or threat appeals. Fear communications included manipulation, in different degrees, of perceived susceptibility to an illness or health condition, perceived severity of that condition, or perceived efficacy of the recommended action. Before presenting the findings of these studies, it is important to briefly review the theory behind the use of fear communications.

Theory of Fear Communications

Two major theoretical paradigms are discussed in the fear communication literature: (1) the fear drive paradigm and (2) the parallel response paradigm. According to Leventhal[49] the fear drive paradigm assumes that the emotional response of fear functions as a drive that mediates belief and behavior change. It suggests that more fearful messages lead to greater persuasion when the recommendations presented are in some degree fear reducing. The performance of recommendations is expected to reduce fear. This reduction of fear is reinforcing and becomes a part of one's permanent response repertoire. This model is largely unsupported by research findings.

The parallel response paradigm, on the other hand, assumes that the perceptual cognitive process mediates reactions to communications and gives rise to fear and adaptive behaviors.[49] In this paradigm fear is not a necessary antecedent of behavior, but both fear and action are consequences of environmental stimulation. Environmental stimulation can lead to a problem solving process to control the danger that Leventhal has called "danger control," or to a "fear control" process in which emotional behavior provides the cues for the selection of the instrumental action and the decision to act. Fear control is thought to be independent of danger control. Actions taken to control fear may be quite different from those taken to control danger. However, interactions between the two processes are thought to exist.

Research Findings

Research findings in the area of fear communications, though complex and inconclusive, showed some empirical regularities worth mentioning. They indicated that threat appeal produced changes in health beliefs, with high-fear messages more likely to produce belief changes in the desired direction than low-fear messages.[36,64–66] Studies also showed that changes in health beliefs mediate subsequent health-related behavior.[57,63,67]

The fear aroused must be related to a personal concern in order to be effective.[57,68,69] A threat is considered useful if it presents a personally relevant danger and is coupled with methods for coping with that danger.[70]

The threat can be counterproductive if other negative feelings (such as anger or high anxiety) are sufficiently aroused or if ways to reduce the threat are not available or are seen as ineffective.[71,72] Fear arousal does not necessarily lead to belief or behavior change in the direction intended, but rather to attempts to resolve the fear. Fear messages may motivate avoidance behavior or denial rather than control of the danger if the person lacks the knowledge of feasible ways of coping with the threat or believes that coping may incur a high cost.[49,73,74] There is some evidence that threat appeals interact with situational and personal factors such as level of initial concern, coping ability, self-esteem, and repetition of threat messages.[63,65,74]

Several questions concerning the use of threat appeals remain unanswered. For instance, what intensity of fear communications is most effective in producing the required change? How do situational and personal factors interact with perception of the threat? Future studies should seek to answer these and similar questions.

RESEARCH ISSUES

The diversity of measures used to indicate certain health beliefs, one of the major problems of research in this field, makes it difficult to establish the validity of these measures and the comparability among studies. For instance, Kirscht et al[40] measured perceived severity of a child's illness in terms of the degree to which the illness is dangerous to the child and interferes with normal activities. Becker et al,[39] in a similar study, measured perceived severity in terms of its impact on the mother's psychological state and ability to carry out a normal routine.

Effects of Time

An increasing number of prospective studies give time ordering to the variables and help throw light on cause and effect relationships. Several of the earlier research projects used a retrospective approach which assumes that the perceptions of the respondents were basically the same prior to taking the health-related action. This assumption may not be valid because the individual's perceptions may have been changed to conform with the present action and achieve cognitive balance, or the action itself may have influenced the beliefs in that the person feels more protected against the disease and less susceptible to it.

Becker et al pointed out that "the relationship between health beliefs and compliance is at least partly bidirectional, with health beliefs becoming congruent with actual compliance as well as the reverse of this."[70(p81)] Retrospective studies also face the problem of memory or inability of respondents to recall, with any degree of certainty, relevant aspects of their behavior in the past.

Replication of previous studies using similar research designs and similar measurements is important for comparability. Intensive testing of the HBM must be conducted in different settings, with different population groups, and with different health regimens, especially those requiring life-style alterations. Prospective designs for these studies seem most appropriate.

Nature of Health Beliefs

More experimental studies are needed to determine the causal role of health beliefs, the conditions under which beliefs may be altered, and the relative efficacies of different intervention strategies that could be used to improve compliance.

Knowledge is needed on conditions under which beliefs are acquired and developed as well as on when children develop concepts of health, illness, causation, and prevention.[75] On the basis of this knowledge, nurses can plan and implement their educational programs for children to help them acquire appropriate health beliefs early in life. Research on stability of beliefs is necessary, since beliefs may change over time.

Thorough investigation of what constitutes cues to action and how they affect behavior is required. For instance, the use of various health education messages can be studied for their differential effect on stimulating health action. The same can be done using a postcard reminder, telephone calls, or other techniques that may seem important in triggering health action. The impact of symptoms on judging a health threat and their relationship to seeking care needs much more study.

Modifying factors should be tested to determine their effect on health beliefs, especially for the influence of significant others and the patient-provider interaction. Health motivation as a variable is still vague and hard to apply. It needs to be clarified through research.

More studies are needed to test interactions among health beliefs and the influence of their various combinations on HRB. The relative importance of each belief variable in accounting for specific HRB also needs to be determined.

Finally, variables other than those in the model should be considered and subjected to investigation, since they may influence HRB. Such variables could be psychological stress and coping style, especially in chronic illness,[4] and locus of control.[70,76,77]

IMPLICATIONS FOR NURSING

Health-related behavior is a particularly relevant issue for the provider concerned with the care of clients.[78,79] Understanding of such behavior is essential if we are to obtain the cooperation and participation of clients in their own care. The HBM provides one approach to the understanding of health-related behavior. It implies that attempts to influence the behavior of clients should be based on better knowledge of their motives and health beliefs.

Problem Identification

The HRB differs from person to person and is dependent on a number of psychosocial factors. Nurses, in the initial assessment of patients, can look closely at these factors and try to identify patients with potential risk of noncompliance. These will need help in following the health care recommendations. This assessment will reveal inappropriate health beliefs among clients or misconceptions about certain health conditions that need to be changed. One example of adapting the HBM variables for use by nurses in assessing a patient's potential compliance is given by Loustau.[78] Although these questions may not accurately reflect some of the health beliefs, they seem to be a good start toward developing a brief and simple assessment tool for nurses' use.

Another useful implication of the model is that intervention should consider individual differences, as individuals may have different combinations of health beliefs. The HBM gives nurses the freedom to choose an intervention strategy that is pertinent to the particular client and the particular situation, based on personal judgment and knowledge of the variables that affect HRB. However, the nurse should be acquainted with the merits and demerits of different intervention strategies in order to make an intelligent choice.

Attitude Development

As suggested by the model, increasing clients' realistic perception of the efficacy of the regimen and the benefits of taking action will enhance compliance. In this respect, the nurse can improve compliance by providing clients with information regarding the benefits of various health actions and helping them select the action with the highest probability of success.

Providing information about an individual's susceptibility to certain health problems for the at-risk groups may be useful in motivating them to protect themselves against that risk. For instance. an individual with a family history of diabetes should know that there is a heightened risk of developing the disease and should have regular check-ups for its early detection. A screening program that was designed and implemented to estimate the risk factors in individuals of having a heart attack at a certain age was presented on TV. The results of that screening were used to inform the target persons of their own susceptibility to heart attacks and of ways to reduce the likelihood of having a heart attack. Marston [77] also noted that the belief that one could have a disease even in the absence of symptoms is currently used in recruiting people to various screening programs.

Manipulating the perceived threat of the disease or health problem (ie, perceived susceptibility and perceived severity) should be accompanied by clear and specific instructions on the various measures the individual can take to reduce the threat and on the available resources that can help in doing so. Such instructions will reduce the anxiety of the person and provide a possibility of doing something about the problem.

Because it is not yet determined whether health motives exist and account for HRB, attempts to modify behavior should not appeal to health motives alone but should consider other motives that do exist and guide the present behavior. In this regard, Becker and Green [80] suggested that appeal to family responsibilities be used to motivate HRB. However, there is some concern that this might arouse feelings of guilt and shame in persons who are unable to follow the prescribed regimen.

Professional Education

Since nurses have more contact with clients than any other health care professional, they have more opportunities to influence clients' HRB. Nurses should keep themselves abreast of theories that attempt to explain HRB and should not apply them uncritically in practice. Rather, nurses are obliged to assess the theory for its applicability in the clinical situation before they use it and to consider the differences among individuals, situations, settings, and cultures. Stetler and Marram pointed out that "each application must be approached as the research in action or as the tentative implementation of theory for the express purpose of evaluation."[81(p563)]

The HBM is partially developed and needs more refinement. Nurses can make an important contribution to the development of the model by refining the operational definitions of its constructs and testing them in clinical situations with various population groups. Having a social psychological background, nurses can accumulate empirical evidence for the model and add to the body of knowledge in this field by engaging in research and creative thinking.

REFERENCES

1. Berkanovic E. Behavioral science and prevention. *Prev Med.* 1976; 5:92–105.
2. Hochbaum GM. Public participation in medical screening programs: A sociopsychological study. *Public Health Service Publication No. 572.* Washington, DC, Government Printing Office, 1958.
3. Rosenstock IM. Historical origins of the health belief model. In Becker JH, ed. *The Health Belief Model and Personal Health Behavior.* Thorofare, NJ: Charles B Slack, 1974.
4. Kasl SV, Cobb S. Health behavior, illness behavior, and sick role behavior. *Arch Environ Health.* 1966; 12:246–266.
5. Kasl SV. The health belief model and behavior related to chronic illness. In Becker MH, ed. *The Health Belief Model and Personal Health Behavior.* Thorofare, NJ: Charles B Slack, 1974.
6. Baric L. Recognition of the "at risk" role—a means to influence health behavior. *Int J Health Ed.* 1969; 12:24–34.
7. Lewin K. *A Dynamic Theory of Personality.* New York: McGraw-Hill, 1935.
8. Hall CS, Lindzey G. *Theories of Personality,* ed 2. New York: John Wiley and Sons, 1970.
9. Rosenstock IM. Why people use health services. *Milbank Mem Fund Q.* 1966;44:94–123.
10. Deutsch M. Field theory in social psychology. In Lindzey G, Aronson E, eds. *The Handbook of Social Psychology, vol 1.* Cambridge: Addison-Wesley Co. 1968.
11. Geiwitz PJ. *Non-Freudian Personality Theories.* Belmont, Calif: Brooks/Cole, 1969.
12. Rosenstock, IM. What research in motivation suggests for public health. *Am J Public Health.* 1960; 50:295–302.
13. Rosenstock IM. Prevention of illness. In Kosa J, et al, eds. *Poverty and Health: A Sociological Analysis.* Cambridge, Mass: Harvard University Press, 1975.
14. Becker MH, Maiman LA. Sociobehavioral determinants of compliance with health and medical care recommendations. *Med Care.* 1975; 13:10–24.
15. Becker MH. The health belief model and sick role behavior. In Becker MH, ed. *The Health Belief Model and Personal Health Behavior.* Thorofare, NJ: Charles B Slack, 1974.
16. Becker MH, Haefner DP, Kasl SV, et al. Selected psychosocial models and correlates of individual health related behaviors. *Med Care.* 1977; 15:27–46.
17. Becker MH, Drachman RH, Kirscht JP. A new approach to explaining sick role behavior in low-income populations. *Am J Public Health.* 1974; 64:204–216.
18. Hochbaum GM. Why people seek diagnostic x-rays. *Public Health Rep.* 1956; 71:377-380.
19. Kirscht JP. The health belief model and illness behavior. In Becker MH, ed. *The Health Belief Model and Personal Health Behavior.* Thorofare, NJ: Charles B Slack, 1974.

20. Rosenstock IM, Kirscht JP. Why people seek health care. In Stone GC, Cohen F, Adler NE, et al: *Health Psychology—A Handbook.* San Francisco: Jossey-Bass, 1979.

21. Gibbs J. *Sociological Theory Construction.* Hinsdale, Ill: Dryden Press, 1972.

22. Hage J. *Techniques and Problems of Theory Construction in Sociology.* New York: John Wiley and Sons, 1972.

23. Hardy ME. Theories: Components, development, and evaluation. *Nurs Res.* 1974; 23:100–107.

24. Schrag C. Elements of theoretical analysis in sociology. In Gross L, ed. *Sociological Theory: Inquiries and Paradigms.* New York: Harper & Row, 1967.

25. Hardy ME. Evaluating nursing theory. In National League for Nursing: *Theory Development: What, Why, How?* Publication No 15-1708. New York: National League for Nursing, 1978.

26. Reynolds P. *A Primer in Theory Construction.* Indianapolis: Bobbs-Merrill, 1971.

27. Cummings KM, Jette AM, Brock BM, et al. Psychological determinants of immunization behavior in a swine influenza campaign. *Med Care.* 1979; 17:639–649.

28. Larson EP, Olsen E, Cole E, et al. The relationship of health beliefs and a postcard reminder to influenza vaccination. *J Fam Pract.* 1979; 8:1207–1211.

29. Rundall TG, Wheeler JRC. Factors associated with utilization of the swine flu vaccination program among senior citizens in Tompkins County. *Med Care.* 1979; 17:191–200.

30. Rosenstock IM, Derryberry M Carriger BK. Why people fail to seek poliomyelitis vaccination. *Public Health Rep.* 1959; 74:93–103.

31. Kegeles SS. Some motives for seeking preventive dental care. *J Am Dent Assoc.* 1963; 67:90–98.

32. Kegeles SS. Why people seek dental care: A test of a conceptual formulation. *J Health Human Behav.* 4:166–173, 1963.

33. Haefner D, Kirscht JP. Motivational and behavioral effects of modifying health beliefs. *Public Health Rep.* 1970; 85:478–484.

34. Becker MH, Kaback M, Rosenstock IM, et al. Some influences on public participation in a genetic screening program. *J Community Health.* 1975; 1:3–14.

35. Fink R, Shapiro S, Roester R. Impact of efforts to increase participation in repetitive screenings for early breast cancer detection. *Am J Public Health.* 1972; 62:328–336.

36. Kegeles SS. A field experiment attempt to change beliefs and behavior of women in an urban ghetto. *J Health Soc Behav.* 1969; 10:115–124.

37. Radius SM, Becker MH, Rosenstock IM, et al. Factors influencing mothers' compliance with a medication regimen for asthmatic children. *J Asthma Res.* 1978; 15:133–149.

38. Becker MH, Maiman LA, Kirscht JP, et al. The health belief model and prediction of dietary compliancy: A field experiment. *J Health Soc Behav.* 1977; 18:348-366.

39. Becker MH, Nathanson CA, Drachman RH, et al. Mothers' health beliefs and children's clinic visits. A prospective study. *J Community Health.* 1977; 3:125–135.

40. Kirscht JP, Becker MH, Eveland JP. Psychological and social factors as predictors of medical behavior. *Med Care* 1976;14:422–431.

41. Kirscht JP, Rosenstock IM. Patient adherence to antihypertensive medical regimens. *J Community Health.* 1977; 3:115–124.

42. Leventhal H, Hochbaum G, Rosenstock I. Epidemic impact on the general population in two cities. In *The Impact of Asian Influenza on Community Life: A Study in Five Cities.* DHEW, Public Health Service Publication No 766. Washington, DC, US Government Printing Office, 1960.

43. Tash RH, O'Shea RM, Cohen LK. Testing a preventive-symptomatic theory of dental health behavior. *Am J Public Health.* 1969; 59:514–521.

44. Gordis L, Markowitz M, Lilienfeld AM. Why patients do not follow medical advice: A study of children on long-term antistreptococcal prophylaxis. *J Pediatr.* 1969; 75:957–968.

45. Becker MH, Drachman RH, Kirscht JP. Motivations as predictors of health behavior. *Health Serv Rep.* 1972; 87:852–862.

46. Becker JH, Drachman RH, Kirscht JP. Predicting mothers' compliance with pediatric medical regimens. *J Pediatr.* 1972; 81:843–854.
47. Taylor DW. A test of the health belief model in hypertension. In Haynes B, Taylor DW, Sackett D, eds. *Compliance in Health Care.* Baltimore: Johns Hopkins University Press, 1979.
48. Ben-Sira Z. Involvement with a disease and health promoting behavior. *Soc Sci Med.* 1977; 11:165.
49. Leventhal H. Findings and theory in the study of fear communications. In Berkowitz L, ed. *Advances in Experimental Social Psychology,* vol 5. New York: Academic Press, 1970.
50. Heinzelman F. Factors in prophylaxis behavior in treating rheumatic fever: An exploratory study. *J Health Human Behav.* 1962; 3:73–81.
51. Becker MH, Radius SM, Rosenstock IM, et al. Compliance with a medical regimen for asthma: A test of the health belief model. *Public Health Rep.* 1978; 93:268–277.
52. Kegeles SS, Kirscht JP, Haefner D, et al. Survey of beliefs about cancer detection and taking Papanicolaou tests. *Public Health Rep.* 1965; 80:815–824.
53. Leavitt F. The health belief model and utilization of ambulatory care services. *Soc Sci Med.* 1979; 13a:105–112.
54. Haynes RB, Sackett DL, Gibson ES, et al. Improvement of medication compliance in uncontrolled hypertension. *Lancet.* 1976; 1:1265–1268.
55. Harris DM, Guten S. Health protective behavior: An exploratory study. *J Health Soc Behav.* 1979; 20:17-29.
56. Ogionwo W. Socio-psychological factors in health behavior: An experimental study on methods and attitude change. *Int J Health Ed.* 1973; 16:supplement.
57. Kirscht JP, Haefner DP. Effects of repeated threatening health communications. *Int J Health Ed.* 1973; 16:3–12.
58. Cummings KM, Jette AM, Rosenstock IM. Construct validation of the health belief model. *Health Educ Monogr.* 1978; 6:394–405.
59. Scriven M. Explanations, predictions, and laws. In Feigl H, Maxwell G, eds. *Minnesota Studies in the Philosophy of Science.* vol 3, Minneapolis: University of Minnesota Press, 1962.
60. Rosenstock IM, Kirscht JP. Practice implications. In Becker MH, ed. *The Health Belief Model and Personal Health Behavior.* Thorofare, NJ: Charles B Slack, 1974.
61. Johnson DE. Development of theory: A requisite for nursing as a primary health profession. *Nurs Res.* 1974; 23:372–377.
62. Kaplan A. *The Conduct of Inquiry.* San Francisco: Chandler, 1964.
63. Kirscht JP, Becker MH, Haefner DP, et al. Effects of threatening communications and mothers' health beliefs on weight change in obese children. *J Behav Med.* 1978; 1:147–157.
64. Evans RI, Rozell RM, Lasater TM, et al. Fear arousal, persuasion, and actual versus implied behavioral change: New perspective utilizing a real life dental hygiene program. *J Pers Soc Psychol.* 1970; 16:220-227.
65. Krisher H, Darley S, Darley J. Fear-provoking recommendations, intentions to take preventive actions, and actual preventive actions. *J Pers Soc Psychol.* 1973; 26:301–308.
66. Rogers R, Mewborn C. Fear appeals and attitude change. Effects of a threat's noxiousness, probability of occurrence, and the efficacy of coping responses. *J Pers Soc Psychol.* 1976; 34:54–61.
67. Mann L, Janis IL. A follow-up study on the long-term effects of emotional role playing. *J Pers Soc Psychol.* 1968; 8:339–342.
68. Leventhal H. Changing attitudes and habits to reduce risk factors in chronic disease. *Am J Cardiol.* 1973; 31:571–580.
69. Leventhal H, Watts J. Sources of resistance to fear-arousing communications on smoking and lung cancer. *J Pers.* 1966; 34:155–175.
70. Becker MH, Maiman LA, Kirscht JP, et al. Patient perception and compliance: Recent studies of the health belief model. In Haynes RB, Taylor DW, Sackett DL, eds. *Compliance in Health Care.* Baltimore: Johns Hopkins University Press, 1979.

71. Dabbs J, Leventhal H. Effects of varying the recommendations in a fear arousing communication. *J Pers Soc Psychol.* 1966; 4:525–531.
72. Janis IL. Vigilance and decision making in personal crises. In Coelho G, Hamburg D, Adams RJ, eds. *Coping and Adaptation.* New York: Basic Books, 1974.
73. Leventhal H, Niles P. A field experiment on fear arousal with data on the validity of questionnaire measures. *J Pers.* 1964; 32:459.
74. Ben-Sira Z, Padeh B. Instrumental coping and affective defense: An additional perspective in health promoting behavior. *Soc Sci Med.* 1978; 12:163–168.
75. Haggerty RJ. Changing life styles to improve health. *Prev Med.* 1977; 6:276–289.
76. Langlie J. Social networks, health beliefs, and preventive health behavior. *J Health Soc Behav.* 1977; 18:224–260.
77. Marston MV. The use of knowledge. In Hardy ME, Conway ME, eds. *Role Theory: Perspectives for Health Professionals.* New York: Appleton-Century-Crofts, 1978.
78. Loustau A. Using the health belief model to predict compliance. *Health Values.* 1979; 3:242–245.
79. Pender N. A conceptual model for preventive health behavior. *Nurs Outlook.* 1975; 23:385–391.
80. Becker MH, Green LW. A family approach to compliance with medical treatment: A selective review of literature. *Int J Health Ed.* 1975; 18:173–182.
81. Stetler CB, Marram G. Evaluating research findings for applicability in practice. *Nurs Outlook.* 1976; 24:559–563.
82. Elling R, Whittemore R, Green M. Patient participation in pediatric program. *J Health Human Behav.* 1960; 1:183–191.
83. Gochman DS. The organizing role of motivation in health beliefs and intentions. *J Health Soc Behav.* 1972; 13:285–293.
84. Nelson AA, Gold BH, Hutchinson RA, et al. Drug default among schizophrenic patients. *Am J Hosp Pharm.* 1975; 32:1237–1242.
85. Carpenter JO, Davis LJ. Medical recommendations—followed or ignored? Factors influencing compliance in arthritis. *Arch Phys Med Rehabil.* 1976; 57:241–246.
86. Nelson EC, Stason WB, Neutra RR, et al. Impact of patient perceptions on compliance with treatment for hypertension. *Med Care.* 1978; 16:893–906.
87. Aho WR. Smoking, dieting, and exercise: Age differences in attitudes and behavior relevant to selected health belief model variables. *Rhode Island Med J.* 1979; 62:85–92.
88. Weisenberg M, Kegeles SS, Lund AK. Children's health beliefs and acceptance of a dental preventive activity. *J Health Soc Behav.* 1980;21:59–74.
89. Hershey JC, Morton BG, Davis JB, et al. Patient compliance with antihypertensive medication. *Am J Public Health.* 1980; 70:1081–1089.

Appendix. Overview of selected studies that used one or more of the HBM variables

Studies	Design	Sample	Behavior	Statistics	Sus	Sev	Ben	Bar
Hochbaum (2)	R, Sur	D 1201	TB x-ray screening	Percentages	+	+/–	+	NM
Leventhal et al (42)	P, Sur	D 86	Influenza vaccination	Percentages	+	+	NM	NM
Elling et al (82)	R, Sur	D 80	Taking penicillin	Chi-square	+	NM	+	NM
Kegeles (31)	R, Sur	D 426	Dental visits	Chi-square	+	+	+	–
Kegeles (32)	P, Sur	D 277	Dental visits	Chi-square	+	0	+	–
Kegeles et al (52)	R, Sur	D 1493	Pap tests to detect cancer	Percentages	NM	NM	+	NM
Tash et al (43)	R, Sur	D 1862	Dental visits	Chi-square	–	+	0	0
Gordis et al (44)	R, Sur	ND 111	Taking penicillin prophylaxis	Descriptive	–	+	0	0
Haefner & Kirscht (33)	P, R, Exp	ND 166	Check-up visits & x-ray for TB, cancer, & heart disease	Chi-square	+	+	+	NM
Becker et al (45)	P, Sur	D 59	Taking med. & appt. keeping	Gamma	+	+	+	NM
Gochman (83)	P, Sur	ND 774	Intention to visit a dentist	Mult Reg	+	NM	0	NM
Becker et al (17)	P, Sur	D 116	Taking med. & appt. keeping	Gamma	+	+	+	0/+
Becker et al (34)	P, Sur	ND 868	Tay-Sachs screening	Chi-square	+	–	+	–
Nelson et al (84)	P, Exp	D 48	Drug taking	ANOVA, Mult Reg	NM	NM	+	–
Carpenter & Davis (85)	P, Sur	ND 54	Following an exercise regimen	Chi-square	NM	0	0	NM
Kirscht et al (40)	R, Sur	ND 251	Use of medical care services	Gamma, Mult Reg	+	+	+	–
Becker et al (38)	P, Exp	ND 182	Following a diet regimen	Gamma, *t* test, ANOVA	+	+	+	–
Kirscht & Rosenstock (41)	R, Sur	D 132	Adherence to med. & dietary recommendations	Chi-square	+	+	+/0	0
Becker et al (39)	P, Sur	D 250	Utilization of pediatric clinic services	Gamma	–/+	–/+	NM	–
Langlie (76)	P, Sur	D 383	Performing preventive H. activity	Mult Reg	–	NM	+	–

Studies	Design	Sample	Behavior	Statistics	Sus	Sev	Ben	Bar
Radius et al (37)	P, Sur	ND 111	Drug taking	Gamma	+	+	0	–
Nelson et al (86)	R, Sur	D 142	Taking med. & appt. keeping	Log linear	NM	+	+	–/0
Ben-Sira and Padeh (74)	P, Sur	ND 956	Tay-Sachs screening	Chi-square	–	NM	NM	NM
Cummings et al (27)	P, Sur	D 286	Swine flu vaccination	Mult Reg, Path.	+	+	+	0
Aho (87)	R, Sur	D 1046	Smoking, wt., physical activity	Chi-square	NM	+	+/0	NM
Leavitt (53)	P, R Sur	D 210	Util. of ambulatory services	Mult Reg	+	0	+	NM
Larson et al (28)	P, R Sur	ND 232	Influenza vaccination	Gamma	+	0	+	–/0
Rundall & Wheeler (29)	P, Sur	D 232	Swine flu vaccination	Logit analysis	0	+	+	–
Taylor (47)	P, Sur	ND 128	Drug taking	Pearson, Mult Reg	0	+	0	–
Weisenberg et al (88)	P, Exp	ND 254	Part. in topical fluoride Rx.	Chi-square	–	0	0	NM
Hershey et al (89)	R, Sur	D 132	Medication taking	Chi sq. & Log linear multivariate	0	0	0	–

Key: P = prospective; R = retrospective; Sur = survey; Exp = experiment; D = random; ND = nonrandom; Sus = prospective susceptibility; Sev = prospective severity; Ben = prospective benefits; Bar = prospective barriers; + = positive relationship; – = negative relationship; 0 = no relationship; NM = not measured.

A Theory of Protection: Parents As Sex Educators

A theory of protection was proposed to organize and explain the dynamic interactions between parents and children as they relate to sex education. Sixteen mothers were interviewed and the data analyzed through the constant comparative method. The optimal goal of sex education was determined to be self-protection, that is, attainment by the child of personal boundary control in order to function positively in society while maintaining his or her own values. The processes of sex education are governed by parents' perceptions of providing protection for the child through the identification and control of boundaries. Major variables moderating the quality of protection are mutuality, knowledge, and values. Using the theory of protection, suggestions are offered for clinical practice, parent teaching, and further investigation.

Eleanor A. Schuster, DNS, RN
Professor
Graduate Nursing Program
College of Nursing
University of North Dakota
Grand Forks, North Dakota
(Former) Director of Graduate Studies
Department of Nursing
Wichita State University

Susan F. Kruger, EdS, MN, RN
Assistant Professor
Department of Nursing
Wichita State University

Julie J. Hebenstreit, MA, RN
Assistant Professor
Department of Nursing
Wichita State University
Wichita, Kansas

Funding for this project was provided through the Office of Research and Sponsored Programs, Wichita State University, Wichita, Kansas. The authors wish to acknowledge the critical reviews of this project by Dr. Catherine M. Norris, Lois V. Rogers, and Dr. Barbara Baker. Dr. Phyllis N. Stern provided valuable suggestions for the relationships proposed in Figure 2, Personal Boundary Control.

Adv Nurs Sci 1985;7(3):70–77

AS SEX EDUCATORS, the investigators were interested in learning what occurs as parents engage in activities related to the sex education of their children. An extensive body of literature[1-4] addresses sex education of children and parents as sex educators. In general, these sources are prescriptive; with the experts assisting parents in assuming the prime educator role with its attendant skills and responsibilities. Little has been written about parents' perceptions of this role. Therefore, the purpose of this investigation was to assess the sex education process through a systematic appraisal of the parental ideas, experiences, convictions, and concerns. The investigators chose grounded theory methodology[5-7] to explain the interrelationships of familiar phenomena and to suggest possible predictive functions of the theory of protection.

The theory of protection proposes that sex education activities of the parents are for the explicit or implicit purpose of protecting their children. Parents devise and carry out protective strategies in infancy and early years. Over time and with assistance, children develop a self-protective mode that enables them to control personal boundaries (physical or psychological limits as defined by or for an individual) while functioning positively in society and maintaining their own values. Thus there is evolvement from protection-by-parent or self-protection by the child, which is proposed as the ultimate goal of all sex education and activity.

The concept of protection has been identified by investigators based on data analysis as the core variable of this theory. The components of the theory are boundary, control of boundary, mutuality, knowledge, and values. The investigators proposed that problems experienced by the parent or child could be pinpointed or anticipated by considering the insufficiencies of one or more of the components or of their linkages and that effective sex education may be attained by strengthening the various components and their interrelationships of variables. The goal of sex education, self-protection, may be obscured by the parent and child's failure to identify the appropriate person who is the focus of protective actions. This happens when a parent is unsure of how to handle a situation so, in effect, protects self by changing the subject or referring the child to someone else.

STUDY METHOD

Subjects

Sixteen mothers were recruited from among parents who had children enrolled in a Head Start Day Care Center. The only criterion for selection was that the participant have at least one child in the home with whom she or he related as a parent. No fathers volunteered for this study, but two male partners participated in the interview. Since social interactions were the focus of the investigation, it was unnecessary to control for additional variables. Human rights of subjects were protected by adhering to the protocol of the Office of Research and Sponsored Programs, of Wichita State University.

The youngest woman was 21; the eldest 46. All were Caucasian and US citizens, although one subject was born in Germany. All had male partners in the home. However, in five instances, this individual was not the biological father. There was one, one-child family and two families with three or more children. The remainder had two children. Nine of the women had attended college or had earned a baccalaureate or higher degree; seven were high school graduates. Two held professional positions, seven held business office positions, and one was a housekeeper. The remaining six were not employed outside the home.

Instrument

A semi-structured questionnaire was developed by the investigators. It was tested on four typical individuals, not the study subjects. Three expert observers knowledgeable about inductive methodology and about human development were recruited to review and criticize the proposed questionnaire and process. The instrument was subsequently shortened and refined based on their recommendations. (See boxed material.)

Procedure

Interviews were conducted by one of the three investigators at a time and place convenient for the subject, ordinarily in the home. Audio recordings were made of the interviews, which lasted from 35 to 90 minutes, and were later transcribed.

A Theory of Protection: Parents as Sex Educators Questionnaire

1. What does the phrase, "sex education," mean to you?
2. What should children be told about sex?
    A. At what age?
    B. By whom?
3. What have you told your child about sex?
4. What do you expect to tell your child about sex?
5. When have you or when do you expect to discuss with your husband/ partner the sex education of your children?
6. In what way(s) would you like your child's sex education to be different from your own?
7. In what areas (topics) do you as a parent think you would like assistance regarding your children and sex education?
8. Where have you or would you expect to go for such assistance?
9. What is your opinion about attending parents' meetings where you could discuss childhood sexuality with other parents and with sex educators?
10. What else comes to your mind that you think is important to say about your child and sex education?

DATA ANALYSIS

The data were analyzed using two major techniques: memo-taking and coding. The three investigators handled the memo-taking, which consisted of writing individual notes about questions, insights, process, and content after all interviews had been completed. A typical memo was "How do parents know that their knowledge is valid?" Relating these memos to interview material assisted the investigators in directing the analysis of data and in determining what information to set aside as extraneous, what to emphasize, and, on occasion, when to return to the literature for a further look at the data collected. Data were classified by determining what processes (teaching, correcting behavior, questioning) were most evident in the interactions between parents and children in matters concerning sexuality and sexual functioning.

Written transcripts of the interviews were coded line for line to identify the various processes in evidence. For instance, a child making comparisons between male and female anatomy was coded as "comparing." Each interaction was stated on a separate file card with the process entered on the lower corner of the card. Multiple processes were often evident, all were listed. An example of multiple processes was one in which a parent reported mutual exploration of body parts by her child and a neighbor's child. This mother was tolerant, considering it a normal developmental activity. The processes could be coded as learning, exploring, tolerating, or boundary-testing. It was important at this juncture to avoid premature selection of one process until all data were examined.

Ultimately, a dominant process emerged and was underscored as the best way to organize and account for the various interchanges between parents and children. In this methodology, all evident categories were named and various possible relationships among them were considered. Again, decisions about which to choose, which to emphasize, and which to set aside were guided by the question, "Which conduct can best account for the process (contained) in the data."

Categories

The coded data produced similarities that were grouped into clusters or categories. Twelve of these categories were dominant in the context of the research: teaching, learning. communicating, mutuality, monitoring, assuming roles, protecting, valuing, establishing boundaries, making ground rules, controlling, and anticipating. They were reviewed to determine which of them were more salient to the investigation—to increase understanding of the processes involved as parents educate their children in sex-related matters. Six categories (protection, boundary, control of boundary, knowledge, values, and mutuality) were dominant and subsumed the other six. In this methodology, categories are reduced in number (category reduction) when it is evident that some are dominant. For example, "making ground rules" is one way to establish a boundary so it can be incorporated into that larger category.

RESULTS

The investigators developed a theory of Protection (Fig 1) to explain the purpose of sex education and to describe the relationship of categories listed above, based on three premises:

1. The optimal *goal* of sex education is the child's attainment of personal boundary control in order to function positively in society while maintaining his or her own values.
2. The *processes* of sex education are governed by parents' perceptions of providing protection for the child through the identification and control of boundaries.
3. The major variables moderating the *quality* of protection are knowledge, values, and mutuality.

Protection

Protection, the ability to defend from injury or destruction, emerged as the primary category. Protection was seen as the goal of sex education, attained through the processes of assigning and controlling boundaries and modified by knowledge, values, and mutuality. The investigators propose that parents, interacting

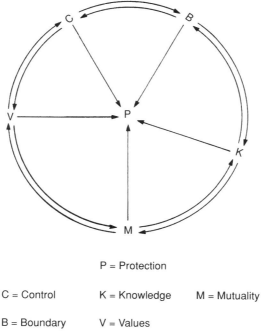

P = Protection

C = Control   K = Knowledge   M = Mutuality

B = Boundary   V = Values

Fig 1. Theory of protection relationship of variables.

with their children in matters relating to sexuality, are engaged in behaviors that protect even though they may not be specifically aware of this. For instance, when parents described the "right kind" and the "wrong kind" of touch or cautioned "never to go with strangers," their intent was to protect the child. Generally, protection meant safeguarding from some outside intrusion, which could be physical, psychological, or both. A variation of protection was occasionally evident as "protection from self" such as touching genital areas only for cleanliness or evacuation. It was determined that parent and child perceptions of protection are formed through their own values and are moderated by knowledge.

Boundary

The principal dynamic in providing protection was the assignment, establishment, and maintenance of a boundary (ie, some form of physical or psychological limit). The most evident mode for this was the specification of family "ground rules." These dimensions represented the limits of acceptability, mainly to parents, of various situations—use of language, nudity, touching, and forming of relationships.

An effective strategy for boundary establishment in one family was called "time out." When asked questions by her daughter of which she was unsure or uncomfortable in responding, the mother called time out specifying when she would resume discussion. This parent reported that she would gather information and visual resource material, if necessary, and become more comfortable with the topic through internal rehearsal. When this was accomplished, she would discuss the question with the child.

Another part of the boundary concept included "being in" or "being out" of bounds. One mother reported rerouting her child's return home from school so they could not view a woman neighbor sunbathing in the nude. Since the mother was unable to alter the neighbor's behavior and reports to the police were futile, she insisted on her children taking another way home. "Out of bounds" was referred to in another sense, namely, the kind of language that was out of bounds in that particular family.

Another aspect of boundary was identified by "putting up." A parent would attempt to keep something out of sight such as explicit pictures, condoms, marriage manuals, or anything else they considered inappropriate for the child to view or too difficult to explain. A response to this strategy on the part of children was curiosity and heightened interest. This, in turn, introduced the notion of "boundary testing," seeking new experiences, trying out new words, and telling stories or jokes about body parts or functions. Often this was in whispers and accompanied by giggling, especially in the presence of an adult.

Boundary Control

"Control" is the ability to institute and maintain a boundary. The study showed parents' greatest concerns about boundary were related to the scope and effectiveness of their control. During early childhood instruction when mobility and geographical constraints coincided with the relatively simple task of naming of body parts, concerns were minimal. As range of mobility increased with school experiences, access to neighborhood and beyond, parental concerns escalated. Concerns related particularly to companionships and to values—"All I can do is tell them what's right and hope they're doing it!"

Strategies for control ranged from permissive to punitive, from effective to ineffective, and were implemented with varying levels of intensity and consistency. A lack of clarity and singleness of purpose frequently emerged, with parents asking themselves, "Why do *I* want this?" Through self-examination, they became more specific and secure in their own values. One contemporary sex education program for parents and children addresses this very issue—"Messages about sexuality: How to give *yours* to your child."[8(p9)]

It was not the investigators' intent to index all forms of boundary and control of boundary but rather to document a common process in the educational interchange between parents and children.

Knowledge

Knowledge, in the context of this study, was the subjects' understanding of sexuality and sex-related facts such as physiological functioning. The parents were concerned about the adequacy and accuracy of their knowledge and, with one exception, wanted their children to be taught facts earlier and more thoroughly than they had. Mothers, rather than fathers, were the primary information sources, a finding supported by recent investigation of children in English-speaking countries.[9]

The interviewees discussed their children vis-à-vis sex education beginning with their ability to verbalize at about two years of age. Neither infant sexuality nor the infant as a sexual being was addressed by any subject. This finding may indicate that the population was unaware of beginning sexuality and early sexual learning. Research in childhood sexuality reveals that, by the age of two years, children have already learned their gender, what body parts are "good" and "bad," and what actions are acceptable to parents.[10-12] Lack of these data may, however, be a function of the questionnaire or the way in which the interview was conducted rather than indication of parental ignorance.

Values

Values for this study were the judgments about "good" and "bad" in the realm of sexuality. Values or convictions provided the rationale and impetus for boundary identification, placement, and control. When parents judged on exposure to information to be good, they took steps to provide it. One example was a mother's reliance on a community health nurse as a source for information. This particular nurse was routinely contacted by the mother to discuss aspects of sexuality with a prepubescent daughter.

The interviewees placed a high value on literature written for the preschool child. Reportedly, 14 parents purchased books or obtained them from the library. This propensity was considered particularly noteworthy by the investigators, since recent research[13] indicates that sex education literature for the preschool child, in the 23 books reviewed, promotes two dominant themes:

- *reinforcement* of traditional sex roles with the mother as caretaker and passive partner in sex relations; and
- *avoidance* where coitus was named but rarely illustrated. When it was depicted, the partners were covered with blankets.

The reason these findings are important, from a sex educator's viewpoint, is the possible need to assist parents in discerning what values they want transmitted to their children through the literature and to choose books accordingly. The fact that coitus was not illustrated may be innocuous, but it is known that children will make up their own myths and theories to explain what they observe.[9]

Mutuality

Mutuality is the level of congruence between the subjects' understandings, values, and expectations. It became apparent, as data were analyzed, that attainment of protection, through teaching or other means, relied on an interactive process—the interchange between and among protectors and those to be protected. One reason the goal of protection was not achieved was a lack of mutuality or congruence in goal specification or in ways to reach the goal. This happened in parent-child and in parent-parent relationships and was particularly evident in stepparent/biologic-parent disagreements. One mother reported, with some vehemence, that she was the only one who handled sex information sessions because her husband, a stepparent, used "raw" vocabulary and crude examples when he discussed matters of sexuality.

DISCUSSION

The theory of protection is the most potentially useful product of this investigation. Significant data could be obtained from counselors or teachers who determine *who* is being protected, by *whom*, through what *means*, and what *intent*, and with what *result*. Assisting individuals and families to examine their world in this way may be useful, keeping in mind that the goal of education is protection through attainment of personal boundary control. The teacher or counselor could assist clients in attaining reliable knowledge, becoming more specific and firm in their espousal of values, and devising strategies for boundary establishment and maintenance, with ultimate relinquishment of this function to the child.

The theory of protection may have predictive as well as explicative value. For instance, the hypothesis that lack of firmness and specificity of personal boundary control by the parent and the child will signal an "at-risk" relationship (for incest

Child boundary control

		+	−
Parent boundary control	+	+ + mutuality of control, comfortable balance	− + potential of child's boundary invaded by parent
	−	+ − potential of parent's boundary invaded by child	− − potential for destructive relationship, mutual lack of boundary control

+ = firm, specific control of personal boundary
− = weak, diffuse control of personal boundary

Fig 2. Personal boundary control.

or other destructive dynamics). Fig 2 depicts the positive and negative aspects of personal boundary control.

The protection theory has been confined in this discussion to parents and children in the sex education relationship. That this theory could be applied more broadly is supported by the umbrella concept of protection, which has been proposed[14] as an organizing framework for a selected group of physiologic phenomena on which to build nursing knowledge. These phenomena are called "basic, human, physiologic protective mechanisms."[14(p385)] Hence, a theory of protection might be relevant to *all* human protective phenomena, the psychosocial and physiologic, thus enlarging the theory beyond the work of Norris and this investigation.

REFERENCES

1. Kirby D, Alter S, Seales P. *An Analysis of U.S. Sex Information Programs and Evaluation Methods.* Bethesda, MD: Math Tech, Inc., 1979, vols 1-5.
2. Carrera M. *The Facts, the Acts and Your Feelings.* New York: Crown, 1981.
3. Otto H. *The New Sex Education.* Chicago: Follett, 1978.
4. Roberts E, Kline D, Gagnon J. *Family Life and Sexual Learning.* Cambridge, Mass: Population Education, Inc., 1978.
5. Glaser B, Strauss A. *A Discovery of Grounded Theory.* New York: Atherton Press, 1965.
6. Glaser B: *Theoretical Sensitivity.* Mill Valley, Calif.: Sociology Press, 1978.
7. Stern PN. Grounded theory methodology: Its uses and processes. *Image.* 1980;12:20–23.
8. *Oh No What Do I Do Now.* New York, Sex Education and Information Council of the US, 1983.
9. Goldman R, Goldman J. *Children's Sexual Thinking.* Boston: Routledge & Kegan Paul, 1982.
10. Money J, Ehrhardt A. *Man and Woman, Boy and Girl.* Baltimore: Johns Hopkins University Press, 1972.

11. Calderone MS. Parents and sexuality in the year of the child. *SIECUS Report.* 1979;8:1, 6.
12. Colonna AB, Solnit AJ. Infant sexuality. *SIECUS Report.* 1981;11:1–2, 6.
13. Rindskopf KD, Cudlip L. Subtle signal: A content analysis of sex education books for young children. *SIECUS Report.* 1982;10:9–11.
14. Norris CM. Synthesis of concepts. Evolving an umbrella concept—protection. In: *Concept Clarification in Nursing.* Rockville, Md: Aspen Systems, 1982.

An Evolutionary-Based Model of Health and Viability

A model of health and viability, as influenced by a wide variety of psychosocial variables, is presented. This model is based on the principle that illness and death sometimes serve an evolutionary function by maximizing natural selection prospects of other group members. Thus, evolutionary viability within the social context (personal contribution to one's social network) is a crucial health factor; life events, life style determiners, control perceptions, and viability emotions are other important concepts within the model. This model points to the possibility that the full scope of clinical practice may require assisting patients in regaining a sense of viability; nursing may be particularly relevant to this need because of the opportunity for intense interpersonal contact with patients.

Jane K. Dixon, PhD
Associate Professor
Program in Nursing Research
Yale University
New Haven, Connecticut

John P. Dixon, PhD
Researcher
Adaptation Research Institute
Branford, Connecticut

IN ATTEMPTS to understand the nature of health and disease, one central issue has been the distinct differences among people in susceptibility to health problems. Some disease-prone persons fall victim to multiple illnesses simultaneously or in quick succession, and others living under similar conditions remain remarkably free of health problems. Hinkle[1] concluded that among similarly aged adults, more than one-half of all illness episodes are experienced by fewer than one-fourth of the subjects. Less healthy individuals not only become ill more frequently and with greater severity, but they also have a greater variety of conditions.

These differences cannot be explained by differences in exposure to disease agents. With many health problems (eg, coronary heart disease), exposure to pathogens is not an issue. With other conditions, exposure rates exceed incidence rates by a wide margin; exposure may be a necessary, but not a sufficient, condition for illness onset. This is true in relation to some acute, infectious conditions,

Adv Nurs Sci 1984;6(3):1–18
© 1984 Aspen Publishers, Inc.

such as clinical mononucleosis. in which the Epstein-Barr virus is implicated, as well as in relation to some chronic conditions, such as cancer. Thus, much health research now emphasizes the identification of risk factors rather than causative agents; such risk factors interact in leading to varying levels of disease susceptibility in the presence of viral, bacterial, chemical, or other agents.

Psychosocial risk factors, such as number of recent life-change events, as well as physiological risk factors, such as elevated serum cholesterol, have been identified. In statistical terms, risk factors are characteristics that increase the probability of a disease condition being detected, but they do not lead to predictions with any certainty. For example, although smoking is a key risk factor in the development of lung cancer, the majority of heavy smokers do not contract this disease, and some nonsmokers do. Similarly, although stressful life events have been consistently related to later illness onset in numerous studies with varied methodologies, correlations have been small, generally accounting for less than 10% of variance.[2]

Both smoking and stressful life events may be general in their effects, leading to any of a variety of diseases, rather than to one specific disease. Based on the understanding that health outcomes are rarely the result of a single cause leading to a single effect, there is some movement toward the development of biopsychosocial models in which multiple biological, psychological, and social variables are considered simultaneously. Within such a model, it is appropriate to focus on overall patterns of health, rather than on specific health problems.

Many biochemical, physiological, and anatomical aspects of health and disease are already well understood, but in the creation of a model of health, psychosocial variables may be of primary importance. The weight of evidence from psychosocial studies of health indicates clearly that emotions, social relationships, and the way persons view their lives affect the degree of healthiness; these are important health behaviors. In addition to stressful life events, the wide variety of psychosocial variables implicated in health outcomes include type A behavior pattern, locus of control, power motivations, contingency hopefulness, activity levels, adaptive flexibility, psychological integrity, transcendent beliefs, alienation from self, anomie, social supports, trust, loneliness, uselessness, pessimism, confusion, depression, and anxiety.

However, such variables are highly interrelated; they are defined and manifested by overlapping sets of behaviors and thought processes. If systematic multivariate research hypotheses are to be created and tested, it is necessary that this assortment of psychosocial variables be organized and integrated into a unified model of health.

EVOLUTIONARY ASSUMPTIONS

Based on review of a wide assortment of studies using psychosocial variables, it is contended that an integration can most successfully be achieved when evolutionary genetic assumptions are used as a key element in the building of a model. First, given that people live in groups (families, tribes, clans, societies, and cultures) and are dependent for survival on others within these groups, it may be assumed that the well-being of any person is tied to the well-being of the groups. Thus, people enmeshed in viable effective groups have advantages over those who are not.

Such advantage refers to having a better chance in the natural selection process. From the evolutionary viewpoint, the greatest significance of a person's life is the role as a depository of genes passed from the former generation. If evolutionary success is attained, these genes or some part of them is passed to the next generation. Group viability is an important factor enabling an individual to achieve such evolutionary success.

Second, group viability is maximized to the extent that there is some built-in mechanism for elimination of members who draw more from the group than they contribute, or are likely to contribute in the future. To the extent that group selection processes have been operative throughout human history, groups have prospered in which there is a tendency for the group to be relieved of the burden of members who make little contribution to group well-being or who actually detract from it. Within such a framework, illness and death serve important evolutionary functions.

The central contention is that evolutionary selection processes have favored the well-being of groups with members who have a genetically determined tendency toward self-destructiveness, among those persons who have a sense of not contributing toward the survival of the group gene pool. This tendency would be an efficient evolutionary mechanism for promoting group survival at the expense of the least productive members. The existence of such a mechanism would be consistent with Darwin's[3] belief that natural selection operates at the level of the family. It is also consistent with such concepts as kin selection, inclusive fitness, and reciprocal altruism propagated in the more modern field of sociobiology.

From this perspective, the assortment of psychosocial variables that have proven valuable in health research can be integrated into a single evolutionary-based model with implications for health practice. If the model is correct, then an important part of clinical nursing practice should be discovery of methods by which a person can re-establish a sense of viability when this viability is threatened.

EVOLUTIONARY MODEL

The unique contribution of this model of health based on evolutionary principles is its integration of a wide assortment of psychosocial concepts and variables. The model inter-relates six major concepts, and each of these has several identified components (Table 1). It is likely that as this model is used and refined,

Table 1. Means of viability model concepts and component elements

Concepts and components	Meaning
Evolutionary viability within social context	Extent to which person functions in promoting survival and well-being of group
Social context	Network of connecting links (eg, communication and interactions) between person as an individual and as member of family, society, and other group
Power	Personal control over life circumstances for oneself and for others (Person cannot contribute to social well-being without power)
Life events	Major happenings determining the nature of a person's life course; some are primarily practical, but most involve shifts in social context
Developmental events	Events resulting from growth, age, or maturation (eg, birth, 1st day of school, or death)
Chance events	Events resulting from personal actions or circumstances (eg, automobile accident or moving to a different country)
Life-style determiners	Elements of personality and learned adaptive strategies that shape the way viability is played out in the face of life events
Activity	Inclination to set and rigorously pursue life purposes and goals
Flexibility	Readiness to shift life pattern when necessary, in order to adapt to practical contingencies to find new satisfactory social contexts
Integrity	Tendency to balance deep internal feelings, preferences, desires, and fantasies with practical external conditions so as to fit the two together with minimal stress and maximal satisfaction
Transcendence	Sense that life has positive purpose in relation to patterns greater than oneself; may be religious, societal, or altruistic
Control perceptions	Perceptions of how circumstances can be controlled in pursuing personal purposes and duties; perceptions may differ from reality of control in social context
Contingency hopefulness	Expectation of ability to shape specific practical circumstances (eg, driving to grocery store or getting high grade on examination)
Power motivation	Desire to achieve and maintain control of significant goods, services, and rewards within wider social context
Moral/ethical power inhibitions	Perceptions of ethical restraints relative to correctness of pursuing or not pursuing control over circumstances in life context
Perception of actual control	General sense of how things have actually worked out in control pursuits; not necessarily accurate reflection of actual control
Satisfaction/ frustration/ balance	Perception of extent of success or blocking of control efforts

continues

Table 1. *(continued)*

Concepts and components	Meaning
Viability emotions	Affective reactions deriving from sense of being viable participant in social order either because of control efforts or because of blessing of having been accepted as viable participant
Acceptance vs abandonment	Feeling of being enmeshed in or excluded from significant social relationships
Usefulness vs uselessness	Feeling of contributing or not contributing in significant social groups
Optimism vs pessimism	Feeling that future does or does not hold positive possibilities
Clarity vs confusion	Feeling of ability or inability to understand life circumstances so that satisfactory life course can be accomplished
Health outcomes	Psychological, behavioral, and physical states resulting from viability emotions in combination with other factors
Psychological comfort vs distress	Extent of experiencing general satisfaction with life or depression and anxiety, which undermines well-being
Self-maintenance vs self-destructive behavior	Extent to which one engages in behaviors that preserve health (eg, proper nutrition) and refrains from activities that show failure to take care of physical self (eg, smoking or suicide) or extent to which one does the reverse
Physiological function vs dysfunction	Extent to which one is in optimal physical condition or has cardiovascular, immunological, and other impairments

new components of these major concepts will be proposed; such modifications would be consistent with the spirit in which the model is offered.

A pictorial representation of the model is presented in Fig 1. The placement of six major concepts indicates their primary, temporal order, and arrows depict major probable causal relationships, which lead to health outcomes.

Some of these concepts (life events and health outcomes) are familiar to most health researchers; others are established concepts organized into a new format (life-style determiners, control perceptions, and viability emotions); and one (evolutionary viability in the social context), although it is firmly grounded in previous research and theory, represents a proposition that may seem novel to some health scholars.

Evolutionary Viability within Social Context

Evolutionary viability refers to the extent to which a person contributes to the evolutionary survival of the group in which that person participates. For such a

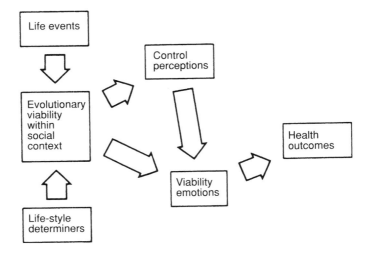

Fig 1. Pictorial representation of relationships between concepts in an evolutionary-based model of viability and health.

contribution to be made, a person must be enmeshed in a social network to which he or she may contribute and must have a degree of power or personal effectiveness such that personal actions or, perhaps, merely presence will have an impact on the welfare of others.

A growing body of evidence is now documenting the role of social connections as a health factor. For example, in a nine-year follow-up of almost 7,000 randomly selected residents of Alameda County in California, those with least extensive social and community ties had a higher death rate than those with most extensive ties.[4] The age-adjusted risk associated with poor social ties was 2.3 for men and 2.8 for women. This relationship between social involvement and mortality was not explainable by initial health status, health practices, or use of preventive health services.

As may be expected based on the concept of evolutionary viability, social contacts seem most relevant to health in times of threat. Some clinical studies have focused on this situation. Nuckolls, Cassel, and Kaplan[5] found that among pregnant women undergoing life crises, lack of social support was associated with a high rate of pregnancy complication. McClelland and Jemmott[6] found that among college students who had social problems, as well as problems in other areas of life, respiratory infections were more frequent. Such studies are supported by animal experimentation in which the presence of the animal's mother[7] or littermates[8] during experimentally induced stress is associated with reduced negative health consequences.

Other researchers have taken the approach of identifying specific personality styles as leading to proneness to specific disease. For example, type A behavior pattern is known to increase the risk of coronary heart disease[9]; and the possibility of a cancer-prone personality, characterized by acquiescence, dependence, and controlled reaction to early loss is receiving increasing attention.[10] Traits of this sort have also been reported to relate to the course of cancer.[11] Pelletier[12] has summarized similar literature related to rheumatoid arthritis, ulcerative colitis, and migraine.

Based on review of studies related to five forms of health problems, Cassel[13] concluded that although the specific descriptions had some variation, all involved deprivation in meaningful social relationships. Another commonality among these descriptions is the possibility that personal effectiveness (ie, the power to influence personal well-being and that of others) is limited. DeCatanzaro,[14] in reviewing the epidemiology of suicide, comes to the even more explicit conclusion that suicide is most prevalent among those whose death is least likely to impact negatively on survival of the gene pool; for example, people who do not have children and those whose ability to care for children (eg, the unemployed) is impaired.

Based on such reviews, it might be legitimate to conclude that the absence of evolutionary viability may lead to any of a variety of self-destructive processes, including suicide and a wide selection of illnesses. The physiological mechanisms through which this occurs remain a mystery, although the work of Bouvard[15] on hypothalamic activity as well as the more recent discovery of brain endorphins might provide some useful clues.[16]

Stressful Life Events

Life for each person is a sequence of developmental happenings and chance events, which determine how well the developmental sequence is played out for the well-being of the person and the social grouping in which the person participates. Some events are primarily practical in their consequences (eg, getting a raise), but more important events often involve direct shifts in the social context (eg, death of a relative or marriage). There is substantial evidence from a variety of sources that such events, especially when they occur in clusters, are often precursors to adverse health changes. For example, in an early study among a group experiencing extraordinary life changes (Indian migrants to Lima, Peru), there was also an extremely high rate of illness.[17] Prospective study has revealed that among enlisted men on naval cruises, life change during the 6-month period prior to deployment is associated with illness during the 6-month cruise.[2] Warren et al[18] found that both perceived stress and occurrence of specific problematic events in seven categories were associated with the onset of multiple sclerosis. Stuart and Brown[19] reported that in a sample of college students, life-change events related to frequency of accidents, as well as to frequency of disease.

Much research on this topic has involved use of the Social Readjustment Rating Scale (SRRS) and its subsequent modifications[20]; in the SRRS, each of 43 events is associated with a numerical weight representing the amount of change required by that event. However, another interesting line of research focuses on the single event considered to be, by far, the most serious in its adaptive consequences: death of a spouse. During bereavement, immune reactions are depressed, and high death rates have been noted, especially as a result of coronary thromboses, other heart disease, and cancer.[21]

Frederick[22] has proposed that during grief, production of ACTH by the pituitary gland is not moderated by the level of circulating cortisol, as it is normally. In this situation, excess ACTH leads to hypersecretion of cortisol, an adrenal hormone known to inhibit immune reactions Among the variety of other physiological and biochemical phenomena implicated in the commonly observed relationships between illness and stressful life events are the general adaptation syndrome described by Selye[23] and the conservation-withdrawal response described by Engel and Schmale.[24]

Stressful life events and the changes in social relationships that such events bring about often present threats to the sense of being a viable, contributing member of groups in which the person participates. This has led, throughout the evolutionary history of humans, to development of numerous biological mechanisms through which stressful life events, especially when clustered, severe, or prolonged, lead to increased susceptibility to a variety of health problems.

Life-style Determiners

Events happen to a person, sometimes as a result of circumstances beyond the person's control, but sometimes as a consequence, at least in part, of personal actions. Despite the intransigence of certain life events (for example, the inevitability of death), a person may do much to shape the course of life and thus to influence viability. Each person develops a style of life, which serves as a pattern for responding to events as they occur and for influencing the nature of future events. These combinations of personality elements and learned adaptive strategies are referred to as life-style determiners. Four crucial life-style determiners with demonstrated relationships to health have been identified: activity, flexibility, integrity, and transcendence. Each of these influences the person's viability within the social context.

Overall, these four life-style determiners seem to act in conjunction with life events to impact on evolutionary viability within the social context. To the extent they are present, they act as health-promoting factors, and they are of special importance in maintaining viability during life crises.

Activity

The setting and pursuing of life goals and purposes is known to mitigate the potentially adverse health consequences of stressful experiences.[25] When a person responds to an unpleasant situation by taking action designed to change the situation or make it more bearable, the likelihood of subsequent health damage is reduced. In animal research, the ability to take aggressive action in response to a stressful stimulus has been associated with limited gastric ulceration.[26] Among humans, those displaying the tendency to express anger when faced with an anger-provoking situation have lower rates of hypertension than those who do not;[27] and a state of high arousal prior to cholecystectomy is correlated with reduced pain and shorter hospital stays.[28]

Two longitudinal studies focusing on dependency, the opposite of constructive activity,[29,30] have concluded that this style of interacting with the environment is associated with general ill health and premature death.[29,30] The evolutionary significance of activity may be that through vigorous pursuit of life goals, a person meets environmental challenges, thus augmenting prospects of genetic survival, not only for the individual, but also for the group in which the individual participates.

Flexibility

The shifting of personal life pattern as necessary to adapt to external contingencies is another crucial variable. The relationship between life change and illness may be limited by the extent to which the person has a general disposition of tolerating changes in life.

Using a scale that differentiates subjects based on optimal stimulation level, Cooley and Keesey found that although a significant relationship existed between life change and illness among those least inclined to seek new experiences, there was no such relationship among those who were most inclined to seek new experiences.[31] In a study by Boyce and associates,[32] inconsistency in daily routines protected children from the negative health changes that often follow major life crises. Totman, Reed, and Craig[33] found, contrary to their expectations, that cold symptoms were more severe, rather than less severe, in research subjects who had experienced a psychological manipulation designed to increase commitment to a particular course of action. Hinkle et al[34] demonstrated that among Chinese residents of the United States, the principal factor differentiating those with a high frequency of illness from those with a low frequency was whether they perceived the changes and difficulties they had faced as threats to a set pattern or as interesting variations in which new opportunities might be discovered.[34]

Taken together, these studies support the suggestion that flexibility as an aspect of life style serves as a health-promoting factor. In evolutionary terms, plasticity of behavior in response to changing circumstances was almost certainly of survival benefit to persons and groups throughout the course of human development, especially in times of crisis.

Integrity

Integrity requires that a person relate to inner subjective experience while accepting the pragmatic contingencies of the external world. Numerous programs of psychotherapeutic intervention with the physically ill are based on the premise that illness occurs when life is not consistent with internally perceived needs; several current research results are consistent with this understanding.

In treadmill testing,[35] persons characterized by the type A behavior pattern, compared with others, pushed themselves closer to their physiological limits while claiming to experience less fatigue. This lack of sensitivity to bodily needs may be a factor in the higher rate of heart disease among type A individuals.

Kasl et al[36] found that among susceptible West Point cadets, lack of consistency between degree of commitment to a military career and academic performance related to the likelihood of contracting mononucleosis. In a study of executives experiencing a high degree of stress, Kobasa[37] demonstrated that those scoring higher on "alienation from self" developed more illness; in a similar study, Marx and associates[38] reported that, among students who had recently experienced a clustering of life changes, those with the highest level of life fulfillment showed the lowest illness rates. In the classic report on research involving 3,500 subjects, it was concluded that among the most ill patients, there often seemed to be a feeling that social obligations interfered with the satisfaction of personal needs.[17]

Overall, there is substantial evidence that the tendency to balance internal feelings with the practical circumstances of life may be associated with better-than-average health. This association is probably derived from the need within any particular social group to depend on various individuals to fulfill various important roles; thus, differences in patterns of behavior among persons is a survival asset to the group, and suppression of these unique inclinations detracts from the probability of low mortality in the group.

Transcendence

Transcendence is the sense that life is oriented toward purposes greater than one-self, whether this involves God, human welfare, or some more limited cause. The health-promoting potential of strong belief systems can be seen in numerous findings, which relate religion to general health,[39] blood pressure,[40] cancer pain,[41] and psychological health.[42] It can also be seen in Frankl's[43] observations on the importance of value commitments to chances of survival among prisoners in Nazi death camps and in the effectiveness of the shaman, who combines the roles of priest and healer, within primitive cultures.[44] The evolutionary foundation of transcendence probably derives from the likelihood that persons with the greatest commitment to religious or socially altruistic purposes contribute most to the well-being of their communities. Thus, the health of such individuals strengthens the genetic survival prospects of the community.

Control Perceptions

The realities of viability in the social context; of the life events experienced; and of the activity, flexibility, integrity, and transcendence with which a person acts affect perceptions of the extent to which a person can influence the circumstances of life. These perceptions may differ from the reality of control in numerous ways, but even when they are inaccurate, these perceptions, themselves, exert an impact on health outcomes.

Contingency hopefulness, the expectation that an action taken will somehow affect existing circumstances, is based on past experience in taking similar actions. Seligman[45] has demonstrated that, when faced with an aversive stimulus, lack of contingency between personal actions and consequences leads to learned helplessness: a syndrome involving a disinclination to attempt to solve personal problems. Visintainer et al[46] have established that, among rats, the experience of contingency reduces cancer susceptibility. Among people, such contingency hopefulness may be a crucial factor in determining the practice of good health habits, which is itself a predictor of physiological health status.

Power motivation, the desire for control over reinforcing elements, influences the extent to which a person strives to obtain rights to goods, services, and rewards from others. Such striving may yield positive results; however, the more control is desired, the greater is the possibility that personal desires will go unrealized and that a sense of failure will result. Thus, in situations in which control cannot be obtained, persons characterized by type A behavior (probably high in power motivation) are more prone to the giving-up behavior accompanying learned helplessness than those with type B behavior.

This extreme response to lack of control may contribute to the association between type A behavior pattern and coronary heart disease. Furthermore, McClelland and Jemmott[6] demonstrated that university students who had a great need for power and were experiencing life events that threatened their sense of power had more severe instances of illness over a semester than did other students.

Power inhibitions, restraints in pursuing achievement of control because of ethical or religious beliefs, serve as a check on excess power motivations. Such restraint has been a theme of the great religions in their frequent urgings that people should accept those elements of life that are beyond personal control; it is also an important philosophical element of the egalitarian principles on which democratic societies are based.

To the extent that power inhibitions are an element in transcendent conceptions, enabling a person to see a positive value in a role involving little potential for control, such inhibitions are of health benefit. When a person accepts a given place in life, he or she avoids the persistent stress that stems from striving for more than can be achieved. However, individuals in whom great power inhibitions are combined with great need for power have increased risk of developing hypertension over a 20-year period;[47] they also experience a high rate of illness as students, especially when they are undergoing life-change events related to power pursuits.[6] Both effects may be attributed to chronic sympathetic arousal in such persons.

Perception of actual control, ie, a sense of how control pursuits have influenced outcomes in life, is best operationalized by the locus of control variable. Since the pioneer study by Seeman and Evans,[48] internality (the perception that personal behaviors generally influence the reinforcements received) has most often been associated with positive health behaviors.[49] Internality appears to protect the type A person from the anxiety reactions sometimes associated with coronary prone behavior. However, Lowery and DuCette[50] found that among persons with diabetes, internally controlled individuals showed poorer health outcomes after the first three years; this may be interpreted to indicate that in situations with a strong element of unpredictability, internality interferes with compliance and, thus, leads to negative health outcomes.

To the extent that a person is successful in control efforts, that person may be said to have a positive satisfaction/frustration balance. This construct may account for the finding of Lowery and DuCette[50] as well as that of Burke and Weir,[51] that although top-level, type A, prison administrators experienced substantial stress, they had notably low physiological risk factors related to cardiac disease. Whereas the internally controlled diabetes patients were frustrated in their attempts to maintain control over the condition, the top-level, type A prison officials probably met relatively few impediments to their exercise of power and, thus, little frustration.

Williams et al[52] found that among the various components of the type A pattern, hostility was the most important in predicting coronary artery disease. This hostility seems to occur in reaction to perceived threats to meeting important goals; it is, thus, a reflection of the satisfaction/frustration balance.

The importance of hostility, engendered by blockage of goal-oriented pursuits, illustrates that the relationship between control perceptions and health outcomes is not direct; rather, as shown in the evolutionary model in Fig 1, control perceptions, as an interacting combination of elements, influence health outcomes indirectly by impacting on personal feelings about a given place in the social order. Control perceptions serve to promote health to the extent that the synthesis of hopefulness, motivation, and inhibitions allow a person to feel maximally viable in relating to life circumstances. But if desires and ambitions exceed their potential to be realized, serious frustration leading to a sense of social inviability may result.

Viability Emotions

As a person processes perceptions of control, which are themselves shaped by personal viability within the social environment as affected by life events and lifestyle determiners, a person either develops a sense of being a viable participant in the social order who may influence the reinforcements received personally and by others or has the sense of not being a viable participant. This sense of viability is emotion laden in its content.

Development of viability emotions is not dependent on cognitive understanding of a situation. For example, reaction of an infant to parental abandonment is not limited by the intellectual developmental level of the infant. Furthermore, viability emotions may become deeply ingrained, based on the early experience or on a small number of key events, so that the emotions are unresponsive to current perceptions or detract from the ability to perceive with accuracy. Although four different bipolar components comprising the substance of viability emotions are identified here, there is some overlap between them, and it appears that the negative pole of each leads to a common outcome: the triggering, to some extent, of self-destructive processes.

Acceptance versus abandonment

The impact of the feeling of acceptance versus that of abandonment is well established in the literature of child development. In the classic study comparing institutionalized children experiencing maternal deprivation and those kept with their mothers in prison, Spitz[53] noted that the deprived children showed not only slowed development but also a high mortality rate, despite hygienic conditions. Harlow's[54] subsequent studies on deprivation in young monkeys indicated that attachment needs are genetically based, independent of the need for food, and most pronounced in stressful situations.

However, such needs are not restricted to the young. Of the five life-change events identified by Holmes and Rahe[20] as requiring the greatest adjustment, four involve abandonment issues (death of a spouse, divorce, marital separation, and death of a close family member). The usefulness of Holmes and Rahe's tool in predicting subsequent illness may result largely from the psychological potency of the abandonment factor. A sense of abandonment appears, also, to be a principle element in voodoo death.[44]

Additionally, studies have documented that illness is associated with distance from others. Thomas[55] found that lack of a close relationship with parents, as reported in early adulthood, predicts later cancer, and in a study of terminally ill children, Spinetta and associates[56] obtained complementary results. A wide variety of illness and handicap conditions have been hierarchically ordered, based on the extent to which they are associated with distance from others.[57] It is commonly understood that illness leads to stigma and abandonment. The sense of having been abandoned also leads to illness in what can become an inescapable cycle.

Usefulness versus uselessness

From control perceptions and evolutionary viability, a personal sense of usefulness or uselessness also develops. Throughout the history of the evolutionary origins of humans, each organism, during its lifetime, faced a series of challenges, and its success in meeting these challenges determined the likelihood of survival, not only for that particular individual, but also for the group. The contention is that the feeling of usefulness that accompanies the meeting of challenges is an emotional necessity. For example, rats who receive escapable electrical shock are less susceptible to cancer than those who are not shocked.[46] Apparently, rats housed in laboratory cages, provided with food and water, and protected from extreme temperatures benefit from the opportunity to respond to an environmental challenge.

In humans, feelings of usefulness derive from the contributions made within the social structure. High mortality rates among the unemployed and the retired, as well as among those who are not socially involved and those who are recently widowed, reflect this quality. When feelings of uselessness rather than usefulness are dominant, self-destructive processes are automatically triggered.

Optimism versus pessimism

Optimism versus pessimism, a function of the person's evaluation of past events and of future prospects, has been identified as a determinant of later goal-directed behavior.[58] In a classic series of experiments, Richter[59] found that rescuing rats from a stressful situation prevented subsequent sudden death, which would otherwise be expected; it appears that the rescued rats developed a hopefulness, which augmented their effectiveness in responding to later threat.

Among recently handicapped persons, tendencies to deny the existence of problems are associated with rehabilitation progress; and in a wide variety of situations, visualizing positive outcomes seems to augment the possibility of success. Among persons with cancer, the patient's image of the disease process is a predictor of subsequent disease state. Endogenous opiate peptides (endorphins) may be among the psychobiochemical links between these psychological and disease processes.[16]

Clarity versus confusion

Clarity is the sense that an adequate understanding of one's life can be achieved, confusion is the sense that it cannot be achieved. Confusion results from the overworked effort to find a solution to a problem, culminating in the conclusion that there is no solution. Such a feeling may be verbally manifested by the declaration, "I just don't understand anything anymore," reflecting a lack of confidence in the ability of one's mind to solve future problems. This emotional response leads to impaired decision making, as the person ceases the effort to predict future outcomes. Persons high in need for power, persons low in transcendental orientation, and persons already experiencing a sense of abandonment, uselessness, and pessimism may be most susceptible to such feelings of confusion.

The possible long-term advantage of the externally controlled person in certain illness situations with an unpredictable course and the health benefit that stems from strong religious commitments may both relate to resistance to the onset of confusion provided by such belief structures.

Overall, the components of viability emotions identified as being of primary importance within the proposed model each carry potential for affect, which ranges from strongly positive to strongly negative. These components derive from combination of control perceptions and the other concepts discussed here; they lead to health outcomes on a variety of levels.

Health Outcomes

When viability emotions are primarily negative, they trigger the onset of a self-destructive process in the forms of (a) psychological distress, (b) malproductive behavior, (c) and physiological dysfunction. Within the evolutionary model, these three phenomena are conceptualized as component elements of health outcomes, and for each element, one may observe signs of maximum health, as well as these indications that pathological, self-destructive processes are operating.

Psychological comfort or discomfort may be a direct result of viability emotions reflecting the presence or absence of feelings of acceptance, usefulness, optimism, and life clarity. When affect is primarily negative, a state of depression or anxiety may be apparent; when affect is primarily positive, the person expresses a general satisfaction with life.

Behavior that is oriented either to self-maintenance or to self-destructiveness is another component of health; the seven health practices identified by Belloc and Breslow[60] are prime indicators of personal status, as is any history of suicidal ideation or reckless, accident-prone behavior. Such behaviors, which constitute observable manifestations of the will to live or the lack of the will to live seem to occur as a general consequence of viability emotions.

Physiological function versus dysfunction, as determined through physical examination, illness history, laboratory procedures, and general fitness is contended also to reflect the viability emotions derived through concepts of the evolutionary model.

The mediation of viability emotions is a necessary connecting link between the variety of psychosocial factors conceptualized here and the variety of physical illness conditions that the psychosocial factors may precipitate. It has been established through numerous research studies that heart disease, cancer, and general illness rates each vary with psychosocial factors. Multiple neurological, hormonal, cardiovascular, and immunological mechanisms are implicated in this effect. These various mechanisms were developed over the eons of evolution because they served to enhance the prospects of group survival by eliminating those group members whose emotions reflected limitations in ability to contribute fully to the group welfare.

FEEDBACK WITHIN THE EVOLUTIONARY MODEL

In the pictorial presentation of the evolutionary model (Fig 1) and in the text, the relationships between major concepts in the model are made to appear somewhat unidirectional. This was necessary for clear exposition in describing the pathway thought to be of primary evolutionary importance in leading to the onset of automatically triggered self-destructive processes. However, the reality of relationships among the six major concepts presented is probably substantially more complex. For example, life events do not occur in a vacuum. They result, in part, from life-style determiners, control perceptions, viability emotions, and even actual viability within the social context. Furthermore, the onset of a serious illness is, itself, a notable life event. Thus, five new arrows could be drawn, each originating at a box representing one of these concepts and each ending at life events.

Likewise, health outcomes influence viability emotions as well as being influenced by them. Personal state of health also has important implications relative to viability in the social context and to personal perception of one's ability to exercise control. Even such matters of life style as the activity with which a person determines and pursues goals and the flexibility with which major life changes are faced may be adversely influenced by an illness.

Rather than specifically mentioning each possible causal/temporal relationship, it may simply be stated that each of six major concepts may be both a cause and an effect of each other concept, so that change in any one element may lead to changes throughout all model elements. In Fig 1, however, an attempt has been made to identify those lines of influence that may be most indicative of the primary causal linear sequence. Establishment of the validity of this model awaits further research.

INTERVENTION POINTS

The use of evolutionary assumptions in the development of a model of psychosocial factors in health is not intended to imply that a laissez-faire approach toward illness should be taken; that would be a serious distortion. Instead, this model is intended to guide creation and refinement of intervention approaches to be used by clinicians in interrupting self-destructive cycles. One central purpose of such intervention would be to impact on health outcomes by restoring the person's sense of viability. These interventions would be based on the assumptions that evolutionary viability is not a static entity and that it is not necessarily perceived accurately by the person.

Intervention may occur in relation to any of the six major concepts identified in this model. Evolutionary viability within a social context may be influenced through psychotherapeutic, educational, or community health intervention designed to improve a person's adaptability relative to the social environment or, as suggested by Norbeck,[61] to enhance social support. For example, programs on parenting skills for adolescent mothers may be expected to augment evolutionary viability in both generations. The potential in this area is not limited to any particular clinical discipline.

In some situations, life-change events are subject to influence by a clinician, as when, for example, a client seeks advice relative to a major personal decision; more often, however, the nature of life-change events serves not as an intervention point, but rather, as an assessment point and possibly as a warning signal that a person may be in a period of high susceptibility. Frequent physical examination, as well as counseling, may be appropriate during periods of bereavement, and more generally, whenever life events of major magnitude are occurring, especially if these events have implications for the person's social relationships.

Life-style determiners, control perceptions, and emotional consequences, like evolutionary viability itself, may be altered through educational, psychotherapeutic, and behavior modification interventions. Programs designed to reduce tendency toward type A behavior and to increase locus of control internality have been the subject of some experimentation; clinical use of relaxation and visualization is well established in some fields (eg, childbirth) and receiving increasing attention in others.[62,63] Interdisciplinary research involving experts in diverse areas (psychotherapy, religion, pharmacology, and clinical nursing) would be needed to determine how a clinician might work to affect such qualities as integrity, power inhibition, or optimism.

Interventions relative to health outcomes, including psychological, behavioral, and physiological components, have been nursing's traditional domain. This evolutionary model indicates that in implementing such interventions, clinicians should be alert to the possibility that as one health problem is resolved, other automatically triggered self-destructive processes may be initiated in the same individual, especially among clients who are most in need. Since such processes are related to a multiplicity of causes, a variety of intervention strategies should be considered. To the extent that the evolutionary model presented here is an accurate reflection of the reality of health and illness causation, intervention relative to evolutionary viability, life-style determiners, and viability emotions would be especially important aspects of health promotion among those who are most frequently ill.

REFERENCES

1. Hinkle LE. Ecological observations of the relation of physical illness, mental illness, and the social environment. *Psychosom Med.* 1961;23:289–296.
2. Rahe RH. Life change and subsequent illness reports. In Gunderson EKE, Rahe RH eds. *Life Stress and Illness.* Springfield, Ill: Charles C Thomas; 1974: pp 58-78.
3. Darwin CR. *The Origins of Species.* London: John Murray, 1859.
4. Berkman LF, Syme SL: Social networks, host resistance, and mortality: A nine-year follow-up study of Alameda County residents. *Am J Epidemiol.* 1979;109:186–204.
5. Nuckolls KB, Cassel J, Kaplan BH. Psychosocial assets, life crisis and the prognosis of pregnancy. *Am J Epidemiol.* 1972;95:431–441.
6. McClelland DC, Jemmott JB. Power motivation, stress and physical illness. *J Human Stress.* 1980;6:6–15.
7. Liddell H. Some specific factors that modify tolerance for environmental stress. In Wolff HG, Wolf SG, Hare CC, eds. *Life Stress and Bodily Disease.* Baltimore: Williams & Wilkins, 1950.
8. Conger JJ, Sawrey W, Turrell ES. The role of social experience in the production of gastric ulcers in hooded rats placed in a conflict situation. *J Abnorm Soc Psychol.* 1958;57:214–220.

9. Friedman M, Rosenman RH. *Type A Behavior and Your Heart.* Greenwich, Conn: Fawcett, 1974.
10. Wellisch DK, Yager J. Is there a cancer-prone personality? *CA.* 1983;33:145–153.
11. Derogatis LR, Abeloff MD, Melisaratos N. Psychological coping mechanisms and survival time in metastatic breast cancer. *JAMA.* 1979;242:1504–1508.
12. Pelletier KR: *Mind as Healer: Mind as Slayer.* New York: Delta, 1977.
13. Cassel J. Psychosocial processes and "stress": Theoretical formulation. *Int J Health Serv.* 1974;4:471–482.
14. DeCatanzaro D. *Suicide and Self-Damaging Behavior: A Sociobiological Perspective.* New York: Academic Press, 1981.
15. Bouvard EW. The effects of social stimuli on the response to stress. *Psychol Rev.* 1959;66:267–277.
16. Hubman M. Endogenous opiates and pain. *Adv Nurs Sci.* 1982;4:62–71.
17. Wolf S, Goodell H. *Harold G Wolff's Stress and Disease.* Springfield, Ill.: Charles C Thomas, 1968.
18. Warren S, Greenhill S, Warren KG. Emotional stress and the development of multiple sclerosis: Case-control evidence of a relationship. *J Chronic Dis.* 1982;35:821–831.
19. Stuart JC, Brown BM. The relationship of stress and coping ability to incidence of diseases and accidents. *J Psychosom Res* 1981;25:255–260.
20. Holmes TH, Rahe RH. The social readjustment rating scale. *J Psychosom Res.* 1967; 11:213-218.
21. Parkes CM, Benjamin B, Fitzgerald RG. Broken heart. A statistical study of increased mortality among widowers. *Br Med J.* 1969;1:740–743.
22. Frederick JF. The biochemistry of bereavement: Possible basis for chemotherapy. *Omega.* 1983;13:295–303.
23. Selye H. *The Stress of Life.* New York: McGraw-Hill, 1956.
24. Engel GL, Schmale AR. *Conversation-Withdrawal: A Primary Regulatory Process for Organismic Homeostasis.* New York: Elsevier, 1972.
25. Gal R, Lazarus RS. The role of activity in anticipating and confronting stressful situations. *J Human Stress.* 1975;1:4–20.
26. Weiss JM, Pohorecky LA, Salman S, et al. Attenuation of gastric lesions by psychological aspects of aggression in rats. *J Comp Physiol Psychol.* 1976;90:252–259.
27. Gentry WD, Chesney AP, Gary HE, et al. Habitual anger-coping styles: Effect on mean blood pressure and risk for essential hypertension. *Psychosom Med.* 1982;44:195–202.
28. Ray C, Fitzgibbon G. Stress arousal and coping with surgery. *Psychol Med.* 1981;11:741–746.
29. Greenberg RP, Dattore PJ. The relationship between dependency and the development of cancer. *Psychosom Med.* 1981;43:35–43.
30. Vaillant GE. Natural history of male psychological health: IV. What kinds of men do not get psychosomatic illness? *Psychosom Med.* 1978;40:420–431.
31. Cooley EJ, Keesey JC. Moderator variables in life stress and illness relationship. *J Human Stress.* 1981;7:35–40.
32. Boyce WT, Jensen EW, Cassel JC, et al. Influence of life events and family routines on childhood respiratory tract illness. *Pediatrics.* 1977;60:609–615.
33. Totman R, Reed SE, Craig JW. Cognitive dissonance, stress and virus-induced common colds. *J Psychosom Res.* 1977;21:55–63.
34. Hinkle LE, Christenson WN, Kane FD, et al. An investigation of the relation between life experience, personality characteristics, and general susceptibility to illness. *Psychosom Med.* 1958;20:278–295.
35. Carver CS, Coleman AE, Glass DC. The coronary-prone behavior pattern and the suppression of fatigue on a treadmill test. *J Pers Soc Psychol.* 1976;33:460–466.
36. Kasl SV, Evans AS, Niederman JC. Psychosocial risk factors in the development of infectious mononucleosis. *Psychosom Med.* 1979;41:445-466.

37. Kobasa SC. Stressful life events, personality, and health: An inquiry into hardiness. *J Pers Soc Psychol.* 1979;37:1–11.

38. Marx MB, Garrity TF, Somes GW. The effect of imbalance in life satisfactions and frustrations upon illness behavior in college students. *J Psychosom Res.* 1977;21:423–427.

39. Shaver P, Lenauer M, Sadd S. Religiousness, conversion, and subjective well-being: The "healthy-minded" religion of modern American women. *Am J Psychiatry.* 1980;137:1563–1568.

40. Graham TW, Kaplan BH, Cornoni-Huntley JC, et al. Frequency of church attendance and blood pressure elevation. *J Behav Med.* 1978;1:37–43.

41. Yates JW, Chalmer BJ, St James P, et al. Religion in patients with advanced cancer. *Med Pediatr Oncol.* 1981;9:121–128.

42. Ness RC. The impact of indigenous healing activity: An empirical study of two fundamentalist churches. *Soc Sci Med.* 1980;14B:167–180.

43. Frankl VE. *Man's Search for Meaning.* New York: Washington Square, 1959.

44. Cannon WB. "Voodoo" death. *Psychosom Med.* 1957;19:182–190.

45. Seligman MEP. *Helplessness: On Depression, Development, and Death.* San Francisco: WH Freeman, 1975.

46. Visintainer MA, Volpicelli JR, Seligman MEP. Tumor rejection in rats after inescapable or escapable shock. *Science.* 1982;216:437–439.

47. McClelland DC. Inhibited power motivation and high blood pressure in men. *J Abnorm Psychol.* 1979;88:182–190.

48. Seeman M, Evans JW. Alienation and learning in a hospital setting. *Am Sociol Rev.* 1962;27:772–783.

49. Arakelian M. An assessment and nursing application of the concept of locus of control. *Adv Nurs Sci.* 1980;3:25–40.

50. Lowery BJ, DuCette JP. Disease-related learning and disease control in diabetics as a function of locus of control. *Nurs Res.* 1976;25:358–362.

51. Burke RJ, Weir T. The type A experience: Occupational and life demands, satisfaction and well-being. *J Human Stress.* 1980;6:28–38.

52. Williams RB, Haney TL, Lee KL, et al. Type A behavior, hostility, and coronary atherosclerosis. *Psychosom Med.* 1980;42:539–549.

53. Spitz RA. Hospitalism: A follow-up report. *Psychoanal Study Child.* 1946;2:113–117.

54. Harlow HF. Love in infant monkeys. *Sci Am.* 1959;200:68–74.

55. Thomas CB. Precursors of disease and death: The predictive potential of habits and family attitudes. *Ann Intern Med.* 1976;85:653–658.

56. Spinetta JJ, Rigler D, Karon M. Personal space as a measure of a dying child's sense of isolation. *J Consult Clin Psychol.* 1974;42:751–756.

57. Harasymiw SJ, Horne MD, Lewis SC. A longitudinal study of disability group acceptance. *Rehabil Lit.* 1976;37:98–102.

58. Tiger L. *Optimism: The Biology of Hope.* New York: Simon & Schuster, 1979.

59. Richter CP. On the phenomenon of sudden death in animals and man. *Psychosom Med.* 1957;19:191-198.

60. Belloc NB, Breslow L. Relationship of physical health status and health practices. *Prev Med.* 1972;1:409–421.

61. Norbeck JS. Social support: A model for clinical research and application. *Adv Nurs Sci.* 1981;3:43–59.

62. Campbell DF, Dixon JK, Sanderford LD, et al. Relaxation: Its effect on the nutritional status and performance status of clients with cancer. *J Am Diet Assoc.* To be published.

63. Nath C, Rinehart J. Effects of individual and group relaxation therapy on blood pressure in essential hypertensives. *Res Nurs Health.* 1979;2:119–126.

Caring for the Frail Elderly at Home: Toward a Theoretical Explanation of the Dynamics of Poor Quality Family Caregiving

Using the grounded theory approach, 39 family caregivers were theoretically sampled using newspaper advertising to explore their perceptions of providing home care for frail elders and to generate a theoretical model that (1) describes the dynamics of good quality and poor quality family caregiving; (2) explains the relationships among certain contextual and perceptual variables and the behaviors exchanged by elders and caregivers; and (3) identifies points where interventions by nurses could be effective. The model consists of five constructs that were identified from the data and were staged within the framework provided by symbolic interactionism and social exchange theory. The five constructs and two related driving forces provide a partial explanation for the quality of family caregiving and a beginning explanation for the phenomenon of elder abuse.

Linda R. Phillips, RNC, PhD
Associate Professor
University of Arizona College of Nursing
Tucson, Arizona

Veronica F. Rempusheski, RN, PhD
Program Director/Nurse Researcher
Gerontological Nursing
Beth Israel Hospital
Boston, Massachusetts

MOST OF THE care for frail elders in our society is managed in the home setting and the bulk of home care and supportive services for the elderly is provided by

The project on which this article is based was partially supported by a Sigma Theta Tau Research Grant, 1981–1982, and the University of Arizona Committee on Gerontology Small Grants Program, 1983–1984.

The first draft of this article was presented at the 12th Annual Nursing Research Conference, Tucson, Arizona, University of Arizona College of Nursing, September 20, 1984.

Adv Nurs Sci 1986;8(4):62–84
© 1986 Aspen Publishers, Inc.

family members.[1-5] For the frail, community-dwelling elder, having a stable relationship with a family caregiver who is willing and able to satisfactorily meet the elder's care needs is critical for the elder's well-being and survival. If all elders received optimal care from their family caregivers, with all of their needs being adequately met, descriptions and explanations of the quality and dynamics of family caregiving would probably be of only passing interest to nurses. This, however, is not the case. Although there is substantial evidence suggesting that for many elders, the quality of their care is supportive, compassionate, and adequate, there is also a body of research evidence to the contrary.[6-11] As a result, nurses practicing in the community are often in the position of needing to intervene in caregiving situations that are less than optimal.

In the past several years, researchers have concentrated their attention on documenting the existence of elder-caregiver relationships and describing the types of services that families provide.[2,5,12-14] Nevertheless, there is still a dearth of theoretical and empirical data that describe the dynamics of elder-caregiver relationships, that account for the quality of these relationships, or that can be used as the basis for nursing intervention models. The purpose of this study was to explore caregivers' perceptions of their caregiving relationships using the grounded theory approach[15] to generate a theoretical model that

- describes the dynamics of caregiving relationships among frail elders and their caregivers in the home setting;
- explains the relationships among certain contextual and perceptual variables and the behaviors exchanged by elders and caregivers; and
- identifies points where interventions by nurses could be effective.

METHODOLOGY

Key features of the grounded theory methodology are that data are collected, coded, and analyzed concurrently, using the technique of constant comparative analysis; that data are fractured into units of analysis, or "data bits," as determined by the concepts guiding the investigation and the evolving theory; and that sampling (of persons and content) is guided by theoretically determined criteria and the evolving theory.[15-17]

This study was conducted in two phases in two separate geographic locations, the Midwestern and the Southwestern United States. The methods used in each location were identical. To ensure maximum variation of the variable "quality of relationship," family caregivers were solicited from those who responded to one of two newspaper advertisements. One advertisement solicited caregivers who had a "good" relationship with the elder for whom they cared and the other solicited caregivers who had an "abusive" or "neglectful" relationship with the elder. Persons who responded to the advertisements were screened to ensure that they had provided at least one intermittent personal, social, or nursing service to a community-dwelling person over the age of 60 years, had had a consanguine or acquired kinship tie with the elder, and were white and English speaking.

The caregivers who volunteered were interviewed at least once after being informed of their rights as participants in a research study. The length of these interviews ranged from one to three hours. With the subject's permission, each interview was tape-recorded. The interviews were conducted in a place of the subject's choice, and for some interviews more than one caregiver participated (for example, both husband and wife participated in describing the caregiving for the husband's mother). The questions for each interview followed the same general format, but as the theoretical sample increased and the data were concurrently analyzed, the questions in subsequent interviews became more refined and focused. Interviews were conducted with subjects until no new data emerged relative to the evolving theory.

SAMPLE

In grounded theory, the researcher samples content, not persons; therefore, in this report, sample size will be addressed from two perspectives: the sample of data bits, or words, phrases, or sentences from subject interviews; and the theoretical sample of subjects, or the persons being interviewed.

Approximately 2,000 large data bits (paragraphs or anecdotes) comprised the beginning working sample. These large data bits were subjected to constant comparative analysis so as to fracture and refine them into the smallest workable units (a technical consideration) and to sort them into categories that emerged from the comparison (a theoretical and model building consideration). The actual mechanics of comparative analysis[16] consisted of open and selective coding of the transcribed interviews. The initial (open) coding of data involved partitioning the interview into relevant phrases, sentences, or anecdotes. Open coding continued until the categories and properties emerged that signaled the start of selective coding. Selective coding involved sorting data bits into the previously determined categories to refine and expand the evolving theory. The majority of the open coding was conducted with the Midwestern data set, though it was used initially with the Southwestern data set to confirm the comparability of the samples.

To estimate the validity of the emerging categories and properties, percent agreement was computed on randomly selected interviews during the open coding phase of the data analysis by comparing the identified responses coded by the two researchers. The percent agreement range was 69 to 81. As methods of refining and validating the evolving theory, Glaser[16] recommends "thinking" about the data and "memoing." These two methods were used with oral and written procedures to ensure relevancy and content validity.

A theoretical sample of 39 caregivers—14 who answered the "good" relationship advertisement and 25 who answered the "abusive" relationship advertisement—were interviewed. Both types of caregivers described elders who had physical and mental disabilities and care needs that ranged from mild to serious. In the Midwestern sample, a total of 19 caregivers were interviewed. Eight caregivers responded to the "good" relationship advertisement and 11 responded to the "abusive" relationship advertisement. The caregivers ranged in age from 15 to 70 years, with a mean age of 46.95 (SD, 15.19). These 19 caregivers provided services to a total of 16 elders who ranged in age from 66 to 92 years (mean, 78.63; SD, 7.36). All but three caregivers lived with the elder for whom they cared. Sixteen caregivers were female and three were male; of the 16 elders, eight were male and eight were female. Twelve of the caregivers were adult children or children-in-law of the elder, three were grandchildren, two were nieces, one was a sibling-in-law, and one was a lifelong significant other.

In the Southwestern sample, a total of 20 caregivers were interviewed. Six caregivers responded to the "good" relationship advertisement and 14 responded to the "abusive" relationship advertisement. The caregivers ranged in age from 32 to 85 years, with a mean age of 58.63 (SD, 13.34). These 20 caregivers provided services to total of 20 elders who ranged in age from 64 to 90 years (mean, 78.84; SD, 6.87). All but two caregivers lived with the elder for whom they cared. Seventeen caregivers were female and three were male; 11 of the elders for whom the caregivers provided service were female and 9 were male. Sixteen of the caregivers were adult children or children-in-law of the elder, two were spouses, one was a sibling, and one was a grandchild.

RESULTS

Several empirical models were generated to describe various facets of caregiving from the caregiver's perspective. This article will focus on a portion of a four-stage model that explains the overall quality of a caregiving relationship based on the caregiver's view of caregiving dynamics. A literature review conducted during the last half of the data analysis confirmed the appropriateness of symbolic interactionism,[18] social exchange theory,[19–21] and dramaturgic theory[22] as the conceptual base for the model. The portion of the generated model that will be discussed (Fig 1) is staged within the McCall and Simmons[18] framework of symbolic interactionism, with stage 1 consisting of the person defining the situation, stage 2 consisting of cognitive processes, stage 3 consisting of expressive processes, and stage 4 consisting of evaluation processes. Five major constructs are set within this framework:

(1) personal identity of the elder (stage 1),
(2) image of caregiving (stage 1),
(3) caregiver's role beliefs (stage 2),
(4) caregiver's behavioral strategies (stage 3), and
(5) perceptions (stage 4).

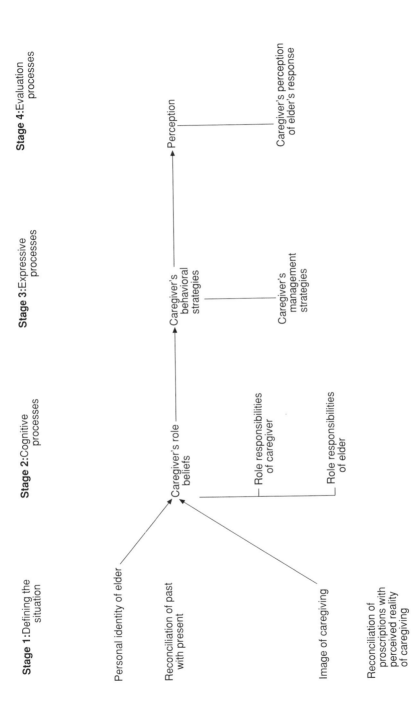

Fig 1. Theoretical model for the dynamics of family caregiving.

Stage 1: Defining the Situation

During the initial contact between two persons, each person defines the situation and establishes and negotiates the background against which plans, actions, and role selections are determined.[18] According to the data from this study, two of the constructs that establish the initial tone of the interactions for the caregiver are the "personal identity of the elder" and the "image of caregiving."

Personal identity of the elder

The personal identity of the elder is partially defined as the mental image that the caregiver has of the elderly person, as derived from past associations, present observations, and the reconciliation of past with present. Goffman[22] presents the conceptualization of personal identity that is most relevant to this induced theory. According to Goffman,[22] as persons interact over time, each develops a constantly evolving "dossier" about the other that contains, among other things, a history of events, impressions, normative role expectations, and evaluations that uniquely identify one person to the other. The "dossier," or image of personal identity, is then used by each person as the basis for his or her ongoing interactions with the other person. From this perspective, the actual behaviors that one person displays have no importance for the other person except as useful illustrations of concrete facets of the individual's personhood.

In this construct, behavioral descriptions such as "he hits me when I try to bathe him" or "she insists on doing the dishes" were found to be important only to the degree to which they described some facet of the elder's image. For example, one caregiver could use a statement such as "she insists on doing the dishes" to illustrate that the elder was remarkable in light of his or her physical limitations, whereas another caregiver could use the same statement to illustrate that the elder was selfishly intruding on the role domain of the caregiver. Therefore, according to these data, the personal identity of the elder has a direct impact on the ways in which the caregiver views the elder's behaviors and the caregiving situation and on the ways in which the caregiver enacts the caregiving role.

The concept associated with the personal identity of the elder is the reconciliation of past with present. This concept subsumes six distinct processes, each of which involves three separate steps:

1. combining or pooling the impressions from the past to derive the past image;
2. combining or pooling the impressions from the present to derive the present image; and
3. formulating a reconciled image of the person by comparing the past image with the present image.

Appendix A provides definitions for these processes and a data-based example of a caregiver engaging in each one. All six processes were represented among persons who responded to the "good" as well as the "abusive" relationship advertisements. In addition, the data from the study provided evidence that most caregivers used all six processes.

During the reconciliation of past with present processes, the caregiver must first derive a past and present image of the elder from which the reconciled image is derived. Consistent with the work of Goffman,[22] Wright,[23] and Thomas,[24] both the past image and present image can be formulated in one of two ways: as a normalized view or as an anormalized view. The normalized view (normalization) is characterized by the caregiver viewing the elder as an adequate human who possesses some strengths and some weaknesses and who is, overall, viewed in a slightly positive light. Deification and stigmatization, on the other hand, are anormalized images of the elder. Deification is characterized by the caregiver viewing the elder as far more than adequate and often almost more than human. The caregiver sees the elder as possessing only strengths and positive attributes and acknowledges no negative traits in the elder. When stigmatized, the elder is viewed as far less than adequate. In fact, the elder may be viewed as far less than human, possessing neither strengths nor positive attributes. Appendix B presents data-based examples that illustrate these views.

The possible outcomes of the caregiver formulating a reconciled image of the elder are schematically represented in Fig 2. The caregiver's reconciled image of the elder is represented by the position achieved in the matrix cells. Empirically, anormalized past images of both deified and stigmatized types tended to be associated with caregivers in the "abusive" relationship group, and normalized images tended to be associated with caregivers in the "good" relationship group. In addition, those who responded to the "abusive" relationship advertisement tended to have a present image that was at least one category lower than the past image; for example, they had a deified past image and a normalized present image or a normalized past image and a stigmatized present image. For them, as Goffman[22] would say, the elder's identity had been "spoiled." The only exceptions were those persons whose stigmatized past image remained stigmatized in the present. Conversely, those who responded to the "good" relationship advertisement tended to have a stable view of the elder from past to present, or they saw the elder's position as a category higher; that is, they had a stigmatized past image and a

Present image \ Past image	Deified	Normalized	Stigmatized
Deified			
Normalized			
Stigmatized			

Fig 2. Matrix of the possible outcomes of the reconciliation process.

normalized present image. No elder in this group was seen as stigmatized in the present.

Image of caregiving

The second construct in stage 1 is image of caregiving, which is partially defined as the degree to which the caregiver's personal imperatives, standards, and values are realized by the caregiving situation. The concept associated with this construct is the reconciliation of proscriptions with the perceived reality of caregiving, which is defined as the degree to which the caregiver's observations and perceptions of the situation diverge from the caregiver's beliefs about propriety. It appears from the data that caregivers come to the caregiving situation with an implicit set of standards for their behavior, the behavior of other persons, and life in general. These standards or proscriptions constitute an ideal against which observations and perceptions of reality are judged.

Several interrelated categories of proscriptions were inferred from the data. The first category relates to general standards for healthy living, including cleanliness, nutritious eating patterns, and moderation in eating, drinking, smoking, and religious activities. The second category relates to general standards for quality of life. For example, many of the caregivers in the sample implied that quality of life is dependent on being productive, performing useful activities, having interests outside of oneself, and having an alert, inquisitive mind. The third category of proscriptions relates to general standards for family behavior. Examples of standards in this category included manners, interests, activities, and expressive patterns appropriate for members of the family. This category was intimately related to expressions of family pride about its perceived status (eg, "because we ascribe to these standards members of our family are better than other people"). The fourth category relates to standards for relationships such as fulfilling obligations and promises, adhering to the norms of reciprocity and fairness, and providing role support and legitimization. Within this category, standards were identified for elders' behaviors (eg, providing a model for and maintaining the standards of family behavior and communicating appropriately) as well as for caregivers' behaviors (eg, assuming responsibility, showing initiative, and being compassionate).

Whereas the caregivers' proscriptions were largely inferred from the data, their descriptions of their perceived reality of caregiving were explicit. According to these descriptions, the perceived reality of caregiving was derived either from ongoing perceptions and observations of elders and caregivers in general or from the caregivers' perceptions and observations of their elders, their situations, and themselves. For example, one subject (identified as "C7"), who implied that cleanliness was a standard of great importance for healthy living, used this standard in her observations of all elders: "Older people tend to forget to take showers. They're really quite lax in their habits. Maybe their sense of smell dulls over the years. I see it all the time in the market. They really need someone to remind *them* about personal hygiene." Another subject (C4), who ascribed to the same standard, used it in his observations of the elder for whom he cared: "She developed a thing—she wouldn't wash. She wouldn't take a bath, and she would have this horrible body odor. You could notice it. We would have people over and she would come through the house and leave a trail of odor."

All caregivers in the sample appeared to engage in reconciling their proscriptions with their perceived reality of caregiving. In addition, for all caregivers, the results of the reconciliation had a direct effect on their expressed role beliefs (stage 2). Among those caregivers who answered the "abusive" relationship advertisement, however, there was more divergence between their proscriptions and their perceived reality. In addition, their proscriptions appeared more rigid and less negotiable than those of the other caregivers. Their perceived reality seemed farther away from their proscriptive ideal and, as a result, their role beliefs reflected a more punitive, controlling attitude than that of the caregivers who responded to the "good" relationship advertisement.

Stage 2: Cognitive Processes

During the cognitive processes of interaction, each person involved improvises a role for himself or herself and imputes a role to the other based on each person's definition of the situation. In stage 2 of the generated model (Fig 1), which focuses only on the perspective of the caregiver, one construct was identified: the "caregiver's role beliefs."

The caregiver's role beliefs as a construct is partially defined as the standards and values held by the caregiver regarding the performance of the caregiver role. The concepts associated with the caregiver's role beliefs are the role responsibilities of the caregiver, which is defined as the role definitions the caregiver improvises for self; and the role responsibilities of the elder, which is defined as the role definitions the caregiver imputes to the elder. Examples of the kinds of role responsibilities of the caregiver identified among these data include doing for, protecting, acting for the good of, monitoring social acceptability, and establishing and enforcing standards. Examples of the role responsibilities of the elder identified among these data include treating the caregiver properly, making contributions, and showing cooperation. Appendix C provides databased examples for some of these role responsibilities.

The personal identity of the elder and the image of caregiving had a direct impact on the caregiver's role beliefs. For example, if the personal identity of the elder was closely reconciled from past to present and the perceived reality of caregiving was fairly close to the proscriptions—which was most commonly the case among those in the "good" relationship—then the role responsibilities of caregiver tended to involve more supportive activities such as protecting and acting on behalf of. The role responsibilities of the elder in the same situation tended to involve fewer expectations for being compliant and cooperative and more understanding about the treatment the elder displayed toward the caregiver.

Conversely, if the personal identity of the elder was not reconciled from past to present and the perceived reality of caregiving was fairly diverse from the proscriptions—which was most commonly the case among those in the "abusive" relationship—then the role responsibilities of caregiver tended to involve more punitive and controlling activities such as monitoring social acceptability and establishing and enforcing standards. The role responsibilities of the elder then tended to involve more expectations for being compliant and cooperative and less understanding about the treatment the elder displayed toward the caregiver.

Stage 3: Expressive Processes

During the expressive processes of interaction, each person involved enacts the role improvised for himself or herself. Stage 3 of the model (Fig 1) identifies one construct to index the caregiver's role enactment: the "caregiver's behavioral strategies." The caregiver's behavioral strategies are partially defined as the behavior the caregiver customarily uses in responding to the elder. The concept associated with this construct is the caregiver's management strategies, defined as the methods the caregiver employs to control the elder's behavior and to resolve conflicts with the elder. Among the caregivers in the sample, three types of management strategies were identified: positive, negative, and neutral strategies. Appendix D provides data-based examples of each of these. The management strategies can be conceptualized on a continuum that ranges from extremely positive to extremely negative. Extremely negative strategies are synonymous with elder abuse, with the caregiver using such behaviors as tripping and slapping in order to control behavior. All caregivers in the sample reported using all three types of management strategies, though for many, one type was predominant, and for those who responded to the "good" relationship advertisement, the extremely negative type was very rare. Frequently, caregivers reported using a progression of management strategies, beginning with positive or neutral strategies and moving down the continuum to more negative strategies until the desired response was elicited.

The nature of the caregiving management strategies chosen and the point on the continuum where the caregiver began attempting to control behavior were related directly to the caregiver's role beliefs and indirectly to both the personal identity of the elder and the image of caregiving. For those caregivers in the "abusive" relationship group, who tended to improvise more punitive role responsibilities for themselves and impute more rigid role responsibilities on the elder, the progression down the continuum was abbreviated to the degree that they attempted to control behavior using more negative strategies. On the other hand, those in the "good" relationship group, who tended to improvise more supportive role responsibilities for themselves and impute less restrictive role responsibilities on the elder, also displayed an abbreviated progression down the continuum because they rarely progressed to negative behaviors.

Stage 4: Evaluation Processes

During the evaluation phase of social interaction, each person judges his or her own and the other's role enactments for adequacy and legitimacy. The evaluation process provides the basis for consensus negotiation as each actor redefines the symbolic meaning of the situation, alters his or her behavior, and allocates or withholds rewards in response to these independent judgments. Over years of interaction, the persons use the feedback obtained from observing the responses of each other and others in the environment to redefine the symbolic meaning of the relationship and reformulate role identities based on anticipated responses. The construct in the model that reflects the evaluation process is "perception," which is partially defined as the caregiver's "representation or image of reality."[25(p94)] The concept associated with perception is the caregiver's perception of the elder's response, which is defined as the caregiver's interpretation of the elder's role support and role enactment. Through interpreting or ascribing meaning to observations of the elder during interactions, the caregiver is able, over time, to positively or negatively modify the present image of the elder and the perceived reality of caregiving (stage 1). Part of the driving force for the model, therefore, is the feedback the caregiver receives from ongoing interactions with the elder. Appendix E provides data-based examples of caregivers using the evaluation process to modify their image of the elder and the caregiving situation.

Mechanisms of Caregiving Dynamics

Whereas the driving force for the model can be partially explained by the feedback mechanism from stage 4 to stage 1, the data indicate that at least two other factors, "currently salient role form" and "role interdependence," contribute to the ways the model works.

Currently salient role form

In addition to providing the specific caregiving anecdotes that generated the model, the interview process employed in this study provided the researchers with an opportunity to derive an overall impression of the caregiver's performance during social interactions other than caregiving. The researchers focused their observations on how the caregiver interacted with the researcher, how the caregiver described interactions with persons other than the elder, and how the caregiver actually interacted with others while in the researcher's presence. From these observations emerged the concept of currently salient role form, which is defined as the dominant interaction mode the caregiver uses in exchanges with others. It would appear from the data that currently salient role form is a concept that affects every construct in the model and delimits the behavioral expressions considered acceptable by the caregiver. Although the individual caregivers displayed a number of different role forms, two types were most strikingly apparent: nurturing-supporting and monitoring-controlling.

The nurturing-supporting role form was displayed by caregivers whose social presentation was characterized by qualities such as attention to comfort, sensitivity, insight, and acceptance. In relationship to the elder, the purist form of the role was termed "earth mother" because these caregivers were generally able to describe the behavior of the elder kindly and empathetically even when the behavior was disturbing or evoked anger. The concept that emerged as a result of interviewing these caregivers was unconditional acceptance which, following Rogers'[26] tradition, was defined as the caregiver's ability to express love, caring, warmth, and respect for the elder regardless of the elder's negative or contradictory behaviors. No caregivers who responded to the "abusive" relationship advertisement demonstrated this type of role form. Appendix F presents examples from the data that illustrate the concept of unconditional acceptance.

The monitoring-controlling role form was displayed by caregivers whose social presentation was characterized by dogmatic expressions and rigidity. In relationship to the elder, the purist form of the role was termed "prison guard" because, although these caregivers verbally expressed their love and concern for the elder, they appeared to be constantly observing the elder for inappropriate behavior that required their corrective action. The concepts that emerged from observing monitoring-controlling caregivers was caregiving dogmatism. Following Rokeach,[27(p195)] caregiving dogmatism is defined as a relatively closed cognitive set of beliefs and disbeliefs about caregiving organized around a central set of beliefs about absolute authority. The central beliefs, in turn, provide a framework for patterns of intolerance and qualified tolerance toward the elder. Among these subjects, caregiving dogmatism was demonstrated by strong, unyielding opinions about how elders and caregivers should be and should behave, closed-mindedness in considering alternative beliefs or behaviors, and a personal projection of right and justice in actions and thoughts. Appendix F presents examples from the data that illustrate caregiving dogmatism. The persons in this study who demonstrated extreme caregiving dogmatism were those who also demonstrated often bizarre negative behavioral management strategies in caring for the elder, usually justifying their actions with expressions about the correctness of their behaviors. Although the elements of caregiving dogmatism were displayed by some persons other than earth mothers in the "good" relationship group, the most extreme examples were found only among those in the "abusive" relationship group.

Role interdependence

Whereas both symbolic interactionism and social exchange theory would predict that a social interaction (and eventually a social relationship) is terminated when the behavior of one person is no longer perceived as reinforcing or supportive by the other, the role interdependence perceived by both individuals in the elder-caregiver dyad prohibited termination of the relationship under any conditions. The caregivers and elders were emotionally bonded and socially intertwined, which had several effects on the caregiving dynamics.

First, because termination of the relationship was not perceived to be an option, it was possible for negative reinforcement cycles to be established and perpetuated in which the mutual withdrawal from negative reinforcement and the secondary gain from providing negative reinforcement became positive reinforcers. Such a negative reinforcement cycle is consistent with Homans'[28] predictions about social exchange. Second, because each participant in the elder-caregiver relationship had a monopoly on certain types of rewards, each had some power advantages and some vulnerabilities. For example, most caregivers provided more instrumental services than did elders, but most elders had the capability of providing needed economic resources and expressive services (eg, giving or withholding love and approval). As a result, among the caregivers who responded to the "abusive" relationship advertisement, issues of power and control were central. Caregivers expressed impotence, embarrassment, and frustration with their inability to control the elder's behavior; similarly, they expressed resentment about the elders' using economic resources to manipulate their behavior and withholding approval and gratitude.

According to Pillemer,[29] abuse arises when the abuser feels powerless and impotent and seeks to compensate for the lack of control or loss of power with the available resources. When personal resources are limited, violence (physical or emotional) is a likely outcome. It is interesting that among the caregivers in the "abusive" relationship group who describe using extreme behavioral strategies usually associated with abuse, the most common reason for answering the advertisement was to describe the abuses perpetrated by the elder.

HYPOTHESES GENERATED FROM THE DATA

1. The more "spoiled" the caregiver's reconciled image of the elder, the more the caregiver's perception will be that the role responsibilities of the caregiver should involve punitive and controlling activities.

2. The more "spoiled" the caregiver's reconciled image of the elder, the more the caregiver's perception will be that the role responsibilities of the elder should involve compliance, making contributions, and treating the caregiver well.

3. The more "normalized" or "deified" the caregiver's reconciled image of the elder, the more the caregiver's perception will be that the role responsibilities of the caregiver should involve supportive activities.

4. The more "normalized" or "deified" the caregiver's reconciled image of the elder, the less the caregiver's perception will be that the role responsibilities of the elder should involve cooperation, making contributions, and treating the caregiver well.

5. The more divergent the caregiver's proscriptions and perceived reality of caregiving, the more the caregiver's perception will be that the role responsibilities of the caregivers should involve punitive and controlling activities.

6. The more divergent the caregiver's proscriptions and perceived reality of caregiving, the more the caregiver's perception will be that the role responsibilities of the elders should involve compliance, making contributions, and treating the caregiver well.

7. The more convergent the caregiver's proscriptions and perceived reality of caregiving, the more the caregiver's perception will be that the role responsibilities of the caregiver should involve supportive activities.

8. The more convergent the caregiver's proscriptions and perceived reality of caregiving, the less the caregiver s perception will be that the role responsibilities of the elder should involve cooperation, making contributions, and treating the caregiver well.

9. The more the caregiver perceives role responsibilities of the caregiver as punitive and controlling, the more frequently the caregiver will use negative behavioral strategies during interactions with the elder.

10. The more the caregiver perceives the role responsibilities of the elder as lacking compliance, lacking contributions, and abusive of the caregiver, the more frequently the caregiver will use negative behavioral strategies during interactions with the elder.

11. The more the caregiver perceives the role responsibilities of the caregiver as supportive, the more frequently the caregiver will use positive behavioral strategies during interactions with the elder.

12. The more the caregiver perceives the role responsibilities of the elder as cooperative, contributing, and treating the caregiver well, the more frequently the caregiver will use positive behavioral strategies during interactions with the elder.

13. When the results of using behavioral strategies are perceived to evoke a positive response in the elder, the present image of the elder and perceived reality of caregiving will be positively affected.

14. When the results of using behavioral strategies are perceived to evoke a negative response in the elder, the present image of the elder and perceived reality of caregiving will be negatively affected.

CONCLUSIONS AND IMPLICATIONS

From this investigation, it is apparent that multiple factors influence the quality of family caregiving. First, the caregiver's perceptions of the history of events, the caregiver's impressions of the elder and his or her behavior, the caregiver's normative role expectations for the elder, and the caregiver's evaluation of both the elder and previous performances appear to have an important impact on the caregiver's role beliefs and on the management strategies the caregiver chooses in everyday interactions with the elder. Second, the caregiver's perceptions of the reality of caregiving as compared with the caregiver's proscriptions for proper living appear to have an important impact on the manner in which the caregiving role is enacted. Third, the caregiver's choice of positive, neutral, or negative caregiving management strategies seems to be associated with the caregiver's beliefs about caregiving, impressions of the elder's past and present behavior, and impressions of the caregiving situation. Last, the quality of family caregiving appears to maintain a dynamic state as a result of the feedback provided by ongoing performance evaluation, factors associated with the caregiver's view of self, and social forces. Although the model generated in this study does not account for all of the variables involved in caregiving dynamics (for example, the effects of caregiving burdens, role conflict, and family support), it does provide a basis for deriving an integrated theoretical view of family caregiving.

The validity of this model is supported by diverse literature sources, and many of the concepts and processes generated from this investigation are consistent with previous empirical findings. For example, the notion of reconciling past with present, though not previously identified per se in the gerontological literature, is not new. Clinically, caregivers' comments like "he is not the man I remember" and "I feel like I'm caring for a stranger" are common enough that Robinson[30] included changes in the caregiver's perception of the elder's image as one of 13 items in the Caregiver's Strain Index. In addition, although caregiving dogmatism has not been previously identified as it relates to family caregiving, researchers (eg, Gelles[31]) of conjugal violence and child abuse have identified as key to the perpetuation of violence within the family offenders' beliefs in their knowledge of "right and proper" behavior and their rights to punish victims to produce proper behavior. The relatively closed structure of beliefs about proper and improper behavior demonstrated by some of the caregivers in this study may represent the same types of beliefs that have been previously identified in the literature on abuse. As with all inductively generated models, however, the validity of the conceptualizations must ultimately be empirically verified by quantitative theory testing.

•   •   •

Family caregivers hold a central position in the quality of care being provided to the frail elderly at home. Without their assistance, many elders would be either prematurely institutionalized or left to their own devices to meet their physical and emotional needs. The assistance of family caregivers, however, adds a complex dimension to providing health care and support services in the home. For the most part, nurses who provide care to elders cannot afford to ignore the role of the family caregiver. Rather, to provide the most therapeutic and cost-effective care, the nurse must understand the family dynamics associated with caregiving and intervene to meet the needs of both the elder and the family members providing the care. The model generated in this research is a first step toward describing some of the dynamics involved in family caregiving that have a direct impact on the quality of the caring situation. Although still in its infancy, this model helps explain some of the behaviors and attitudes displayed by caregivers. With testing and refinement, it holds promise for predictive power in identifying caregivers who are at high risk for providing less than optimal care and for prescriptive power in identifying the points where the interventions by nurses will be most effective in ameliorating high-risk caregiving situations.

REFERENCES

1. Brody EM. Women in the middle and family help to old people. *Gerontologist.* 1981;21:471–480.
2. Brody S, Poulshock SW, Masciocci CF. The family caring unit: A major consideration in the long-term support system. *Gerontologist.* 1978;18:556–561.
3. Kohen JA. Old but not alone: Informal social supports among the elderly by marital status and sex. *Gerontologist.* 1983;23:57–63.
4. Shanas E. The family as a social support system in old age. *Gerontologist.* 1979;19:169–174.
5. Stoller EP, Earl LL. Help with activities of everyday life: Sources of support for the noninstitutionalized elderly. *Gerontologist.* 1983;23:64–70.
6. Hickey T, Douglass RL. The mistreatment of the elder in the domestic setting: An exploratory study. *Am J Public Health.* 1981;71:171–176.
7. Hickey T, Douglass RL. Neglect and abuse of older family members: Professionals' perspective and care experiences. *Gerontologist.* 1981;21:171–176.
8. Phillips LR. Abuse/neglect of the frail elderly at home: An exploration of theoretical relationship. *J Adv Nurs.* 1983;8:379–392.
9. Phillips LR, Rempusheski VF. A decision-making model for diagnosing and intervening in elder abuse and neglect. *Nurs Res.* 1985;34:134–139.
10. Lau EE, Kosberg JI. Abuse of the elderly by informal careproviders. *Aging.* 1979;299:10–15.
11. Pillemer K. The dangers of dependency: New findings on domestic violence against the elderly. Special report. Family Research Laboratory and Department of Sociology, University of New Hampshire, 1985.
12. Archbold PG. Impact of parent-caring on middle aged offspring. *J Gerontol Nurs.* 1980;6:78–85.
13. Archbold PG. Impact of parent-caring on women. *Fam Relations.* 1983;32:39–45.
14. Cantor M. Strain among caregivers: A study of experience in the United States. *Gerontologist.* 1983;23:597–604.
15. Glaser B, Strauss A. *The Discovery of Grounded Theory: Strategies for Qualitative Research.* Hawthorne, NY, Aldine, 1967.
16. Glaser B. *Theoretical Sensitivity.* Mill Valley, Calif: Sociology Press, 1978.
17. Stern PM. Grounded theory methodology: Its uses and processes. *Image.* 1980;12:20–23.
18. McCall GJ, Simmons JL. *Identities and Interaction.* New York: Free Press, 1976.
19. Blau PM. *Exchange and Power in Social Life.* New York: Wiley, 1967.
20. Dowd JJ. Aging as exchange: A preface to theory. *J Gerontol.* 1975;30:584–595.
21. Dowd JJ. Exchange rates and old people. *J Gerontol.* 1980;35:596–602.
22. Goffman E. *Stigma.* Englewood Cliffs, NJ: Prentice-Hall, 1962.
23. Wright BA. *Physical Disability—A Psychological Approach.* New York: Harper & Row, 1960.
24. Thomas EJ. Problems of disability from the perspective of role theory. In Glasser PH, Glasser LN, eds. *Families in Crisis.* New York: Harper & Row, 1970, pp 252–272.
25. King I. *Toward a Theory of Nursing.* New York: Wiley, 1971.
26. Rogers CR. *Client-Centered Therapy.* Boston: Houghton Mifflin, 1951.
27. Rokeach M. The nature and meaning of dogmatism. *Psychol Rev.* 1954;61:194–204.
28. Homans G. *Social Behavior: Its Elementary Forms.* New York: Harcourt, Brace & World, 1961.
29. Pillemer K. The dangers of dependency: New findings on domestic violence against the elderly. Special report. Family Research Laboratory and Department of Sociology, University of New Hampshire, 1985.
30. Robinson BC. Validation of a caregiver strain index. *J Gerontol.* 1983;38:344–348.
31. Gelles RJ. *The Violent Home.* Beverly Hills, Calif: Sage, 1972.

Appendix A

Data-Based Examples Supporting the Reconciliation of Past with Present Processes

Processes	Definitions	Examples
Normative comparison	Process by which the caregiver determines how the elder compares to other individuals based on the caregiver's personal observations of others in a similar role (eg, other mothers or others who are depressed) or of some other important person (eg, other parents or parents' siblings).	"She did something which I vowed I'd never do to [control] my children and never did. She used scare tactics. When I was very small, I can remember her doing 'something will get you.' I think a lot of people did that back then. It was sheer ignorance; they didn't realize." (C4)*
Consistency	Process by which the caregiver determines how the elder's present behavior is similar or dissimilar to the elder's past behavior.	"Her table manners are atrocious today compared to what I remember her table manners being. You wouldn't dare take her out to a restaurant because she will take a piece of bread and put it on the plate and sop up the grease on the plate or the au jus from the roast beef. She would never let her children do that. If I had tried to do it, she'd have broken my arm. But today, that's perfectly acceptable to her." (C7)*

continues

Processes	Definitions	Examples
Ledgerkeeping	Process by which the caregiver determines the degree to which the elder's past debts and credits are reconciled with present debts and contributions and with the caregiver's debts and contributions.	"I think Mother was always very much interested in my welfare. When my husband and I were married, and my husband was in school, we were at the state university. I remember Mother doing canning and things for us, so that we'd have a winter supply of fruits and vegetables. I mean, Mother has always been very loyal to us, and wanted to see that we had the necessities of life." (C2)*
Identification	Process by which the caregiver determines the degree to which the caregiver's own identity is attributable to the elder's influence.	"She's a very caring person. The best qualities she has she has instilled in us. We're very much alike in our general outlook, she has a very good sense of humor, she likes people, she's pleasant to be with most of the time." (C14)*
Rationalization	Process by which the caregiver analyzes the elder's behavior and creates reasons that satisfactorily explain particularly disturbing facets.	"I call my husband a real man outside of his violent nature. At first, I excused his violent nature because he had been in the war. I tried to find some excuses for his violent nature because he came from a good family. He had a wonderful mother. I named my daughter after his mother. And, he had a quiet, home-loving family, and he turned out like that with that violent nature. So I blamed it on the war. I said, 'Well, if it is the war's fault, I'll put up with that because maybe he can't help himself.' But that's not true. That is not true!" (C17)*

continues

Processes	Definitions	Examples
Evaluation	Process by which the caregiver determines the overall worth, goodness, and effectiveness of the elder based on behavioral observations.	"She's always been ill. I don't remember a time that she could have been independent. When we were young children I don't know what she would have done if my father had left then. She wouldn't have been independent enough to handle herself." (C14)*

*Code representing subject or caregiver number.

Appendix B

Data-Based Examples Supporting the Caregiver's View of the Elder's Image

Image types	Past image	Present image
Normalization	"I can remember my mother spanking me when I was very small and I thought she was terribly, terribly cruel. Looking back now I don't think the lady was terribly cruel. I think she *did* what she felt she had to do." (C4)*	"He has some very strong religious beliefs, and he can argue the Bible right down the line with anybody. He remembers texts. He swears some." (C6)*
Deification	". . . as far as I know, just an eighth grade education. He went to school and became an electrician and he's a pretty bright person. He wrote the code book for the electrician union. He worked with his brother and did that for years—he kept the business going for years because his brother lived in the hospital. They didn't make a lot of money because most of it went for his care, but my dad kept it going and if it hadn't been for him—I'm quite proud that he's my dad." (C6)*	"She has a keen sense of humor. She's a very intelligent woman. Very sympathetic, very interested in what's going on and in people. Over the years she made many, many friends. Most people that come in contact with my mother are very fond of her. She corresponds with a number of women, all of our friends really like her. They keep in touch with her. I guess because of her illness and problems and sense of humor that people can talk to her and come away comforted, being as she could match them or surpass them or give them some hope that things might be better." (C13)*

continues

Image types	Past image	Present image
Stigmatization	"I don't know that she's a terribly bright lady. I don't know what her IQ would have been. Her mother died when she was very small and she lived with her grandmother. The grandmother died of cancer when she was 10 years old. When my mother lived with her grandmother she was very happy. After that she went to live with her step-mother and her father and it's like her development just stopped." (C4)*	"It was my grandfather's birthday and we took him over to that restaurant. And he just grunted and growled. He roared at the waitress and said he'd never come back. He said the food was outrageous. I mean, when he gets going he's really nasty, verbally nasty. He doesn't use harsh words, but he can really diminish somebody if he wants to." (C1)*

*Code representing subject or caregiver number.

Appendix C

Data-Based Examples Supporting the Caregiver's Beliefs about Caregiving

Role responsibilities of caregiver	Role responsibilities of elder
Doing for: "I have to do laundry every day, I bathe her, and do complete care. I mean, I have to feed her, I have to see that her food is soft or pureed, so that she can handle it." (C2)*	*Being pleasant.* "I think everybody should be nice to one another. It doesn't get you anywhere to be mean. It only hurts the other person. That is not her attitude. If she isn't pouting, it's a nasty attitude." (C8)*
Establishing and enforcing standards: "Now, when we get into the cooler months, she doesn't need to [take a bath every other day]. But, by God, during the summer months it's going to be every day." (C7)*	*Demonstrating cooperation:* "We knew that we would need help with the bookkeeping, the paying of bills, the banking, that sort of thing. I did not expect resistance in the area of personal cleanliness. It never occurred to me that I would have trouble getting her to take showers. I never thought she'd proceed to urinate outside instead of using the bathroom. I did not think we'd meet with as much obstinance as we did. I thought that I would suggest something and she would follow through with it. But it didn't work that way. It was as if it was a power struggle." (C4)*

continues

Role responsibilities of caregiver	Role responsibilities of elder
Monitoring social acceptability: "So it was like a little game to say to me that she didn't have to use the bathroom. She'd go out in the back-yard. The first time I said, "Oh, Mother, we don't *live* in the country. You can't do that. You'll have the Health Department down around our ears if you do that.' 'Well, nobody saw me.' I said, 'Mother, there are people. There's a pharmacist who lives next door; there's a teacher who lives behind me; the fire chief lives on the other side.' I said that there are people all around and they know us, and I said, 'It would be embarrassing if somebody saw you.' "(C4)*	*Showing interest in life.* "I knew that he was limited, but I didn't realize that he was as limited as he is. I thought surely a man of his age would read the newspaper." (C10)*

*Code representing subject or caregiver number.

Appendix D
Data-Based Examples Supporting the Three Types of Caregiving Management Strategies

Strategies	Examples
Positive	"I used to tell her, 'You know, you are a fine person. You have every right to expect good things for yourself, too. You shouldn't put yourself down all of the time, because you are a fine human being. And, there's no reason to feel that you are any less a person than anybody else.' "(C4)*
Neutral	"I think my attitude was different. I was a little more relaxed about it this time. Part of it was I figured he's done all the damage he can do. There's not much left for him to repair or punch holes in. And also, I wasn't home very much at all. And unless it was absolutely the most pressing problem, I just ignored it." (C12)*
Negative	"I'm still going to *make* her ask me. As long as she is able to do this, she is going to *ask* me for a bath. She shouldn't have to be reminded to take a bath. Even if it's just once a week. Just the same way if she wants an extra cup of coffee, I want her to ask for an extra cup of coffee—I'm not her maid." (C8)*

*Code representing subject or caregiver number.

Appendix E

Data-Based Examples Supporting Feedback Supplied during Evaluation Process

Example 1:
"She's hard of hearing and she will *not* wear her hearing aid. She makes you scream; she *deliberately* makes you scream. You can be within two feet of her and she'll just sit there and stare at you and not answer you and will *not* say a word to you. And after repeating yourself for about six times you'd say, finally, 'Did you hear what I said?' 'Yeah, I heard you.' Upon which, I'd just turn on my heels and leave. Or I'd lose control of myself because I just want to grab her by the shoulders and shake the living daylights out of her. She's not sick.'' (C8)*

Example 2:
"You'd think a person in his own home would be interested in the elements out-side. One night there was an absolutely gorgeous sky. It was kind of a pinky golden sunset and there was lightning in it. I wanted him to come out and see it. Well, I thought, maybe when you get to be 82 years you've seen everything there is to see, but that's kind of sad, too, because there's no feeling of wonder left.'' (C10)*

Example 3:
"Well, Mother is coming out of this stroke that she had, and it's nice to see. She was so depressed and everything, when she had this stroke. And now she is com-ing back. She's warm now that she's recuperating. She is smiling, and she'll wave at us. It's nice to see her happy.'' (C2)*

Example 4:
"I was asked to help him learn the skills again. Well, he'd get angry. He'd say 'I don't want to learn how to read and write again.' I said, 'Forget it.' Because I was trying to help but he thought it was too much to learn. He wasn't motivated to help himself. I figured forget it. There was nothing really pushing him." (C9)*

---

*Code representing subject or caregiver number.

Appendix F

Examples of Concepts Related to Currently Salient Role Forms

Concept	Examples

Unconditional acceptance

Example 1:

"Mother requires a consistency of being there. I give her the privacy of her own room and I do not interfere. I have not gone into her room and have not started the habit of sleeping in there with her. I have felt that I will have my own side of the house. I will keep it, try to keep that privilege for her too. A feeling of privacy which I think that deep down we all—it's a nucleus of our being—that small amount of privacy we must have." (C5)*

Example 2:

Everything is hard. I wake up in the morning at 5:30. Normally I would get up at 6:30, but I wake up with a whole lot of things on my mind that are going to be done during the day. Plus I have to realize that there is going to be something every day which I didn't anticipate. I set that aside and I play it this way: I'll meet it when it gets here. Otherwise you drive yourself crazy. You cannot sit and anticipate what's going to happen. I've had to learn. With a new situation for her, I have to change all the things that I do. I have to fit her. She can't fit me, 'cause she is disabled. 'What's going to make her easy?" That's all there is to think about. What else is there in the world but her? If you've got a good marriage, you become one single unit and you're only part. And you never, ever get away from it." (C15)*

Caregiving dogmatism

Example 1:

"She goes to the market and she'll bring home three jars of marshmallow whip, Twinkies, tortilla chips, Cheetos, containers of various types of dip, garlic dip, onion dip, bacon and onion dip—junk food, things that you wouldn't allow anybody to eat including the dog. When I *catch* her eating some of that food I say, 'Mother, you're not going to eat that are you?" She says, 'Oh no, I was going to give it to the dog.' I say, 'Don't give it to the dog, you'll kill the dog.' Then she walks outside eating her

continues

Concept	Examples
Caregiving dogmatism	junk food. It's selective senility. She knows damn well it's not good for her. But, by God, she's going to eat it anyway. She must have the stomach of a shark because it would kill a normal person.'' (C7)*

Example 2:
"Give her a piece of bread to use as a pusher, she'll eat three fourths of it. Then she'll finally end up eating with her fingers until I call her down. I tell her, 'You don't eat with your fingers. Not in my house.' Did you ever see anyone try to eat oatmeal? A baby! But she's perfectly capable of eating with utensils.'' (C8)*

*Code representing subject or caregiver number.

Toward a Theory of Helpfulness for the Elderly Bereaved: An Invitation to a New Life

The purpose of this study was to generate a theory of helpfulness for the elderly bereaved. The theory is grounded in data from responses of 30 participants concerning the advice they would give others who have lost a spouse and how others were helpful to them. Participants responded during six interviews following death of their spouses. A content analysis of responses was the basis of a dialectical theory of helpfulness: *An Invitation to a New Life*.

Imogene S. Rigdon, RN, PhD
Associate Professor

Bonnie C. Clayton, RN, PhD
Associate Professor

Margaret Dimond, RN, PhD
Professor
College of Nursing
University of Utah
Salt Lake City, Utah

A YOUNG MOTHER delivers a stillborn daughter. A father watches helplessly as his teenage son dies, and the grandparents stand near to comfort him. A child grieves the death of a parent, and widows and widowers bear the pain of losing a spouse. The death and loss of a loved one is a common event. "For all pairs of lovers without exception, bereavement is a universal and integral part of our experience of love."[1(p41)] The universality of the experience, however, in no way lessens the impact of grief or an individual's suffering. The bereaved person is a vulnerable person, vulnerable to the loss of self-identity[2,3] as well as to increased health problems[4] and elevated mortality risk.[5] The elderly bereaved are vulnerable to the simultaneous experience of other losses, which may include the death of

The bereavement study on which this article is based was supported by grant No. R01 AG 02193 from the National Institute on Aging.

Adv Nurs Sci 1987, 9(2), 32–43
© 1987 Aspen Publishers, Inc.

friends, illness, loss of acuity, retirement, loss of social value, and economic uncertainty. These accumulations of losses among the elderly are so profound that the phenomenon has been described as "bereavement overload."[6] As such, the bereaved elderly are a high-risk group who have a unique need for helpfulness from nurses, health care providers, families, and friends.

For centuries the nursing profession has sought ways to assist vulnerable persons or persons in need. The care of the dying person is a familiar experience for most nurses. Dimond proposes that a "logical and integral part of nursing care to the dying person is 'bereavement care' of the spouse."[7(p469)] The nurse is in a pivotal position, not only to provide bereavement care of the spouse, but also to allow, encourage, and mobilize other people who can be of assistance as an inherent aspect of that care. In concert with the long tradition of nursing, the purpose of the bereavement study discussed here was to develop a beginning theory of helpfulness for the elderly bereaved. The theory was generated from the content analysis of bereaved persons' interview responses concerning the advice they would offer to others who have lost a spouse and how others were helpful to them. The study was intended to increase nurses' awareness of the need to incorporate the care of bereaved persons more fully into their practice and to generate further nursing theory of bereavement care of widowed elderly persons.

CONTEXT OF THE STUDY

The human experience of bereavement has a time, a place, and a history. The context of bereavement is crucial to understanding this human experience. Patton stated: "One of the cardinal principles of qualitative methods is the importance of background and context to the processes of understanding and interpreting data."[8(p9)] This principle is addressed through the presentation of the bereavement context of the research participants as well as the theoretical and conceptual context of the researcher.

Bereavement Context

Despite the hospice movement, dying is institutionalized. The task of caring for the dying is primarily given to health professionals. Early grief experiences frequently begin with the pronouncement of death by the physician, followed by the announcement of death to the family. The manner of sharing the "bad news" of the death of a loved one with the family is often with the hope that the bereaved will quietly accept the death.[9] Like death, funerals have been organized away from the home and the family.[10] Freud, in his classic work "Mourning and Melancholia,"[11] was among the first to conceptualize a theory about the responses of the bereaved to the loss of a loved one. Freud saw grief as normal and self-limiting. Unresolved loss or pathological mourning became precursors of depression.[11]

Normal grief is a natural human process in response to the loss of a cherished person, uncomplicated by distorted or delayed reactions. "Normal grief" is described in the acute or beginning phases as having five characteristics: somatic distress, preoccupation with the image of the deceased, guilt, hostile reactions, and loss of usual patterns of activity. When traits of the deceased appear in the behavior of the bereaved, they are considered to border on pathological mourning.[12(p148)]

Grieving, like dying, has been conceptualized as a process of flexible phases or stages, denoting grief as dynamic and evolving. Periods of numbness, yearning, disorganization, and despair, and finally reorganization are postulated as phases the bereaved experience.[13(p85)]

Grieving is also conceptualized as a time of crisis, a short period of disequilibrium.[14] However, bereavement as a short-term process of weeks or months is not validated by more recent studies,[15,16] which indicate that some symptoms of grief are evident as much as two to four years after the death of a spouse. Parkes[17] suggests that bereavement should be viewed as a psychosocial transition rather than a crisis.

The length of time required to finish the work of grief may be best expressed by a bereaved spouse who said:

I have a new life, but though I have a new life, I have an old relationship still struggling in my mind toward some resolution I know it will never find. It has been 15 years since my wife died—the struggle goes on, and I imagine it will go on as long as I live.[18(p82)]

It is apparent that theorists have described grief in varying ways. Grief is normal. Grief can be delayed and pathological. Grief is a crisis time, a time of psychosocial transition, or even a lifetime companion. Grieving is a dynamic, evolving, and fluctuating process.

Theoretical and Conceptual Context

Keat and Urry[19] present scientific knowledge as both interpretive and explanatory modes of understanding. Explanatory understanding is grounded in the empirical. The interpretive mode provides understanding of subjective meaning. It involves knowledge of the kinds of beliefs and values present in the society being studied. Hermeneutics is central to interpretation.

Nursing is a human science and bereavement is a subjective experience. The issue of meaning cannot be ignored; therefore, this bereavement study followed the canons of hermeneutic interpretation. "These are not canons in the same sense as canons of traditional logic; they do not lead automatically to a correct result. They are rather guidelines which lead toward an acceptable intersubjective validity."[20(p133)]

The five canons of hermeneutic or interpretive understanding are identified by Kockelmans.[21] The autonomy of the object is the first canon. Meaning is derived from the phenomenon itself. This study involves the phenomenon of bereavement, and the bereaved participants are the source and criteria of the analysis. Making the phenomenon "maximally reasonable" in human terms is the second canon.

Only the participants and the readers could evaluate the success with which the study met this canon.

Achieving the "greatest possible familiarity with the phenomenon" is the third canon. Personal experience, shared communications of bereaved participants, and the literature review offer the opportunity for familiarity with the phenomenon.

The fourth canon of interpretive understanding is to show the meaning of the phenomenon for the researcher's own situation. Researchers choose phenomena to study. Tucker calls this point in the research process the "problem selection context."[22(p7)] These choices are made for personal, social, or institutional reasons, and this study clearly evolved from the researcher's personal and professional experiences. Seeing an aged father suffer the loss of his wife and caring for many depressed persons in a psychiatric nursing practice strengthened a desire to help others suffering loss. This study is viewed as a way to fulfill that desire.

The last canon is the hermeneutic circle. The hermeneutic circle involves dialectic reasoning. "The dialectic method works by taking as its perspective a whole that it organizes. Whatever whole is so organized governs the relationship and provides coherence to the parts of the whole. . . . Contradictory views are resolved by progression to a higher level from which contradictions are seen as compatible components in a larger unit."[23(p35)] It is within these hermeneutic canons of understanding that the study was conducted.

Methodological Context

This study is a unique part of a larger research project, *Bereavement in the Elderly: Factors in Adaptation*, which was a descriptive longitudinal study of the elderly bereaved by the University of Utah College of Nursing (National Institute of Aging Research Grant No. R01 AG02193). The setting was Salt Lake County, Utah, with a population of 619,066 (1980 Census). Recently bereaved persons over the age of 50 were identified through local newspaper obituaries. To be eligible for the project, the recently bereaved had to be a survivor of a spouse whose death was neither homicide nor suicide and had to consent to participate.

For the purposes of this study, the sample consisted of 30 bereaved persons randomly selected from the larger research group who were personally interviewed (N = 78). Personal interviews offered the bereaved an opportunity to elaborate on their answers, and a recent study indicates that the interviewer does not have a significant effect on bereavement outcomes.[24]

The bereaved who participated were usually over the age of 60 and primarily middle-income widows and widowers. Most were bereaved after long years in a married relationship. More than half of the bereaved were widows who had attended college or a trade school, but few were presently employed.

The bereaved participants were scheduled to be interviewed in their homes six times during a 2-year period following the death of a spouse. The initial interview was approximately 4 weeks after the death. The remaining five interviews were scheduled at the 2-month, 6-month, 1-year, 18-month, and 2-year time periods following the death of the spouse. Attrition was minimal, and 162 of a possible 180 interviews were completed. Each interview was tape recorded and transcribed. The data were responses to the following questions:

1. Is there any advice that you would give someone else who has lost a spouse?
2. Have others (family, friends, etc.) been helpful to you during the past few weeks?
3. What have they done?

The responses from the interviews were content analyzed to present a systematic and objective description of the attributes of the participants' communication.[25] The process of content analysis is primarily inductive. Hence, no preconceived theoretical construct was consciously imposed, and the researcher allowed the theory to emerge from the empirical data. The content analysis began by repeatedly reading responses to the three questions in the series of six interviews. The purpose of the rereadings of the interview data was to allow the researcher to achieve the greatest possible familiarity with the data. Simultaneously, a search was made for data that recurred repeatedly, representing patterns or themes that could be clustered into categories. The frequency of recurring data in each of the six interviews and the total percentage of the bereaved who provided the recurring data were used to determine with some degree of certainty that the data represented patterns or themes.

Single semantic relationships were used to structure the process of identifying and clustering themes of the responses and developing categories. From the universal semantic relationships proposed by Spradley,[26] "means-end" and "strict inclusion" were chosen. Means-end expresses the relationship: X is a way to do Y. The first interview question elicited advice the bereaved would give to others who lose a spouse (X) as ways to help themselves (Y). For example, the bereaved advised others to go for walks and listen to music (X) to keep their minds off the grief (Y). Likewise, the responses to the second and third questions, "How do others help?" and "What have they done?" reflect ways (X) the bereaved are helped (Y). For example mowing the lawn, shoveling snow, and grocery shopping were identified by the bereaved as ways others had helped them. Using strict inclusion, which expresses the semantic relationship, X is a kind of Y, these ways of helping (X) were clustered together as kinds of physical help (Y).

In content analysis, the utility of a category set is largely a function of internal homogeneity among items in any particular category and the external homogeneity among categories. The items in a category should be logically related and defensible as encompassing a single concept, that is, unidimensional, to meet the criteria of internal homogeneity. The criteria of external homogeneity is met by clear, bold differences and lack of overlapping data among the categories.[27]

With these criteria in mind, the researcher continued to analyze the data for similarities and differences. For example, mowing the lawn, vacuuming, and fixing the car are similar in that they all require some degree of physical labor. The category of physical labor as a helpful act was clearly different from other helpful behaviors, such as visiting the bereaved, which did not require physical labor. Using single semantic relationships facilitated the identification of similarities and differences. After completing the content analysis, an outside expert, an experienced clinical nurse who works with people in distress, analyzed ten randomly selected interviews by following the rules that the researcher used to determine whether data fell within the boundaries of a category. This process established 89% intercoder reliability of the study.

In addition, the internal validity of a qualitative study can be strengthened by the confirmation and critique of the study by the participants.[28] In view of this, the theory of helpfulness generated from the content analysis was presented to the interviewed bereaved for their validation and critique. The theory was validated by all but one of the participants (N = 20) who could be located.

Advice to Others

The advice the bereaved gave to others who lost a spouse was divided into five categories, which were unidimensional but not mutually exclusive. The following describes the inductive process the researcher used to ultimately identify mutually exclusive, as well as unidimensional, categories of advice. The five categories of advice and their themes are:

1. Keep busy: engage in solitary activities, accept and extend social invitations, and help someone else;
2. Be individual: grief is different for each person and grief is an individual experience, so make your own decisions slowly;
3. Talk with others: engage in casual conversations and express feelings of grief;
4. Have faith: maintain religious beliefs and practices and philosophical beliefs; and
5. Give yourself time: time is healing; take one day at a time.

During at least one interview, most (93% [28]) of the elderly bereaved participants advised others who lose a spouse to *keep busy*. The essence of keeping busy is to engage in solitary activities, to accept social invitations, and to help someone else. This advice appeared with repeatable regularity in the interviews between the two-month and two-year periods following the death of a spouse. The advice to keep busy was strikingly minimal during the first interview, with only four bereaved advising it. Perhaps the grief was too new and mobilizing the energy to keep busy was not yet possible.

Grief by its very nature is perceived as *individual*, as "one's own grief" differs from the grief of others. This advice reflects rugged individualism, which is a distinct derivative of the Puritan ethic. More than half of the participants described the uniqueness of grief for each person, such as:

Well, it's hard to answer that question because circumstances are different in different cases. My case is entirely different from, maybe, a young man who dies a violent death of some kind and leaves a young woman with several small children and not much means of support. That is an entirely different thing than I have to face.

Well, every situation is different. It depends on the marriage, you know, how deep the marriage was, how they got along.

Similar to the perception that the grief experience is different for each person were responses describing grief as an individual experience that is essentially solitary and lonely. This was poignantly expressed in these descriptive data:

I think each person has to work it out for himself and by himself, in his own way. You have to go through it yourself. I don't think that advice would help anyone because it's something that you have to go through and make your own adjustments.

Individuality was also expressed in the advice to make one's own decisions and not to make decisions hastily:

You get all sorts of advice, and I think you just decide what's best for you. What someone else thinks is best for you isn't necessarily.

Don't take advice from people that rush around the first month telling how you should do it. If you've got a brain at all, sit down and take a little inventory on what you're doing first.

I wouldn't take a trip immediately, like I did. I would have stayed and settled things, got everything in order, and then taken a trip. Rather than to go when your heart is so full and heavy and there's so much waiting for you when you get back to do, I'd advise people to wait.

Making one's own decision, grieving in one's own way, and the solitary uniqueness of grief itself comprise the initial category of being an individual.

The third category of advice is to *talk with others*. Twenty-one of the bereaved participants offered this advice at least once during the six interview sessions. The greatest single frequency (50%) of bereaved offering advice to communicate with others occurred during the interview six months following the death of a spouse. A widow expressed this need:

I just feel like I could hold out my hand to another human being and say, "Yes, it's hell. Oh, it's really rotten. But let me talk to you. Tell me how you feel. I'll cry with you. I'll laugh with you. But let's talk."

Have faith is the fourth category. No one person offered the advice to abandon religious beliefs or practices as meaningless during bereavement. On the contrary, during the first year of bereavement, religious beliefs and practices were recommended to others by nearly half of the bereaved participants, but only one person did so during the second year of bereavement. It is possible that the pain of the early phases of grief is a potent reminder of a person's dependency and need for God, prayer, and faith or metaphysical beliefs, but as the pain lessens, the feelings of helplessness decrease and metaphysical beliefs take on an ordinary role in a person's everyday life.

The fifth and last category, reflected in the advice of only nine bereaved partici-pants, is *give yourself time*. Six participants expressed this during the one-year interview. The essence of this advice is described by a widow:

Just take one day at a time. I look ahead and I get panicky. There's no way I can live another year. There's no way. I think, I've made it today. I'll make it tomorrow. Sometimes I take a half a day at a time.

Conceiving time as irreversible and continuous is intolerable to many people. Durations are time intervals or regularities of time created by persons to control the unpredictability and irreversibility of time and to maintain social and political order.[29] These concepts apply to the time of grieving. Living one day at a time creates discontinuous time so that pain is more bearable. People earnestly seek to define the duration of grieving time partially because experiencing grief as on-going and irreversible creates social havoc and intolerable living.

In summary, the five categories and themes of the advice of the bereaved to others who lose a spouse can be expressed in two unidimensional and mutually exclusive categories of advice: Be individual and be involved with others. To be individual requires only the initiative of the bereaved. It reflects the things that only the bereaved can do for themselves. The second key category, to be involved with others, requires the initiative of the bereaved and reciprocal response from others. (See boxed material.)

HELPFUL BEHAVIORS OF OTHERS

There are seven categories that describe the behaviors of others that elderly be-reaved perceived as helpful: (1) being available, (2) expressing concern, (3) keep-ing in touch, (4) extending social invitations, (5) providing physical labor, (6) providing transportation and financial and legal assistance, and (7) giving "care packages."

Knowing that others are available if needed was reported to be very helpful to the elderly bereaved participants. Offering to help is the surest way of confirming availability. The participants indicated that others had offered to help, especially during the initial interviews, but offers to help were strikingly minimal as noted in the interviews after six months. This suggests that others offer their help immedi-ately after the death but do not continue to do so. It is conceivable that other per-sons commonly perceive grief as a crisis of short duration rather than as an ex-tended process of transition.

Key Categories of Advice

Be individual
Engage in solitary activities
Realize grief is different for each person
Grieve in your own way
Make your own decisions
Have faith
Give yourself time

Be involved with others
Accept social invitations
Help someone else
Talk with others

Eighty-seven percent of the bereaved (26) describe the expressed, personalized concern of others for them as individuals as helpful. Some examples are: "Ask how I feel about things and his death and that"; "Check on me and make sure everything is okay"; and "Say 'We want you, we want to laugh, you make it happy,' things like that. It builds my ego."

All but one of the bereaved participants identified that others had helped them by keeping in touch or communicating with them. The kinds of keeping in touch are telephoning the bereaved, visiting them in their homes, and writing letters and cards.

Extending social invitations was described by all of the participants as a way others help them. These social invitations are opportunities for the bereaved to get out and do something socially, to be involved with others, and to keep busy. A widower expressed this helpfulness:

Well, for one thing, the family, like on weekends, always calls and invites me to come to dinner. They don't like me to be alone, they say, through the week it isn't so bad, but we don't like you alone on Sunday. Oh, they include me in things that they're doing.

They won't let me stay home and pine away.

In the study, 20 participants identified *strong-arm help*, providing manual labor, as a way others helped. The specific kinds of "strong-arm help" were in four areas: yard work, homemaking, house maintenance, and car maintenance. As one bereaved person said: "Well, since my heart attack, I've needed manual labor help, strong-arm help."

Financial and legal assistance were identified by 40% (12) of the bereaved as ways others helped them, primarily in the first six months after the death of the spouse. Legal assistance consisted of helping with estate settlements and business affairs, undoubtedly most pressing in the early months after the death of a spouse. Financial assistance included monetary assistance, that is, helping to pay medical and funeral expenses, or simply assisting the bereaved to fill out Medicare and Veteran's benefit forms. As one bereaved person stated:

Helping me with all the paper work and things and making sure I had them—because a time like that (two months after death of spouse), you feel so numb or so discombobulated that you don't know if you're filling out anything exactly right.

Providing transportation, as a way of helping the bereaved elderly, was identified by 37% (11) of the research participants The bereaved persons' requests for transportation were to take them to church, to the physician's office, to the grocery store, or wherever they needed to go. No access to a car, lack of friends or relatives, fear of traveling alone at night, poor eyesight, and reluctance to impose on others are contributing factors to transportation difficulties among the elderly bereaved.

Thirty-seven percent of the bereaved mentioned that *giving gift of food* was one way others had helped them. One of the bereaved named such gifts "care packages." Undoubtedly, the gifts are perceived as helpful because they are symbols of a nourished caring, as expressed by this participant:

Last winter I had swine flu and pneumonia. The neighbors opened the front door and called back to me. Nobody wanted to come in and I didn't blame them. I told them not to. But they opened the front door and said, "Your lunch is on the mantel." They'd brought a bowl of soup or clam chowder.

These seven categories of helpfulness can be expressed in two unidimensional and mutually exclusive categories: be there and do something. The categories be available, express concern, and keep in touch are kinds of being there. The kinds of things that others do for the bereaved are expressed in the last four categories: extending social invitations, providing strong-arm help, providing transportation and offering legal and financial assistance, and bringing care packages.

Being there is essential to helping but it is not enough. Being there is like using words in a conversation. Doing something is like putting those words into action.

Being there without "doing something" is only partially helpful to the bereaved. This is most vividly expressed by the following:

I have a lot of people ask me if I need things done, and the thing is you just tell them "no." Blessed is the person who just comes in and does something.

Thousands of people asked me if I needed anything done. But there's only three that I can think of who really did something.

Showing the relationships among the categories and building toward an integrated theory are the essential parts of content analysis. The categories of advice and helpful behavior of others and their relationships were conceptualized as invitations. Invitations are a dialogue, a call and a response.[30] To be helped, the bereaved person needs a call and a response from self to the self, and from others to the self.

AN INVITATION TO A NEW LIFE

"An invitation to a new life" was given to the research participants in a lovely and unique way. After completing the analysis, phone calls were made to the experts on helpfulness—the bereaved participants— for the purpose of validating the content analysis and the proposed theory of an invitation to continue living. During the second phone call, one widow agreed with the conceptualization of helpfulness as an invitation, but said: "Honey, you're dead wrong. It is not an invitation to continue living. It is an invitation to a new life." All but one of the participants agreed with the widow.

When someone we love dies, our lives are permanently changed. We also die a little, wonder if our lives are still worth living, and question how we can continue living without our loved one. Life as we knew it is gone. We face a new life.

It is, however, naive to believe that this wondering and questioning occurs for every bereaved person following the death of a spouse. Love in a marriage can die long before the death of a spouse. The lives of the bereaved whose marriages were not very satisfying are also permanently changed by the death of their spouses. They too face a new life without their spouses. Inviting the elderly bereaved to embrace a new life without their spouse is the essence of the theory of helpfulness during bereavement.

The *invitation to a new life* is a dialectic. On the one hand, the bereaved have the primary responsibility to invite themselves to a new life, to help themselves after the death of a spouse by being an individual and by being involved with others. On the other hand, others must invite the bereaved person to become a part of their lives by being there and by doing something for or with them. Without this invitation from others, the new life of the bereaved is diminished and the invitation is only partial. An invitation to a new life is the larger unity of the opposite poles of I and Thou, of giving and receiving, and of being there and doing something.

IMPLICATIONS FOR NURSING

The theory is rich in that it taps a human dimension, the elderly bereaved person's experiences of helpfulness, and leads to new perspectives and questions for nursing. It is common for nurses to realize that bereaved people need care and concern from others. It is surely less often that we realize that bereaved people also want and need to help others. Nurses are in a unique position to encourage families and friends to allow widows and widowers to give help, not only to receive it.

The theory suggests that helpfulness from others during bereavement is primarily crisis oriented. Continuing help for a longer time seems like a more plausible approach to intervening with elderly widows and widowers.

New studies can be designed to discover the similarities and differences of helpfulness in other cultures and in other kinds of losses. Nurses can test the theory in their clinical practice. An "invitation to a new life" is grounded in the human experience of grieving people. It is a conceptualization that made sense to the bereaved research participants. It is hoped that the theory will also have meaning for nurses providing bereavement care.

REFERENCES

1. Lewis CS. *A Grief Observed.* New York: Seabury Press, 1961.
2. Lopata HZ. *Widowhood in an American City.* Cambridge, Mass: Schenkman, 1973.
3. Saunders JM. A process of bereavement resolution: Uncoupled identity. *West J Nurs Res.* 1981;3:319–336.
4. Gerber I, Rusalem P, Hannon N, et al. Anticipating grief and aged widows and widowers. *J Gerontol.* 1975;30:225–229.
5. Jacobs S, Ostfeld A. An epidemiological review of the mortality of bereavement. *Psychosom Med.* 1977;239:344–357.
6. Kastembaum R. Death and bereavement in later life. In Kutscher HE, ed. *Death and Bereavement.* Springfield, Ill: Charles C Thomas, 1969.
7. Dimond M. Bereavement and the elderly: A critical review with implications for nursing practice and research. *J Adv Nurs.* 1981;6:461–470.
8. Patton MQ. *Qualitative Evaluation Methods.* Beverly Hills, Calif: Sage, 1980.
9. Sudnow D. *Passing on : The Social Organization of Dying.* Englewood Cliffs, NJ: Prentice-Hall, 1967.
10. Charmaz K. *The Social Reality of Death.* Reading, Mass: Addison-Wesley, 1980.
11. Freud S. Mourning and melancholia, in *Collected Papers,* Riviere J, trans. New York: Basic Books, 1959;4:152–170.
12. Lindemann E. Symptomatology and management of acute grief. *Am J Psychiatry.* 1944;101:141–148.
13. Bowlby J. *Attachment and Loss: Loss, Sadness and Depression.* New York: Basic Books, 1980, vol 3.
14. Caplan G. *Principles of Preventive Psychiatry.* New York: Basic Books, 1964.
15. Lund DA, Dimond ME, Caserta MS, et al. Identifying elderly with coping difficulties after two years of bereavement. *Omega.* 1985;16(3):213–224.
16. Weiner A, Gerber I, Battin D, et al. Process and phenomenology of bereavement. In Schoenberg B, ed. *Bereavement: Its Psychosocial Aspects.* New York. Columbia University Press, 1975.
17. Parkes CM. *Bereavement: Studies of Grief in Adult Life.* New York: International Universities Press, 1972.
18. Anderson R. Notes of a survivor. In Troup JB, Green WA, eds. *The Patient, Death, and the Family.* New York: Charles Scribner's; 1974:73–82.
19. Keat R, Urry J. *Social Theory as Science,* ed 2. London: Routledge & Kegan Paul, 1982.
20. Rowan J, Reason P. On making sense. In Reason P, Rowan J, eds. *Human Inquiry.* Chichester, England: Wiley; 1981:113–137.
21. Kockelmans J. Toward an interpretative or hermeneutic social science. *Grad Faculty J.* 1975;5:73–96.
22. Tucker RW. The value decisions we know as science. *Adv Nurs Sci.* 1979;1(January):1–12.
23. Stevens BJ. *Nursing Theory.* Boston: Little, Brown, 1979.
24. Caserta MS, Lund DA, Dimond MF. Assessing interviewer effects in a longitudinal study of bereaved elderly adults. *J Gerontol.* 1985;40:637–640.
25. Holisti OR, Loomba JK, North RC. Content analysis. In Lindzey G. Aronson E, eds. *The Handbook of Social Psychology.* Reading, Mass. Addison-Wesley; 1968.
26. Spradley JP. *The Ethnographic Interview.* New York: Holt, Rinehart & Winston, 1979.
27. Guba EG. *Toward a Methodology of Naturalistic Inquiry in Educational Evaluation.* CSE Monograph Series in Evaluation, Los Angeles, Center for the Study of Evaluation, University of California, 1978, no. 8.
28. Miles MB, Huberman AM. *Qualitative Data Analysis: A Sourcebook of New Methods.* Beverly Hills, Calif: Sage, 1984.
29. Leach ER. Two essays concerning the symbolic representation of time. In Leach ER, ed. *Rethinking Anthropology.* London: Athlone Press; 1961.
30. Paterson JG, Zderad LT. *Humanistic Nursing.* New York: Wiley; 1976.

Relapse among Ex-Smokers: An Example of Theory Derivation

Theory derivation, the use of analogous concepts from other disciplines to derive theory about a particular phenomenon, has been described as an effective strategy for building nursing theory, especially where existing theory bases are limited. This article provides a detailed, step-by-step description of how the theory derivation process was used to develop a theory of smoking relapse from an analogous theory of recovery after alcohol abuse. Empirical testing revealed partial support for the derived theory. Advantages and limitations of theory derivation as a strategy for constructing nursing theory are described.

Mary Ellen Wewers, RN, PhD
Assistant Professor
Department of Life Span Process
College of Nursing
Ohio State University
Columbus, Ohio

Elizabeth R. Lenz, RN, PhD
Professor; Director, Doctoral Program
University of Maryland
School of Nursing
Baltimore, Maryland

AS NURSES strive to expand the knowledge base for nursing practice, emphasis is being placed on constructing and testing sound, middle-range nursing theories.[1] Although various authors have discussed the components and desirable properties of theories,[2-4] few concrete strategies are available to assist nurses who wish to develop theory to guide their research and practice. A notable exception is Walker and Avant's[5] explicit description of three strategies that can be used to construct nursing theories: theory analysis, theory synthesis, and theory derivation. Theory derivation is defined as "the process of using analogy to obtain explanations or predictions about a phenomenon in one field from the explanations or predictions

The study on which this article is based was partially funded by the American Lung Association of Maryland. The authors wish to thank Frederick Suppe, PhD, for his comments on this article.

Adv Nurs Sci 1987, 9(2), 44–53

in another field."[5(p163)] Walker and Avant described the steps involved in theory derivation and included some illustrative examples; however, their examples were hypothetical, partially developed, or had not been empirically tested. This article describes how theory derivation was employed as a strategy for developing the theoretical basis for a study of relapse among ex-smokers. The results of empirically testing the derived theory are also presented.

THEORY DERIVATION PROCESS

In theory derivation, an entire set of interrelated concepts or an entire theoretical structure is moved from one area of interest and modified to fit another. This process requires the theorist to identify analogies between the concepts in the two areas or fields and to transpose the content or structure from Field 1 to Field 2. According to Walker and Avant,[5] derivation differs from borrowing theory in that the former involves modifying the content or structure of an existing theory, whereas borrowed theory is unchanged. Theory derivation is especially useful when available data are limited or when a theorist has identified concepts that may be related to the phenomenon of interest but has not identified their relational structure.

Walker and Avant[5] depicted the theory derivation process as involving five steps: (1) becoming familiar with the literature concerning the phenomenon of interest (Field 2) and evaluating the suitability of current theories for explaining the phenomenon, (2) reading the literature from other disciplines (including Field 1) to discover potential analogies, (3) selecting a parent theory from Field 1 to transpose and restate in order to explain the phenomenon of interest in Field 2, (4) identifying the content or structure from the parent theory that will be used in Field 2, and (5) modifying the concepts or structure from the parent theory and restating them in terms of the phenomenon of interest. Each of these steps was followed to derive a theory of relapse among ex-smokers.

Step 1: Phenomenon of Interest—Relapse among Ex-smokers

Investigators have used different criteria to describe the term "smoking relapse." Broadly defined, it is a person's return to smoking after a period of cessation and abstinence from cigarettes.[6] It has been reported that, in most clinic programs, 70% to 75% of ex-smokers resumed smoking nine to 18 months after treatment.[7] For the most part, experts believe that the return to smoking is motivated by physiological and psychological factors.[8] Those who cite physiological factors emphasize the symptomatology experienced by smokers withdrawing from nicotine as the basis for relapse.[9] The smoker, deprived of nicotine and experiencing symptoms such as inability to concentrate, insomnia, and craving, resumes smoking as a way to relieve these unpleasant sensations.

On the other hand, proponents of psychological factors believe that smoking behavior is a learned process. Smoking serves as a strong reinforcer that is not easily replaced.[10] It has been suggested by those who subscribe to a social learning theory basis for relapse that smokers have learned to manage such things as "affect" by smoking.[8] For example, if a person usually smoked when tense, he or she may not know how to deal with tension upon cessation and may resume smoking in order to manage it. In addition, recent studies have suggested that factors such as stressors, coping responses, and lack of social support may contribute to resumption of smoking.[11–13]

Although several potentially important variables emerged from a review of the smoking relapse literature, it was apparent that most studies examined the role of a specific factor in the relapse process. No multivariate theories of relapse were evident. Such theories could provide valuable insights to nurses working in this important area of preventive health. Information that further characterizes the relapse process would enable nurses to design more effective smoking cessation techniques aimed at maintaining long-term abstinence from cigarettes.

Step 2: Review of Literature from Other Fields—Alcohol Relapse

It seemed appropriate to review the literature regarding a closely related phenomenon, alcohol abuse, since commonalities between the two behaviors have been suggested. Among these commonalities are (1) similar relapse rates; (2) assertion that use of the substance is due, in part, to addiction; (3) occurrence of a reported withdrawal syndrome upon cessation of the substance; (4) notion that use of the substance is related to the presence of certain cues or stimuli; and (5) treatment interventions that center around behavior modification techniques.[8]

Two comprehensive multivariate theories were found to dominate the alcohol literature. The first was a cognitive-behavioral model of relapse that attempted to characterize the individual s reaction to a relapse and to examine the relationship between the first relapse episode and subsequent use of alcohol.[12] The model included numerous variables, such as cognitive antecedents, life-style factors, high-risk situations, coping responses, self-efficacy, and an abstinence-violation effect. Only the variable of high-risk situation had been submitted to empirical testing. The second theory (termed a conceptual framework by its originators) was developed by Cronkite and Moos[14] to describe relationships among patient characteristics, treatment experiences, posttreatment factors, and treatment outcome. In the causal model developed to represent the theory, six sets of interrelated factors were hypothesized to be associated directly and indirectly with four outcome variables, all indicators of recovery. Patient-related characteristics included sociodemographic characteristics and pretreatment symptoms (eg, type and severity of drinking). Treatment experience referred to the type and amount of therapy obtained by the alcoholic client. Posttreatment factors included stressors that can trigger a relapse, coping responses that can decrease the negative impact of stressors, and the family environment that may provide support for or interfere with functioning.

In a longitudinal study to test their model, Cronkite and Moos[14] asked 120 alcoholic clients to complete questionnaires that measured each of the six factors. The model was examined in relation to each of the four outcome variables: alcohol consumption, abstinence, depression, and occupational functioning. The predictors related, with varying degrees, to recovery, their relative importance differing for each of the four outcomes. Path analyses revealed that posttreatment stressors and coping responses were more strongly associated with outcome than was family environment. Pretreatment symptoms were the best predictor of occupational functioning and alcohol consumption, but positive coping response was the strongest predictor of abstinence. Although treatment characteristics were not significant direct predictors of outcome, indirectly they were important through posttreatment characteristics of stressors and coping responses. Treatment reduced stressors and increased the use of effective coping responses that lead to better outcome.

Step 3: Selecting a Parent Theory—Conceptual Framework

The Cronkite and Moos theory was selected as the more appropriate of the two potential parent (Field 1) theories to use as the basis for deriving a theory of smoking relapse for several reasons. First, it had been empirically tested in its entirety. Second, each of the six factors had been studied separately in smoking research and put forth as a possible determinant of relapse. Finally, the model incorporated a multivariate structure deemed desirable for a theory of smoking relapse.

Steps 4 and 5: Identification and Modification of Analogous Content or Structure from the Parent Theory—Restatement as a Theory of Relapse among Ex-smokers

According to Walker and Avant,[5] it is permissible to use all or part of the parent theory as the basis for derivation; the content or the structure of the parent theory may constitute the analog. The Cronkite and Moos[14] theory has a complex structure that details relationships among the predictor variables, as well as their relations to the outcome. Given the dearth of multivariate theories to explain smoking relapse, a decision was made to employ a simplified theory structure, which specified only the direct effects of the six predictive factors to the outcome. It was anticipated that once the key explanatory variables had been validated, attention could be directed in subsequent theory development and research toward specifying indirect as well as direct linkages. Although the structure of the parent theory was simplified for the initial study, it seemed to represent an appropriate analog to be used for guiding future smoking cessation research.

Minor modifications made in the content of the parent theory to make it meaningful to the phenomenon of smoking relapse are described below. They were based on empirical literature in the smoking cessation field that paralleled the six factors contained in the parent theory.

Patient-Related Characteristics

Sociodemographic factors

Several demographic variables have been shown to be related to relapse among ex-smokers.[15] For example, women have much higher rates of relapse than men, and divorced and separated persons have higher relapse rates than either married or single individuals. In addition, socioeconomic status is known to be associated with smoking cessation. Successful cessation is associated with higher status, and education and occupation are positively correlated with abstinence. The content of this component of the parent theory, therefore, was changed little in the derived theory.

Pretreatment symptoms

In the Cronkite and Moos[14] framework, the pretreatment symptoms factor was represented by four aspects of functioning: alcohol consumption, type of drinker, depression, and occupational functioning. Alcohol consumption and type of drinker symptoms were chosen and modified since cigarette consumption and type of smoker have been empirically supported as determinants of relapse.[16] In addition to using an analogous measure of cigarette consumption, a variable categorizing smokers by type was added to describe pretreatment symptoms. Smokers have been categorized as primarily (1) positive affect, those who smoke in pleasurable or relaxing situations; (2) negative affect, those who smoke to reduce feelings of tension, anger, frustration, and anxiety; (3) addictive, those who smoke to relieve the unpleasant side effects associated with nicotine withdrawal; and (4) habitual, those who smoke in response to environmental cues.[17-18] Several studies have suggested that negative-affect smokers have much higher rates of relapse, since it is difficult to replace smoking with effective substitutes for dealing with negative feelings.[13,16]

Treatment-Related Characteristics

Treatment for smoking cessation involves interventions that are similar to alcohol abuse treatment. The various structured treatment programs in both areas include behavioral modification therapy (either individual or group), hypnosis, aversion therapy, and medication. Surprisingly, the type of smoking cessation treatment program has been shown to have little effect on relapse, in that similar relapse rates have been reported for all types of programs. Of persons who quit smoking by means of these methods, only 25% to 30% were still abstinent at 9 to 18 months.[16,19] Treatment programs that included behavior modification plus the use of nicotine gum have reported success rates ranging from 13% to 31% at six to 12 months.[20] People who are able to quit smoking on their own without formal treatment have success rates of up to 65%.[21]

Because the effect of different types of formal treatment on smoking relapse has not been substantiated, the factor of treatment-related characteristics has questionable utility as a component of a theory of smoking relapse. This component of the Cronkite and Moos model may be highly relevant for comparing the effects of self-treatment and treatment programs, but has limited value for explaining and predicting relapse among those who participate in formal treatment.

Posttreatment Characteristics

Stressors

The Cronkite and Moos[14] model included stressors after treatment as predictors of outcomes, and their research confirmed that stressful life events were negatively associated with some aspects of recovery. The smoking cessation literature suggests that stressful life events and other stressful conditions, such as alcohol consumption and interpersonal conflicts, are associated with increased risk of relapse.[12,13,22] In addition, elements of the tobacco withdrawal syndrome may be considered stressors that are conducive to relapse.[13] The withdrawal symptom of craving has been cited as a major reason for resuming smoking. In a review of smoking cessation programs, Hunt and Matarazzo[7] reported that over one half of recidivists cited craving as their reason for relapse. The derived theory included both the social contextual stressor of major life events and the internal stressor of craving.

Coping responses

Shiffman[13] described two basic coping styles (behavioral and cognitive) that emerged from his interviews with ex-smokers. Behavioral styles involved taking an action, such as leaving a room filled with smokers; cognitive styles included thoughts that help the ex-smokers get through a stressful period. After examining the relation of these coping styles to smoking relapse, Shiffman concluded that coping responses are key determinants of relapse. Their presence distinguished recidivists from those who successfully maintained cessation; and the performance of any coping response was successful in forestalling relapse. The coping responses factor was, therefore, retained in the derived theory.

Family environment

A strong body of evidence suggests that successful, long-term smoking cessation is associated with having family members and friends who are nonsmokers or who had previously been able to quit smoking.[11,23,24] Although Cronkite and Moos[14] found family environment, measured as a multifaceted phenomenon, to be only weakly related to alcohol recovery, this factor was included in the derived theory of smoking relapse. Its scope of meaning was limited to the presence of significant others who had never smoked or had successfully quit smoking, and thus was more restrictive than Cronkite and Moos's conception.

SUMMARY OF DERIVED THEORY

To summarize the derived theory, the likelihood that an individual who had quit smoking would relapse was theorized to be a function of six factors: sociodemographic and pretreatment smoking characteristics, nature of the treatment received, and three posttreatment characteristics—stressors, coping responses, and family environment. There were four major differences between the parent theory of alcohol recovery and the derived theory of smoking relapse.

1. The structure of the derived theory was temporarily simplified for the initial study to emphasize *direct* effects, rather than the more complex *indirect* effects, of predictors on the outcome.
2. Stressors were expanded to take into account not only those emanating from the social context (eg, stressful life events), but also those more physiological in nature arising from within the individual.
3. Several variables were operationalized differently to render them specific to smoking, eg, type of smoker and family environment.
4. The treatment-related characteristics factor was assigned a minor explanatory role in the derived theory because of empirical evidence countering any differential effect of various treatment techniques.

EMPIRICAL TEST OF THE DERIVED THEORY

To test the derived theory, a study was conducted to examine the relationships between smoking relapse and five of the six major components of the theory. The treatment-related characteristics factor was controlled by the design of the research, hence was not a variable in the study. The hypothesis deduced from the theory was that social background, type of smoker, presence of stressors, number and type of coping responses used, and nature of the family environment would differentiate those who relapse from those who abstain from smoking following participation in a smoking cessation program. The study and findings are briefly described below.[25]

Study Design

The convenience sample was comprised of 150 adults who attended American Lung Association smoking cessation clinics in the Baltimore area and who volunteered to participate. The prospective one-group-only design involved assessing subjects prior to and three months after treatment. The following variables were measured before treatment: (1) self-reported frequency of current smoking behavior; (2) social background characteristics of sex, age, marital status, and education; (3) type of smoker, measured by a modification of the Horn-Waingrow[17] instrument, which categorizes smokers as positive affect, negative affect, addictive, or habitual; and (4) family environment, measured by the number of nonsmokers and ex-smokers among family members and close friends. Three months following treatment, subjects were reassessed regarding their smoking behavior. Posttreatment measures of stressors included number of stressful life events (measured by the Life Change Inventory)[26] and degree of craving (measured by the Shiffman-Jarvik Craving Subscale)[27] experienced following treatment. Coping response was operationalized as the number of problem- and emotion-focused coping responses the subject used when tempted to smoke. This typology and the Ways of Coping Checklist[28] were used instead of Shiffman's typology because they have been better substantiated theoretically and empirically.

Study Findings

At follow-up, 39% of the subjects (59) were abstinent; 34% (51) had partially relapsed (ie, smoking, but at a rate less than before treatment), and 27% (40) had totally relapsed, ie, were smoking at a rate equal to or greater than before treatment. Discriminant analysis revealed that stressors, particularly the degree of craving experienced, effectively predicted smoking behavior group membership at the three-month follow-up ($P < 0.01$). Analysis of variance with post hoc comparisons revealed that abstinent subjects had lower mean craving scores than both partially and totally relapsed subjects. Although the three groups did not differ in total number of coping responses utilized, analysis of variance revealed that abstinent subjects employed more problem-focused (efforts that attempt to alter or alleviate the source of stress) and fewer emotion-focused (efforts to alleviate the unpleasant emotions that accompany a stressful event) coping responses than either partially or totally relapsed smokers. Three of the five hypothesized predictors—sociodemographic characteristics, pretreatment symptoms, and family environment—were unrelated to relapse; thus, the model received only partial support. It is possible that these three predictors may have had indirect effects on smoking cessation through their influence on stressors and coping.

The results suggest that understanding the role of the posttreatment characteristics, stressors (particularly craving), and type of coping response may prove useful in helping nurses design effective treatments to help ex-smokers maintain long-term abstinence. Clients experiencing symptoms of craving should be considered to be at increased risk for relapse. In addition, teaching ex-smokers to rely on problem-focused versus emotion-focused coping responses may improve success rates.

There were similarities between the present findings and those of Cronkite and Moos[14] regarding outcomes of alcohol treatment, particularly the abstinence outcome that is most directly comparable to the outcome measure used in the smoking study. The findings of both studies revealed that the posttreatment characteristics of stressors and coping responses were related directly to abstinence, whereas pretreatment characteristics were unrelated to this outcome. In neither study did social background or family environmental characteristics relate directly to outcome; however, Cronkite and Moos did discern a significant total (direct plus indirect) effect of social background on abstinence. The indirect effects of the six predictive factors on relapse of ex-smokers were neither addressed in the derived theory nor examined in the present study.

Logical next steps in continuing the process of deriving a theory of smoking relapse include (1) extending the analogy to include the entire structure of the Cronkite and Moos framework and testing the total model, which includes direct and indirect effects; (2) determining the extent to which the derived theory can successfully predict additional outcomes of smoking cessation treatment programs; and (3) examining the role of the treatment-related characteristics component of the theory by expanding it to include self-treatment.

IMPLICATIONS FOR THEORY DEVELOPMENT IN NURSING

This study demonstrated that theory derivation is a useful strategy for developing theory to guide nursing research. It represents a rather quickly and easily applied approach to theory development. However, theory derivation should not be viewed as an easy shortcut to developing theory. It requires not only becoming well versed in literature about the phenomenon of interest and several related fields of inquiry, but also engaging in creative and insightful thinking.

A major asset of theory derivation is that it calls attention to similarities among phenomena in different fields of study. Identified patterns can then be incorporated in more generic descriptive or practice-oriented theories. For example, similarities discerned through the process of deriving a theory of smoking relapse from a theory of alcohol recovery could, with future testing and refinement, provide the basis for a more general theory of recovery from substance use and related nursing practice theories. The focus on similarities among phenomena may have the disadvantage of encouraging theorists to overlook or de-emphasize important dissimilarities or "dis-analogies" in the parent theory,[5(p169)] or to ignore negative analogies.[29] There may be a tendency to assume erroneously that identical forces are operating to influence phenomena that are merely analogous. Where noted, dissimilarities can be used advantageously to refine and specify the derived theory and to qualify more generic theories and their application.

Theory derivation can be an important springboard to the more complex and difficult process of theory synthesis. Particularly in areas of interest where little prior work has been done or, as in the present example, where discrete findings need to be integrated, the process of theory derivation can help clarify the phenomenon, structure the theorist's thinking, and point out gaps in explanation and prediction that require amplification. Whether used alone or in combination with other theory-building strategies, theory derivation represents a promising approach to developing the middle-range theories that are badly needed to guide nursing practice and research.

REFERENCES

1. Kim HS. *The Nature of Theoretical Thinking in Nursing.* Norwalk, Conn: Appleton-Century-Crofts, 1983.
2. Stevens BJ. *Nursing Theory: Analysis, Application, Evaluation,* ed 2. Boston: Little, Brown, 1984.
3. Torres G. *Theoretical Foundations of Nursing.* Norwalk, Conn: Appleton-Century-Crofts, 1986.
4. Fawcett J, Downs FS. *The Relationship of Theory and Research.* Norwalk, Conn: Appleton-Century-Crofts, 1986.
5. Walker LO, Avant KC. *Strategies for Theory Construction in Nursing.* Norwalk, Conn: Appleton-Century-Crofts, 1983.
6. Shipley RH, Rosen TJ, Williams C. Measurements of smoking: Surveys and some recommendations. *Addict Behav.* 1982;72:99–102.
7. Hunt WA, Matarazzo JD. Three years later: Recent developments in the experimental modification of smoking behavior. *J Abnorm Psychol.* 1973;81:107–114.
8. Pomerleau O. Commonalities in the treatment and understanding of smoking and other self-management disorders. In Krasnegor NA, ed. *Behavioral Analysis of Treatment and Substance Abuse.* US Dept of Health, Education, and Welfare publication No. 79–893. Government Printing Office, 1979.
9. Schacter S. Pharmacological and psychological determinants of smoking. *Ann Intern Med.* 1978;88:104–114.
10. Lichtenstein E. Social learning, smoking, and substance abuse. In Krasnegor NA, ed. *Behavioral analysis of treatment and substance abuse.* US Dept of Health, Education, and Welfare publication No. 79–893. Government Printing Office, 1979.
11. Horwitz MB, Hindi-Alexander M, Wagner TJ. Psychosocial mediators of abstinence, relapse, and continued smoking: A one-year follow-up of a minimal intervention. *Addict Behav.* 1985;10:29–39.
12. Marlatt GA, Gordan JR. Determinants of relapse: Implications for the maintenance of behavior change. In Davidson, P, ed. *Behavioral Medicine: Changing Health Lifestyles.* New York: Brunner/Mazel, 1979.
13. Shiffman S. Relapse following smoking cessation: A situational analysis. *J Consult Clin Psychol.* 1982;50:71–82.
14. Cronkite RC, Moos RH. Determinants of the post-treatment functioning of alcoholic patients: A conceptual framework. *J Consult Clin Psychol.* 1980;48:305–316.
15. Green DE. Patterns of tobacco use in the United States. In Krasnegor NA, ed. *Cigarette Smoking as a Dependence Process.* US Dept of Health, Education, and Welfare publication No. 79–800. Government Printing Office, 1979.
16. Pomerleau O, Adkins D, Pertschuk M. Predictors of outcome and recidivism in smoking cessation. *Addict Behav.* 1978;3:65–70.
17. Ikard F, Green DE, Horn D. A scale to differentiate between types of smoking as related to the management of affect. *Int J Addict.* 1969;4:649–659.
18. Tomkins SS. Psychological model of smoking behavior. *Am J Public Health.* 1966;56:117–120.
19. McFall R, Hammen C. Motivation, structure, and self-monitoring: Role of specific factors in smoking reduction. *J Consult Clin Psychol.* 1971;37:80–86.
20. Schneider NG, Jarvik ME, Forsythe AB, et al. Nicotine gum in smoking cessation: A placebo-controlled, double-blind trial. *Addict Behav.* 1983;8:253–261.
21. Schacter S. Recidivism and self-cure of smoking and obesity. *Am Psychol.* 1982;37:436–444.
22. Gunn RC. Smoking clinic failures and recent life stress. *Addict Behav.* 1983;8:83–87.
23. Graham S, Gibson RW. Cessation of patterned behavior: Withdrawal from smoking. *Soc Sci Med.* 1970;5:319–337.

24. Mermelstein R, Lichtenstein E, McIntyre K. Partner support and relapse in smoking cessation programs. *J Consult Clin Psychol.* 1983;51:465–466.

25. Wewers ME. *Factors Associated with Relapse among Ex-Smokers.* Dissertation. University of Maryland at Baltimore, 1986.

26. Dohrenwend BS, Dohrenwend BJ. Life events as stressors. A methodological inquiry. *J Health Soc Behav.* 1973;14:167-175.

27. Shiffman S, Jarvik ME. Smoking withdrawal symptoms in two weeks of abstinence. *Psychopharmacology.* 1976;50:35–39.

28. Folkman S, Lazarus RS. An analysis of coping in a middle-aged community sample. *J Health Soc Behav.* 1980;21:219–239.

29. Hesse M. *Models and Analogies in Science.* South Bend, Ind: University of Notre Dame Press, 1966.

Identity of Self As Infertile: An Example of Theory-Generating Research

This article presents results of a study using grounded-theory methodology to explore the meaning of infertility to those persons experiencing it. Thirty-two persons were interviewed, including 15 married couples and two married women whose husbands were either unable or unwilling to participate in the study. Forty-five semistructured interviews were conducted, as each person was interviewed separately and 13 couples were interviewed conjointly. Through the ongoing process of data collection and analysis, a substantive grounded theory was generated, with a core concept being that as persons experience unwanted infertility they take on a central identity of themselves as infertile. The process of taking on and managing this identity is described.

Ellen Frances Olshansky, RNC, DNSc
Assistant Professor
Department of Parent and Child Nursing
University of Washington
Seattle, Washington

THE CONTINUING development of the discipline of nursing requires a variety of ways of knowing.[1] One such way is to generate theory through an inductive mode of inquiry. In a recent presentation, Melia[2] stated that nursing is in need of theories that are generated from inductive research and grounded in the data obtained through such research.

This article presents results of an inductive research study that was conducted to better understand the human responses to infertility and to generate a substantive grounded theory that helps explain some of these responses. This study has relevance for the discipline of nursing for two primary reasons. First, nursing is con-

The author acknowledges the assistance of the following people with the research conducted for the study on which this article is based: Katharyn A. May, RN, DNSc; Ramona T. Mercer, RN, PhD; and Leonard Schatzman, PhD. The author also thanks Jeanne Q. Benoliel, RN, DNSc, for her critique of the article.

Funding for the study presented in this article was provided by a National Research Service Award, #1F31 NU-05785-01, US Dept of Health and Human Services, Division of Nursing; and an award from Sigma Theta Tau, Alpha Eta Chapter.

This article is adapted from presentations at The National Symposium of Nursing Research, San Francisco, Calif, Nov 14, 1985, and The International Nursing Research Conference, Edmonton, Alberta, Canada, May 9, 1986.

Adv Nurs Sci 1987, 9(2), 54–63

cerned with the diagnosis and treatment of human responses to actual or potential health problems, and understanding the human responses to infertility contributes to nursing knowledge.[3] Second, theory-generating research is an important aspect of scholarly inquiry that contributes to nursing knowledge and to the discipline of nursing.[2]

LITERATURE REVIEW

Approximately 20% of US couples experience difficulty trying to have a child.[4] While research on infertility is predominantly medically oriented, a growing body of literature exists pertaining to psychosocial and emotional aspects of infertility. Until recently, this literature only examined psychosocial antecedents of infertility, searching for causes of infertility, with the focus being on females almost to the exclusion of males. Rarely did researchers emphasize the psychosocial consequences of infertility or how infertility influences the lives of those experiencing it, or focus on both females and males. Recently, however, interest has heightened regarding the influence of infertility on the lives of infertile persons. Menning[5-10] noted that the process of resolving the emotional conflicts surrounding infertility involves several stages. Wiehe[11] discussed similar findings, and Sawatsky[12] discussed psychological tasks through which infertile couples must work in order to resolve their conflicts. Others[13-25] have addressed the emotional impact of infertility, emphasizing the need for sensitivity in those providing health care for infertile persons. The research presented in this article represents a new understanding of the consequences of infertility, adding to existing literature by exploring the meaning of infertility from the perspective of infertile persons themselves.

STUDY METHODOLOGY

The sample consisted of 32 informants, including 15 married couples and two married women whose husbands were either unable or unwilling to participate in the study. Informants were recruited from a large university infertility clinic on the West Coast as well as from RESOLVE, an infertility support organization. A total of 45 interviews was conducted, as each person was interviewed separately and 13 couple units were interviewed conjointly. Two couple units were not available for the conjoint interview. The women ranged in age from 28 to 41, and the men from 29 to 47. All were Caucasian from various religious backgrounds, and most were employed in professional occupations. The characteristics of the sample indicated an important limitation to the ability to generalize this study since persons from lower socioeconomic backgrounds and various ethnic groups were not represented. Infertility treatment is expensive, and the question arises concerning whether this limitation related to the study sample may, in fact, represent a larger societal problem of inaccessibility to infertility treatment by a significant portion of the population. This issue deserves further attention.

The sample was not limited to a particular kind of infertility problem. Couples who were infertile due to a physiological problem in the female, in the male, or a combined physiological problem, and those infertile due to unknown causes were included in the study. The key factor was the couples themselves perceiving that they had an infertility problem. They were at various stages of an infertility workup, including those beginning a medical workup and those actively seeking alternative solutions.

STUDY PROCEDURES

Grounded-theory methodology was used in collecting and analyzing data.[26,27] In conducting an inductive research study, the goal of the research is to generate theory that explains the phenomenon in question. Thus, a theoretical framework is not determined a priori to be tested. Inductive research is not atheoretical, however, as it is guided by certain philosophical underpinnings. Grounded-theory methodology is rooted in the theoretical perspective of symbolic interactionism. The basic premise of symbolic interactionism is that persons construct meanings for phenomena based on their interpretations of interactions that they have with one another within a social context.[28] Thus, the interactions of infertile persons will influence the meaning they attach to infertility.

With grounded-theory methodology, qualitative data are collected through observation and interviews "in the field," meaning the natural environment of the informants being studied. In this case, data were collected in the homes of infertile persons. Data were analyzed according to the technique of "constant comparative analysis," in which "slices of data" were constantly compared against other "slices of data," and each informant was compared against other informants.[26,27]

Data collection and analysis are not two discrete processes, but rather they are related in a circular fashion. Data are analyzed as they are collected, and this initial analysis guides further data collection, leading to more refined data analysis and more focused data collection. In this study, data were collected using broad, open-ended questions. The interviews were tape-recorded and transcribed for data analysis. The researcher constructed codes or words that captured the meanings of the transcripts, a process referred to as open coding.[27] Eventually several codes were grouped into categories that subsumed these codes. These categories guided further data collection, providing focus for subsequent interviews, as questions became directed toward understanding and verifying these categories. The initial interview questions were

- How would you say that infertility has affected your life?
- How has infertility affected your relationships with significant others in your life?
- In what ways do you deal with the feelings you have about infertility?

The interview questions used toward the end of the study after data were analyzed from the majority of informants were more focused.

- Does it seem accurate to you to describe the treatments and procedures surrounding infertility as "work"?
- Do you feel that infertility has taken a central focus in your life?
- In what ways are you able to carry on with other important things in your life while experiencing infertility?
- How do you view the various options available to you in dealing with infertility?

As data analysis continued, certain categories became more evident and the researcher focused on them, a process referred to as selective coding.[27] Eventually certain categories emerged consistently with less and less new information elicited, a point at which the researcher had reached theoretical saturation.[27] In this research, the categories that emerged consistently were "the work of fertility" and "the central identity of self as infertile." The categories and their subcategories were linked, a process termed theoretical integration, to form a substantive theory.[26,27]

As stated, the goal of this methodology is to generate substantive theory that is grounded in the data collected and explains the phenomenon in question. Ultimately, the goal is to generate formal theory in which the substantive theory has application to other substantive areas, thus becoming more formalized. Melia,[2] in advocating this kind of theory in nursing, describes substantive and formal theory as theories of the second and third kind, respectively, with theory of the first kind being that derived by the logico-deductive method.[2] The analysis in this study led to the generation of a substantive theory, or theory of the second kind, that provides an explanation and understanding of the meaning of infertility to those experiencing it.

STUDY FINDINGS

The findings of this study consist of an organizing scheme constructed from the data that represented a beginning substantive theory explaining the process of taking on and managing an identity of self as infertile. Before presenting this organizing scheme, it is important to indicate that an underlying assumption in this study, derived from symbolic interactionism (the framework guiding grounded-theory methodology), is that self is conceptualized as being composed of multiple identities.[29] These identities are dynamic, constantly shifting their positions within the self, with some identities taking on a central position and others taking on a peripheral position. The positions assumed by the various identities can and do change under differing circumstances.

Findings of this study suggest that infertile persons who are distressed by their infertility undergo a process of "taking on" an identity of self as infertile. This identity becomes central. They eventually attempt to "shed," "push," or "diminish" this identity to the periphery and "get on with their lives." For these individuals, infertility becomes all-encompassing, taking on a central focus in their lives as they "work" actively to intervene in this problem. Other important identities and their related activities, such as career identity, are "pushed" to the periphery (Fig 1).

Paradoxically, in contrast to those for whom infertility is relatively unimportant, the infertile couples in this study had to confront directly their identities as infertile in order to make these identities less central. The paradox is that in order to rid themselves of the central identity as infertile and make this identity peripheral, infertile persons must initially take on this identity centrally.

Fig 2 conceptualizes the process of taking on and managing an identity of self as infertile.[30] This process is highly interrelated with and influenced by biological, sociocultural, and psychological processes in the infertile person's life. Many variations occur as a result of individual experiences, strategies employed, and consequences experienced. The commonality, however, is the taking on and focusing on the identity of self as infertile to deemphasize this identity. This process is key in the larger process of managing infertility.

TAKING ON AN IDENTITY OF SELF AS INFERTILE

Symbolic Rehearsals

Initially there are symbolic rehearsals of becoming pregnant or becoming a parent. These symbolic rehearsals refer to a period of imagining what it would be like to be pregnant or to be a parent, imagining such specific instances as holding a baby, feeding a baby, clothing a baby. These symbolic rehearsals occur under the influence of sociocultural factors. Symbolic rehearsals may have begun years before, often during childhood play. Some examples of symbolic rehearsals are seen in the following quotes from informants in this study:

I think I have really come down to a very basic, very primitive idea that this (having children) is the way life is supposed to be, and you do it because it's natural to do, because not doing it feels very unnatural.

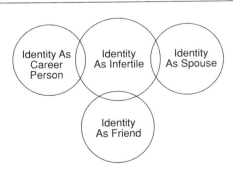

Fig 1. Conceptualization of the central identity of self as infertile.

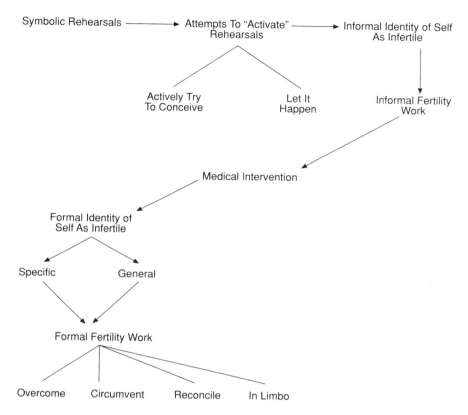

Fig 2. The work of taking on and managing an identity of self as infertile. Reprinted with permission from Olshansky EF: *The Work of Taking on and Managing an Identity of Self as Infertile,* dissertation. University of California, San Francisco, Calif, 1985.

I think we've all grown up with the idea that pregnancy is what a woman does, it's the most natural thing, and we have a whole 2,000 years of literature and culture that have always pointed in that direction. So there has been this tradition, and it's very hard at times to redefine oneself as a woman.

I figured I could sit in the backyard and make quilts and do handwork that I love to do, which in some ways I haven't done because now I see no purpose—it is more something to do if you're pregnant. There are some things I still haven't done, like fix up the patio with astro turf, which would be nice for a child to play in. And some things I would do in the house that now really aren't needed since there are no kids. I had images and plans of things I would do.

Such critical rehearsals of identity in relation to pregnancy and child rearing most frequently lead to a decision to "activate" these rehearsals by becoming parents, either by "letting it happen" or by "trying" to conceive. That is, some people decide only to discontinue contraceptive use, while others decide to discontinue contraception and consciously "time" sexual intercourse around the expected ovulatory phase of the woman's menstrual cycle. How couples choose to try to "activate" these rehearsals may be related to how they perceive their infertility's effect on their lives.

Informal Identity of Self As Infertile

After a period of letting it happen or trying to conceive with no resulting pregnancy, the couple (or at least one member of the couple) may begin to suspect a problem. There is a persistent "thwarting" of attempts to realize the symbolic rehearsals; the couple then begins a process of "reluctant acceptance" of an identity of self as infertile. This identity is cast upon them biologically and socially. Initially this identity is of an informal nature, as it has not been "confirmed" and "formalized" through medical diagnosis. This informal identity leads to "informal work" of attempting to push aside the identity. This informal "fertility work" includes strategies related to "playing probabilities" by modifying their diets, changing positions and timing of sexual intercourse, and generally following suggestions they have received informally from friends, literature, or media.

The following example from the data illustrates this concept:

You kind of have this anticipation; and when it doesn't happen, you get tired of it and you figure you can't live the rest of your life like this. So just in general reading about it, you realize that something might be wrong and that you have to work on it.

Formal Identity of Self As Infertile

As a result of the reluctant acceptance of self as infertile, the couple (or one member of the couple) takes on the role of self as infertile, acting on it by making a commitment to "work" on de-emphasizing this identity. This fertility work involves strategies of searching for a cause as well as a remedy for the infertility. Through the process of searching, these couples seek medical intervention for diagnosis and treatment. As a result of the medical diagnosis and the clinical confirmation, they take on a more formal identity of self as infertile. This formal identity can be either specific, referring to explained infertility (diagnosed cause), or general, referring to unexplained infertility (no specific diagnosed cause).

Each of these types of formal identity has its own consequences. Once clinically confirmed as infertile, the individual or couple undertakes "formal fertility work." This formal work involves following the medical regimen prescribed, such as undergoing specific treatments or taking certain drugs. The formal fertility work often has profound effects on the lives of infertile couples. A poignant example of this is evidenced in the following quote from an informant:

Our sexual life hasn't recovered yet. When I finally failed the last time with Pergonal, I was so depressed that I didn't want to have anything to do with sex at all, and he was so depressed that he had been through all of this for nothing that he didn't want to have anything to do with sex. Sex was a pain. Pleasure? Are you kidding me? I'd rather go take a shot of Pergonal rather than have sex, which was so rife with emotion. So we just decided let's not even do it, if we never do it again, it's O.K. Let's just forget about it and take this negative aspect away from it, and we went for many months with no sex, and I didn't miss it at all and he didn't miss it at all either. Slowly, it's coming back, very, very slowly. Sometimes I think it's never going to be the same because of my association with it. I don't know when there is ever going to be a time in our lives when we can be relaxed enough to get back into sex as a pleasure. It became a focus for all of our rage and anxiety and fears.

Expansion of the Identity of Self As Infertile

Taking on a formal identity and role of self as infertile leads to a greater commitment to this fertility work. With greater commitment comes a greater focus on this identity. The identity as infertile eventually takes on a greater focus in the lives of infertile couples, thus their identity of self as infertile is expanded. Paradoxically, their infertility becomes all-encompassing as couples become more absorbed in the work of letting go of this identity. The following quote offers an example:

It could be getting my period, or it could be finding out that somebody else is pregnant, or it could be having to do a test that I just didn't feel like thinking about and I was just feeling sorry for myself, like that time around my birthday and finishing the second year of trying to become pregnant. Now that I'm spending such an inordinate amount of time noticing my temperature and all that other stuff, I feel like everything is under a microscope.

MANAGING THE IDENTITY OF SELF AS INFERTILE

As the identity of self as infertile is taken on centrally, the search for remedies escalates. The search for causes continues for those identified as falling into the category of "unexplained-general" infertility. In analyzing the data, it was apparent that the desired results of this search were to resolve the infertility, allowing other identities to regain a central focus as the infertile identity assumed a peripheral position. The data revealed that the infertile couples used three distinct modes of managing infertility: overcoming infertility, circumventing infertility, and reconciling infertility. Regardless of the mode of managing infertility, varying degrees of success were achieved by the couples in this study. The infertile identity began to assume a greater or lesser peripheral position for various individuals as they resolved their feelings and conflicts surrounding infertility to a greater or lesser degree.

Overcoming the Identity of Self As Infertile

Some people managed infertility by becoming pregnant, either as a direct result of, or in spite of, medical intervention. This process is viewed conceptually as "overcoming" infertility as this identity is "shed" to the periphery, while the underlying cause of the infertility is corrected, allowing pregnancy to occur. Two couples in this study fell into this category.

Circumventing the Identity of Self As Infertile

Some manage infertility through technological means such as in vitro fertilization or artificial insemination, thus circumventing the underlying cause, but still achieving pregnancy. In this case, the identity as infertile is "pushed" to the periphery, with pregnancy occurring though the underlying cause is still present. Two couples in this study fell into this category, with one couple achieving pregnancy through in vitro fertilization, and another couple currently attempting to conceive through artificial insemination. Two other couples were in the process of trying to overcome infertility. A woman in this study who became pregnant as a result of in vitro fertilization described herself as "an infertile fertile woman."

Reconciling the Identity of Self As Infertile

A third group of persons managed infertility by choosing alternative measures such as adopting, or choosing to be childfree. These strategies represent methods of reconciling infertility because the underlying cause of the infertility is not corrected nor is pregnancy achieved through technological means. These people, however, are able to come to terms with their inability to have biologically linked children. This reconciliation process allows the identity as infertile to "diminish," taking on a peripheral position in their lives. Six couples fell into this category, with three adopting children, two in the process of adopting, and one choosing to be without children.

Remaining in Limbo

A fourth mode observed does not represent a way of managing successfully the identity of self as infertile. Some infertile persons remained "in limbo" as they continued unsuccessfully to try to conceive, without attempting other strategies described above. This group of people persistently tried to overcome infertility, though they were unsuccessful. Some persons in this group discontinued actively trying to overcome infertility but had not resolved their feelings about infertility. Five couples in this study fell into this group. This group requires further study.

An initial substantive grounded theory, referred to as the work of taking on and managing an identity of self as infertile, was generated from data collected and analyzed using grounded-theory methodology. Such a theory contributes to nursing knowledge and the discipline of nursing in that it provides an understanding of the human response to infertility from the perspective of those persons experiencing it. More study is needed to build on this substantive theory in order to better understand the phenomenon of infertility, as well as to attempt to formalize this theory by testing it in other substantive areas that are relevant to nursing. In addition, other areas of infertility deserve study, such as the influence of infertility on a marital relationship, as well as on the larger family unit. This study represents an initial effort at understanding and explaining the human response to infertility.

REFERENCES

1. Carper BA. Fundamental patterns of knowing in nursing. *Adv Nurs Sci.* 1978;1:13–23.
2. Melia K. *Theories of the second and third kind.* Read before the 2d International Nursing Research Conference, Edmonton, Alberta, Canada, May 8, 1986.
3. ANA. *A Social Policy Statement.* Kansas City, Mo, American Nurses' Association, 1980.
4. Peindl C. The expanding nursing role in infertility. *Insights into Infertility.* Serono Symposia Publishers, 1985.
5. Menning BE. The psychosocial impact of infertility. *Nurs Clin North Am.* 1982;17:155–163.
6. Menning BE. The emotional needs of infertile couples. *Fertil Steril.* 1980;34:313–319.
7. Menning BE. Counseling infertile couples. *Contemp Obstet Gynecol.* 1979;13:101–108.
8. Menning BE. *Infertility: A Guide for the Childless Couple.* Englewood Cliffs, NJ: Prentice-Hall, 1977.
9. Menning BE. RESOLVE: A support group for infertile couples. *Am J Nurs.* 1976;76:258–259.
10. Menning BE. The infertile couple: A plea for advocacy. *Child Welfare.* 1975;54:454–460.
11. Wiehe V. Psychosocial reactions to infertility: Implications for nursing in resolving feelings of disappointment and inadequacy. *J Obstet Gynecol Neonatal Nurs.* 1976;5:28–32.
12. Sawatsky M. Tasks of infertile couples. *J Obstet Gynecol Neonatal Nurs.* 1981;10:132–133.
13. Bernstein J, Mattox JH. An overview of infertility. *J Obstet Gynecol Neonatal Nurs.* 1982;11:309–314.
14. Frideman BM. Infertility workup. *Am J Nurs.* 1981;81:2040–2046.
15. Kraft AD, Palombo MA, Mitchell D, et al. The psychological dimensions of infertility. *Am J Orthopsychiatry.* 1980;50:618–628.
16. Mazor MD. Emotional reactions to infertility. In Mazor MD, ed. *Infertility: Medical, Emotional and Social Considerations.* New York: Human Sciences Press, 1984.
17. Mazor MD. The problem of infertility. In Notman M, Nadelson C, eds. *The Woman Patient.* New York: Plenum Press, 1978.
18. Mocarski V. The nurse's role in helping infertile couples. *Am J Maternal Child Nurs.* 1977;2:264–266.
19. McCormick TM. Out of control: One aspect of infertility. *J Obstet Gynecol Neonatal Nurs.* 1980;9:205–206.
20. McCusker MR. The subfertile couple. *J Obstet Gynecol Neonatal Nurs.* 1982;11:157–162.
21. Rosenfeld DL, Mitchell E. Treating the emotional aspects of infertility: Counseling services in an infertility clinic. *Am J Obstet Gynecol.* 1979;135:177–180.
22. Williams LS, Power PW. The emotional impact of infertility in single women: Some implications for counseling. *J Am Med Women's Assoc.* 1977;32:327–333.
23. Wilson EA. Sequence of emotional responses induced by infertility. *J Kentucky Med Assoc.* 1979;77:229–233.
24. Woods NF. Infertility. In Fogel I, Woods NF, eds. *Health Care of Women: A Nursing Perspective.* St. Louis: Mosby, 1981.
25. Woods NF. *Human Sexuality in Health and Illness.* St Louis: Mosby, 1979.
26. Glaser B, Strauss AL. *The Discovery of Grounded Theory.* Hawthorne, NY: Aldine, 1967.
27. Glaser B. *Theoretical Sensitivity.* Mill Valley Calif: Sociology Press, 1978.
28. Blumer H. *Symbolic Interactionism: Perspective and Method.* Englewood Cliffs, NJ: Prentice-Hall, 1969.
29. Mead GH. *Mind, Self, and Society.* Chicago: University of Chicago Press, 1934, vol 1.
30. Olshansky EF. *The Work of Taking on and Managing an Identity of Self as Infertile.* Dissertation. University of California, San Francisco, Calif, 1985.

Being Healthy: Women's Images

Although the concept of health is central to nursing practice and science, measurement of the concept has lagged far behind theory development. The study presented extends Laffrey's earlier work by describing the meaning of health for a population of women representing multiple ethnic groups residing in the Pacific Northwest. A sample of 528 women from a cross-section of a community who had participated in a study of women's health was asked to respond to the question, "What does being healthy mean to you?" In addition to evidence of the clinical, role performance, and adaptive models of health, the women's responses yielded nine dimensions consistent with the eudaemonistic model. Each dimension included multiple descriptors identified through content analysis of the women's verbatim responses. The women's images of health were consistent with Smith's and Laffrey's four conceptions, but the eudaemonistic category included multiple dimensions. The women reported images of health consistent with contemporary nursing theorists' views. Moreover, their emphasis on eudaemonistic images crossed all categories of age, education, income, ethnicity, and employment status.

Nancy Fugate Woods, PhD, RN, FAAN
Professor and Chair
Department of Parent and Child Nursing
University of Washington

Shirley Laffrey, PhD, RN
Associate Professor of Mental Health,
Community and Administrative Nursing

Mary Duffy, PhD, RN
Assistant Professor of Mental Health,
Community and Administrative Nursing
University of California at San Francisco
School of Nursing
San Francisco, California

Martha J. Lentz, RN, PhD
Research Assistant Professor
Department of Physiological Nursing

Ellen Sullivan Mitchell, ARNP, PhD
Research Assistant Professor
Department of Parent and Child Nursing

Diana Taylor, ARNP, PhC
Doctoral Candidate

Kathryn Ann Cowan
Research Assistant
Department of Parent and Child Nursing
University of Washington
Seattle, Washington

The research on which this article was based was supported by Grant No. NU01054 from the Center for Nursing Research, US Department of Health and Human Services. The authors appreciate comments from Lydia Kotchek, PhD, RN, on the coding schema for health images, as well as the technical assistance of May Phifer in preparing this article.

Adv Nurs Sci 1988; 11 (1):36–46

DESPITE THE centrality of the concept "health" to nursing practice and science, assessment of health has lagged far behind theory development. Health, as well as discussions of person, environment, and nursing, appears in most contemporary theoretical works. Common to these works is an integrated view of human health that is inconsistent with the particularistic view of physical, mental, or social health discussed in other literature.[1]

Images of health have differed over the course of nursing history. Nevertheless, there is consensus among nurse theorists that health is a state or a process of the whole person existing independently of disease. Nightingale's views of health,[2] published in the 19th century, reflected the major social challenge of the time: hygiene. She advanced the laws of health, which emphasized the relationship of the environment and the human being. Nightingale believed the individual possessed inherent reparative powers and that nursing placed the person in the best condition for the environment to influence these powers. Peplau,[3] influenced by 20th-century theories of human development, defined health as forward movement of the personality and other ongoing human processes in the direction of creative, constructive, and productive personal and community living. She was the first to emphasize health as a dynamic developmental process. Theorists writing in the 1960s viewed health in relation to human needs. Orlando[4] identified dimensions of human needs, such as physical limitations, adverse reactions to a setting, and experiences that prevent communication of needs. Henderson[5] elaborated a functional view of health, identifying 14 areas for nursing care, such as breathing, eating, drinking, and engaging in recreation. Likewise, Wiedenbach's work[6] reflected a needs orientation to human health.

Theorists writing in the late 1960s and early 1970s emphasized health as a positive rather than a negative state. Hall's work,[7] focusing on recovery from acute illness, emphasized self-actualization. Levine[8] advocated the concept of balance. She saw the individual as a holistic being and based her nursing therapies on the conservation of energy, structural integrity, personal integrity, and social integrity. Johnson[9] advocated a view of health as interacting behavioral systems.

Recently Parse[10] has distinguished two paradigms in nursing: the Man-Environment totality paradigm and the Man-Environment simultaneity paradigm. The Man-Environment totality paradigm sets forth a view of humans as total summative organisms whose nature is a combination of bio-psycho-social-spiritual features. This paradigm includes a view of health as a dynamic state or process of physical, psychological, social, and spiritual wellbeing. Parse believes Roy's, Orem's, and King's words[11-13] reflect the totality paradigm. Roy emphasized human's adaptive capacities, equating health with a dynamic state of adaptation to internal and external forces. King defined health as a dynamic state of wellbeing, implying continuous adjustment to stressors in the internal or external environment through use of one's resources to achieve maximum potential for daily living. Orem defined health as a dynamic state of soundness or wholeness of structure and function.

The Man-Environment simultaneity paradigm sets forth a view of humans as more than and different from the sum of their parts, beings in continuous multiple interrelationships with the environment.[10] This view defines health as a process of becoming and a set of lived value priorities, man's unfolding. Parse believed Rogers and her own works reflected the simultaneity paradigm. Although Rogers[14] did not define health, she advocated a view of unitary human beings and health as an expression of the life process. Parse devised a concept called "Man-Living-Health," which is a unitary phenomenon expressing how humans relate to the world through revealing-concealing, enabling-limiting, and connecting-separating behaviors. Health is a constantly changing process that humans participate in cocreating.

Paterson and Zderad,[15] Watson,[16] and Newman[17] have defined health from a perspective linked closely to the simultaneity paradigm. Paterson and Zderad viewed health as a process of growth toward authentic awareness and the making of responsible choices. Newman saw health as expanded consciousness, explicating the underlying pattern of the person-environment. Watson defined health as a concept of unity and harmony with the mind, body, and soul: congruence between the self as perceived and the self as experienced. Health implies harmony with the world and an openness to increased diversity.

In a recent review of the idea of health, Smith[18] proposed four models of health: eudaemonistic, adaptive, role performance, and clinical. The eudaemonistic model of health connotes exuberant well-being, whereas the adaptive model connotes flexible adjustment to the environment. The role performance perspective emphasizes one's socially defined roles, and the clinical model emphasizes health as the absence of disease. Throughout nursing's theoretical literature, the description of health reflects a progression from ideas concerned with clinical, role-performance, and adaptive models to those reflecting adaptive and eudaemonistic visions. Consistency is implied in some of the theoretical works between the definitions that undergird efforts to develop nursing theory and the visions of health commonly held by the people nurses serve, yet little information about these visions of health exists.

There are two exceptions to the unrelatedness of empirical work and nursing theory development about health: Laffrey's work on health conceptions[19] and Parse's study of the lived experience of health.[10] Laffrey defined health conception as "the personal meaning of health for an individual." Her Health Conceptions Scale, based on Smith's philosophical inquiry about health,[17] includes clinical, role-performance, adaptive, and eudaemonistic dimensions of health. Laffrey developed items for the Health Conceptions Scale from a sample of 78 midwestern adults participating in evening adult education courses. She selected for inclusion in a 28-item scale the responses to the question, "What do you mean when you say you are in good health?", that were consistent with Smith's four models of health. She did not include responses that were inconsistent with one of the four models of health. Although Laffrey sought the meaning of health to individuals, her imposition of Smith's four models on her health conceptions data may have closed out a number of health conceptions held by a wide cross-section of the population. Moreover, her use of well-educated midwestern subjects may restrict the meaning of health to one held by those who share membership in a homogeneous cultural and geographical group.

Parse and colleagues[20] studied the lived experience of health based on questionnaires inviting 400 individuals to describe a situation in which they experienced a feeling of health. These people were asked to share their thoughts, perceptions, and feelings about the situation. Parse used phenomenological analysis to derive structural definitions of health for men and women in four age groups: under 19 years, 20 to 45 years, 46 to 65 years, and 66 years and older. For adults 20 to 45 years of age, 291 descriptive expressions reflected three common elements that Parse labeled: spirited intensity (being enthusiastic, feeling in peak condition), fulfilling inventiveness (accomplishment, ability to extend the limits of endurance), and symphonic integrity (feeling of worth, peaceful attitude). Parse's definitions of health reflected her perspective of health as a "rhythmically constituting process of the man-environment interrelationship. . . an intersubjective process of transcending with the possibles. . . a synthesis of values.[20(p28)] Parse's analytical approach involved identifying common elements and structural definitions based on coders' interpretations of descriptive expressions rather than using an emic coding approach in which codes closely reflected people's own words.

The purpose of the study on which this article is based was to extend Laffrey's work by describing the meaning of health for a population of women of multiple ethnic groups residing in the Pacific Northwest. The steps to that goal were

- to assess the consistency of the dimensions of health identified in the study with Smith's four models and the ideas of health as proposed in nursing theory;
- to determine the variation in health conceptions related to women's age, ethnicity, income, education, and employment status; and
- to refine the instrumentation for the measurement of health in nursing studies.

SUBJECTS AND METHODS

This report is one component of a larger study on the prevalence of perimenstrual symptoms.[21] Women who participated in an initial home interview regarding their social environment, socialization, reproductive health experiences, health practices, and health status were asked to keep a 90-day health diary and to be interviewed again by telephone at the end of the study. Of 656 women who participated in the initial interview, 528 completed the telephone interview.

The sampling framework used in this study involved multiple steps. The research team identified census block groups in which there were high proportions of women who were between 18 and 45 years of age, black or Asian, and educated at the high school level. The street segments within each selected block group were then identified and randomly ordered with a computer program. The numbers of the street segments within the block groups provided the link between the initial criteria and a directory of all addresses in Seattle, from which the telephone numbers of all potential participants were chosen. From this pool of potential subjects, 656 women completed interviews, a response rate of 58%. Of these women, 528 completed the telephone interview and the initial in-person interview. This approach generated a sample of women comprising 64 Asians, 80 blacks, 291 whites, and 19 Native Americans, Hispanics, and others. The women ranged in age from 18 to 45 years, with a mean age of 32.6 years. They reported a mean educational level of 14.2 years and a mean income range of $29,000 to $30,999. In this group of women, 78% reported some level of employment outside the home. Currently, 63% were married or partnered; 24% had never been married, and 12% were divorced or separated.

A single question was used to elicit health images: "What does being healthy mean to you?" Data were divided into phrases with any phrases with complete ideas as constituting units of analysis. Each phrase was reviewed by two reviewers and assigned an emic code, closely reflecting the woman's own words. This approach yielded over 100 codes. In order to establish reliability of the emic codes, two coders assigned codes to a sampling of 261 phrases. The coders attained 88% agreement, reached consensus on coding differences, and then coded each phrase contained in each woman's response. Codes were then aggregated by six individuals, yielding 12 discrete clusters of health conceptions. Definitions for each cluster, including its dimensions, were proposed. The individual phrases were then coded by two additional analysts using the definitions for each cluster.

RESULTS

Categories of Health Images

Content analysis of the health images data produced over 100 codes. These individual codes, grouped according to the consensus of six analysts, appear in the Appendix.

The categories of clinical, role performance, and adaptive health perceptions, as described by Smith[18] and Laffrey,[19] along with their definitions, appear in the boxed material. The women interviewed also reported multiple dimensions of health that reflected the eudaemonistic model. These included actualizing self, practicing healthy life ways, self-concept, body image, social involvement, fitness, cognitive function, positive mood, and harmony.

The multiple-content categories of the eudaemonistic health images prompted the exploration of a second dimension of coding that differentiated the categories according to negating, being, and doing. The "negating" category denoted the association of health with the absence of behaviors, signs, symptoms, or problems.

This dimension was restricted exclusively to the clinical category of health conception. The "being" category included health images that specified a state, such as the presence of desirable attributes or the possibility of wish fulfillment. The "doing" category denoted health images that specified activity, specifically, health-related activities, such as exercising, role functions, such as working, and social involvement, such as doing with and for others. The content dimensions of health images intersect with the action dimension such that the dominant dimension associated with clinical images is "negating," whereas "doing" is the dimension that dominates the role performance category. Both "being" and "doing" apply throughout the adaptive and eudaemonistic images.

The frequencies with which women reported categories of health images were calculated. The most frequently cited health images included the clinical (56.5% of the 528 women), positive affect (49.2%), fitness (43.8%), practicing healthy life ways (23.9%), and harmony (23.6%) categories. The least frequently reported health images were the positive self-concept (0.9%), cognitive function (10.1%),

---

Health Images and Definitions

Image	Definitions
Clinical	Health as the absence of illness; absence or infrequency of symptoms, illness, disease, or bad feelings; freedom from addiction; ability to recover quickly from illness; absence of need for medical care or medication(s); normalcy.
Role performance	Health as the ability to perform one's activities of daily living at an expected level.
Adaptive	Health as the ability to flexibly adjust to the environment, to cope with stressful events.
Eudaemonistic	Health as exuberant well-being; includes ability to actualize self; healthy life ways; positive self-concept and body image; capacity for positive social involvement; fitness; cognitive functioning; positive mood; harmony.
Actualizing self	Reaching one's optimum, achieving one's goals.
Practicing healthy life ways	Taking action to promote health or to prevent disease.
Self-concept	Feeling good about oneself; a positive sense of one's worth.
Body image	Feeling good about one's body; appearance.
Social involvement	Having ability to interact; love; care; enjoy relationships; to give and receive pleasure in relationships.
Fitness	Feeling stamina, strength, energy; in good shape.
Cognitive function	Thinking rationally, being creative, having many interests, being alert, being inquisitive.
Positive mood	Feeling positive affect, such as happiness, joy, affection, excitement, exhilaration.
Harmony	Feeling spiritually whole, centered, in balance, content.

social involvement (6.1%), and actualizing self (6.6%) categories. The remaining images reported were role performance (17.9%), adaptive (13.6%), and positive body image (13.8%). The nine categories in the eudaemonistic model totaled an 88% frequency of report.

Demographics

The women's ages did not influence the variety of health images they reported. However, women who were older reported more role performance ($\tau = 0.17$, p < .05) and adaptive health images (r = 0.11, p < .05) and fewer eudaemonistic health images ($\tau =-.08$, p < .05) than younger women.

Women who had completed more formal education tended to report a greater variety of health images than those with less formal education ($\tau=-0.11$). They also reported more eudaemonistic ($\tau = 0.12$, p < .05), but fewer role performance ($\tau =-0.11$, p < .05) images than did women with less formal education.

Women with greater family income reported a significantly greater variety of health images ($X^2 = 43$, 24 *df*; p < .05). The women with the highest income reported the most eudaemonistic images ($\tau = 0.08$, p < .05).

Women who were employed at the time reported neither a greater variety, nor different frequencies of health images. Likewise, Asian, white, black, Native American, and Hispanic women reported a similar variety of health images and similar frequencies of each category.

When the women's frequency of reporting one category of health images was cross-tabulated with their reports of other categories, it was evident that women reporting the most eudaemonistic descriptors reported fewer clinical images ($\tau = -0.21$, p < .00) and fewer role performance images (=-0.19,p < .00); reports of eudaemonistic images were unrelated to reports of adaptive images. The frequency of clinical images was not associated with frequency of role performance or adaptive images. Adaptive and role images were unrelated.

DISCUSSION

The most striking finding of this study was the rich variety of health images the women reported. The four categories of health images described by Smith[18] and Laffrey[19] were represented. The women reported nine additional images of health reflecting the eudaemonistic model. Moreover, the most frequently reported categories included clinical, positive affect, fitness, practicing healthy life ways, and harmony, all of which, except clinical, were from the eudaemonistic model. Clearly, women's images reflected a strong emphasis on exuberant well-being, not merely the absence of symptoms, role performance, or management of their environments. The variability in women's health images is consistent with Parse's assertion that health is each person's own experience of valuing that can be known only through a personal description.[10]

Despite the variety of descriptions derived from an emic coding approach, women's health images resembled those advanced by many nurse theorists. Many of the descriptors included in the dimensions of actualizing self, practicing healthy life ways, positive self-concept, fitness, cognitive function, positive affect, and harmony resemble the descriptors for the categories developed by Parse and associates[20] of spirited intensity, fulfilling inventiveness, and symphonic integrity.

Considering individual categories of health images, there is also consistency with works reflecting the totality paradigm. The most commonly mentioned category was "positive affect" descriptors, reflecting what Orem termed "wellness." The categories "fitness" and "practicing healthy life ways" probably reflect contemporary emphasis on health promotion,[1] but neither is mentioned in nursing's contemporary theoretical works. "Harmony" is consistent with Watson's emphasis on unity of mind, body, and soul, in harmony with the world. "Positive body image" does not figure prominently in any of the theorists' definitions of health but does reflect the Cartesian dualism represented in contemporary media about women.

The categories "cognitive function," "positive affect," "positive body image," and "fitness" can also be evidence that women use language to describe their health that represents the totality paradigm. The totality paradigm may, indeed, reflect how contemporary women view their worlds: as environments with which they are not in mutual simultaneous interaction, but to which they must adapt. Given the influences of sexism in women's lives, there is good justification for the totality paradigm to prevail in their thinking. The predominance of eudaemonistic images, however, is encouraging. Moreover, the finding that women who reported eudaemonistic images reported the lowest frequency of clinical and role performance images may suggest that a shift in how women define their health may be occurring. Perhaps this shift can be attributed to the expanded possibilities for women associated with the Women's Movement.

Older women reported more role performance and adaptive images but fewer eudaemonistic images than their younger counterparts. This may reflect a cohort effect attributable to the recent social emphasis on health promotion and changing norms for younger women.[1]

Women who had more formal education and/or higher income reported more eudaemonistic images than their less educated and/or less well-off counterparts. Perhaps this pattern is a function of the opportunity socially advantaged women may have to develop images of health that transcend the limits of clinical, role performance, and adaptive images.

Of interest was the negligible effect of ethnicity and employment on health images. The lack of evident effect may result from the similarity in socioeconomic status of the racial and ethnic groups included in the study. Likewise, employment may be less influential in shaping women's health images than in shaping their health behaviors.

In sum, women reported a rich diversity of health images. Their emphasis on eudaemonistic images was consistent with the definitions of contemporary nursing theorists and was in evidence regardless of the women's ages, education, income, ethnicity, or employment status.

REFERENCES

1. Pender N. Health and health promotion: The conceptual dilemmas. In Duffy M, Pender N, eds. *Conceptual Issues in Health Promotion. Report of Proceedings of a Wingspread Conference.* Indianapolis: Sigma Theta Tau International, 1987.
2. Nightingale F. *Notes on Nursing: What It Is and What It Is Not.* New York, Dover unabridged republication of the 1st American edition as published in 1860 by Appleton, 1969.
3. Peplau H. *Interpersonal Relations in Nursing.* New York: Putnam, 1952.
4. Orlando I. *The Dynamic Nurse-Patient Relationship: Function, Process and Principles.* New York: Putnam, 1961.
5. Henderson V. *The Nature of Nursing.* New York: Macmillan, 1966.
6. Wiedenbach E. *Clinical Nursing: A Helping Art.* New York: Springer, 1984.
7. Hall I. Another view of nursing care and quality. In Straub K, Parker K, eds. *Continuity of Patient Care: The Role of Nursing.* Washington, DC: Catholic University Press; 1966:47–60.
8. Levine M. *Introduction to Clinical Nursing,* ed 2. Philadelphia: F.A. Davis, 1973.
9. Johnson D. The behavioral system model for nursing. In Roehl J, Roy C, eds. *Conceptual Models for Nursing Practice,* ed 2. New York: Appleton-Century-Crofts; 1980:206–216.
10. Parse R. *Nursing Science: Major Paradigms, Theories and Critiques.* Philadelphia: W.B. Saunders, 1987.
11. Roy C. *Introduction to Nursing: An Adaptation Model.* Englewood Cliffs, NJ: Prentice Hall, 1976.
12. Orem D. *Nursing: Concepts of Practice.* New York: McGraw-Hill, 1985.
13. King I. *A Theory of Nursing: Systems, Concepts, Process.* New York: Wiley, 1981.
14. Rogers M. *An Introduction to the Theoretical Basis of Nursing.* Philadelphia: F.A. Davis, 1970.
15. Paterson J, Zderad L. *Humanistic Nursing.* New York: Wiley, 1976.
16. Watson J. *Nursing: Human Science and Human Care.* Norwalk, Conn: Appleton-Century-Crofts, 1985.
17. Newman M. *Health as Expanding Consciousness.* St Louis: Mosby, 1986.
18. Smith J. The idea of health: A philosophical inquiry. *Adv Nurs Sci.* 1981;3(3):43–50.
19. Laffrey S. Development of a health conception scale. *Res Nurs Health.* 1986;9(2):107–113.
20. Parse R, Coyne A, Smith M. The lived experience of health: A phenomenological study. In Parse R et al: *Nursing Research: Qualitative Methods.* Bowie, Md: Brady Communications; 1985: 27–37.
21. Woods N, Lentz M, Mitchell E, et al. Perimenstrual symptoms: Another look. *Public Health Rep.* 1988 (suppl):106–112.

Appendix
Health Images Grouped
by Category

CLINICAL

No lowered appetite
No tiredness or laziness
No bothersome symptoms
Not ill or sick, disease free
No chronic illness
No bad feelings
No pain
Infrequent illness
Only occasional colds
Not incapacitated
Normal
No guilt
Don't need medications
Not bedridden
No addictions
Not having to see a physician
Quick recovery, no lingering
    memories from illness
Not susceptible to disease
No aches, pains, or headaches
Pap smear ok
Health examinations ok

ROLE PERFORMANCE

Able to do work, do usual functions
Able to do anything physical
Able to move
Ability to get through it
Able to exercise
Able to get up in the morning
Able to perform

Able to get around
Able to do things
Able to function without discomfort,
    fatigue
Predictably being able to do things
Able to be as active as you want
Able to tackle anything mentally

ADAPTIVE

Flexibility
Sense of humor
Able to put things in perspective
Don't let things get you down
Acceptance of life's situation(s)
Adaptability to change
Able to take care of things easily
Ability to cope
Able to handle/manage life
Able to take anything mentally
Stress management
Adequate money to meet needs
Financial adequacy
In control
Control over life
Control over mind, health, and body
Self-discipline

ACTUALIZING SELF

Able to achieve goals
Going for it
Reaching optimum
Productive
Self-awareness

continues

PRACTICING HEALTHY LIFE WAYS

Not smoking
Taking care of self
Exercising
Wanting to do good things for your
  body
Moderate consumption of alcohol,
  chocolate
Good eating habits
Eat balanced diet
Good nutrition

POSITIVE SELF-CONCEPT

Sense of self-worth
Self confident
Feel good about self
High self-esteem

BODY IMAGE

Ideal weight
Good feelings re: body
Look good
Nice appearance
Nice body

SOCIAL INVOLVEMENT

Liked by others
Involved in community
Interesting to be with
Outgoing
Having many friends
Able to enjoy family
Feel good about relationships
Being with healthy people
Able to love and care

FITNESS

Stamina
Strength
Physically fit

Able to be active
Feel strong
In good shape
Rested
Energetic

COGNITIVE FUNCTION

Think rationally
Creative
Having many interests
Alert
Clear headed
Inquisitive

POSITIVE AFFECT

Positive mental attitude
Sense of well-being
Happy
Joyous
Cheerful
Exciting
Exhilarating
Wonderful
Affectionate
Feel good

HARMONY

Spiritually whole
Sense of purpose
Centered
Peaceful
Relaxed
Calm
In harmony
Life in balance
Carefree
No worries
Peace of mind
Body/mind in harmony
Satisfied
Content

Refining an Emergent Life-Style—Change Theory through Matrix Analysis

Matrix analysis is a methodologic tool used by researchers to systematically enter qualitative data into matrices and to simultaneously perform the complex integrative functions of data analysis and verification of findings. The article focuses on (1) the steps of qualitative data analysis that can be achieved by using matrix analysis, (2) the appropriate conditions for using matrix analysis, (3) the procedure for constructing a matrix, (4) the application of matrix analysis to a research problem that involved refining an emergent theory of the health life-style–change process, and (5) the use of matrix analysis to meet the criteria for trustworthiness of research findings.

Gene W. Marsh, PhD, RN
Assistant Director of Nursing for Research
Rose Medical Center
Assistant Professor
University of Colorado
School of Nursing
Denver, Colorado

THE RESEARCHER using qualitative methods frequently suffers from the pains of data overload. Disentangling and assigning meaning to collected verbiage and establishing the trustworthiness of findings are tedious challenges requiring tenacity. As a result, the path to conclusion drawing and verification may be neglected or omitted when research findings are presented. Such omissions jeopardize the publication of qualitative studies. Conversely, the length of research papers that retain rich descriptions and elaborate audit trails may also prohibit publication. The purpose of this article is to demonstrate the use of a methodologic tool that will permit the researcher to perform analysis functions, demonstrate and communicate those functions so that others can understand and evaluate how decisions and conclusions were reached, and assess the trustworthiness of findings.

The problem of establishing the trustworthiness of induced research findings is intricately interwoven into the scientific fabric of measurement theory. Regardless

The research on which this article was based was supported by a National Research Service Award No. NRO 5886-03 from the Center for Nursing Research, US Department of Health and Human Services. The author acknowledges the guidance of Linda Phillips, PhD, RN, in conducting the research.

Adv Nurs Sci 1990; 12(3): 41–52
© Aspen Publishers, Inc.

of the methodology employed, establishing trustworthiness of findings (reliability and validity) is a necessity. Researchers using qualitative methods have grappled with the problem in a variety of ways. For example, Knafl and Howard[1] identified the problem as lack of standardization in reporting. They suggested that findings be presented in strict adherence to the purpose of the qualitative research. For example, if the purpose is conceptualization, the researcher must demonstrate how an emergent theory guided data collection. However, if the purpose is instrumentation, discussion of the interview guide, observer role, methods of collecting and categorizing data, and use of data in instrument development may be of greater importance.[1]

Others have demonstrated how traditional notions of reliability and validity may be established within qualitative studies. For example, Atwood and Hinds[2] applied the evaluative strategies of measurement theory (reliability and validity criteria) to the products of grounded theory. Using a panel method of assigning data to categories, they estimated interrater reliability among judges to demonstrate evidence of reliability and validity.[2]

Lincoln and Guba[3] established criteria for assessing the trustworthiness of qualitative data. The criteria refer to four categories of trustworthiness that correspond to the rationalistic paradigm: (1) truth value (internal validity), (2) applicability (external validity), (3) consistency (reliability), and (4) neutrality (objectivity). Lincoln and Guba suggest strategies for establishing trustworthiness within each of the categories. For example, to establish consistency, the researcher may have an inquiry auditor examine and attest to the extent the process and product of the inquiry are supported by data.[3]

However, convincing others of the trustworthiness of qualitative research findings is further complicated because the researcher using qualitative methods does not work in a linear manner.[4,5] For example, grounded theory is an interactive methodology consisting of simultaneous data collection, coding, analysis, literature review, and hypothesis formation and testing.[6] The constant comparative analysis method of grounded theory requires that the researcher compare each data bit with every other bit. The process can be compared to the interitem analysis conducted in an instrumentation study, whereby the reliability of a measure is estimated by comparing the correlation of each item with every other item of a measure. The computer simplifies the analysis procedure and generates a matrix of interitem correlations and summary statistics from which the researcher may infer meaning. When qualitative methods are employed, the researcher serves as the computer by performing the comparative analysis, storing the information, discovering or inferring meaning as it emerges from the data, and creating summaries of the findings. The critical reader may be unconvinced about the trustworthiness of the research findings unless he or she is presented with sufficient data to draw similar conclusions. While researchers using qualitative methods concur on the necessity of estimating the degree of a study's reliability and validity, or trustworthiness,[1-8] limited information is available on methods the researcher can use to succinctly present sufficient qualitative data to involve others in the verification process. By using matrix analysis, the researcher may address many of the problems of qualitative data analysis.

Matrix analysis is a methodologic tool derived and adapted by this researcher from the data display techniques of Miles and Huberman.[9] The method involves systematically entering raw data into matrices so that the complex steps of conducting qualitative data analysis and verification may be carried out simultaneously. Specifically, matrix analysis may be used to help simplify the analysis of qualitative data, condense findings so that they may be more easily communicated, create an audit trail of how credibility was established, and obtain confidence in the trustworthiness of findings for both the subjects and the contexts with which qualitative methods are used.

This article focuses on the steps of qualitative data analysis that the researcher can achieve by using matrix analysis, the appropriate conditions for using matrix analysis, the procedure for constructing a matrix, the application of matrix analysis to an actual research problem, and the use of matrix analysis in establishing the trustworthiness of findings.

STEPS OF QUALITATIVE DATA ANALYSIS

Miles and Huberman[9] view qualitative data analysis as being composed of three steps: (1) data reduction, (2) data display, and (3) conclusion drawing and verification. Data reduction refers to the process of selecting, focusing, simplifying, and transforming raw data. The step includes the researcher's choices of which data to code, which to extract, and which portions of data yield patterns.[9] Data reduction organizes data into a format that facilitates conclusion drawing and verification.

Data display is a spatial representation that allows the researcher to organize data into a compact form and that establishes the framework for conclusion drawing and verification. The entry of data into a matrix (a gridlike display of rows, columns, and cells) facilitates viewing enormous amounts of data simultaneously and provides a new context, consisting of visual cues, for analyzing the data. The presentation may stimulate the researcher to approach the data in innovative ways. For example, new patterns may become evident when all data are viewed simultaneously.

Conclusion drawing refers to the process of inferring substantive meaning from the data. Conclusions must also be verified, that is, trustworthiness must be established. A major advantage of using matrix analysis is that it permits the researcher to carry out all three steps simultaneously, and thus to perform the nonlinear functions necessary when using qualitative methodologies.

USE OF MATRIX ANALYSIS

Matrix analysis may be used to address a primary research question during the initial phase of data reduction. However, this researcher found it was more useful in the analysis of secondary research questions that emerged during initial data reduction. During the primary phase of data analysis, the researcher's emerging questions may necessitate focusing on secondary research questions such as determining whether an underlying process is similar across subjects, determining similarities and differences of a phenomenon across contexts, closely examining an emerging category or concept in depth, or testing hypotheses about an emerging theory. An important point to remember is that the matrix itself represents an analysis function and depicts the researcher's best hunch or hypothesis of what is happening. Therefore a matrix is a format for addressing issues about the data as they emerge and is not, by itself, a representation of the final conclusion.

Few limitations exist to the variety of research questions that may be addressed by matrix analysis. While most of the examples in this article are from grounded theory, the researcher may easily adapt matrix analysis to other qualitative methods such as ethnography or phenomenology.

CONSTRUCTING A MATRIX

Constructing a matrix is a function of the researcher's own analysis needs and creativity. However, two general steps are necessary in creating any matrix: selecting a format and establishing decision rules.

Selecting a Format

Format selection is a decision about what type of matrix to use and is dependent on a clear statement of the research question and the relationship of the research question to the passage of time. Although many types of matrices exist,[9] the three that may be most useful to nursing research are a descriptive matrix, an outcome-oriented matrix, and a process-oriented matrix.

The descriptive matrix depicts an existing situation and either captures a cross-sectional view of a site at one point in time or allows in-depth analysis of one concept or category as depicted across several subjects. The outcome-oriented matrix focuses on end results and facilitates drawing conclusions about what happened, such as changes that occurred in a specific dependent variable. The process-oriented matrix illustrates the dynamics of change. The focus is on the forces that bring about change, the reasons for change, or the relationships among independent, intervening, and dependent variables. Process-oriented matrices help to draw conclusions about why a particular phenomenon or process occurred.

Decision Rules

Once a decision has been made about the type of matrix that will satisfy the researcher's purpose, decision rules about data entry must be established. Decision rules guide the researcher in deciding what variables to include in the rows and columns of the matrix and how and under what conditions data will be entered into the matrix cells. Decision rules help to clarify the trustworthiness issues that must be addressed. They also help the researcher to work consistently by establishing criteria for addressing each piece of data in the same manner. Because qualitative data analysis takes a long time, it is important that each time the researcher resumes analyzing data, he or she approaches it in exactly the same way. Therefore decision rules must be written down prior to creating the matrix and must be strictly followed.

RESEARCH APPLICATION

Purpose

Matrix analysis was used to analyze emerging research questions from a study of positive health life-style changes. The nation's health statistics reflect an urgent need to address the widespread problem of chronic disease risks attributed to unhealthy life styles.[10] Nursing is concerned with life-style practices that reduce the risk of disease and disability among individuals. Understanding how health behavior is maintained and changed is a necessary first step toward addressing the problem. Much of the nursing research is derived or deduced from psychologic theories such as social learning theory.[11] However, knowledge about life-style change in nursing may be advanced by using alternative theoretic and methodologic approaches. Therefore the purpose of the research was to discover the underlying process individuals experienced while making or sustaining a positive health life-style change. Because discovery of an underlying process was the objective and because this researcher sought a new perspective of the life-style—change problem, grounded theory was the preferred methodology for this exploratory study.

Subjects and Methodology

Seven individuals (with a mean age of 55 years) who were making or sustaining a health life-style change were each interviewed for about 45 minutes. Interviews were loosely structured and focused on the process of life-style change. Four subjects were trying to lose weight and three were trying to quit smoking. Three of the seven subjects were also self-proclaimed recovering alcoholics. One subject had previously quit smoking. The interviews were recorded and transcribed. Phrases relating to the lifestyle-change process were extracted from interview transcriptions and sorted into conceptually similar categories. Categories were labeled and arranged in chronologic order.

Findings

The time-ordered categories represented an emerging theory and depicted the life–style-change process as collectively viewed by the seven informants. Following is a description of the process: An individual, aware of the need and desiring to alter his or her life style, makes one or more attempts to change over time. The attempts result in relapse. A self-monitoring process mediates between awareness of the individual's need to change and his or her relapses in the process of change. At some point tension mounts over the need to change. This tension, labeled "readiness," is characterized by a combination of personal and environmental variables, such as low self-esteem or support from significant others. Following readiness, the individual experiences a profound self-revelation. The revelation is characterized by a dramatic self-insight, a coming to as if shaken by a new understanding of reality. The revelation is followed by a belief system change about personal power, following which the individual makes and sustains a health lifestyle change. An individual who experiences no revelation remains in the initial pattern of attempted change and relapse.

Revelation appeared to be the emerging core variable of the life-style—change process. The following are two descriptions of the revelation process that were extracted from the interview data of two subjects:

I never had any problem at all with alcohol. Very strange things happened, but I never thought those insane things were caused by alcohol. Those funny quirks would go on. So suddenly one day it dawned on me. I had a beer in my hand. I had the flu, I thought . . . the doctor told me I had the flu . . . but he told my wife it was alcohol. I had many hours at home from work and—it suddenly hit me—*that I didn't like me anymore.*

It's so subtle . . . but when it happens it's like the 4th of July, the fireworks . . . it's everything that comes together, and all of a sudden you switch one side of the magnetic pole and things are pulled together. It's just that subtle. I can't say that one particular thing had to do with it. I can't pinpoint it.

Matrix Analysis

This researcher used matrix analysis to test and to confirm conclusions about the emergent theory of life-style change, that is, to clarify categories and emerging concepts, and to examine the life-style-change process among subjects both individually and collectively. The secondary research question that emerged from the data and was examined using matrix analysis was: What variables, critical incidents, processes, individuals, stressors, or forces propelled the life-style—change process forward for each subject?

The question reflects the need to explore the dynamics of change. Therefore a process-oriented matrix was selected for the format. Following format selection, decision rules were established about the variables to be included in the matrix columns and rows. This researcher was interested in exploring change within and between subjects. Both process and subjects needed to be viewed simultaneously. Therefore each stage of the change process was represented by a matrix column, while each subject was represented by a row. A reduced version of the original matrix appears in the Appendix. To better grasp the change process for each subject, each health life-style change made by a subject was identified by subdividing rows. For example, the row for subject 2 was subdivided into three smaller rows. Each subrow represented one life-style change made by subject 2. Subject 2 made three lifestyle changes: weight reduction, alcohol abstinence, and smoking cessation. The first subrow for subject 2 represented the most recent or current change and was identified by an asterisk. The same procedure was used to identify the life-style changes of the remaining subjects. For the total sample this resulted in four examples of smoking cessation, four of weight reduction, and three of alcohol abstinence. An additional column was added to the far right of the matrix to allow the researcher to make predictions, based on findings, about the subjects' anticipated future behavior.

Cell entries consisted of condensed data bits (obtained from the coded transcriptions) that specifically referred to the change process that each subject experienced for each health life-style change. Perhaps the researcher's most important decision rule was that each data bit would be assigned to only one cell. Data that did not fit or that fit into more than one cell were examined for alternative theoretic explanations and spurious relationships. No data were discarded. The original matrix contained excerpts from all data bits that reflected any new ideas or information. The reduced matrix in the Appendix presents summaries of the data bits that were entered into the matrix cells.

Findings and Discussion

The completed matrix made it easy for the researcher to visualize and to conclude that all subjects fit within the life-style—change context. Closer analysis of the matrix involved comparing the matrix rows (life-style change process) and columns (autonomous categories) across subjects. The researcher must remain open to discovering similarities, differences, and emerging patterns in the data. For example, subjects 1, 2, 3, and 4 represented the individuals who were trying to lose weight. By examining the matrix, this researcher observed that subjects 1, 2, and 4 had experienced revelations about overeating:

Subject 1. I can use my power with God's to conquer the demon overeating.
Subject 2. If that woman can do it, so can I.
Subject 4. All of a sudden everything was pulled together; I realized I can control my life.

The revelation was followed by a belief system change:

Subject 1. I have strength in working with God. This gives me power.
Subject 2. I don't need to eat to be happy.
Subject 4. Food controlled me. Now I can control it. I can ask my inner power and God for strength and help. Help from others is okay.

The behavioral outcome for these individuals was weight losses of 60 to 75 lbs that had been sustained for 4.5 months to 1 year. In addition, the three individuals expressed confidence in continued success. The third subject had experienced no revelation and no success in weight loss.

When all of the data were displayed in matrix form, patterns that might otherwise have been overlooked seemed to become obvious. Two examples follow and illustrate how subjects repeatedly described a phenomenon in a consistent but unexpected manner and how empty cells attracted attention.

During initial data reduction the researcher hypothesized that a belief-system change occurred that enabled the individual to make a life-style change. The researcher assumed that this was a health-belief change. Data in the belief-system—change column illustrated a contradiction to the assumption. In all cases in which a belief-system change occurred, the change was one of personal empowerment. Beliefs about self, not health, moved the process forward to a behavioral change. The researcher might have overlooked this finding had the matrix not been used.

The decision rule that specified that data fit into only one cell led to another finding. The researcher repeatedly had difficulty deciding whether data belonged in the revelation column or in the belief-system—change column. These two categories seemed to have some similarities. Perhaps revelation and belief-system change were part of the same phenomenon, with self-empowerment actually indexing revelation. The finding identified the need to obtain a greater degree of conceptual clarity between these two emerging categories.

The life-style—change process of the smokers was examined in a manner similar to that of the overeaters. Subjects 5 and 7 had experienced revelations but not with respect to smoking. Their revelations were related to their alcohol consumption habits. Examination of the matrix revealed that subjects 5 and 7 also experienced revelations followed by belief-system changes about self-empowerment. Their belief-system changes were followed by successful life-style changes (ie, abstaining from alcohol for 3 and 6 years, respectively). Subject 6 experienced no revelation and no sustained success in smoking cessation.

When the data were entered into the matrix, an interesting finding emerged. The smokers had not experienced revelations, nor had they successfully stopped smoking. Subject 2 was the one exception to this finding. Examining the three subrows assigned to subject 2 revealed the following: Revelation had not preceded the individual's smoking cessation, and the revelation that occurred with weight reduction had a less intense quality to it than the revelations experienced by other subjects. However, the revelation that was related to alcohol consumption seemed to be so great that it either reinforced subsequent behaviors that resulted in successful life-style change or else subject 2 applied learning from altering the alcohol-related behavior to both smoking and weight reduction. Consequently a conclusion was made that revelation may influence subsequent life-style changes through reinforcement or learning.

To summarize these findings, five out of seven subjects had experienced a revelation. The two who had not experienced a revelation also failed to make the desired life-style change. The most remarkable finding was that when revelation had occurred, each subject subsequently encountered, first, a belief-system change about self-empowerment and, second, a successful life-style change outcome. There were no exceptions to this finding. Therefore in answer to the research question about what propelled the change process forward, the conclusion was drawn that revelation had an impact on subsequent success in making and sustaining life-style changes among study subjects.

In addition to the initial findings, new questions emerged during matrix analysis that were addressed in subsequent research.[12] While space does not permit a full description of the research that followed, the emergent questions are briefly summarized. First, regarding the relapses of the smokers, subsequent research revealed that smokers also experienced the revelation process.[12] Second, peers reviewing the matrix challenged the finding that individuals had to experience relapse before achieving a successful life-style change outcome. A subsequent quantitative study revealed that individuals who had made successful life-style changes had made a mean of four previous attempts at change prior to experiencing success.[12] Third, the findings from the process-oriented matrix suggested that a more in-depth understanding of the readiness concept was necessary. Data in the readiness column supported the conceptualization of readiness as consisting of several variables acting together. The emerging research question was: What is the nature of readiness? An in-depth analysis of the readiness category was performed using a descriptive matrix that helped the researcher analyze readiness across subjects at one point in time. The analysis of the data in the readiness column facilitated the identification of nine variables that appeared to be components of readiness. These were (1) social support from significant others, (2) social support from groups, (3) isolation, (4) low self-esteem, (5) despair, (6) concern over the impact of behavior on significant others (influence on others), (7) health concerns, (8) loss of control, and (9) chance.

The life-style—change process identified in this research represents the ground work for the development of theory that describes how individuals make and sustain positive health life-style changes. Current research focuses on obtaining conceptual clarity between revelation and belief-system change and operationally defining readiness and revelation.[12] Once the theory is more accurately specified, the full theoretic model will be tested. The emergent theory has implications for nursing practice. For example, nurses may need to reconceptualize their understanding of relapse behavior. In addition, the readiness variables reflect areas for nursing intervention that may promote the occurrence of a revelation, such as mobilizing or becoming a social support system for the individual. This new research endeavor may entail traveling many paths of inquiry.

ESTABLISHING TRUSTWORTHINESS

Matrix analysis is not a panacea for addressing all questions of reliability and validity. Reliability and validity analysis must still be superimposed on matrix analysis, as is the case in using other data reduction techniques. Lincoln and Guba's[3] criteria for assessing the trustworthiness of findings from qualitative data are useful for identifying the relationship between matrix analysis and the assessment of reliability and validity. The operationalized criteria include credibility (internal validity), transferability (external validity), dependability (reliability), and confirmability (objectivity).[3] Following is a brief discussion of how the researcher may use matrix analysis to help satisfy the criteria.

Credibility

Credibility deals with establishing confidence in the findings for both subjects and the contexts in which the inquiry is conducted.[3] Using matrix analysis, the researcher can display and analyze the subjects and contexts simultaneously. Three examples of how a matrix may be used to establish credibility follow. First, the researcher may compare a matrix with cell entries consisting of interview data to a matrix with cells containing data from memos or field notes. Comparison of the two matrices constitutes a form of triangulation or the analysis of multiple sources of information. Second, negative case analysis, or the process of accounting for all known cases without exception,[3] can be addressed by making a decision rule that all data must fit the matrix. Since the matrix is similar to the researcher's hypothesis about an existing situation, misfitting data may illustrate a disproved hypothesis, and the researcher must consider alternative explanations. Third, a matrix is an organization of data in a format that may be easily evaluated by others. Therefore matrices may be presented to other members of the research team, expert judges, or original subjects to test categories, interpretations, and conclusions.

Transferability

Transferability refers to the degree to which findings in one context may hold true or be applied to other subjects or contexts.[3] Because so much data can be displayed and analyzed simultaneously, matrix analysis is well suited for cross-site and between-subject comparisons. Data that do not fit the matrix or the occurrence of empty cells represent questions about transferability. In the life-style—change study, transferability was demonstrated between subjects. Although the sample size was inadequate for analyzing life-style change across contexts, the absence of the revelation experience among smokers emerged as a transferability issue that future research must address.

Dependability

Dependability refers to achieving the same or similar findings in inquiries that are repeated with the same or similar subjects in the same or similar context.[3] As with transferability, observations comparing subjects, contexts, or observations from other investigators can be displayed in matrix form, thus simplifying the analysis process. For example (within the same matrix), a replicated study can be compared with the original study. The researcher can detect variations between the two studies and can precisely identify where variations occurred.

Confirmability

Confirmability refers to the degree to which the investigator's bias, motivation, interest, and perspective influence the interpretation of findings.[3] Even though matrix analysis creates an audit trail of the investigator's decision-making process, the researcher's personal bias can still threaten the initial processes of reducing, coding, categorizing, labeling, and interpreting data. During matrix analysis, bias may affect decisions about which data bits to enter in the matrix cells, or the researcher may be tempted to justify the squeeze and fit of all data into the existing cells. While matrix analysis may help the researcher to account for decisions that are made, it is not a substitute for other methods such as triangulation, the use of colleagues and expert judges to confirm findings, or replication of studies with other subjects and contexts.

Matrix analysis is a methodologic tool for addressing specific research questions, for providing a structure for systematic and consistent analysis of qualitative data, for analyzing the fit of emerging research findings, for testing hypotheses, for documenting decision-making processes, and for concisely communicating findings to others. The researcher using matrix analysis has flexibility in producing matrices so that a variety of research questions may be depicted and analyzed in matrix format. In addition, matrix analysis may prove useful as the researcher addresses issues that focus on the trustworthiness of findings.

REFERENCES

1. Knafl AK, Howard MJ. Interpreting and reporting qualitative research. *Res Nurs Health.* 1984;7:17–24.
2. Atwood JR, Hinds P. Heuristic heresy: application of reliability and validity criteria to products of grounded theory. *West J Nurs Res.* 1986;8:135–147.
3. Lincoln YS, Guba EG. *Naturalistic Inquiry.* Beverly Hills, Calif: Sage; 1985.
4. Stern PN. Grounded theory methodology: its uses and processes. *Image.* 1980;12:20–23.
5. Chenitz WC, Swanson JM. *From Practice to Grounded Theory.* Menlo Park, Calif: Addison-Wesley; 1986.
6. Glaser B, Strauss A. *The Discovery of Grounded Theory.* New York, NY: Aldine; 1986.
7. Wilson H. Qualitative studies: from observations to explanations. *J Nurs Adm.* 1985;15(5):8–10.
8. Aamodt AM. Problems in doing research: developing criteria for evaluating qualitative research. *West J Nurs Res.* 1983;5:398–401.
9. Miles MB, Huberman AM. *Qualitative Data Analysis: A Sourcebook of New Methods.* Beverly Hills, Calif: Sage; 1984.
10. National Center for Health Statistics. *Health United States.* 1985. Washington, DC: Government Printing Office, US Dept of Health and Human Services publication No. (PHS) 86–1232.
11. Rotter JB, Crance JE, Phares EJ. *Applications of Social Learning Theory to Personality.* New York, NY: Holt, Rinehart, and Winston; 1972.
12. Marsh GW. *The Development of Instruments to Measure Concepts in the Revelation Readiness Model of Lifestyle Change.* Tucson, Ariz: University of Arizona Press; 1989. Dissertation.

Appendix
Process-oriented Matrix of Life-style Change

Subject no.	Life-style change	Problem awareness	Relapse	Readiness
1	Overeating*	In 8th grade, I was conscious of being overweight I need to do something for myself	I have no time to care for I have character defects I didn't want to commit and fail	My husband was supportive I got friend to go to meeting with me People at group were honest I want to live Success of others in group was inspirational
2	Overeating*	I feel uncomfortable and short of breath	I tried all new diets My spouse supported my failure, both have poor will power	I got help from spouse I got help from group
	Alcohol	None	None	I got support from spouse I have low self-esteem I got group support—I went willingly, with no expectations
	Smoking	I have a bad cough	I made two failed attempts	My father's health was bad I had a bad cough I really wanted to quit
3	Overeating*	Eating is a sin—I love it, I hate it At a group I was obsessive/compulsive over food	I had many, many failures Food controls me, I have little control I tried groups; I like the support but can't keep with it	I have low self-esteem I am concerned for my child Group gives me hope and strength I have been depressed, I hate my life When I'm okay, everything else is
4	Overeating*	I was a fat slob and an introvert since I was a small child	I wanted a magic cure with no responsibility	I felt depressed and suicidal I have low life satisfaction I'm a miserable, hurting person not in touch with self

Appendix
Process-oriented Matrix of life-style change

Revelation	Belief-system change	Behavioral outcome	Predicted future outcome
I can use my power along with God's power to conquer demon, overeating	I have strength in working with God; this gives me power and I can use it	60-lb weight loss sustained for 4.5 months, confident of continued success	Will sustain
I realized, if that woman can do it, so can I	I no longer need to eat to be happy	75-lb weight loss sustained over 1 year	Will sustain
It suddenly hit "I didn't like *me* any more"	I have personal power I find support in group	Alcohol abstinence	Will sustain
None	I can do it by myself (strength from alcohol problem)	Sustained smoking cessation for several years	Will sustain
None	None	Repeated relapses	Escalation of readiness
I realized I can control my life and it's okay to seek guidance from others "All of a sudden everything was pulled together"	Asked my higher power for strength and help (higher power = God = inner self) Food controlled me, now I can control it. I'm proud of me	Sustained 65-lb loss 8 months Still needs group support, seeks reinforcement from others	Success if group support continued

Subject no.	Life-style change	Problem awareness	Relapse	Readiness
5	Smoking*	I was tired of it It was a hassle	I have no one to share problem with, no pats on back, no group support I'm a failure	I have low self-esteem I joined group from fear of death I felt group inspira-tion, I'm not alone I'm joining groups to meet people in similar situation
	Alcohol	I was sneaking I was hiding problem from family	None	I feel concern and love from little sister
6	Smoking*	I was thinking about change I feel scared, angry I need a focus My body and health are changing It's filthy I'm ambivalent	I made it convenient I quit in past, started again I want others to help	I am grasping a focus, letting others know once you start you need to keep going
7	Smoking*	It's expensive It's filthy I risk getting cancer of the mouth	I've made many attempts I'm angry I don't want to give it up	I want group help Support of my son helps I'm concerned for effect of my smoking on my granddaughter and son
	Alcohol	I was hiding bottles I was a closet drinker	I tried quitting for 6 years	I have low self-esteem

*Change currently being made.

Revelation	Belief-system change	Behavioral outcome	Predicted future outcome
None	None	Never got the group support sought Another relapse	Success with right group
I was shaken by my little sister's concern I suddenly knew I needed help	I want help at any cost Group support will help; joined group 3–4 years old I'm making written commitment	Reformed alcoholic no backsliding 3 years of sustained change	Will sustain
None	None	Smoking cessation for 4 days Has not told family or friends, is afraid of failure	Relapse
None	None	Relapse	Continued relapse
I realized no one could do it for me. I could do it by myself	I only have myself to blame I'm the only one who can do anything about it	Alcohol abstinence 6 years	Will sustain

Toward a Nursing Theory of Self-Transcendence: Deductive Reformulation Using Developmental Theories

The purpose of this article is to explicate the development of an emerging middle-range nursing theory of self-transcendence. The process of developing the theory was based largely on the method of "deductive reformulation." Using this strategy, theoretic knowledge derived from life span developmental psychology was reformulated based on Rogers' conceptual system. Clinical experience and empirical investigations were also important in the theory development process. The theory of self-transcendence is potentially useful for application in various nursing settings where clients' well-being my be compromised by end-of life issues.

Pamela G. Reed, RN, PhD
Associate Professor
College of Nursing
The University of Arizona
Tucson, Arizona

AS RECENTLY AS 1975, therapeutic approaches for the mental health of adults did not account for the developmental differences now known to exist throughout adulthood. In contrast, an understanding of developmental phenomena was considered critical in addressing problems of early life. There is a distinct need for theories about developmental phenomena as related to well-being in later life phases. The life span movement within developmental psychology, coupled with the rich heritage of knowledge in the nursing conceptual models, provided the opportunity to undertake construction of a nursing theory that links mental health at the end of life with a developmental phenomenon, namely self-transcendence. Self-transcendence refers broadly to a characteristic of developmental maturity whereby there is an expansion of self-boundaries and an orientation toward broadened life perspectives and purposes.

This little-studied phenomenon is significant to well-being for those facing end-of-life issues, whether through aging, terminal illness, or other experiences. This

Adv Nurs Sci 1991; 13(4):64–77

article explicates the development of an emerging middle-range nursing theory of self-transcendence.

Middle-range theory, the boundaries of which are neither too broad nor too narrow,[1] is particularly suited for enhancing understanding about a particular phenomenon for utilization in nursing practice. Middle-range theory is specific enough to have meaning in the clinical context, yet general enough to allow the nurse to integrate other ways of knowing in applying the scientific theory.

The process of developing the theory of self-transcendence was based largely on the method of "deductive reformulation."[2,3] Deductive reformulation is a strategy for constructing middle-range theory whereby existing knowledge, derived from nonnursing theory on the phenomenon of interest, is reformulated using knowledge obtained deductively from a nursing conceptual model. The aim was to build a nursing theory that incorporated extant knowledge in life span developmental psychology in a manner congruent with the unique perspective of nursing. Life span theories on adult social-cognitive and transpersonal development were the primary sources of theory derivation. A synthesis of life span theories was used, as no one theory was considered adequate for the derivation. Martha Rogers's conceptual system provided the nursing perspective of human development for reformulating knowledge about self-transcendence derived from the life span theories. In addition to these theoretic sources of knowledge, clinical experience and empirical work were important sources of knowledge at different steps of the theory development process.

CLINICAL SOURCES OF KNOWLEDGE: LINKING HUMAN DEVELOPMENT AND MENTAL HEALTH

The theoretic idea about the significance of developmental phenomena in general to the mental health of individuals at the end of life had its inception in successful clinical encounters with individuals at the beginning of life, children and adolescents. Mental health problems of young clients were approached from a developmental framework constructed by Fagin[4] that integrated interpersonal, psychoanalytic, and cognitive theories of development. This framework outlined the developmental tasks of each phase of life through late adolescence and the developmental tools normally available to a child to meet the challenges of each life phase.

A major assumption of Fagin's framework was that the mental health of a child is linked to salient developmental issues of his or her given phase of life. Problems in development were reflected in the child's mental health status, and solutions resided in part in understanding the client's developmental profile. Assessing developmental strengths and deficits was prerequisite to planning intervention strategies, which were aimed toward exploiting the child's developmental potential. Thus knowledge gained through clinical practice with children sensitized one to the potential significance of developmental issues in mental health at other phases of life. Subsequent clinical experiences with young, middle, and older adults reinforced this understanding.

THEORETIC SOURCES OF KNOWLEDGE: LIFE SPAN DEVELOPMENT AND LATER LIFE

The life span perspective of psychological development came into being in the early 1970s and challenged long-held views about adult development and aging.[5] These biologically based views of human development depicted aging as a decremental process in which physical decline was assumed to cause concomitant, inevitable decline in psychosocial competence. Assumptions about aging were modeled after the second law of thermodynamics, which identified the tendency of matter to decay toward disorder and equilibrium. Older adults were regarded generally as closed systems who, having reached their zenith much earlier in life, were running out of energy and becoming increasingly disordered to the point of debilitation and death. A paradigm shift occurred in adult developmental theory—later reinforced by Prigogine's[6,7] theory of dissipative structures—whereby mechanistic views of aging were supplanted with a world view in which living systems were conceptualized as open, self-organizing, and thriving on disequilibrium, creating "order out of chaos."

Development came to be more clearly understood as a lifelong, nonlinear process of increasing complexity and integration, as Werner[8] and others had explained in the 1950s. Development was not a linear process of accretion and loss but rather a nonlinear process of transforming the old and integrating the new. Thus the change in world view about human development set the stage for increased efforts to identify developmental issues relevant to health that characterize later phases of development.[9] Late adulthood, like early childhood or other phases, was regarded as possessing a repertoire of challenges and resources.

SELF-TRANSCENDENCE: A CONCEPT DERIVED FROM LIFE SPAN THEORIES

One particular resource of later life is the propensity toward transcendence of boundaries posed by the immediate situation, by physical limitations, or by constricted perspectives of life and self. This idea was derived largely from empirically based life span developmental theories on social-cognitive development in later life, which extended Piaget's developmental framework on reasoning.[10–13] It was commonly understood that development entailed movement from concrete thinking to abstract and symbolic thought, known as "formal operations."[14] However, research in the past decade has revealed another level of reasoning ability that characterizes developmental maturity in adults, referred to as "postformal" thought,[15,16] a unique form of reasoning in later life reflective of a self-transcendent perspective. In contrast to formal logic, which is essentially a hypothetic-deductive approach to solving abstract problems, postformal thought is a more encompassing form of logic that applies to real-life experiences of a social, personal, and moral nature.[10,17] In postformal thought, objective, externally oriented logic gives way to a relativistic, interdependent mode of thought. Thinking patterns transcend a purely scientific approach; the individual is able to confront existential concerns and metaphysical issues and synthesize the paradoxic and conflicting elements of life. Postformal reasoning enables the person to step beyond the concrete aspects of an event to derive meaning from that event. Wisdom draws in part from a broadened view of time in which past experience and anticipation of the future provide perspective on the present. Life perspectives are pragmatic yet visionary. Postformal thought emerges in adulthood and particularly in later adulthood.

Transpersonal theorists also have explicated a criterion of developmental maturity respective of self-transcendent perspectives. This criterion extends beyond achievement of "self-identity" as the developmental goal to include an interdependent self-definition based on a strengthened sense of identity with the greater environment.[18,19] Mature development in later adulthood is characterized by ego transcendence and body transcendence (ie, the capacity to transcend a preoccupation with the self in general and with the physical body despite increasing problems).[20-22] Thus social-cognitive and transpersonal theories on developmental maturity in later adulthood provided a basis for deriving ideas about self-transcendence as a developmental pattern at the end of life.

SELF-TRANSCENDENCE: A THEME IN PSYCHOSOCIAL AND NURSING THEORIES

Other theorists have given specific attention to self-transcendence as an important, if not pivotal, theme in the human process. Erikson explained that mature individuals transcend personal interests and need to be needed.[23] He recently extended his "generativity" phase by 20 years into late adulthood. Lifton described a basic human press for self-transcendence directed toward gaining a sense of continuity and vital participation in the larger human process when faced with the end of one's life.[24] Creative work, children, religious beliefs, an identification with nature, and mystical experiences were identified as five modes of transcendence for expanding self-boundaries. Similarly, Frankl[25] proposed that people make meaning through three modes of self-transcendence: by contributing to the world, by being receptive to others, and by accepting inevitable life events. Allport[26] proposed that extension of self beyond one's immediate needs and duties was a key characteristic of the mature personality.

The theme of self-transcendence is evident in nursing theories as well. Parse[27] defined health in part as a process of transcending with the possibles, similar to one of Maslow's definitions of transcendence as a "rising to the realm of the possible as well as of the actual."[28(p60)] Watson's[29] theory of human care is based on a view of person as having the capacity to transcend time and self-interests through intrapersonal and interpersonal experiences. In Newman's[30] theory on health as expansion of consciousness, transcendence of temporal and ego boundaries is integral to achieving maturity and expansion of one's consciousness.

These theorists may offer somewhat competing explanations of the underlying dynamics of self-transcendence. Taken collectively, however, they represent a rich and unifying perspective on the potential significance of self-transcendence. Psychosocial and nursing theories provided conceptual support for deriving ideas about self-transcendence from life span developmental theories to construct the nursing theory.

THE NURSING PERSPECTIVE: BASIS OF REFORMULATION

Theoretic knowledge derived from the life span developmental theories was reformulated based on knowledge deduced from Rogers' conceptual system.[31-33] In many respects, the life span development perspective is congruent with the nursing perspective of human beings. In other areas there are important differences. The reformulation process entailed (1) determining general areas of congruence in understandings about human development between the two theoretic systems,(2) delineating specific differences between the two systems to further clarify the emerging theory, and (3) specifying the major elements of the emerging theory.

Theoretic Parallels: Identifying Basic Assumptions of the New Theory

Rogers[31] clarified nursing's perspective of development as an open system process in which change did not obey the second law of thermodynamics. In doing so, she generated an optimistic view of aging that contrasted with the decremental view that prevailed when her first book was published. Rogers' assumptions about human development as outlined in her three principles of homeodynamics[32,33] are paralleled by key principles of the life span developmental framework. Points of convergence among these principles marked basic theoretic assumptions about the nature, characteristics, and mechanism of human development.

Rogers' *principle of integrality* identifies the nature of development in terms of a mutuality of human and environmental processes.[33] Congruent with this is the life span developmental view that change is a function of both human and contextual factors. This contextual view is a departure from the traditional emphasis on epigenesis (an unfolding from within the organism) as the primary impetus for development. Environmental processes, such as those related to "history-graded" and "nonnormative" events, are no less important and likely are more important in advanced development than biologically based processes (called "normative age-graded events") originating within the organism.[34] Moreover, the conflict or disequilibrium inherent in this process between person and environment is viewed as fundamental to developmental progress.[31,35]

Rogers' *principle of helicy* characterizes human development as innovative and unpredictable.[33] Innovative change is possible throughout the life span; there is no "prime of life" per se. Developmental phases in life are not linearly related in terms of being better or worse than another. Rather, the innovativeness gives rise to developmental phases that are qualitatively different. The helicy principle is reinforced by life span developmentalists' findings on the "plasticity" of the older adult, referring to a capacity for intraindividual variability that is often productive within the given context.[36] This variability is particularly evident in later phases of life, whereby older adults as individuals and as a group display increased diversity and unpredictability.

Rogers' homeodynamic *principle of resonancy* describes the mechanism of human development, which is based on a process of movement from "lower to higher frequency wave patterns."[33(p8)] Werner's "orthogenetic principle" parallels Rogers' principle of resonancy in depicting development as a process characterized by rhythm and pattern.[8] According to the orthogenetic principle, developmental change in a structure occurs by an organized, irreversible process of movement from lower to higher levels of organization as the structure becomes increasingly complex. "Higher" does not necessarily mean "better"; it simply refers to the degree of articulation (or organization) among the elements of the system needed for development, given a certain level of complexity. For example, as complexity in life increases, higher levels of organization are needed to accommodate the increasing complexity in a way that supports continued development, lest decremental or chaotic change occur. Lower levels of organization are appropriate for lower levels of complexity in earlier phases of development. Organization or pattern exists at all levels of development and identifies the structure.

Development entails a "nonlinear (or hierarchical) organization"[8(p126)] whereby less developed patterns are subordinated by or traded away for more highly developed patterns that are then integrated into the structure. Through this rhythmic process, new patterns of higher levels of organization emerge that are more appropriate and productive in the current context. When the rhythm of this process is inhibited—as, for example, through a failure to trade away outdated patterns for new—developmental progress may be compromised.[37] Thus distinct life perspectives of mature development entail a transformation of formal reasoning and focus on self-identification into a postformal approach to reasoning about oneself and the world. Self-transcendence, then, was assumed to be a manifestation of a new human pattern representative of a level of organization appropriate for contexts of increased complexity (eg, later adulthood).

Key Theoretic Assumption: Conceptual Boundaries of the Self

A cornerstone of the emerging theory on self-transcendence, deduced from Rogers' conceptual system and influenced by life span theories and clinical experiences, was based on the idea of conceptual boundaries of the self that define the human field. Specifically, there was the assumption that human beings, as open systems, impose conceptual boundaries on their openness to define their reality and provide a sense of wholeness and connectedness within themselves and their environment. The "human field is characterized by continuously fluctuating imaginary boundaries."[32(pp331,332)] These conceptual boundaries may or may not correspond with concrete experience. For example, through one's perspectives about death, reaching out to others, actualizing one's potential, or learning to live with a debilitating illness, a person can step beyond and redefine traditional spatial-temporal boundaries of the "physical body."

Rogers' description of human development included the idea that the human field "extends beyond the discernible mass perceived of as the human being . . . at times extending farther into the environment and at other times retreating toward the person's visible core."[31(p90)] Although Rogers has emphasized that the human and environmental fields are infinite and have no real boundaries, conceptual boundaries of the self can be regarded as an artifact of the human process of organizing experience within a multidimensional reality.[38] The potential importance of the person's conceptual boundaries is conveyed through two fundamental questions for inquiry posed by Rogers: "Where do individuals perceive their boundaries to be?" and "In what ways and under what conditions do these boundaries vary?"[31(p113)] In general, conceptual boundaries of the self vary in form across development, from the self-diffuseness of newborns, the self-consciousness of youth, and the self-identity of adulthood to the self-transcendence of maturity.[22,23,39,40] It was assumed, then, that conceptual boundaries of the self are relevant to human health and development. Self-transcendence was identified as one important indicator of this abstract concept.

Areas of Incongruence: Clarifying Elements of the Emerging Theory

A particularly useful step in developing the theory entailed examination of areas of incongruence between Rogers' system and the life span developmental system. These areas represented critical junctures for reformulation. Three major areas were identified:

1. The multidimensionality of conceptual boundaries;
2. The developmental context of self-transcendence; and
3. Health as the correlate of interest.

Decisions made regarding these incongruencies reflect the uniqueness of nursing theories about developmental phenomena. Reformulations led to a more specific definition of the concept of self-transcendence and to identification of the major boundaries and propositions of the new theory.

The multidimensionality of conceptual boundaries: defining self-transcendence

A pattern of fluctuations in conceptual boundaries of the self is generally evident ontogenetically across the life span as a whole (ie, from concrete to more abstract self-boundaries). However, how conceptual boundaries may be specifically manifested in later life is a point of incongruence between the life span developmental theory and Rogers' theoretic system. Developmental theories of aging do not reflect the diversity of pattern in conceptual boundaries at the end of life that can be deduced from Rogers' concept of multidimensionality (originally named "four-dimensionality"), in which the perception of reality transcends spatial and temporal boundaries.[32,33] In developmental theories, conceptual boundaries generally are presented as fluctuating unidirectionally in later adulthood; that is, the self-boundary either expands from an egocentric stance toward a self-beyond-the-self perspective[20,41] or contracts toward an inner self focus.[21,39] In contrast, deductions from Rogers' model suggest that the conceptual boundaries of the self are multidimensional, particularly in developmental phases of increased complexity.

Reformulation based on Rogers' system then led to a clarification of the definition of self-transcendence as expansion of self-boundaries multidimensionally: inwardly (eg, through introspective experiences), outwardly (eg, by reaching out to others), and temporally (whereby past and future are integrated into the present).[42] Further, self-transcendence was distinguished from meanings that implied detachment of self from others. Rather, the term referred to a transcendence of less complex (and more concrete) conceptual boundaries of the self that dichotomize person and environment, body and soul, past and present, conflict and solution, knower and known.

The developmental context of self-transcendence: identifying a boundary of the theory

With few exceptions, developmental phenomena are typically regarded in psychology as occurring longitudinally over a period of years, preferably decades, linearly spanning the individual's life (ie, ontogenesis). Ontogenesis is studied predominantly from one of two focuses: normative events related to changes in chronologic age and normative events associated with historical change.[34] However, the nature of nursing is such that knowledge is needed also and perhaps primarily in reference to "microgenesis"[8(p143)] (ie, developmental phenomena that occur within a time period of months, days, weeks, and even hours, minutes, seconds—as within a "relative present").[32]

Microgenesis, which is sometimes quite dramatic, occurs within the context of nonnormative (unexpected) as well as normative events, particularly health-related events frequently encountered in nursing. Examples of health events include timely and untimely death and birth, loss, illness, and other health-related crises. Thus development is not necessarily associated with chronologic age, a marker of linear time. It is instead the life event, the "dialectical moment"[12] that is the context of development. Given this, the idea of self-transcendence as a healthy characteristic only of advanced age was reformulated to clarify self-transcendence as a pattern associated with advanced development that can occur in the context of a significant life event. In particular, life experiences that increase awareness of personal mortality—that one's life as is commonly understood will end some-day—were identified as the developmentally maturing context.

The perspective of microgenesis, then, was translated into a consideration of end-of-own-life experiences rather than age per se as a developmental context of self-transcendence. This reformulation was supported by several who associated death involvement with developmental maturity and self-transcendence, regard-less of age.[23,27,43,44] Thus the major "boundary-determining criterion"[45] of the theory was identified in terms of persons currently dealing with end-of-own-life events. Experiences of terminal illness, life-threatening events, chronic illness, suicidal ideation, and the aging process represent potential domains within that boundary.

Making the health connection: identifying a proposition of the theory

The study of human phenomena among psychologists is done primarily as it relates to the development and function of certain cognitive, social, or personality structures over the life span.[34,46] Questions posed about developmental phenomena within Rogers' conceptual system are studied for the distinct purposes of gaining understanding of the life process of human beings and acquiring knowledge about phenomena as they relate to human health and well-being. Within this nursing perspective then, a primary focus on developmental phenomena was reformulated to incorporate the link to health and well-being.

The relationship of a person's conceptual boundaries to well-being, particularly in terms of mental health, has been recognized clinically. Clinical terminology exists to describe the pathologic conditions that can occur when conceptual boundaries are ill defined, too expansive, or too restrictive for a given phase of development (eg, autism, symbiosis, narcissism, paranoia, egocentricity, with-drawal). There are also terms that imply healthy conceptions of one's self bounda-ries at given phases of development (eg, object constancy, individuation, empa-thy, generativity). Thus a major proposition of the theory was that conceptual boundaries were related to well-being. Specifically, it was proposed that self-tran-scendence, as representative of a conceptual boundary, is positively related to mental health as an indicator of overall well-being in persons confronted with end-of-own-life issues.

Specification of the Emerging Theory

Assumptions about the nature, characteristics, and mechanism of development underlying the theory were identified, based on a convergence of principles of human development from life span developmental psychology and Rogers' con-ceptual system. In addition, a corner stone of the theory dealt with self-boundaries that are constructed by human beings and characterize the human field. It was theorized broadly that there is a relationship between the fluctuations of conceptual boundaries and well-being over the life span. Distinct patterns of conceptual boundaries of the self are evident over development. Life events that increase the person's awareness of the end of life, such as terminal illness and aging, were conceptualized as a context of development during which an expanded self-boundary may occur. This context was identified as the major boundary of the theory.

Self-transcendence was identified as a particular pattern of expansion of conceptual boundaries. It was theorized that expansion of conceptual boundaries through intrapersonal, interpersonal, and temporal experiences was developmentally appropriate in individuals confronted with end-of-own-life issues. Secondly, it was theorized that expansion of self-boundaries was positively related to indicators of well-being in these individuals. Fig 1 summarizes the key steps in developing the theory.

Empirical Sources of Knowledge: The Double Helix

The linkage between research and theorizing is critical to theory development. Although much theorizing preceded empirical investigation, the research process, including instrument development necessitated by the uncharted focus of the theory, played a key role in the emerging theory. Two "strategic propositions," which are propositions put forth to test the theory,[45] were identified:

1. Self-transcendence is greater in persons facing end-of-own-life issues than in individuals not confronted with such issues.
2. Self-transcendence is positively related to indicators of well-being in persons facing end-of-own-life issues.

Collateral sets of studies were undertaken to examine the propositions. Examining the first proposition tested the boundary of the theory, one of the most important empirical tests of a theory.[45] In addition, specification of the boundary of the theory was important in ensuring "comparability across studies"[45(p134)]; in other words, participants in both series of studies were selected because they were representative of persons currently facing end-of-own-life issues.

Spiritual self-transcendence studies

The first set of studies focused on spiritual perspective, as one manifestation of self-transcendence during end-of-own-life events. Spiritual perspective was defined in terms of a sense of relatedness to a dimension greater than the self without devaluing the individual. Spiritual perspective represented one meaningful way of expanding personal boundaries multidimensionally through such experiences as prayer, meditation, forgiveness, and belief in a transcendent dimension or being. The Spiritual Perspective Scale was developed to measure these indicators. Two studies were conducted in which the significance of spiritual perspective at the end of life was examined.[47,48] The first involved 114 ambulatory adults from a large

Life-span theories
  Social-cognitive and transpersonal development
  Psychosocial and nursing theories
Clinical practice

Martha Rogers's conceptual system

Assumptions:
  On the nature, characteristics, and mechanism of developmental phenomena
  On construction and fluctuation of conceptual boundaries over development
  Self-transcendence is a pattern of expansion of conceptual boundaries
  Microgenesis, applied in terms of end-of-own-life experiences comprising a developmentally maturing context

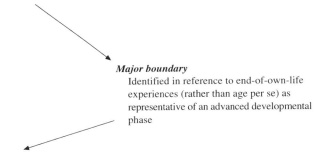

Major boundary
  Identified in reference to end-of-own-life experiences (rather than age per se) as representative of an advanced developmental phase

General and strategic propositions:
  1. Expansion of conceptual boundaries is developmentally appropriate in persons facing end-of-own-life issues.
     Self-transcendence is greater in persons facing end-of-own-life issues than in persons not confronted with such issues.
  2. There is a relationship between fluctuations in conceptual boundaries and well-being across developmental phases.
     Self-transcendence is positively related to indicators of well-being in persons facing end-of-own-life issues.

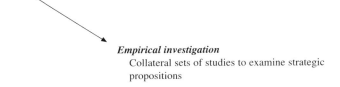

Empirical investigation
  Collateral sets of studies to examine strategic propositions

Fig 1. Main elements of theory development process.

midwestern city, half of whom were outpatients who had incurable cancer and were expected to live less than 1 year, and half of whom were well adults. In the second study, 300 adults from a southwestern city participated; they were distributed into three groups: 100 terminally ill hospitalized cancer patients who were critically ill and aware of the terminal nature of their illness; 100 nonterminally ill hospitalized patients; and 100 well nonhospitalized adults.

Results of both studies supported the hypothesis that terminally ill adults who have awareness of their nearness to the end of life report higher levels of spiritual perspective than other adults. regardless of age, sex, years of education, religious background, or event of hospitalization. Also, a significant positive relationship between spiritual perspective and sense of well-being was found in the critically terminally ill group of adults.

Findings from these and other studies on spiritually related variables supported the conceptualization of the end of life as an experience during which self-transcendent perspectives are particularly salient and correlate with well-being.

Psychosocial self-transcendence studies

Concurrent with the spiritual perspective research, a second set of studies was initiated on another group of adults confronting end-of-life issues: middle-old and oldest-old adults, who ranged in age from 60 to 100 years.[37,42,49] The Self-Transcendence Scale (a shortened version of the Developmental Resources of Later Adulthood Scale) was developed to measure psychosocial expressions of self-transcendence in later life. Examples include sharing wisdom with others, helping others in some way, and finding meaning in one's past experiences. The theorized relationship between self-transcendence (originally referred to as a developmental resource of later adulthood) and mental health was examined in studies of well elderly persons and depressed elderly persons who were hospitalized for psychiatric treatment. Correlational and longitudinal designs were used.

Significant inverse relationships of moderately high magnitude were found between the level of self-transcendence and mental health symptomatology among both clinically depressed and mentally healthy elderly groups. Also, depressed older adults exhibited significantly lower levels of self-transcendence than did the mentally healthy older adults. All findings held up over time. In addition, a significant link was identified between self-transcendence and subsequent occurrence of depression among mentally healthy older adults.[37] Content analysis of qualitative data indicated that problems related to developmental issues of aging such as self-transcendence are perceived by the clients as precipitating psychiatric hospitalization.[49]

Results of research into self-transcendence in the oldest-old, those age 80 to 100, further supported the significant inverse relationship between self-transcendence and various measures of mental health problems. Also, examination of qualitative data using a matrix analysis scheme yielded four patterns of self-transcendence reported by the participants as being particularly important to their well-being at this time of their lives: innerdirectedness, generativity, temporal integration, and body-transcendence.[42] In sum, evidence from these series of studies supported both strategic propositions and provided a beginning empirical base for the emerging theory.

CONCLUSIONS: THEORY-RESEARCH-PRACTICE LINKS

The emerging theory proposes that in individuals who have an increased awareness of personal mortality through such experiences as terminal illness or advanced age, self-transcendence is a salient pattern and a correlate of well-being. The process of theory construction was facilitated early on by opportunities posed by a paradigm shift in developmental psychology and by a visionary thinker in nursing. The strategy of deductive reformulation was used as adapted to incorporate clinical experience and use of multiple life span theories in derivation of the theoretic base. Theory development entailed considerable attention to conceptual issues, tempered with findings from collateral sets of empirical work and inspired by clinical experiences with clients across the life span. The nursing theory reflected perspectives of human development that were both congruent with other disciplines and unique to nursing.

A theory of self-transcendence is potentially useful as rationale for nurses to attend to spiritual and psychosocial expressions of self-transcendence in clients who for various reasons are confronted with end-of-own-life issues. Relevant nursing therapies that help clients to expand self-boundaries have yet to be tested for their effectiveness in enhancing well-being during confrontations with personal mortality. Potential nursing approaches might entail making use of current practices such as meditation, self-reflection, visualization, religious expression, peer counseling, journal keeping, and life review processes, all of which help clients expand self-boundaries temporally, inwardly, and outwardly. Other therapeutic approaches may include providing opportunities for clients to reach out and share their experiences and wisdom with others. The theory is broad enough to allow for the individualization of therapies appropriate for each client situation.

Continued progress toward a middle-range theory of self-transcendence requires research designed to identify additional boundary-determining criteria and to support (or alter as needed) the linkages specified in the propositions. For example, is the theory bounded in any way by chronologic age (adults versus children who face end-of own-life issues), gender, temporal distance from the death-related experience, or health status? In what other death-related contexts is self-transcendence significant to well-being? With continued research, other manifestations of self-transcendence may be described and measured. These refinements will enhance the theory's middle-range status, with the ultimate goal of providing a distinct base of knowledge for application in a wide variety of nursing settings where clients' well-being may be compromised by end-of-life experiences. This emerging theory may also generate ideas for nursing theories and research that address forms of conceptual boundaries related to well-being during other developmental contexts of life.

REFERENCES

1. Merton RK. *Social Theory and Social Structure.* New York, NY: Free Press; 1949.
2. Fitzpatrick J, Whall A, Johnston R, Floyd J. *Nursing Models and their Psychiatric Mental Health Applications.* Bowie, Md: Brady; 1982.
3. Whall AL. *Family Therapy Theory for Nursing: Four Approaches.* Norwalk, Conn: Appleton-Century-Crofts; 1986.
4. Fagin CM, ed. *Nursing in Child Psychiatry.* St Louis, Mo: CV Mosby; 1972.
5. Lemer RM, ed. *Developmental Psychology: Historical and Philosophical Perspectives.* Hillsdale, NJ; Erlbaum; 1983.
6. Brent SB. Prigogine's model for self-organization in nonequilibrium systems. *Hum Dev.* 1978;21:374–387.
7. Prigogine I, Stengers I. *Order Out of Chaos: Man's New Dialogue with Nature.* New York, NY: Bantam; 1984.
8. Werner H. The concept of development from a comparative and organismic point of view. In: Harris DB, ed. *The Concept of Development.* Minneapolis, Minn: University of Minnesota Press; 1957:125–148.
9. Reed PG. Implications of the life-span developmental framework for well-being in adulthood and aging. *ANS.* 1983;6:18–25.
10. Arlin PK. Cognitive development in adulthood: A fifth state? *Dev Psychol.* 1975;11:602–606.
11. Labouvie-Vief G. Logic and self-regulation from youth to maturity: A model. In: Commons ML, Richards FA, Armon C, eds. *Beyond Formal Operations: Late Adolescent and Adult Cognitive Development.* New York, NY: Praeger, 1984;158–179.
12. Pascual-Leone J. Growing into human maturity: Toward a metasubjective theory of adulthood stages. In: Baltes PB, Brim OG Jr, eds. *Life-Span Development and Behavior.* Vol 5. New York, NY: Academic Press; 1983:117–156.
13. Sinnott JD. Life-span relativistic postformal thought: Methodology and data from everyday problem-solving studies. In: Commons ML, Sinnott JD, Richards FA, Armon C, eds. *Adult Development: Comparisons and Applications of Developmental Models.* Vol 1. New York, NY: Praeger, 1989:239–278.
14. Piaget J. Intellectual evolution from adolescence to adulthood. *Hum Dev.* 1972;91:133–141.
15. Commons ML, Richards FA, Armon C, eds. *Beyond Formal Operations: Late Adolescent and Adult Cognitive Development.* New York, NY: Praeger, 1984.
16. Commons ML, Sinnott JD, Richards FA, Armon C, eds. *Adult Development: Comparisons and Applications of Developmental Models.* Vol 1. New York, NY: Praeger, 1989.
17. Rybash JM, Hoyer WY, Roodin PA. *Adult Cognition and Aging: Developmental Changes in Processing, Knowing and Thinking.* New York, NY: Pergamon; 1986.
18. Vaughan F. Discovering transpersonal identity. *J Human Psychol.* 1985;25(3):13–38.
19. Wilber K. *The Atman Project: A Transpersonal View of Human Development.* Wheaton, Ill: Theosophical; 1980.
20. Chinen A. Modal logic—a new paradigm of adult development and late-life potential. *Hum Dev.* 1984;27:42–46.
21. Jung CG. The stages of life. In: Read H, Fordham M, Adler G, eds; Hull RFC, trans. *The Collected Works of C.G. Jung.* Princeton, NJ: Bollingen; 1969:749–795.
22. Peck RC. Psychological development in the second half of life. In: Neugarten BL, ed. *Middle Age and Aging.* Chicago, Ill: University of Chicago Press; 1968:88–92.

23. Erikson EH. *Vital Involvement in Old Age.* New York, NY: Norton; 1986.
24. Lifton RJ. *The Broken Connection.* New York, NY: Simon & Schuster; 1979.
25. Frankl VE; Lasch I, trans. *Man's Search for Meaning.* New York, NY: Pocket Books; 1963.
26. Allport GW. *Pattern and Growth in Personality.* New York, NY: Holt, Rinehart & Winston; 1961.
27. Parse R. *Man-Living-Health: A Theory of Nursing.* New York, NY: Wiley; 1981.
28. Maslow AH. Various meanings of transcendence. *J Transpersonal Psychol.* 1969;1:56–66.
29. Watson J. *Nursing: Human Science and Human Care.* Norwalk, Conn: Appleton-Century-Crofts; 1985.
30. Newman M. *Health as Expanding Consciousness.* St Louis, Mo: CV Mosby; 1986.
31. Rogers ME. *An Introduction to the Theoretical Basis of Nursing.* Philadelphia, Pa: FA Davis; 1970.
32. Rogers ME. Nursing: A science of unitary man. In: Riehl JP, Roy C, eds. *Conceptual Models for Nursing Practice.* 2nd ed. New York, NY: Appleton-Century-Crofts; 1980;329–337.
33. Rogers ME. Nursing: Science of unitary, irreducible human beings: Update 1990. In: Barrett EAM, ed. *Visions of Rogers' Science-Based Nursing.* New York, NY: National League for Nursing; 1990:5–12.
34. Baltes PB, Reese HW, Lipsitt LP, eds. Life-span developmental psychology. *Annu Rev Psychol.* 1980; 31:65–110.
35. Riegel KF. The dialectics of human development. *Am Psychol.* 1976;31:631–647.
36. Lerner RM, Hood KE. Plasticity in development: Concepts and issues for intervention. *J Appl Dev Psychol.* 1986;7:139–152.
37. Reed PG. Developmental resources and depression in the elderly. *Nurs Res.* 1986;35:368–374.
38. Koplowitz H. A projection beyond Piaget's formal-operational stage: A general systems stage and a unitary stage. In: commons ML, Richards FA, Armon C, eds. *Beyond Formal Operations: Late Adolescent and Adult Cognitive Development.* New York, NY: Praeger; 1984;272–296.
39. Erikson EH. *Childhood and Society.* 2nd ed. New York, NY: Norton; 1963.
40. Mullahy P. *The Beginnings of Modern American Psychiatry: The Ideas of Harry Stack Sullivan.* Boston, Mass: Houghton Mifflin; 1970.
41. Acklin MW. Adult maturational processes and the facilitating environment. *J Religion Health.* 1986;25:198–206.
42. Reed PG. Self-transcendence and mental health in oldest-old adults. *Nurs Res.* 1991;40:1–7.
43. Andrews P. Developmental tasks of terminally ill patients. *J Religion Health.* 1981;20:301–311.
44. Hood R, Morris R. Toward a theory of death transcendence. *J Sci Study Religion.* 1983;22:353–365.
45. Dubin R. *Theory Building.* New York, NY: Free Press; 1978.
46. Brent SB. *Psychological and Social Structures.* Hillsdale, NJ: Erlbaum; 1984.
47. Reed PG. Religiousness among terminally ill and healthy adults. *Res Nurs Health.* 1986;9:35–42.
48. Reed PG. Spirituality and well-being in terminally ill hospitalized adults. *Res Nurs Health.* 1987;10:335–344.
49. Reed PG. Mental health of older adults. *West J Nurs Res.* 1989;11:143–163.

A Theory of Mastery

Mastery is a human response to difficult or stressful circumstances in which competency, control, and dominion have been gained over the experience of stress. The goal
of the theory of mastery is to explain how individuals who experience illness or other
stressful health conditions may emerge, not demoralized and vulnerable, but healthy
and possibly stronger. The human response to stress is fundamentally an existential
problem. As such, the theory of mastery has philosophic as well as conceptual roots.

Janet B. Younger, PhD, RN
Associate Professor of Nursing
Department of Maternal & Child Nursing
Medical College of Virginia/Virginia Commonwealth University
Richmond, Virginia

WHEN A STRESSFUL LIFE EVENT such as serious illness is experienced, it
evokes a number of human responses. There is an important, painful interval between the first pangs of recognition of loss and the adaptation to circumstances as
they must be.[1] People appraise the event and the changes it will require.[2] They
attempt to attribute the event to some cause.[3–10] When the event taxes or exceeds
the individual's resources and is thus stressful, personal and environmental resources are called forth in an attempt to cope.[2] Commonly, though not always,
there follows a period of alternating confrontation with and retreat from the impact
of the event.[11–13] During this period, there are unusual levels of both the intrusion
of ideas and feelings and the denial of ideas and numbing of emotions, which
appear to fluctuate in ways particular to each person. Nonetheless, there is phasic
tendency.[1] In confronting the event, a process of "working through" ensues, in
which the event is compulsively repeated in both the conscious and dream states.
During the working-through phase, the event is imbued with some meaning, daily
life is reconstructed in accordance with the change, life meanings in general are
reconsidered, and personal identity is altered.[1,14] There is a revision of inner models that represent the self, the self in relation to others, and ideas of the world.
Models are checked and rechecked for fit with past reality and with the new reality. In time, which may vary from moments to a lifetime, some adjustment is
achieved and the experience of stress and dysphoria is relieved.

The circumstances of events vary and those differences require different types
of coping;[11] some events require the individual to struggle with the environment to
change the event or its characteristics, while other events, being immutable, re-

Adv Nurs Sci 1991;14(1):76–89
© Aspen Publishers, Inc.

quire the person to struggle with himself or herself to accept the facts. Thus, some events require more coping and others require more grieving. Falek and Britton described the similarity between coping and grieving, both being "phenotypic expressions of the psychological mechanisms attempting to reestablish the dynamic steady state."[15(p2)] Reality-oriented adaptation and mastery require that we alter the threats we can alter and accept the things we cannot control. However, with all of these situations and responses, mastery may be an outcome.

In spite of events such as personal illness or the death of a family member, most people ultimately achieve a quality of life or level of fulfillment equivalent to or even exceeding their prior level.[7,16] Furthermore, they often do so substantially on their own. Not everyone readjusts,[13,17] but most do, and they gain mastery over the event in particular and over life more generally.[7]

The goal of the theory of mastery is to explain how individuals who experience illness or other stressful health conditions and enter into a state of stress may emerge, not demoralized and vulnerable, but healthy and possibly stronger. In the theory of mastery, illness is viewed as a special case of stress. When mastery occurs in an illness experience, it is similar to Moch's concept of health-within-illness.[18] It is a theory that provides an additional basis for the diagnosis and treatment of human responses to stress and is aimed at the promotion of health and enhancement of the quality of life. Through better understanding of mastery, patients may be assisted in their efforts to help themselves. This is an important element in the quality of life and health of an individual and thus is a goal of nursing.

This article sets forth the philosophic and historical foundations of the theory of mastery, defines the conceptual elements of mastery, and explains the relationships among these elements. An additional purpose is to set forth the theoretic basis for the Mastery of Stress instrument (J.Y., unpublished data, 1990).

PHILOSOPHIC AND CONCEPTUAL FOUNDATIONS OF MASTERY

Stoic philosophy reflects the way in which some of the noblest figures in antiquity and their followers in modern times have resolved the problem of existence and conquered the anxieties of fate and death.[19] Epictetus, a Greek stoic philosopher, observed in his manual for Roman soldiers, *Encheridion*,[20] that peace of soul is gained through self-control and self-mastery. These are obtained through learning to accept what cannot be changed and tolerating any loss so that the sting will diminish and fade away.[21] Serenity can be preserved by understanding the true nature of things:

Of all existing things some are in our power, and others are not in our power. In our power are thought, impulse, will to get and will to avoid, and, in a word, everything which is our own doing. Things not in our power include the body, property, reputation, office, and, in a word, everything which is not our own doing. Things in our power are by nature free, unhindered, untrammelled; things not in our power are weak, servile, subject to hindrance, dependent on others.[20(p331)]

Epictetus said that difficult problems should be embraced; one must never run away from them, for they are desirable spiritual exercises.[21] Thus, some of the philosophic underpinnings of this theory of mastery may be traced to stoicism. This theory also may be traced to existentialists, particularly Kierkegaard, Nietzsche, Jaspers, and Heidegger, in their dealing with issues of fate, freedom, decision, and the place of will in human existence.[22,23] Existentialism can be defined as participating in a situation "with the whole of one's existence . . . and it includes the finite freedom which reacts to these conditions and changes them."[19(p124)] The existential attitude is that "man is able to transcend, in knowledge and life, the finitude, the estrangement, and the ambiguities of human existence."[19(p125)] Existentialism also recognizes that persons are unique beings who choose, contemplate, and suffer. People create themselves in their engagement with life and in the decisions they make.[21] The theory of mastery is based on these notions. Further, much of the concept of mastery focuses on inner experience as the crucial reality and on the motivation of people by anxiety.

The natural complementarity between stoicism and existentialism was observed by Allport,[24] in his introduction to Victor Frankl's book, *Man's Search for Meaning*.[25] He refers to Frankl's view of freedom, which is that, when all the familiar goals in life are snatched away, what alone remains is "the last of human freedoms—the ability to choose one's attitude in a given set of circumstances."[24(pxi)] This freedom was recognized, Allport noted, by the ancient Stoics as well as by modern existentialists. Finding meaning is a part of choosing one's attitude. "To live is to suffer, to survive is to find meaning in the suffering. If there is a purpose in life at all, there must be a purpose in suffering and in dying."[24] Frankl quotes Nietzsche, who said, "He who has a why to live can bear with almost any how,"[25(p121)] and, "That which does not kill me, makes me stronger."[25(p130)] These ideas are the essence of mastery.

Historical Development of the Concept of Mastery

There have been other descriptions of mastery, but they differ in some ways from the present conceptualization and from its theoretic orientation. Freud[26] first described mastery in his discussion of the compulsive repetition of traumatic events as a belated attempt at mastery. According to Freud, the repetitive and intrusive thoughts that are characteristic of traumatic neurosis, although unpleasant, are but a postponement of satisfaction, a temporary endurance of pain on the long and circuitous road to pleasure. The pleasure is that of mastery.

Maslow[27] observed that forward growth is made possible by the feeling of being safe. Assured safety permits higher needs and impulses to emerge and to grow toward mastery. Experiencing higher or more advanced delights has a feedback effect on the self, in feelings of certainty, capability, mastery, self-trust, and self-esteem.

Both Rapoport[28] and Parad and Caplan[29] pointed out that a crisis presents an opportunity for personality growth as well as a danger of increased vulnerability to mental disorder. Studies of outcomes of difficult human experiences have often emphasized the impact, distress, and incapacity of the experience. However, Andreasen and Norris,[30] reporting on the experiences of burn patients, and Hamburg,[31] who studied the parents of leukemic children, noted that persons recovering from crisis reported resolution that included positive changes. Many of the patients felt their difficult experiences had made them better persons. In fact, Hamburg[31] found that mastery of profoundly stressful challenges had, in the long run, produced a sense of resourcefulness and compassion. In a longitudinal study of selected children from birth to young adulthood, Murphy[32] found that when children master early experiences of stress, it reinforces their confidence and develops resilience. This resilience gained through guided coping with failure produced greater strength.

A number of authors have defined mastery. White[33] applied the term to behavior in which frustrations have been surmounted and adaptive efforts have come to a successful conclusion. Bandura[34] described mastery as arising from effective performance. He said that expectations of personal mastery affect both initiation of and persistence in coping behaviors and are, in turn, altered by the cumulative effects of one's efforts. Pearlin and Schooler,[35] who developed a measure of mastery, defined it as a psychologic resource, the extent to which one regards one's life changes as being under one's own control, in contrast to being fatalistically ruled. Caplan defined mastery as behavior that reduces emotional arousal, mobilizes the individual's resources, and develops new capabilities that "lead to his changing his environment or his relation to it, so that he reduces the threat or finds alternate sources of satisfactions for what is lost."[36(p413)] Other definitions have included one's sense of control over the important circumstances of life[37,38] and the extent to which one imagines oneself capable of acting effectively on the environment to meet one's felt needs.[39] Hobfoll and Leiberman[40] emphasized the direct-control aspects of mastery, observing that a sense of mastery may actually cause frustration in situations in which exerting control is inappropriate. Taylor[7] acknowledged that mastery includes beliefs about personal control or a feeling of control over a threatening event so as to manage it or keep it from occurring again. However, he also said that a sense of mastery can be fulfilled by other than direct efforts to control the event; acquiring information, for example, is an indirect effort at control.

Related Concepts

Lazarus and Launier[41] defined *coping* as consisting of efforts, both action-oriented and intrapsychic, to manage environmental and internal demands and conflicts among them that tax or exceed a person's resources. Lazarus and Folkman[2] later refined the definition to one of constantly changing cognitive and behavioral efforts to manage specific external and/or internal demands that are appraised as taxing or exceeding the resources of the person. These changes were designed to define coping as process-oriented rather than trait-oriented. Further, they emphasized that this definition avoids the problem of confounding coping with outcome; thus the use of the word "manage" rather than "mastery."

Adjustment, a closely related concept, has been defined as the goodness of fit between the characteristics of the person and the properties of his or her environment.[42] In this definition, environment includes both the objective and subjective environment. The definition of adjustment does not, however, convey the necessity for growth, as does the definition of mastery presented here.

Efficacy,[34] *resilience*,[32,43] and *hardiness*[44] refer to relatively stable traits of the personality that may predispose an individual to master difficult circumstances. Self-efficacy arises from the perception of successful performance and in turn gives rise to persistence in coping. Resilience is an ability to recover from or adjust easily to misfortune or change. Hardiness is a composite of traits consisting of commitment, challenge, and control.

Control is a concept that is related to mastery, but lacks the focus on outcome and growth. Much of the literature on control often takes the implicit position that it is better to believe that you can control events than to think you cannot.[45–48] White,[33] in a now classic review of the literature on effectance motivation, referred to a pervasive, intrinsic need to exercise control over the environment; DeCharms[49] argued that the urge to be effective in changing the environment is man's primary motivational propensity. Moch[50] used the term "personal uncontrol" to refer to the realization that one does not have power over all, which is a type of letting go. However, in stressful situations, people strongly value and are reluctant to relinquish the perception of control.[6] Theorists of both helplessness and locus of control interpret various inward behaviors (passivity, withdrawal, and submissiveness) as signs of relinquished perceived control. In fact, such behavior may be initiated and maintained in an effort to sustain perceptions of control. This is particularly likely when the inward behavior helps prevent disappointment, when it leads to a perception of alignment with forces such as chance or powerful others, and when it is accompanied by attempts to derive meaning from a situation. Because control is so valued, the quest for it is rarely abandoned; instead, individuals are likely to shift from one method of striving for control to another.[6] Rothbaum and colleagues[6] proposed a two-process model of control. The first process involves attempts to change the world so that it fits the self's needs (primary control). The second process, attempts to fit with the world, is referred to as secondary control. Neither process is thought to exist in pure form; often the two are intertwined.

Thus, in many cases, mastery has been conceptualized as either largely or entirely involving change of the event or environment. Previous definitions of mastery are often trait-oriented and appear to be closely aligned with earlier ideas of locus of control. The present theory includes mastery by changing the stressor but also addresses mastery in those situations in which the event cannot be changed and mastery occurs over the experience of stress. This theory also emphasizes the growth that may result with mastery.

MASTERY AND ITS COMPONENTS

The Concept of Mastery

The definition of mastery proposed here is congruent with the root-word, "master," which means one who has control, defeats another, possesses consummate skill or dominion, and is in full command. Mastery is a human response to difficult or stressful circumstances in which competency, control, and dominion are gained over the experience of stress. It means having developed new capabilities, having changed the environment, and/or reorganized the self so that there is a meaning and purpose in living that transcends the difficulty of the experience. One who is beset by threatening circumstances and overcomes is tempered by the experience and emerges with greater strength and resilience. It includes having rebuilt shattered assumptions about self and the world and having a greater feeling of harmony and purposefulness.[7,51]

There are a number of defining characteristics of mastery. They include 1) the achieved sense of control, perceived or actual, over a situation that created a sense of vulnerability and over one's life;[7] 2) having an answer to the question, how can I keep this or a similar event from happening again, when that is appropriate to the circumstances; 3) having recovered self-esteem, feeling good about oneself again, and having a competent self-image; and 4) having found alternative sources of satisfaction for what is lost. These become a personal resource enabling one to "imagine oneself capable of acting effectively on the environment to meet one's felt needs."[39(p185)]

Mastery may also be characterized by the higher quality of life it generates. Taylor[7] observed that, following devastating experiences, many individuals achieve a quality of life or level of fulfillment equivalent to or even exceeding their prior level of satisfaction. The shock of discovering one's personal vulnerability may be replaced by a decrease in the need to believe in one's invulnerability and by an acceptance of life on those terms, without abandoning the opportunity to exert personal influence on events.

Although mastery is expressed in the intrapersonal mode, that is, in the way the person experiences himself or herself, it is also expressed in the interpersonal mode, in the person's relationships with others. As such, it is characterized by stronger family and other interpersonal ties and a greater sense of community with others. This is often reflected in an ability to immerse oneself in productive activity, both work and leisure, coupled with a greater awareness and understanding of life experiences and thus more compassion and understanding of others. These bonds of connectedness with others forge greater social strengths with which to engage both present and future challenges.

Antecedents of mastery include successful coping and the self-curing and self-caring activities required for recovery. In consequence, mastery results in a change in the perception of the self as more efficacious, strong, and enduring. It also results in the anticipatory appraisal of similar future events as less threatening and of available resources as more adequate. The effect of mastery on the state of health is that the net flow of personal energies is directed toward living, upward aspirations and toward expanding human potential (anabiotic) rather than defending against threat (catabiotic).

Mastery is not the absence of stress in a given set of circumstances. Nor does mastery imply that the individual experiencing it does not react. It also does not mean that an individual has coped with a stressful experience with ease. Instead, it means that, in spite of suffering, anguish, and perhaps a number of missteps, the attempt to overcome is eventually successful. It does imply that there is no continuing hypervigilance, compulsive repetition or sleep disturbances, or continued dysphoria resulting in catabiotic effect. Nor does any continued longing for what has been lost exert such catabiotic effect as to prevent the formation of new attachments. Rather, the love invested in old attachments is freed and becomes more universal and therefore available for future attachment, both to individuals and to society. Mastery also implies that not only are previous levels of personal integration regained, but new growth occurs. Also, although mastery is a process and does change, it is not coping. It is not the efforts to deal with the situation, but rather the product of those efforts. Thus the mode of coping or even temporary, ineffective efforts are not directly relevant to mastery.

Not all individuals emerge from a stressful experience with mastery. Absence of mastery is characterized by fearfulness, passivity, alienation, and an indistinct sense of self. The full opposite of mastery is to become a slave of circumstance, neither experiencing choice and control nor maintaining dominion over self. With some mastery, individuals may adjust to events and regain equilibrium but fall short of growth or any sense of control or dominion. Absence of mastery often includes failure to regain the sense of community with others.

Mastery contains the following conceptual elements: certainty, change, acceptance, and growth.

Certainty

The root word certainty means to be, on the basis of thorough examination, definite, sure, not in doubt. Thus, certainty is a state of having adopted a particular view that is free of troublesome doubts. The particular view is complex: it is the product of an internal model that incorporates previous life events and self-perceptions but has been revised in the face of new realities pertaining to the event and to changes in self, in others, and in the relationship between self and environment. Changes in the relationship between self and environment include changes in the perception of what is possible in life, what may occur in life, and what is the nature of human beings. This view may be very realistic, but it also contains all of the faith, hope, and illusion (denial) needed to sustain an intact view of the self and the world.[52] It is a negotiated view. The negotiation maximizes the following:

- a view of self that maintains the level of self-esteem necessary to continue coping,
- a degree of agreement with others that minimizes negative feedback and disconfirmation, and
- a critical degree of agreement with the verifiable history of the events (the video camera test or written documentation).

Thus, this view is an internally and externally consistent "theory" of the event. It is a general principle, not handicapped by individual circumstances or by disconfirmation of comparatively minor aspects of the situation. In short, certainty is the mastery of meaning.

Wittgenstein[53] likened certainty to a tone of voice in which one declares how things are. He said that what is important about the certainty of an idea is "what it connects up with." That is, "When we first begin to believe anything, what we believe is not a single proposition, it is a whole system of propositions; light dawns gradually over the whole."[53(p141)] Belief in this system of propositions is essential. One cannot make experiments if there are not some things one does not doubt. However, it is not necessary for everyone to hold the same system of propositions. For example, very intelligent and well-educated people believe in the story of creation in the Bible, or an afterlife, while others hold it as proven false, and the grounds of the latter are well known to the former.[53]

The defining characteristics of certainty are shown principally in the integration of the past model with the revised view. Certainty involves having assigned causes for the event—even if the assigned cause is fate—sufficient to understand, predict, and if possible control the environment. There is also an understanding of the significance of the event and what it symbolizes about one's life. Thus, the person can answer the questions: What impact has it had? What does my life mean now?[7] Hope is sustained.[54] Doubt and confusion are sufficiently reduced to avoid catabiotic effects, and decisions can be made and actions taken that are life promoting.

Certainty includes knowledge but is not fully determined by it. Knowledge assists in categorizing the present situation, accurately determining the potential for change, and forming a strategy for problem solving. However, in the absence of knowledge, preexisting cognitive categories developed through experience and existing belief matrices fill the gap. Thus, certainty is an integration of all of the philosophy, theology, and science (knowledge) previously used in directing one's life with the recent revision of inner models (views of the self, the self in relation to others, and ideas of the world). All of these are brought into conformity with the new reality. The new model is consistent and can serve as the dominant organizer of experiences for the present and the future.

Most of the foundations of certainty are present before the onset of the stressful event. Certainty may be partially attained through preexisting developmental maturity. In the negotiation of some developmental states, some questions acquire a categorical or generic answer. For example, some people acquire a generic answer to the question, am I going to die? and are less troubled than others by the specific cause or even the specific date. Thus, knowledge about diagnosis and prognosis are merely details and not the death sentence itself.

Certainty has interactional components. Relationships with others provide bonds of connection through which existing knowledge and culturally mandated beliefs are passed. They also provide a fabric of love that envelops the individual and gives constancy in the face of the seeming disconfirmation produced by the event. Further, others serve to maintain the reality orientation of the belief matrix. They characteristically whittle away at denial, excuses, and any lack of initiative in pursuing information.

Mishel[55] defined uncertainty as a perceptual state that occurs when internal or external stimuli are vague or unclear. Interpreting and assigning meaning to such stimuli are difficult; the ability to cognitively structure the stimuli, to assign value to them, or to predict their outcome is hindered. Individuals may simply not know whether events are really threatening or can be changed,[56] and uncertainty is associated with greater emotional distress. Further, Mishel and Braden[57] reasoned that high degrees of uncertainty decreased the use of direct actions and information seeking and encouraged modes of coping, such as vigilance and avoidance.

Although uncertainty and doubt exist in the working-through phases of stress, for the state of certainty to exist, the models and the view must be predominantly free of self-doubt or dispute with others who are significant in the present and future. Past disputes are less important. Certainty does not exist when a person is unable to categorize or understand the event because mental foundations do not include sufficiently similar categories, that is, when the event seems unique because it is so inconsistent with what was expected (this may occur even with events that are relatively common, such as labor or sudden illness). Not achieving certainty results in a state of continued doubt. It is characterized by the inability to reconcile the "old me" with the "new me" and, often, with the inability to reconcile one's view of circumstances with that of others. It results in an inability to make decisions for change or to accept circumstances and move on.

Certainty is present in mastery. It enables one to plan, to make decisions, and to know one's direction.

Change

To change is to directly affect the demands or resources of the objective environment and thus to reduce the impact of a stressor. Change entails effective problem solving, decision making, and action. It is exercising primary control and influence on the environment. It is more than minor modification or incremental problem solving. It involves transformative change requiring skills and solutions that were not previously a part of the repertoire. Change achieves mastery of stress through the mastery of the stressor or the relationship between the stressor and the resources. Thus, change is the mastery of fate.

The attributes of change include (a) possessing an accurate appraisal of what can be changed, which is generally validated by the opinion and assistance of significant others; (b) having the necessary knowledge and skills to deal directly with stressors; (c) planning and problem solving; (d) choosing actions from among the possibilities based on careful evaluation of alternatives; (e) employing resources for specific assistance; (f) having a sense of personal responsibility for effecting the change; and (g) persisting in acting and in refining of actions to effect control. Change also involves, in an existential sense, authenticity, that is, a commitment to do what is needed and what is true to the self.

Antecedents of change are both personal and situational. Personal characteristics required for change include sufficient problem-solving and analytical abilities to assess the situation and make a useful plan, the ability to accrue and use knowledge and skills, and a sense of personal efficacy and persistence. Situational antecedents require that there be a number of significant elements in the situation that have not been permanently lost. Change often results in self-actualization in the face of challenge, the acquisition of new skills, and a heightened sense of personal efficacy.

When the situation permits change but the individual does not enact it, victimization and a sense of personal ineffectiveness occur. Unnecessary resignation is experienced. Usually the individual's self-evaluation and the evaluation of others reduce self-esteem. When lack of self-confidence causes an individual to flee from the new learning or the risks entailed by change, that lack of self-confidence continues. Growth does not take place. In some stressful situations, a number of attempts are made to change the situation before it is concluded that, for the most part, it cannot be changed. This attempt to change may be necessary, particularly for some people, before the process of acceptance can begin.

Acceptance

Acceptance is to acknowledge events as true and normal and to agree to the terms of a situation. To accept is to

- admit that crucial aspects of an event cannot be changed,
- suffer the impact of that realization,
- give up any hopeless causes and expectations in the situation,
- be predominantly free of longing for what has been lost,
- change the self rather than the event,
- reinvest in new goals and relationships, and
- find alternate sources of satisfaction for what is lost.

Kubler-Ross described acceptance as the last stage in the process of grieving and defined it as "an existence without fear and despair."[58(p120)] Thus, acceptance is the mastery of self. Philosophically, the concept may be traced to Nietzsche's *amor fati*, embracing our destiny, which is the existentialist's commitment and fidelity when assuming a personal situation in the world.[22]

A condition of acceptance as a component of mastery is, first, doing what can be done to prevent a situation or correct it. The usual sequence of events following a stressful event includes attempting to change the situation, then longing, searching, and even raging for what has been lost. This state entails suffering. Further, the state is characterized by remissions and exacerbations for a considerable time, with gradual reductions in the frequency and severity of the state. At some point, the proportion of personal energy engaged in preoccupation with loss decreases, and energy is invested in new pursuits. Thus, acceptance is a product of the complete and successful grieving of losses.

The effects of acceptance include adjusting one's expectations realistically, giving up attempts to change events that cannot be changed, and making a decision to go forward. Using the interpretation that is given the event, some meaning is derived from the situation, and there is a reorganization of the meaning of one's life in general. New psychologic attachments exist. Hope and optimism return.

In the absence of acceptance, it is difficult to develop new relationships. Lack of acceptance also impedes the investment of life with energy. There is continued prominence of grieving and longing for what was lost, sometimes accompanied by continued efforts to change a situation that cannot be changed. The failure to accept is accompanied by feelings of defeat, despair, depression, helplessness, and hopelessness.

Growth

Growth is a state in which the individual has attained new competencies and feels stronger, more purposeful, and more efficacious than before the event. New strategies developed in the situation are likely to become available for use in future crises and may broaden the individual's adaptive capability.[31] Therefore, growth means possessing new skills or attachments, having meaning and purpose to living that transcend the difficulty of the experience, and participating in appropriate forward movement. Growth is a state of health in which the net flow of personal energies is directed toward upward aspirations (anabiotic) rather than toward defending against threat or illness (catabiotic). Growth is, therefore, the mastery of a life transition.

Growth involves transformation, in the developmental sense of a qualitative change or new stage, a feeling of having found new meaning, endured, or overcome. For example, Erikson[59] described developmental crises that, when successfully confronted, lead to accrued strengths of the ego and growth. Lane described transcendence as "the ability of the human spirit to step beyond who and what we are,"[60(p333)] the "rising above and beyond" one's immediate circumstances to a higher level of personal and shared communion. Under these circumstances, an individual has more awareness of life as well as more knowledge of self and others, and often, there is a creative outgrowth of the difficult experience itself. There is also a perception of the self as more efficacious, stronger, and more enduring. Human beings are predisposed to grow, to become more differentiated, and to master circumstances. Growth often occurs in situations of novelty and stress, developmental transitions, threats to self, and loss of previously comfortable ways.

The implication of growth is that future difficulties will be met with less shock and with greater competence, resilience, and endurance. The anticipatory appraisal of similar future events will be less threatening, and available resources will be seen as more adequate. Growth results in an individual having more experience and compassion to offer others in similar circumstances. Therefore, the cumulative effect of growth among a number of people will be a strong, healthier community. The healthier community may be observed in families, in groups or in organizations.

THE RELATIONSHIPS AMONG THE CONCEPTS OF MASTERY

All of the elements of mastery—certainty, change, acceptance, and growth—are processes. Each begins early in a stressful experience and evolves over time. A critical dose of certainty is necessary for change and acceptance, and a critical dose of those two elements is necessary for growth. Increases in certainty are completed before changes in the other elements are completed, and so on throughout the process of mastery. Because the elements have a period of temporal overlap, it is likely they also have periods of reciprocal causation, which is typical of theories that describe human development. Thus, change, acceptance, or growth may feedback to increase levels of certainty. Growth may also feedback to increase levels of change or acceptance.

In the case of particularly significant life events, it is unlikely that any of these elements is ever "complete." Rather, each reaches a level of stability at which it may remain permanently or, more probably, until another stressful event evokes memories and similar circumstances. The individual may then engage in additional working-through of the first event and achieve greater mastery.

Certainty is a necessary condition for both change and acceptance. It is the basis for a decision to change. It is also the basis for the revision in internal models that ultimately leads to acceptance. Either change or acceptance must occur for mastery to be achieved. However, change and acceptance rarely, if ever, occur as either/or phenomena; they are intertwined in dynamic coordination that is ever responding to the circumstances of a situation. They may vacillate; either change or acceptance may be in the forefront. However, change is primary in the sense that, if it can reasonably occur, it must occur in order to satisfy the conditions of growth. Acceptance occurs largely in relation to what cannot (or ought not to) be changed.

Change, because it entails the acquisition of new knowledge and skills, is a sufficient condition for growth. Acceptance, when it is characterized by the investment of life energies in new people or new pursuits, is also sufficient for growth. However, a balance between change and acceptance that is appropriate for the circumstances of the situation is a necessary condition for growth.

The person engaged in mastery of stress may be likened to a sailor in a storm. Stress is the storm, certainty is the compass, change is the rudder, acceptance is the angle of the sail set against the wind, and growth is the progress toward a destination. Mastery suggests that the sailor may not only avoid being blown off course, but may in fact use the wind with such effectiveness as to make greater progress than was expected.

The theory of mastery addresses phenomena of considerable importance to nurses whose concern is the human response to health and illness. As patients confront difficult health circumstances, mastery is a critical link in wellness and in quality of life. Nursing scholarship has addressed many aspects of coping behavior as the process with which patients manage stress. The theory of mastery addresses the outcome. A theory of mastery may guide the development of specific interventions to assist the self-curing activities of patients. Researchers may measure and study the progression of mastery and the effects that specific interventions may influence on its development. The goal of these activities is knowledge of human responses to difficulty, effective assistance of patients, and health in the face of illness.

REFERENCES

1. Horowitz M. Psychological response to serious life events. In: Breznitz S, ed. *The Denial of Stress.* New York, NY: International Universities Press, 1983.
2. Lazarus RS, Folkman S. *Stress, Appraisal, and Coping.* New York, NY: Springer-Verlag, 1984.
3. Affleck G, Tennen H, Gershman K. Cognitive adaptations to high-risk infants: The search for mastery, meaning and protection from future harm. *Am J Ment Defic.* 1985;89(6):653–656.
4. Lewis F. Experienced personal control and quality of life in late-stage cancer patients. *Nurs Res.* 1982; 31(2):113–119.
5. Lowry B, Jacobsen B, Murphy B. An exploratory investigation of causal thinking of arthritics. *Nurs Res.* 1983;32(3):157–162.
6. Rothbaum F, Weisz J, Snyder S. Changing the world and changing the self: A two-process model of perceived control. *J Pers Soc Psychol.* 1982;42(1):5–37.
7. Taylor SE. Adjustment to threatening events. A theory of cognitive adaptation. *Am Psychol.* 1983;38:1161–1173.
8. Taylor S, Lictman R, Wood J. Attributions, beliefs about control and adjustment to breast cancer. *J Pers Soc Psychol.* 1984;46:489–502.
9. Watson D. The actor and the observer: How are their perceptions of causality divergent? *Psychol Bull.* 1982;92(3):682–700.

10. Wong PTP, Weiner B. When people ask "Why" questions, and the heuristics of attributional search. *J Pers Soc Psychol.* 1981;40(4):650–663.
11. McCrae RR. Situational determinants of coping responses: Loss, threat, and challenge. *J Pers Soc Psychol.* 1984;46(4):919–928.
12. Shontz FC. *The Psychological Aspects of Physical Illness and Disability.* New York, NY: Macmillan, 1975.
13. Wortman C, Silver R. The myths of coping with loss. *J Consult Clin Psychol.* 1989;57(3):349–357.
14. Katz S, Florian V. A comprehensive theoretical model of psychological reaction to loss. *Int J Psychiatry Med.* 1987;16:325–345.
15. Falek A, Britton S. Phases in coping: The hypothesis and its implications. *Soc Biol.* 1974;21:1–7.
16. Caplan G. Loss, stress and mental health. *Community Ment Health J.* 1990;26(1):27–48.
17. Silver R, Wortman E. Coping with undesirable life events. In: Garber J, Seligman MEP, eds. *Human Helplessness: Theory and Application.* New York, NY: Academic Press, 1980.
18. Moch S. Health within illness: Conceptual evolution and practice possibilities. *ANS.* 1989;11(4):23–31.
19. Tillich P. *The Courage To Be.* New Haven, Conn: Yale University Press, 1952.
20. Epictetus; Higginson T, trans. *Discourses and Encheridion.* New York, NY: Walter J. Black, 1944.
21. Sahakian W, Sahakian M. *Ideas of the Great Philosophers.* New York, NY: Barnes & Noble, 1966.
22. Blackham HJ. *Six Existentialist Thinkers.* New York, NY: Harper & Row, 1959.
23. Gadamer H; Linge D, trans. *Philosophical Hermeneutics.* Berkeley: University of California, 1976.
24. Allport G: Introduction. In: Frankl V. *Man's Search for Meaning.* New York, NY: Pocket Books, 1959.
25. Frankl V. *Man's Search for Meaning.* New York, NY: Pocket Books, 1959.
26. Freud S. *Beyond the Pleasure Principle.* London, England: Hogarth Press, 1920.
27. Maslow A. *The Psychology of Being.* New York, NY: Van Nostrand, 1968.
28. Rapoport L. The state of crisis: Some theoretical considerations. In: Parad HJ, ed. *Crisis Intervention: Selected Readings.* New York, NY: Family Service Association of America, 1965.
29. Parad H, Caplan G. A framework for studying families in crisis. In: Parad HJ, *Crisis Intervention: Selected Readings.* New York, NY: Family Service Association of America, 1964.
30. Andreasen N, Norris J. Long-term adjustment and adaptation mechanisms in severely burned adults. *J Pers Soc Psychol.* 1972;154:352–362.
31. Hamburg DA. Coping behavior in life-threatening circumstances. *Psychother Psychosomat.* 1974;23:13–25.
32. Murphy L. Coping, vulnerability and resilience in childhood. In: Coelho G, Hamburg D, Adams J, eds. *Coping and Adaptation.* New York: Basic Books, 1974.
33. White R. Motivation reconsidered: The concept of competence. *Psychol Rev.* 1959;66:297–333.
34. Bandura A. Self-efficacy: Toward a unifying theory of behavioral change. *Psychol Rev.* 1977;84:191–215.
35. Pearlin L, Schooler C. The structure of coping. *J Health Soc Behav.* 1978;19:2–21.
36. Caplan G. Mastery of stress: Psychosocial aspects. *Am J Psychiatry.* 1981;138:413–420.
37. Eliott D, Trief P. Stein N. Mastery, stress and coping in marriage among chronic pain patients. *J Behav Med.* 1986;9(6):549–558.
38. Pearlin L, Radabaugh C. Economic strains and the coping functions of alcohol. *Am J Sociol.* 1976;82:652–663.
39. Hobfoll S, Walfisch S. Stressful events, mastery, and depression: An evaluation of crisis theory. *J Community Psychol.* 1986;14:183–195.

40. Hobfoll S, Leiberman J. Personality and social resources in immediate and continued stress resistance among women. *J Pers Soc Psychol.* 1987;52(1):18–26.

41. Lazarus RS, Launier R. Stress-related transactions between person and environment. In: Peravin L, Lewis M, eds. *Perspectives in Interactional Psychology.* New York, NY: Plenum Press, 1978.

42. French J, Rodgers W, Cobb S. Adjustment as person-environment fit. In: Coelho G, Hamburg D, Adams J, eds. *Coping and Adaptation.* New York, NY: Basic Books, 1974.

43. Kadner K. Resilience: Responding to adversity. *J Psychosoc Nurs.* 1989;27(7):20–25.

44. Kobosa SC. Stressful life events, personality, and health: An inquiry into hardiness. *J Pers Soc Psychol.* 1979;37(1):1–11.

45. Fleishman JA. Personality characteristics and coping patterns. *J Health Soc Behav.* 1984;25:229–244.

46. Lefcourt H. The function of the illusions of control and freedom. *Am Psychologist.* 1973;28:417–424.

47. Rotter JB, Seeman M, Liverant S. Internal vs. external locus of control of reinforcement: A major variable in behavior theory. In: Washburne NF, ed. *Decisions, Values and Groups.* London, England: Pergamon Press, 1962.

48. Thompson SC. Will it hurt less if I can control it? A complex answer to a simple question. *Psychol Bull.* 1981;90(1):89–101.

49. DeCharms R. *Personal Causation.* New York, NY: Academic Press, 1968.

50. Moch S. Towards a personal control/uncontrol balance. *J Adv Nurs.* 1988;13:119–123.

51. Janoff-Bullman R, Freize I. A theoretical perspective for understanding reactions to victimization. *J Soc Issues* 1983;39:1–17.

52. Dufault K, Martocchio B. Hope: Its spheres and dimensions. *Nurs Clin North Am.* 1985;20(2):379–391.

53. Wittgenstein L, Anscombe GEM, von Wright GH, eds. *On Certainty.* New York, NY: Harper & Row, 1969.

54. Scanlon C. Creating a vision of hope: The challenge of palliative care. *Oncol Nurs Forum.* 1989;16(4):491–496.

55. Mishel M. Perceived uncertainty and stress in medical patients. *Res Nurs Health.* 1984;7:163–171.

56. Christman NJ, McConnell EA, Pfeiffer C, Wells KK, Schmitt M, Ries J. Uncertainty, coping, and distress following myocardial infarction: Transition from hospital to home. *Res Nurs Health.* 1988;11:71–82.

57. Mishel M, Braden C. Uncertainty: A mediator between support and adjustment. *West J Nurs Res.* 1987;9(1):43–73.

58. Kubler-Ross E. *Death and Dying.* New York, NY: Macmillan, 1969.

59. Erikson E. *Childhood and Society.* New York, NY: Basic Books, 1963.

60. Lane JA. The care of the human spirit. *J Prof Nurs.* 1987;3:332–337.

A Theoretical Perspective on Attention and Patient Education

Understanding how people learn is critical to effective patient education. This article addresses the central role of attentional processes in supporting effective mental functioning and learning. The theoretical perspective provides a basis for examining attentional requirements associated with illness and the detrimental effects of multiple mental demands on attentional capacity and learning. Through therapeutic approaches that conserve and restore attentional capacity, patient teaching and learning can be improved.

Bernadine Cimprich, PhD, RN
Assistant Professor
School of Nursing
University of Wisconsin-Madison
Madison, Wisconsin

Everyone knows what attention is. It is the taking possession by the mind in a clear and vivid form of one out of what seems several simultaneously possible objects or trains of thought. Focalization, concentration, of consciousness are of its essence. It implies withdrawal from some things in order to deal effectively with others, and is a condition which has a real opposite in the confused, dazed . . . state . . . called Distraction . . .

William James[1(pp381,382)]

THE DEVELOPMENT of effective educational interventions is an enormous challenge in health and illness care. With increased treatment and care in day hospitals and ambulatory care settings, people are expected to learn new information, skills, and strategies for immediate self-care and long-term changes in life style within short periods of time and often under highly stressful conditions. Despite considerable emphasis on patient teaching, people are often confused by the volume and complexity of information they are confronted with in illness and health care transactions.[2,3] Furthermore, the efficacy of many current patient educational interventions for achieving difficult changes in life style remains questionable.[4] Although considerable emphasis in practice and research has been placed on the development of patient educational interventions, much less attention has been

The author thanks Mary Keller, PhD; Linda Baumann, PhD; and Marilyn Oberst, EdD, for their comments during the preparation of this article.

Adv Nurs Sci 1992;14(3):39–51
© Aspen Publishers, Inc.

given to pursuing and using knowledge of the way people learn to improve the process of patient teaching. A notable exception is the body of work done by Jean Johnson and colleagues,[5] which has provided a strong theoretical basis for preparation of patients for surgery and other stressful procedures.

The effectiveness of patient learning in any circumstances is dependent on complex neurocognitive processes involving innate human informational needs, biases, and limitations. First and foremost is attention, that is, the capacity to focus and concentrate. Although, as James[1] noted over 100 years ago, everyone intuitively knows what attention is, there is still little understanding of the complexity of attentional processes or the critical role of attention in supporting effective functioning in daily life. The same attentional capacity that supports acquisition and use of information in the learning process also is needed for critical mental activities that are an integral part of therapeutic self-care, such as planning, problem solving, initiating, and carrying out effortful tasks and self-monitoring. Clinical data from varying sources indicate that people can experience significant and persistent loss of the capacity to focus and concentrate during and following periods of treatment,[2,6,7] suggesting that attentional capacity often cannot support informational demands associated with current patient educational approaches.

An extensive literature on patient education suggests a common understanding that attention is necessary for learning and that attention (often referred to as attention span) may be affected by various factors associated with illness such as stress, pain, or medications. However, there is no reference to the complexity of attentional processes or to how such processes normally function to support or hinder learning. Such understandings are critical for advancing patient education practice and research. The purpose of this article is to propose a theoretical perspective on attention pertinent to patient education and learning. The view presented here provides a basis for examining the attentional requirements associated with illness, the detrimental effects of multiple mental demands on attentional capacity and functioning, and ways to conserve or restore attention. By looking at how attentional processes support or hinder effective learning, it is hoped that a better understanding of approaches to enhance patient teaching will be achieved.

SELECTIVE ATTENTION: CLARITY AND COSTS

Attention operates to increase sensitivity to information, or selected stimuli, in the external and the internal environments. In this context, sources of information refer to people, objects, and events in the external environment and stored knowledge and memory in the internal environment. The simple act of "paying attention" involves complex neurocognitive processes.[8] One component of attention is selectivity, that is, the ability to focus awareness on (analyze and perceive) some information in the internal or external environment while ignoring other information. Thus attention is akin to a mental searchlight that focuses on one neural activity to the exclusion of others. The selective operation of attentional processes permits coherence of thought by protecting an individual from endless confusion that would otherwise be generated by random bombardment with environmental stimuli. Attention also involves a sustaining component that permits an individual to concentrate, that is, develop and maintain optimal sensitivity to a focus of stimulation (thus one can hold a train of thought). Finally, attention involves a component of limited capacity that refers to the amount of information a person can actively attend to at one time. Attentional theorists have observed and widely agree that while the capacity for storage of information appears to be vast, human attentional capacity is limited and thus permits active processing of only a few "chunks" of information at any one time—five plus or minus two under optimum healthy conditions.[9]

The successful operation of attention results in mental clarity, characterized by strong focus and concentration or suppression of distraction.[10] Clarity of focus permits effective mental activity required for learning or other purposeful activity. On the other hand, impairment of attention results in lack of clarity, or confusion, which undermines human effectiveness and learning in any situation.

Human capability to actively focus and concentrate on pertinent information in the environment has some associated costs. The concept of attentional costs is critical in understanding the possible impact of illness on attentional capacity and functioning. A common dictionary definition of cost is the price paid to achieve something. The cost of attention refers to the mental effort that is required to clearly focus on active selection of information. The concept of cost may be more readily understood in the context of kinds of selective attentional processes, the functional significance of each, and the related operational expense of mental effort.

Two Kinds of Selective Attention

In a classical analysis of attention, James[1] first distinguished two kinds of selective attentional processes: involuntary and voluntary. (Voluntary attention is more commonly referred to as directed attention.) Both kinds of attention presumably involve neural inhibitory mechanisms that intensify sensitivity to selected information, but major differences exist between them in terms of function and cost in mental effort.

As distinguished by James,[1] involuntary attention is a spontaneous and apparently effortless response to sensory or intellectual stimuli of interest resulting in the effect of "captured attention." James proposed that such spontaneous attention is given to instinctively dangerous, novel, or exciting stimuli such as "strange things, moving things, wild things, bright things, pretty things, metallic things, blows, blood, etc".[1(p394)] Laboratory and field studies have supported James's early description of sources of involuntary attention. Stimuli that received involuntary attention were characterized by vividness, that is, high emotional interest or imaginability of information[11,12]; novelty; brightness; movement; or complexity of objects or people in the visual field.[13,14]

In everyday life, sources of involuntary attention are thought to include both *contents* and *processes* that people find fascinating in transactions with their environment.[10] Contents that are fascinating are the potentially dangerous (e.g., things that cause bodily injury or pain), survival-related phenomena (shelter, food, weather), as well as aspects of nature epitomized in living green things of all kinds (plants, gardens, parks) and water in the environment. Processes that are fascinating relate to coping with uncertainty in the environment and involve two crucial facets: (1) making sense, that is, being able to recognize and predict; and (2) involvement reflected in exploration or curiosity. Making sense and involvement are complementary facets of a person's interaction with an environment, which together encourage acquisition and utilization of information likely to foster human survival. Thus involuntary attention strongly influences the pattern of human responses to information and supports adaptive responses to potentially dangerous, potentially educational, and potentially valuable information in the environment.

Despite its adaptive value, involuntary attention also can interfere with effective functioning. Involuntary attention to salient information in the environment can act as a powerful distraction when the information does not serve a person's purposes or intended activity. In such instances, involuntary attention becomes costly because increased mental effort is needed to suppress the distractions to permit purposeful mental activity. For example, many facets of health care environments are associated with pain or discomfort and thus capture involuntary attention. Increased mental effort is needed to overcome such powerful distraction to attend to other information in the environment.

In contrast, voluntary or directed attention derives from our intentions and purposes and requires mental effort to sustain. It has been proposed that directed attention is needed to deal with much of what is necessary and important but intrinsically uninteresting in daily life.[10] The ability to direct attention presumably depends on a global, neural, inhibitory mechanism that acts to block competing stimuli or distractions.[10,15,16] When a person directs attention to important information in the environment, competing or distracting stimuli are actively inhibited. As distractions increase, greater inhibitory (mental) effort is needed to prevent the competing stimuli from interfering with intended activity. Because directed attention requires effort to sustain, it is subject to fatigue.

Theoretically, directed attention supports purposeful mental activity such as ongoing train of thought and action by suppressing competing stimuli or distraction. At the same time, this same capacity permits delay of action, such as keeping from saying or doing something, when such a response is important or desired. Although often taken for granted, directed attention is crucial for effective functioning in daily life. Lezak[17] and others[18] distinguished four components of effective human functioning: goal formulation, planning, carrying out activities, and self-monitoring of performance. These components have been termed "executive functions" because they determine how a person does something or whether an activity is done at all.[17] Goal formulation requires self-awareness on several levels involving internal states, experience, and relation to the environment and the ability to conceptualize purposes before acting. Goal-directed activity, regardless of its nature, requires sustained focus and control of interference or distraction. Planning requires the ability to think of alternatives, to make choices, and to construct a conceptual structure that serves as a guide for action. Thus planning, or manipulating thoughts, requires suppression of distracting stimuli in the immediate external environment. Carrying out purposeful activity involves directed attentional capacity in initiating and maintaining intended activity and in stopping in an orderly manner. Finally, directed attention is crucial for self-monitoring, including keeping track of what one is doing and perceiving mistakes, and for adapting behavior to meet intended goals. Thus without the support of directed attention, a person would be unable to function independently or to pursue personal purposes in life. In the context of illness, directed attention is crucial not only for learning new information but also for carrying out therapeutic self-care and making necessary, but often difficult, adjustments in daily life.

In summary, two patterns of attentional responses are involved in selection of pertinent information in the environment. Involuntary attention is powerful and effortless; however, it becomes costly when increased mental effort is needed to suppress distractions that are highly salient but irrelevant to intended purposes. Directed attention functions to mitigate conflicts among different sources of information (i.e., to suppress distraction) and requires mental effort to achieve clarity. Because directed attention is critical to effective learning and mental functioning, it becomes important to better understand how illness and health care transactions may increase the demands or requirements for use of directed attention.

Attentional Requirements in Illness

Attentional requirements may be delineated based on the concept of person-environment compatibility.[19] Compatibility refers to the extent to which an environment, internal and external, supports or hinders an individual in meeting basic human informational needs in any purposeful activity. As person-environment compatibility increases, the demand or requirement for directed attention and expense of mental effort decreases. When compatibility is high, for example, when there are no distractions that attract involuntary attention in the external or internal environment, a person can function, think clearly, and learn with minimal need for directed attention and exertion of mental effort. Conversely, as sources of incompatibility in the environment increase, the requirements for directed attention and expense of mental effort also increase. Sources of incompatibility can arise from both the external environment and from within an individual. Incompatibilities commonly occur when (1) available information is inadequate to carry out one's purposes (is lacking or is difficult to make sense of); (2) the environment contains distractions that must be overcome to function effectively; (3) thoughts or emotions interfere with efforts to gain needed information or carry out activity; and (4) desired activity is thwarted or other action is required in a particular setting.

From this perspective, multiple factors associated with illness and health care transactions can increase attentional requirements. Generally, informational needs associated with illness are intense. Pertinent information concerning the disease, illness, treatment, and self-care often is unfamiliar and complex, must be acquired under considerable time pressure, and often is inherently threatening. At the same time, affective factors such as worry about the future, anticipated or actual losses, and associated painful thoughts can act as continuous distractions to purposeful activity. Mental preoccupation with distressing thoughts can be a powerful distraction, and increased mental effort would be needed to successfully attend to important or urgent information in the environment. Furthermore, illness imposes multiple constraints on usual activity stemming from physical discomfort or pain, from losses of privacy and territory, and from disruptions or changes in day-to-day life that increase the need for directed attention over long periods of time.

Transactions with the health care environment also may increase the need for directed attention at times when the person's attentional capacity is already diminished. For example, at times of personal vulnerability, people are commonly expected to adjust rapidly to complex health care environments in which almost everything is unfamiliar—the physical environment, language, and customs. At the same time, the sheer volume and complexity of information provided about a disease or treatment often requires considerable directed attention. In case study analyses of coping with cancer, Weisman[20] has provided vivid accounts of how communications from health care providers that were meant to be helpful actually increased confusion and distress. Such instances included providing detailed information that was too difficult to comprehend, use of statistics to describe favorable outcomes, and a ubiquitous use of language that sounded foreign to the patient. In another clinical study, a lack of clarity about the illness and treatment was so profound that although individuals desired more information, they did not ask questions because they could not think of what questions to ask.[21] In physical or intellectual environments in which information is lacking or is too difficult to comprehend, one is continually in danger of becoming confused, or getting lost, and increased mental effort is needed to carry out purposeful activity, whatever it may be.

In summary, multiple person and environmental factors associated with illness and health care transactions may interact to increase attentional requirements over prolonged periods of time. When attentional requirements are high, increased mental effort must be expended to maintain effective functioning and to learn under any circumstance.

ATTENTIONAL FATIGUE

Prolonged demands on attention can lead to attentional fatigue and related impairment in key areas of functioning. Two conceptualizations of mental or attentional fatigue are salient in the current literature. The term mental fatigue has been previously used by theorists when referring to attentional fatigue. The term attentional fatigue was adopted, however, because it is more specific. Cohen[22] defines mental fatigue as a decrease in total available attentional capacity resulting from information overload, while Kaplan and Kaplan[10] propose that mental fatigue is the result of excessive use of the neural inhibitory mechanism underlying the capacity to direct attention resulting in reduced effectiveness in purposeful activity. A critical difference in these two theoretical perspectives is the proposed process underlying development of mental fatigue.

Although the idea of information overload is common, Cohen's[22] conceptualization of mental fatigue appears to have limited explanatory value in relation to predisposing conditions or the scope of related effects. In Cohen's[22] definition of mental fatigue, attention and mental effort are assumed to be synonymous (i.e., all attention is effortful). Depletion of attentional capacity and rate of fatigue, then, are proposed to increase with both the amount of attention allocated to an activity and the duration of the activity. When demands exceed attentional capacity, information overload is thought to occur, resulting in reduction in performance and increased narrowing or focusing of attention on fewer environmental stimuli. The underlying assumption of attention as a single, or unitary, process does not seem to fare well under empirical scrutiny. Empirical evidence suggests that there are various kinds of attentional processes, and both effortless and effortful operations of selective attention have been demonstrated under laboratory conditions.[23] For example, a person who is mentally fatigued can still attend to something of interest because it requires no exertion of mental effort. Furthermore, from a purely theoretical perspective it is difficult to reconcile the idea of an "information overload" with attentional processes that are widely considered to be selective.[24]

Kaplan and Kaplan[10] propose that mental fatigue is a manifestation of overuse of the neural inhibitory mechanism underlying directed attention, the capacity to actively block competing or distracting sources of information. The development of mental fatigue suggests some baseline of directed attentional capacity (i.e., inhibitory capacity) that supports normal functioning, including inhibition of distractions occurring much of the time. When distracting stimuli increase, greater inhibitory effort is needed to suppress competing mental activity to maintain clarity of focus and effective functioning. The characteristic effect of overuse and fatigue of such a mechanism would be distractibility and a decline in the capacity to direct attention. Attentional fatigue would affect all activities that require directed attention, including acquiring new information, goal setting, planning, problem solving, initiating and carrying out tasks, and self-monitoring of behavior. Thus a person who has fatigue of directed attention would tend to avoid such mentally effortful activities or, if compelled, would be unable to carry them out effectively. On the other hand, a person who has fatigue of directed attention may not be physically tired and may even engage in physical activity to relieve the mental strain.

Converging evidence from diverse areas of research[25-27] supports the theoretical conceptualization of mental fatigue as a decline in the capacity to direct attention. In healthy adults, intense use of directed attention has been associated with subsequent impairment of ability to perceive, interpret, and respond to environmental stimuli when attempting to carry out purposeful activity. Thus this theoretical view appears to have strong explanatory power in relation to conditions that predispose to loss of attention and the scope of related effects. Furthermore, this theory has direct implications for patient teaching and learning because it suggests ways to conserve and restore directed attention.

CONSERVING AND RESTORING DIRECTED ATTENTIONAL CAPACITY

Given the critical role of directed attention in effective mental functioning, approaches that would help conserve or restore directed attentional capacity when people are chronically ill or recovering from acute illness would have high therapeutic value. Two conceptual approaches are pertinent to patient learning and teaching. The first approach involves limiting sources of attentional requirements in the environment to conserve directed attentional capacity. The second approach is restorative and involves interventions that promote rest and recovery of directed attention to control overall level of attentional fatigue.

CONSERVING ATTENTION

The approach to conserving directed attentional capacity is embodied in the concept of the supportive environment.[19] In terms of person-environment compatibility, an environment high in compatibility with a person's needs and purposes supports an individual in meeting basic human informational needs with minimal attentional costs or expense of mental effort. A supportive environment, then, is responsive to the basic need to make sense (i.e., to be able to comprehend and predict) and to the human need for choices and self-determination. From this view, patient learning may be considered as a process of making sense or forming a coherent understanding of the mental and physical responses that might be expected and the actions that might be taken to regain or to maintain health or to increase physical and mental well-being. Similarly, patient teaching may be considered as the process of helping an individual to make sense (comprehend, anticipate, and predict events) and to participate meaningfully (make choices, act, decide) in activities that are critical to well-being.

Making sense involves a natural process of exploration, of finding order, and of uncovering connections or relationships.[19] For example, asking questions reflects a process of exploration. Once important points and relations are readily discerned, then predictability, that is, knowing what follows what, or what to expect, also is increased. Thus being able to make sense of things provides a knowledge foundation, or coherent structure, from which a person can comprehend and learn. In unfamiliar or complex circumstances, making sense places a premium on economy of information, so that important points and their relations can be readily discerned, without danger of confusion or getting lost in the details. Even under optimal conditions, the amount of new information that can be efficiently and accurately processed at any one time is limited.[9] One has only to recall initial encounters with a computer to appreciate the amount of time and effort that was needed to learn even the most basic operating procedures. Furthermore, when directed attention is compromised, the amount of new information that can be efficiently and accurately processed is greatly reduced.

Although directed attentional capacity may be severely limited in illness, current trends in patient education involve the development of myriad written and audiovisual teaching materials containing detailed information and requiring intense use of directed attention to make sense and to determine personal relevance. Moreover, the information often is provided from an expert viewpoint (nurse), and the main points that are obvious to the expert may not be apparent to the novice (patient). These points were illustrated in a study of day-to-day problems experienced by 78 patients with various types of cancer.[28] All of the patients felt they had access to health-related information from physicians and nurses, but the majority expressed difficulty in comprehending the information received. Finally, current approaches to patient education rarely incorporate the opportunity for pacing of instruction to accommodate individual levels of understanding of pertinent information and attentional capacity. From this perspective many current approaches to patient education are antithetical to the idea of conserving attention and may even hasten fatigue and loss of attentional capacity.

Given that directed attention requires effort to sustain, patient teaching strategies that are designed to engage spontaneous, effortless attention could facilitate the learning of important information. Information that is vivid and concrete, that is, easily imaged and involving personal interest or experience, is more likely to receive spontaneous, effortless attention than information that is abstract and impersonal. In fact, a large body of evidence shows that people value concrete and vivid information, even when it is unreliable, and tend to ignore abstract information, even when highly reliable.[11] When the capacity for directed attention is diminished, exertion of mental effort can be painful, and a person may avoid dealing with abstract information, even when motivated to learn. In this instance, avoidance would be an adaptive response. Thus strategies that include the use of concrete and vivid information would facilitate learning. An excellent example of this is the work of Johnson and colleagues,[5] which has shown that preparatory sensory information can be effective in reducing distress in unfamiliar, threatening situations. Theoretically, sensory information is vivid, concrete, and thus would receive spontaneous, effortless attention. Other ways to increase vividness and concreteness of information would be to use examples, stories, and anecdotes to illustrate points and simple graphics or models of objects, environments, and events that permit a person to see easily the main points and their connections.

Another concept that is particularly important for teaching self-care is that of meaningful participation. Meaningful participation serves the basic human need to decide for oneself, to make choices, and to act on one's own behalf.[10] The importance of patient participation in goal setting, planning, and decision making is frequently emphasized in patient education literature. However, meaningful participation assumes that choices and alternatives are present and that information needed to make choices is readily available. When directed attentional capacity is low, choices and alternatives that are obvious to the health care professional may not be visible to the patient. Furthermore, the ability to plan or to problem solve, which requires directed attention, may be impaired. From this perspective then, an important strategy in teaching self-care would be to assist an individual to identify or "see" meaningful choices or alternatives that realistically might be pursued in the particular situation, resulting in real individualization of care. One way to communicate possible choices or alternatives for dealing with necessary but difficult life changes might be through examples or personal accounts depicting how others in similar circumstances have dealt effectively with a particular problem or situation. A prime benefit of this type of approach is that what is considered important information from the health care professional's point of view also becomes a matter of personal interest to the patient, and spontaneous effortless attention can be used in learning and carrying out necessary self-care.

Finally, patient teaching is often viewed only in the context of providing specific instruction, while the deleterious effects of health care environments on attentional capacity and learning have been ignored. Health care environments, in which learning is often expected to occur, contain multiple distractions in the form of noise, traffic, multiple caregivers (teachers), and impersonal, technological surroundings, to name but a few. Given that such conditions coerce attention and are difficult or impossible to ignore under any condition, considerable mental effort is needed simply to make sense of the environment and to overcome distractions before any other learning can occur. The impact of the health care environment on attention was illustrated in one clinical study in which the effectiveness of discharge preparation for patients being treated on a hematology oncology unit was examined.[29] When interviewed in the immediate postdischarge period, a significant proportion of patients had no recollection of receiving instruction while in the hospital. People continually learn about their environments, but what patients learn in health care settings may not always be what is intended. There is a need for better understanding of the deleterious effects of health care environments on directed attentional capacity[30,31] and of ways to modify these environments to support learning and effective mental functioning.

Restoring Attention

When patients have difficulty thinking clearly and learning new information, the solution may not be to increase patient educational efforts. In such instances, well-intended educational efforts are often ineffective and may even increase levels of attentional fatigue and impairment. Rather, interventions might be focused on restoring directed attentional capacity to support effective mental functioning. In this way patients could be helped to help themselves.

A conceptual approach for dealing with fatigue of directed attention involves restorative experiences that promote rest and recovery of directed attention.[32] Although sleep is necessary to restore directed attention, it is not considered sufficient when demands are intense or prolonged. Consider the experience of feeling mentally tired when awaking from a full night's sleep. The possibility for rest and restoration of directed attentional capacity lies in the use of involuntary attention. Because involuntary attention is powerful and effortless, it provides a critical resource for resting directed attention. Such possibility is intuitively understood when people seek experiences that are interesting or fascinating, when they feel mentally strained and in need of a "rest." The concept of restorative experiences for recovery of directed attention has considerable significance in health and illness care.

Kaplan and Kaplan[32] theorize that four factors are important for a restorative experience: fascination, coherence, sense of being away, and compatibility with inclinations and goals. Because involuntary attention provides the basis for resting directed attention, some source of interest or fascination is critical to the restorative experience. Random fascinations, however, may be a source of confusion or distraction. Thus coherence, or being able to see or imagine the relation of the parts, also is necessary, so that the experience becomes one of wholeness rather than of competing stimuli. In addition, a sense of being away allows relief from the concerns that normally occupy the mind. From this view, being away may relate to escape from a particular *content* rather than a particular physical environment. Finally, compatibility with an individual's inclinations is required, since what is a source of fascination for one person may be boring or incoherent for another.

A growing body of empirical literature suggests that the natural environment contains factors necessary for a restorative experience. The perceived psychological benefits of wilderness experiences have been well documented and include opportunities for reflection, sense of tranquility, and improved mental functioning.[32–34] Everyday experiences involving the natural environment, such as gardening and tending plants, also hold inherent fascination and restorative qualities. Even a natural view from a window when an individual is sick or confined has been associated with restorative benefits that are often unrecognized.[35] Furthermore, the findings of an initial clinical study involving women with breast cancer suggest that regular participation in activities deemed to be restorative may enhance attentional capacity and mental functioning over time.[36] Although the conceptualization of the restorative experience is recent in the literature, Nightingale,[37] over 100 years ago, observed the importance of a variety of experiences, for example, tending plants, caring for pets, painting, view from a window, as a means of providing relief for the mind, as well as bodily pain. Theoretically, the therapeutic use of restorative experiences may provide a way to help people to manage information more effectively. Ultimately such experiences may help people who are suffering from fatigue of directed attention to regain effective functioning.

RESEARCH DIRECTIONS

The theoretical perspective on attention suggests at least four new avenues of research pertinent to patient teaching and learning. First, there is a need to determine clinically useful measures for assessment of directed attentional capacity and functioning. Research in this area is already in progress, and preliminary findings indicate that directed attentional capacity may be assessed using a short battery of tests requiring inhibition of competing stimuli.[36] In addition, in an initial study of individuals treated for cancer, the attentional measures appeared to be sensitive and reliable indicators of changes in directed attentional capacity and functioning over time. Second, there is a need to systematically determine both illness and environmental factors that increase requirements for directed attention. This knowledge could then be used to identify specific populations at high risk for developing attentional fatigue and to modify educational experiences to meet individual needs and capacities. For example, in people with cancer, the combination of multiple life changes, prolonged periods of intensive treatment, and requirements for rapid acquisition and use of information in therapeutic self-care would seem to place exceptional demands on directed attentional capacity even under the most favorable circumstances. Third, from the perspective of serving basic human informational needs, current methods of patient teaching and education are especially in need of scrutiny. In particular, there is a need to explore ways to design educational interventions that facilitate ease of comprehension of important information without intense exertion of mental effort. Finally, little is known about the therapeutic use of "restorative experiences" in illness and health care. In relation to patient teaching and learning, there is a need to determine the differential effects of a variety of possible restorative experiences on the capacity to direct attention when informational demands associated with illness are intense or prolonged. Given the potential benefits to patient teaching and learning, such research would seem to be well worth the effort.

REFERENCES

1. James W. *The Principles of Psychology.* Cambridge, Mass: Harvard University Press, 1983.
2. Cohen F, Lazarus R. Coping with the stresses of illness. In: Stone G, Cohen F, Adler N, eds. *Health Psychology—A Handbook.* San Francisco, Calif: Jossey-Bass, 1979.

3. Northouse LL. The impact of breast cancer on patients and husbands. *Cancer Nurs.* 1989;12(5):276–284.

4. Oberst MT. Perspectives on research in patient teaching. *Nurs Clin North Am.* 1989;24(3):621–628.

5. Leventhal H, Johnson JE. Laboratory and field experimentation: Development of a theory of self-regulation. In: Wooldridge P, Schmitt M, Skipper J, Leonard R, eds. *Behavioral Science and Nursing Theory.* 2nd ed. St. Louis, Mo: Mosby; 1983.

6. Mages NL, Mendolsohn GA. Effects of cancer on patients' lives: A personological approach. In: Stone G, Cohen F, Adler N, eds. *Health Psychology—A Handbook.* San Francisco, Calif: Jossey-Bass, 1979.

7. Oberst M, James R. Going home: Patient and spouse adjustment following cancer surgery. *Top Clin Nurs.* 1985;7(1):46–56.

8. Posner MI, Boies S. Components of attention. *Psychol Rev.* 1971;78(5):391–408.

9. Mandler G. Consciousness: Respectable, useful and probably necessary. In: Solso RL, ed. *Information Processing and Cognition.* Hillsdale, NJ: Erlbaum, 1975.

10. Kaplan S, Kaplan R. *Environment and Cognition.* New York, NY: Praeger, 1982.

11. Nisbett RE, Borgida E, Crandall R, Reed H. Popular induction: Information is not necessarily informative. In: Carroll SJ, Payne JW, eds. *Cognition and Social Behavior.* Hillsdale, NJ: Erlbaum, 1976.

12. Kaplan S. Adaptation, structure and knowledge. In: Moore GT, Golledge RG, eds. *Environmental Knowing.* Stroudsburg, Pa: Dowden, Hutchinson and Ross, 1976.

13. Taylor SE, Fiske S. Salience, attention and attribution: Top of the head phenomena. In: Berkowitz L, ed. *Advances in Experimental Social Psychology Vol II.* New York, NY: Academic Press, 1978.

14. McArthur L. What grabs you? The role of attention in impression formation and causal attribution. In: Higgins ET, Herman CP, Zanna MP, eds. *Social Cognition.* Hillsdale, NJ: Erlbaum, 1981.

15. Posner MI, Snyder CR. Attention and cognitive control. In: Solso RL, ed. *Information Processing and Cognition.* Hillsdale, NJ: Erlbaum, 1975.

16. Posner MI. Hierarchical distributed networks in the neuropsychology of selective attention. In: Caramazza A, ed. *Cognitive Neuropsychology and Neurolinguistics.* Hillsdale, NJ: Erlbaum, 1990.

17. Lezak MD. The problem of assessing executive functions. *Int J Psychol.* 1982;17:281–297.

18. Stuss DT, Benson DF. *The Frontal Lobes.* New York, NY: Raven Press, 1986.

19. Kaplan S. A model of person-environment compatibility. *Environ Behav.* 1983;15:311–332.

20. Weisman AD. *Coping With Cancer.* New York, NY: McGraw-Hill, 1979.

21. Messerli ML, Garamendi C, Romano J. Breast cancer: Information as a technique of crisis intervention. *Am J Orthopsychiatry.* 1980;50:728–731.

22. Cohen S. Environmental load and the allocation of attention. In: Baum A, Singer J, Valins S, eds. *Advances in Environmental Psychology.* Hillsdale, NJ: Erlbaum, 1978.

23. Fiske AD, Schneider W. Control and automatic processing during tasks requiring sustained attention: A new approach to vigilance. *Hum Factors.* 1981;23(6):737–750.

24. Johnston WA, Dark VJ. Selective attention. *Ann Rev Psychol.* 1986;37:42–75.

25. Mackworth NH. The breakdown of vigilance during prolonged visual search. *Q J Exp Psychol.* 1948;1:6–21.

26. Cohen S, Spacapan S. The after effects of stress: An attentional interpretation. *Environ Psychol Nonverbal Behav.* 1978;3:43–57.

27. Parasuraman R. Vigilance, monitoring and search. In: Boff K, Kaufman L, Thomas JP, eds. *Handbook of Perception and Human Performance. Vol II. Cognitive Processes and Performance.* New York, NY: Wiley, 1986.

28. Heinrich RL, Schag CC, Ganz PA. Living with cancer: The cancer inventory of problem situations. *J Clin Psychol.* 1984;40:972–980.

29. Arenth L, Mamon J. Determining patient needs after discharge. *Nurs Manage.* 1985;16(9):20–24.

30. Williams M. The physical environment and patient care. *Ann Rev Nurs Res.* 1988;6:61–84.

31. Kaplan S. Mental fatigue and the designed environment. In: Harvey J, Henning D, eds. *Public Environments.* Washington, DC: EDRA, 1987.

32. Kaplan R, Kaplan S. *The Experience of Nature: A Psychological Perspective.* New York, NY: Cambridge University Press, 1989.

33. Kaplan S, Talbot J. Psychological benefits of wilderness experience. In: Altman I, Wohlwill JF, eds. *Behavior and the Natural Environment.* New York, NY: Plenum, 1983.

34. Mang M. The restorative effects of wilderness backpacking. *Dis Abstr Int.* 1984;45(9):3057-B.

35. Ulrich R. View through a window may influence recovery from surgery. *Science.* 1984;224:420–421.

36. Cimprich B. Attentional fatigue and restoration in individuals with cancer. *Dis Abstr Int.* 1990;51B(4):1740.

37. Nightingale F. *Notes on Nursing.* London, England: Duckworth, 1959.

Nursing Practice Model for Maternal Role Sufficiency

In 1975 Meleis set forth a conceptual framework for nursing practice centered on the concepts of role insufficiency and role supplementation. Later, Millor introduced a parental role sufficiency model for nursing research in child abuse and neglect. Based on the works of Meleis and Millor, a nursing practice model is proposed that focuses on maternal role sufficiency. It includes assessment of prenatal characteristics, measurement of developmental and health–illness outcomes, and preventive role supplementation intervention.

Kathleen Flynn Gaffney, RN, PhD
Associate Professor
School of Nursing
George Mason University
Fairfax, Virginia

NURSING PRACTICE models serve as an organizing framework for clinical practice and research. The purpose of this article is to present a model for maternal–child nursing practice and research that addresses the need for primary prevention of special developmental and health problems of families with infants and children. Specifically, the model represents an expansion of earlier models developed by Meleis[1] and Millor.[2]

BACKGROUND

In 1975 Meleis[1] set forth a theoretical basis for nursing practice based on the concept of role insufficiency. She explained that role insufficiency was a phenomenon individuals experienced during role transition and was accompanied by developmental and health–illness implications. She defined role insufficiency as "any difficulty in the cognizance and/or performance of a role or the sentiments and goals associated with the role behavior as perceived by self or by significant others."[1(p266)] These significant others included health care providers, such as the community health nurse who made a nursing diagnosis and planned care for an expectant mother.

The author thanks Drs. Linda Cronenwett and Doreen Harper for their critical review. Special recognition is extended to Drs. Georgia Millor and Afaf Meleis for contributions to the development of this work. Support for this article was provided by the National Center for Nursing Research, Grant Number 1-KO7-NR00014.

Adv Nurs Sci 1992;15(2):76–84
© Aspen Publishers, Inc.

Central to the Meleis model were specific nursing actions designed to prevent or ameliorate role insufficiency, referred to as role supplementation. The latter were described as a deliberate process that included conveying information or providing experiences for the role incumbent to become aware of anticipated role behaviors and goals, as well as the interrelationships between the new role and the roles of others.

Later, Millor[2] developed a nursing model for the complex phenomenon of parental role sufficiency. Specifically, Millor designed an organizing framework for nursing research in child abuse and neglect, the extreme manifestation of parental role insufficiency. Her model encompassed the transactional relationships among individual, family, and community characteristics and parent role behaviors, as perceived by self and significant others. Millor's approach was an eclectic one that drew from symbolic interaction, stress, and temperament theories.[3–6] The core of her model was stress-appraised transactions between parent and child that, tempered by multifactorial individual and ecological components, led to a range of parental role behaviors, from normative nurturing (parental role sufficiency) to neglect and abuse (parental role insufficiency).

RATIONALE FOR THE EXPANDED MODEL

Fig 1 depicts Millor's original nursing model for parental role sufficiency with the proposed expansion. The expanded model includes assessment of prenatal characteristics and measurement of developmental and health–illness outcomes, as well as direction for role supplementation intervention as described in the Meleis model.[1]

The primary reason for the proposed expansion of these models to the prenatal period is to provide nursing and related practice disciplines with a model for more fully examining the developmental and health–illness implications of role sufficiency throughout the period of transition to motherhood. To initiate examination of role sufficiency when the stress-appraised transactions between mother and child have already begun is to have missed the unique contribution of prenatal factors that occur early in the process of role transition. Examples of factors derived from the original model that may be assessed prenatally include the pregnant woman's perception of the mothering she received as a child with respect to nurturing and discipline (Parent's Own Childrearing History), her perception of current difficult life circumstances and her personal resources to cope with them (Parent Self-Characteristics), and her expectations of the maternal role and infant competencies (Parent Role Expectations).

In expanding the examination of role sufficiency, consideration is also given specifically to the impact of prenatal maternal role sufficiency on later role behavior. The term prenatal maternal role sufficiency is proposed to encompass the

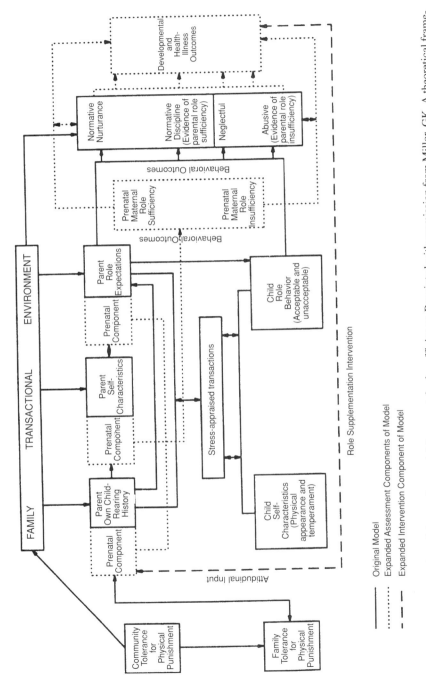

Fig 1. Proposed expansion of the nursing model for parental role sufficiency. Reprinted with permission from Millor, GK. A theoretical framework for nursing research in child abuse and neglect. *Nurs Res.* 1981;30(2):78–83. © 1981, American Journal of Nursing Company.

spectrum of prenatal behaviors that range from warm, affiliative nurturing to risk behaviors that may be deleterious to infant health.

ASSESSMENT COMPONENT OF THE EXPANDED MODEL

Parent's Own Childrearing History is one component of the original Millor model that may be expanded for prenatal assessment. Gaffney[7] compared prenatal plans for child discipline with pregnant women's own perceptions of having been disciplined as a child by their mothers and found a significant association. Further study is needed to determine the extent to which these prenatal plans predict later practices of childhood discipline.

However, the child abuse and neglect literature supports the notion that a woman's experience of having been maltreated as a child may put her at risk for continuing an intergenerational cycle of abuse and neglect. Based on their longitudinal, prospective study of the antecedents of child maltreatment, Egeland, Jacobvitz, and Papatola[8] concluded that the experience of being maltreated as a child may be a circumstance that leads mothers to lose control with their own children and neglect their physical or emotional needs. Their observation was that women who had been maltreated as children had suffered significant psychologic trauma that impaired their capability for close interpersonal relationships. Sroufe and Fleeson[9] emphasized that women who were victimized as children often thought of themselves as victims and acted out the observed role of victimizer when caring for their own children.

However, studies[10,11] of maltreating parents also indicated that healthy parenting outcomes are possible despite earlier maltreatment, particularly when women have gained knowledge about relationships, relearned self–other concepts, and developed secure, emotional relationships that allowed them to deal with earlier traumas of childhood.

These findings support the notion that intervention to break the intergenerational cycle of abuse can be effective. It also argues favorably for early assessment and preventive intervention that supports the development of nurturing relationships *before* the mother is faced with stress-appraised transactions generated by an infant who may at times appear to be overly dependent and noncompliant.

A second concept from the nursing model for parental role sufficiency that may be assessed during pregnancy is Self-Characteristics. Specifically, a woman's perception of her chronic and current stressors, coupled with her perception of her own coping skills and supportive resources, may be considered within this concept.

The Children's Defense Fund[12] links dramatic rises in the incidence of child abuse and neglect with such stressors as poverty, homelessness, substance abuse, and domestic violence. Beckwith[13] cautions that most parents who experience high degrees of stressful circumstances do not abuse or neglect their children. In fact, a comparison of parents experiencing high stress found that those who did abuse or neglect their children were more likely to have also had a history of violence in their own childhood or current violent episodes with their partner and few satisfying social supports.

The utility of prenatal assessments of perceptions women have of their own stressors and supportive resources has not been fully explored. However, Booth et al[14] conducted a study of maternal competence that included prenatal assessment of both difficult life circumstances and perceived social support among women at social high risk. They found that women with low social skills who received individually planned, therapeutic home visits from nurses demonstrated improved competence in relation to both adult social skills and maternal–infant interactive skills. The researchers concluded that a connection may exist between these two outcomes. Specifically, they suggested that mothers who improved their own ability to communicate with adults were better able to reach out for the effective support needed to deal with difficult life circumstances and, in turn, became more emotionally available to respond to infant needs.

A third concept from the Millor model that may be extended for prenatal assessment when considering prevention of child maltreatment is Parent Role Expectations. According to Millor (personal communication, June 1992), this concept refers to the mother's expectations of herself in the maternal role and her expectations of her own infant's competencies.

By means of prenatal assessment of these factors, clinicians and researchers may be afforded a view of the distortions that contribute to a stressed relationship and heightened vulnerability to maternal role insufficiency. Snyder et al,[15] for example, examined prenatal maternal expectations of infant capabilities with respect to early maternal–infant interaction. They found that inappropriate expectations by mothers during pregnancy were associated with lower scores on a measure of maternal provision of infant stimulation at 4, 8, and 12 months of age. The latter may be considered a measure of maternal role sufficiency. The Snyder et al findings were confirmed in a later study by Gaffney,[7] using a larger sample at data collection points during pregnancy and 4 months infant age.[2]

Since the original Millor model identifies nurturing behaviors as evidence of parental role sufficiency and abusive and neglectful behaviors as evidence of parental role insufficiency, the concept of prenatal maternal role sufficiency is proposed to address entities, such as prenatal maternal attachment, that may be early indicators of later maternal role insufficiency.

Mercer and Ferketich[16] found that prenatal maternal attachment was a predictor of early maternal–infant attachment. Although studies are not available that link prenatal attachment levels with later parenting outcomes, it is increasingly clear that disorders of attachment lie at the root of abusive and neglectful parenting behaviors.[10,17,18] Consequently, early identification of normal and dysfunctional patterns of early attachment are warranted.

INTERVENTION COMPONENT OF THE EXPANDED MODEL

Beginning with the first prenatal assessment, role supplementation intervention may be initiated to prevent or ameliorate the incidence of maternal role insufficiency. As described by Meleis,[1] role supplementation intervention consists of two components. The first, role clarification, is defined as the mastery of knowledge to perform the role. In order to efficiently target specific role clarification needs of new mothers, clinicians and researchers may use available indices including the Knowledge of Infant Development Inventory (MacPhee D, 1982, Unpublished data) and the Developmental Expectations Scale.[15]

The second component of role supplementation intervention, role taking, addresses the "empathetic abilities of self."[19(p372)] In the case of maternal role insufficiency, this component incorporates the woman's capacity to understand her role in relation to her infant's feelings and needs. The Maternal–Fetal Attachment Scale[20] addresses this phenomenon during pregnancy. The Nursing Child Assessment Feeding and Teaching Scales[21] with their Sensitivity to Cues subscales tap the role taking component.

In addition to the two components of role supplementation, three specific strategies for intervention have been described: role modeling, role rehearsal, and reference group interactions. All three were used in a study of couples expecting their first baby.[22] Role modeling consisted of teaching participants how to learn appropriate role behaviors from family, friends, and professionals who knew and utilized the behaviors and values of the expected role.

Role rehearsal was facilitated with the use of case studies. Couples were asked to think about and explain how they might handle a specific situation related to infant care. This intervention strategy helped the couples anticipate behaviors and sentiments associated with the parental role.

Reference group interactions were generated through weekly meetings with the couples and two nurse group leaders. The group forum allowed members to test ideas, receive reinforcements, and understand the normal range of feelings, fears, and experiences of others in a similar point of role transition.

Study findings supported the notion that role supplementation intervention had a positive effect on maternal role sufficiency.[2] Specifically, the mothers who received role supplementation intervention were less likely to show an attitude of ignoring infant cues and more likely to demonstrate an attitude of responding to infant needs than were mothers in two similar groups who did not receive the intervention.

More recent intervention studies provide some additional support for the use of role supplementation strategies to promote maternal role sufficiency. For instance, Unger and Wandersman[23] tested the effects of a resource mothers program for socially disadvantaged pregnant teenagers. The resource mothers were role models in that they were experienced mothers and paraprofessionals similar in race

and socioeconomic status to the teenagers. The resource mothers visited the expectant mothers regularly during pregnancy and infancy and provided them with
needed information about the anticipated maternal role. The researchers found
that the visited mothers demonstrated greater knowledge of infant development,
more satisfaction with the mothering role, and greater responsiveness to infant
needs than did a control group. By using the expanded model as an organizing
framework to conduct and evaluate nursing practice, a potential conclusion from
these findings is that the role modeling strategy was effective in supporting maternal role sufficiency.

Olds[17] also conducted an intervention study of a prenatal home visit program for
pregnant teenagers. His intervention involved the role rehearsal strategy. That is,
nurses helped pregnant teenagers anticipate and recognize differences in infant
temperament, especially crying behavior. The pregnant teenagers were helped to
understand the meaning of crying from the child's point of view and not misinter-
pret it as an indication of the mother's failure in caregiving or a deliberate attempt
by the baby to disrupt the mother's life. The teenagers in the home visit intervention program that experienced this role rehearsal strategy demonstrated fewer in-
cidences of child abuse and neglect than did a similar control group. Olds concluded that subjects in the treatment group were able to interpret infant behavior
more correctly and respond more appropriately, "thus forming the basis for secure
attachments which may protect the child from abuse and neglect."[17(p752)]

Although studies that demonstrate the effectiveness of the reference group interaction strategy in preventing or ameliorating maternal role sufficiency are limited, nursing has long used the group process as an intervention strategy.[24,25] Future nursing studies of the effectiveness of reference group interactions may
consider injecting the focus group interview technique into this intervention strategy. The purpose of the focus group interview is to gather "information which,
when performed in a permissive nonthreatening group environment, allows the
investigation of a multitude of perceptions on a defined area of interest."[26(p1282)]
The purpose of the reference group is to provide members with a nonthreatening
situation for testing their ideas and for receiving positive reinforcements from others who are experiencing similar role transitions. By wedding the intervention
strategy with the qualitative research technique, nursing is afforded the opportunity to meet the needs of clients in an immediate practice setting and to simultaneously generate data that leads to the ongoing evaluation and refinement of practice in a wider range of practice settings.

SCOPE OF THE EXPANDED MODEL

The proposed nursing practice model for maternal role sufficiency has potential
application for clinical problems in addition to child abuse and neglect. Specifically, researchers may find it a useful framework for organizing studies of many
health and developmental outcomes of infancy that have maternal precedents in
the prenatal period. As an example, researchers who have studied causes and cor-

relates of the incidence of low birthweight collectively present prenatal variables that fall within the umbrella of the expanded model. That is, just as the self-characteristics of prenatal perception of adverse life circumstances and prenatal perception of social support have been associated with later child maltreatment, these prenatal variables have been associated with the incidence of low birthweight. Bullock and McFarlane[27] examined the impact of one specific difficult life circumstance, battering during pregnancy, on later incidence of low birthweight (LBW) and found a significantly greater incidence of LBW among women who had been battered compared to a control group. This finding concurs with the report of the Public Health Service Expert Panel on the Content of Prenatal Care[28] that indicated that living in abusive or other high stress situations and experiencing inadequate personal support systems places a pregnant woman at risk for poor birth outcomes.

LBW researchers may find it useful to investigate prenatal behaviors such as abstention from smoking and alcohol, regular prenatal checkups, and healthy eating patterns within the expanded model concept of prenatal maternal role sufficiency. Each behavior fits within the definition of prenatal maternal role sufficiency and has been found to be a significant factor in reducing the incidence of low birthweight babies.[29-33]

Further, the role modeling intervention strategy has been shown to have promising results in encouraging these behaviors and preventing or reducing the incidence of LBW. Konafel[34] reported that, through the use of a resource mothers program with socially disadvantaged pregnant teenagers, the incidence of LBW dropped to 6%, compared to the prevailing rate of 9.6% in Virginia where the program was conducted.

By using the expanded model as an organizing framework, researchers are afforded an opportunity to examine multiple clinical outcomes with the same data set, thus yielding greater contributions to the current body of nursing knowledge. The intertwining nature of predictor variables and outcomes will yield information about interrelatedness that is unavailable with separate studies.

The proposed nursing practice model is directed specifically toward the prevention of health and developmental problems, such as child abuse and neglect, that may have underpinnings evident during pregnancy. Since the model includes a strong theoretical base, early prenatal assessment of maternal role sufficiency, simultaneous initiation of preventive role supplementation intervention, and an overall framework for ongoing empirical evaluation of health and developmental outcomes, it is considered to be a comprehensive model for maternal–child nursing practice.

REFERENCES

1. Meleis AI. Role insufficiency and role supplementation: a conceptual framework. *Nurs Res.* 1975;24(4):264–271.

2. Millor GK. A theoretical framework for nursing research in child abuse and neglect. *Nurs Res.* 1981;30(2):78–83.
3. Mead GH. *Mind, Self, and Society, I.* Chicago, Ill: University of Chicago Press; 1934.
4. Sarbin T. Role theory. In: Lindzey G, ed. *Handbook of Sociology.* Reading, Mass: Addison-Wesley; 1954.
5. Lazarus R, Launier R. Stress-related transactions between person and environment. In: Pervin LA, Lewis L, eds. *Perspectives in Interactional Psychology.* New York, NY: Plenum; 1978.
6. Carey WB. A simplified method of measuring infant temperament. *J Pediatr.* 1970;77:188–194.
7. Gaffney KF. *Prenatal Predictors of Maternal Role Sufficiency.* Final Report to the National Center for Nursing Research. Washington, DC: National Institutes of Health; 1991.
8. Egeland B, Jacobvitz D, Papatola K. *Intergenerational Continuity of Parental Abuse.* Proceedings from Conference on Biosocial Perspectives of Child Abuse and Neglect. York, Me: Social Science Research Council; May 20–23, 1984.
9. Sroufe LA, Fleeson J. Attachment and the construction of relationships. In: Hartum WW, Rubin Z, eds. *Relationships and Development.* New York, NY: Cambridge University Press; 1986.
10. Planta R, Egeland B, Erickson MF. The antecedents of maltreatment; results of the Mother-Child Interaction Research Project. In: Cicchetti D, Carlson V, eds. *Child Maltreatment.* New York, NY: Cambridge University Press; 1989.
11. Ricks M. The social transmission of parental behavior: attachment across generations. In: Bretherton I, Waters E, eds. *Growing Points of Attachment Theory and Research.* 50(1-2, Serial No. 209). *Monographs of the Society for Research in Child Development.* Chicago, Ill: University of Chicago Press; 1985.
12. Children's Defense Fund. *The State of America's Children 1991.* Washington DC: Children's Defense Fund; 1991.
13. Beckwith L. Adaptive and maladaptive parenting: implications for intervention. In: Meisels S, Shonkoff JP, eds. *Handbook of Early Childhood Intervention.* New York, NY: Cambridge University Press; 1990.
14. Booth CL, Mitchell SK, Barnard KE, Spieker SJ. Development of maternal social skills in multiproblem families: effects on the mother–child relationship. *Dev Psychol.* 1989;25(3):403–412.
15. Snyder C, Eyres SJ, Barnard K. New findings about mothers' antenatal expectations and their relationship to infant development. *MCN.* 1979;4:354–357.
16. Mercer RT, Ferketich SL. Predictors of parental attachment during early parenthood. *J Adv Nurs.* 1990;15:268–280.
17. Olds DL, Henderson CR. The prevention of maltreatment. In: Cicchitti D, Carlson V, eds. *Child Maltreatment.* New York, NY: Cambridge University Press; 1989.
18. Main M, Goldwyn R. Predicting rejection of her infant from mother's representation of her own experience: implications for the abused–abusing intergenerational cycle. *Child Abuse Negl.* 1984;8:203–217.
19. Meleis AI. The sick role. In: Hardy ME, Conway ME, eds. *Role Theory: Perspectives for Health Professionals.* Norwalk, Conn: Appleton & Lange; 1988.
20. Cranley M. Development of a tool for the measurement of maternal attachment during pregnancy. *Nurs Res.* 1981;30(5):281–284.
21. Barnard KE, Hammond MA, Booth CL, Bee HL, Mitchell SK, Spieker SJ. Measurement and meaning of parent–child interaction. In: Morrison F, Lord C, Keating D, eds. *Applied Developmental Psychology, III.* New York, NY: Academic Press; 1989.
22. Meleis AI, Swendsen LA. Role supplementation: an empirical test of a nursing intervention. *Nurs Res.* 1978;27(1):11–18.
23. Unger DG, Wandersman LP. Social support and adolescent mothers: action research contributions to theory and application. *J Soc Iss.* 1985;41:29–45.
24. Fullar SA, Lum B, Sprik MG, Cooper EM. A small group can go a long way. *MCN.* 1988;13(6):414–418.

25. Snyder D. Peer group support for high-risk mothers. *MCN.* 1988;13(2):114–117.
26. Nyamathi A, Schuler P. Focus group interview: a research technique for informed nursing practice. *J Adv Nurs.* 1990;15:1281–1288.
27. Bullock L, McFarlane J. The birthweight/battering connection. *Am J Nurs.* 1989;89(9):1153–1155.
28. *Caring for Our Future: The Content of Prenatal Care.* Report of the Public Health Service Expert Panel on the Content of Prenatal Care. Washington, DC: US Department of Health and Human Services; 1989.
29. Haglund B, Cratingius S. Cigarette smoking as a risk factor for sudden infant death syndrome: a population based study. *Am J Public Health.* 1990;80(1):29–32.
30. Harwood HJ, Napolitano DM, Kristiansen PL. Economic costs to society of alcohol and drug abuse and mental illness: 1980. *Res Triangle Institute.* 1984;June.
31. Kleinman JC, Pierre MB, Madams JH, Land GH, Schramm WF. The effects of maternal smoking on fetal and infant mortality. *Am J Epidemiol.* 1988;27:274–282.
32. Koop CE. *Memorandum from Surgeon General of Public Health Service.* Washington, DC: US Department of Health and Human Services; March, 1989.
33. National Commission to Prevent Infant Mortality. *Troubling Trends: The Health of America's Next Generation.* Washington, DC: National Commission to Prevent Infant Mortality; 1990.
34. *Home Visiting: Opening Doors for America's Pregnant Women and Children.* Washington, DC: National Commission to Prevent Infant Mortality; 1989.

The Triandis Model for the Study of Health and Illness Behavior: A Social Behavior Theory with Sensitivity to Diversity

The Triandis model of social behavior offers exceptional promise to nurse researchers whose goal is to achieve cultural sensitivity in their research investigations. The model includes six components: consequential beliefs, affect, social influences, previous behavioral habits, physiologic arousal, and facilitating environmental resources. A directed methodology to include culture-relevant items in the measurement of each of these model components allows researchers to capture the diverse explanations of health and illness behavior that might pertain in diverse populations. Researchers utilizing the model can achieve theory-based explanations of differences they observe by gender, race/ethnicity, social class, and sexual orientation. The Triandis model can provide studies to target variables for future intervention studies, as well as highlight areas for needed political action to equalize access to and delivery of nursing care.

Noreen C. Facione, RN, MSN, FNP
Doctoral Candidate
University of California, San Francisco
San Francisco, California

CULTURAL SENSITIVITY IN NURSING SCIENCE

What factors will improve the use of mammography in elderly Latina women? How can a cancer home care program serve a diverse urban population? What approach to prenatal services will most effectively decrease the number of low-birth-weight infants? How can human immunodeficiency virus/acquired immunodeficiency syndrome (HIV/AIDS) education programs and the use of condoms be promoted in drug-addicted, homeless individuals? To answer these and other questions, nurses have piloted, often successfully, grass roots intervention

The author thanks Drs. Afaf Meleis and William Holzemer, both of the University of California, San Francisco, School of Nursing, for their helpful comments.

This article was supported by doctoral training grants from the American Cancer Society and the University of California Regents.

Adv Nurs Sci 1993;15(3):49–58

projects designed to address gaps in primary prevention and health care delivery. However, rarely are these pilot projects grounded in theory. In the absence of a theoretical base to explain and predict likely outcomes, there is little to guide clinicians in the replication of pilot intervention strategies and much concern that the reported success of a project was perhaps overly dependent on the personalities of the expert clinicians involved in the pilot study. This article presents a well-developed theory with exceptional potential for culturally sensitive research investigations that is still productive of generalizable findings.

SOCIAL BEHAVIORAL THEORY APPLIED TO HEALTH AND ILLNESS BEHAVIOR

How a person might behave in response to an illness symptom or why an individual might find one treatment plan more acceptable than another are questions that defy answers when divorced from the personal, social, environmental, and health status context of the individual. This appreciation of the importance of all the diverse aspects of culture as key to the development of nursing knowledge and effective nursing care is certainly not a new perspective for either the nurse clinician or the nurse scientist.[1–9]

Acknowledging the complexity of human behavior and the range of cultural diversity within current American society, many researchers might despair of even the *possibility* of a culturally sensitive theoretical model to guide the study of health and illness behavior. However, nursing research is not for the faint of heart, and promising models do exist that challenge the nurse researcher to design studies to both guide clinical practice and provide directives for political action. It is not necessary to create these models "from the ground up." Social psychologists have provided a base of empirical inquiry that can be adapted to health and illness research. Some of these existing theoretical models offer more than others in terms of concept development, logic of structure, and utility for research in diverse cultures. The reader is referred to comparative analyses of the use of social behavioral theory for the study of health and illness and other more generic critiques.[10–18]

Researchers have most frequently used Rosenstock's Health Belief Model (HBM)[19] to examine perceptions of the seriousness of, susceptibility to, benefits of, and barriers to performing a given health or illness behavior. Survey instruments based on the HBM have typically been constructed to measure culture-neutral or Euro-American beliefs about health and illness behaviors and do not attempt to capture variation in beliefs that arise within culturally diverse groups. Rather than indicating a weakness within the HBM itself, this is perhaps a result of a research tradition that has (1) tended to ignore culture as a variable, (2) studied predominantly Caucasian groups, (3) designed across-culture rather than within-culture studies, and (4) tended to view many aspects of diversity as deviance rather than variance. As a result, behavioral studies utilizing the HBM frequently fail to examine powerful sociocultural factors such as poverty or religious beliefs that might be important to the behavioral outcome. Nurse researchers who use the HBM as a tool for studying health and illness behavior need to broaden the conceptualization of the HBM variables to accommodate the diversity of beliefs about health and illness behaviors that are present, particularly in marginalized patient populations.

TRIANDIS MODEL OF SOCIAL BEHAVIOR

One social-psychological model with superior promise for culturally sensitive research is the Triandis model of social behavior.[20,21] Beginning with the assumption that most behaviors that attract the interest of researchers are rational, reflective behaviors (rather than reflexive, automatic behaviors), the Triandis model builds on Kurt Lewin's motivational theory.[22] Arising from Triandis's research interest in diversity,[21,23-26] the model acknowledges cultural diversity as contributing to differences in behavior.

The box lists the variables included in the Triandis model along with their conceptual definitions. According to the model, the determinants of an individual's performing (or *not* performing) any given behavior (B) are one's intention (I) to perform (B), one's previous habit (H) of performing (B), relevant physiologic arousal (P) to perform (B), and the facilitating factors (F) in the environment that assist (or constrain) the performance of (B). The following equation represents the relationship between model variables as originally suggested by Triandis:

$$(B) = [w(I) + w(H)] \, (P) \times (F)$$

The w's are weights expressing individual differences. Triandis conceptualized (F) as being scaled between 0 and 1. When facilitating conditions are most favorable for (B) to occur, (F) = 1. When they are most unfavorable, (F) = 0. Similarly, (P) ranges from 0 to 1. When there is no arousal to perform (B), (P) = 0. When there is sufficient arousal to perform (B), (P) = 1. Researchers who have tested the Triandis model to study health and illness behaviors have chosen to express the relationship between variables somewhat differently. Montano,[27] for instance, gauged (F) with 7-point Likert scale items measuring familiarity with immunization procedures and access to the immunization site in his study of influenza vaccination behavior.

Although the (P) variable seems quite central to the prediction of (B) in Triandis' model, it has not been extensively developed, and studies testing the model frequently omit this variable. Lauver and Chang[28] deleted consideration of this variable in their study of seeking care for a breast cancer symptom, considering it to be redundant to the affect (A) variable. Montano[27] omitted discussion of the (P) variable, as did Valois et al[15] in their study of exercise intention. Adequate grounds for eliminating the (P) variable, considering how few tests of the complete Triandis model have been reported, remain to be established. In future model testing, nurse researchers might explore ways to operationalize (P) to capture

Triandis' Conceptual Definitions of Behavior, Behavioral Intention, and Six Predictor Variables Included in the Model

Behavior (B): The criterion behavior, also referred to as the "Act" by Triandis. The researcher is typically concerned with predicting the performance or nonperformance of (B).

Behavioral Intention (I): Instructions that individuals give to themselves to behave in certain ways. More specifically, the instruction to perform or not to perform (B). The researcher may also be concerned with predicting the likelihood of (I). Depending on the research question, the prediction of (I) may be a higher immediate priority than the prediction of (B).

Predictor Variables

Perceived Consequences (C): An individual's estimation of the certainty of the positive or negative consequences of performing or not performing (B).

Affect (A): The feelings associated by an individual with (B): joy, elation, pleasure, depression, disgust, displeasure, hate, fear, embarrassment, etc.

Social Factor (S): The individual's internalization of the referent group's subjective culture and specific interpersonal agreements that the individual has made with others regarding (B).

Physiologic Arousal (P): Either high drive to perform (B) or a situation that is relevant to the individual's values that may increase the probability of (B).

Habit Hierarchies (H): Situation behavior sequences that have become automatic so that they occur without self-instruction. (H) reflects both the individual's ability relative to performing (B) and past learning experience, such as rewards or punishments, associated with performing (B).

Facilitating Factors (F): These (F) factors may ultimately be the reason for (B) not being performed, even if the intention (I) is high, habits (H) are well established, and physiologic arousal (P) is optimal.

Triandis' sense of situational stimulus to action. Depending on the behavior in question, this variable might prove more or less critical. For instance, a measure of symptom characteristic or severity might be the appropriate indirect measure of (P) for a study of help-seeking behavior, or perhaps the (P) variable might be used to capture situation-specific influences in studies of substance abuse behavior. Creative exploration of this variable will answer the question of its importance to the model.

The investigators in the studies cited above typically used multiple regression analyses, as suggested by Triandis, to examine the predictive power of the model. Prediction, in this discussion, refers to explanation of shared variance in a regression analysis and as such is, strictly speaking, an associational relationship rather than predictive. The equation that correctly expresses a regression analyses of these predictor variables is:

$$(B) = w\,(I) + w\,(H) + w\,(F) + w\,(P)$$

A multiple regression model is also suggested to predict the intention (I) variable as a function of one's beliefs about the consequences (C) of performing (or not performing) the behavior, one's affect (A) toward the behavior, and the social influences (S) one experiences in relation to the behavior. Again, the regression weights (ws) are expressions of individual difference. This relationship is expressed in the equation:

$$(I) = w\,(C) + w\,(A) + w\,(S)$$

The Triandis variables typically are measured through the use of Likert style item scales or semantic differential scales. The scales are constructed with a balance between inclusion of all salient items and concern for responder burden. Scale totals are used as variable values for inclusion in the regression analysis.

Researchers are directed by Triandis to match model variable scales with the cultural context of the intended study population. When choosing or designing instruments to measure the model variables, the researcher must endeavor to exhaustively measure the salient, culturally relevant aspects of the variable that relate to whatever behavior is being studied. The operationalization of each model variable might be expected to differ depending on how the study population is defined in terms of gender, age, racial/ethnic group, or class. Theoretically, the amount of explained variance obtainable in a given investigation is directly related to the representation of salient aspects of each variable in the measurement tool(s). It can be seen that this model is structured to examine health and illness behavior *within* cultural groups rather than *across* cultural groups. The goal here is not to measure communalities between cultural groups that account for health and illness behavior, but rather to examine health and illness behavior in a context that will permit unique cultural differences to be discovered and analyzed for their power to predict the behavior under study.

CAPTURING CULTURE

In a forthcoming publication from the American Academy of Nursing (AAN),[9] cultural sensitivity in nursing care and nursing science is defined as an awareness of, and utilization of knowledge related to, ethnicity, culture, gender, or sexual orientation in explaining and understanding the situation and the responses of clients and their environments. In this context, culturally competent nursing care is similarly defined as care that is based on knowledge and theories that explain clients' responses and situations within the context of ethnicity, culture, gender, and sexual orientation.

Through these definitions the AAN highlights the need for theory to connect culture variables to behavioral outcomes in nursing research investigations. Theory-based models that clearly specify the interrelationships of cultural context variables and behavioral outcomes are needed to supply the framework for nursing science inquiry. Nurse scientists who aspire to culturally sensitive investigations of health and illness behavior need to utilize models that capture the uniqueness of diverse groups. Only then can subsequent intervention studies be expected to effectively produce desired health outcomes in today's culturally diverse society.

As an example of how Triandis's model might be used to examine a health-related behavior within a culturally sensitive context, consider how a study might be designed to examine the use of condoms for the prevention of transmission of HIV/AIDS in a population of Latina women ages 15 to 50. Items measuring consequential beliefs (C) would need to include beliefs about the potential threat of HIV infection, potential alienation or loss of a sexual partner, potential religious implications of contraception, and so forth. Items measuring social influences (S) would need to probe the perception of how well the use of condoms fit with a woman's self-concept, what behavior is mandated by the normative beliefs of significant others, and what perceived role constraints might be operative with respect to the use of condoms. Affect (A) items would need to probe the range of emotions associated with the actual behavior of using (purchasing, touching, applying, etc) condoms, the emotions associated with requesting her sexual partner use a condom, and the emotions elicited by religious norms. Items measuring the habit (H) variable might need to explore previous use of all types of contraception, as well as typical circumstances under which sexual intercourse occurs. Measurement of facilitating factors (F) in this case would include an assessment of the ease or difficulty of obtaining condoms, whether poverty or lack of personal financial resources was a factor, the ability to keep a condom in her possession in the event of sexual intercourse, and perhaps even to what extent the woman controls when and if sexual intercourse will occur. How might the physiologic arousal (P) variable be most meaningfully operationalized in relation to the use of a condom? Is (P) redundant to the affect (A) variable, as suggested by Lauver and Chang?[28] Or might this variable be used to capture additional situation-specific factors such as, for instance, familiar versus unfamiliar sexual partner, or sexual encounters at home versus in the workplace.

Other investigators designing such a study might have chosen to explore different or additional aspects of any of the above variables. This example is intended only as an exercise to suggest how the Triandis model might be used as a framework to design a survey investigation of an important health or illness behavior with sensitivity to the context of a particular cultural group. The fact that the nurse researcher may not be able to identify the culturally salient items that should be included in the survey is a testimony to how well or poorly we have done culturally sensitive research in the past on the particular health or illness behavior. If salient beliefs can only be speculated on (such was the case with the above example), then preliminary qualitative key informant interview or focus group work can be used to inform the structuring of a new instrument or the possible modification of an existing instrument. The subsequent empirical study can then be used to test the proposed relationships and to add support for the generalizability of small study reports to larger within-culture populations.

The richness of the Triandis model is readily apparent. Investigators utilizing this model will necessarily go beyond previous studies that merely reported demographic variable associations with less desirable health or illness behavior. Gender, age, race, class, and sexual orientation are not variables amenable to change. What is needed is an understanding of *why* these demographic descriptors might be associated with certain less desirable behaviors. Triandis's model identifies beliefs, social influences, feelings, habits, and resource gaps, all variables that can be targeted for change. More important, it specifies a methodology that customizes studies for the populations they target.

Research on women would be enriched by the examination of the influences included in Triandis's (S) variable: self-concept, social normative influences, and role constraints. Because more than 37 million Americans are currently without health insurance,[29] and because even the possession of health insurance is not synonymous with the affordability of health services, research on health and illness behavior must include measures of resource factors facilitating or constraining utilization behavior, the Triandis (F) variable. Through skillful operationalization of the (F) variable, the nurse scientist could hope to separate the effects of race or ethnic grouping from the effects of socioeconomic status in studies of health and illness behaviors. This design consideration is of paramount importance for scientists who wish to decrease the likelihood of attributing the behavioral outcomes arising from poverty to the factor of race. Such incorrect interpretations, common in the literature, only serve to further disadvantage racial or ethnic groups overly represented in the lower socioeconomic groups. To the extent that the (F) variable is found to explain significant variance in desired behavioral outcomes, clear political directives might emerge regarding the equalization of resources to address particular health care problems.

Because rarely, if ever, are health or illness behaviors entirely unique, the inclusion of experiential learning or habit formation (H) is a strength of the model. This is apparent when one considers investigations of health services utilization, preventive cancer screening behaviors, or substance abuse behavior. In the operationalization of the Triandis (H) variable, nurse researchers may select or design instruments to capture these context-specific considerations.

Harrell[30] reported that being treated without respect by staff was a strong influence on the utilization of prenatal services in a sample of black women. Haynes,[31] former director of the Drew Cancer Center in Los Angeles, reported that 43% of the blacks and Latinos in his setting felt that they had been treated curtly and without respect, a fact that constrained their help-seeking behavior. Studies of these groups' utilization of preventive health services that did not examine this aspect of the (H) variable might be expected to fail to explain much of the observed variance in their behavior.

CRITIQUE OF THE TRIANDIS MODEL

The Triandis model exhibits the linearity common to models that predate later insights on the recursive nature of cognitive processing. Critics of the model have suggested a more recursive modeling of directional relationships between Triandis model variables.[12,16] Previous learning from performing the given (or a similar) behavior might in this case be expected to influence one's consequential beliefs about the behavior (C), one's affect toward the behavior (A), one's perceptions of the social norm or one's role expectations in relation to the behavior (S), the formation of the habit of performing the behavior (H), and one's awareness of one's resources in relation to the behavior (F).

The recursivity of reflective judgment and decision making becomes particularly important when the concern is to predict the intention (I) to perform a given health or illness behavior rather than the behavior (B) itself. Rather than including only the (C), (A), and (S) variables to predict (I), the variables (H) and (F) are also included. The theoretical rationale for this maneuver is an acknowledgment that one's foreknowledge of available facilitating resources (F) and one's previous behavior (H) will affect one's intention to perform the behavior. Several groups of researchers utilizing the Triandis model to study illness behavior have assumed a more recursive model.[11,15,27,28] Other researchers have reported using Ajzen and Fishbein's theory of reasoned action,[32,33] with the addition of the Triandis model (A), (H), and/or (F) variables, effectively creating the Triandis model.[34–36]

The assumption of variable independence is somewhat problematic in the Triandis model. Miniard and Cohen[13] point out that in models of behavior that contain personal and social components, these components are not independent, and therefore such models cannot be used to measure the separate contributions of one's personal beliefs and one's social normative beliefs on behavior. If this is the researcher's task, an altogether different theoretical approach is perhaps warranted. However, this criticism does point to the likelihood of at least some degree of collinearity between (C) and (S) in the model and opens a discussion of multicollinearity between model variables in general. Hopefully, researchers using social behavioral models to guide regression analyses are interested in more than percentages of explained variance, important as that might be.

If the interest is rather to identify meaningful factors for future study or factors amenable to change for inclusion in future intervention studies, then investigators must examine the full regression model for all variables contributing significant variance and then examine each significant variable for the potential knowledge it can provide. For example, it would not be enough to report a finding such as, "The (F) variable contributed the most explained variance (25%) in attendance at prenatal clinics by black women in Detroit." To guide nursing interventions to improve attendance in prenatal clinics, it is necessary to report what *specific* differences in facilitating resources pertained between clinic attenders and nonattenders.

By now the demands placed on the researcher by the artful use of the Triandis model must be readily apparent. To achieve the goal of a well-designed, correctly interpreted, and culturally sensitive study, the nurse researcher or research team must be adept at study design, tool development, and data analysis. This might seem an exceedingly large demand, but it is certainly not beyond the expertise of nurse scientists concerned with high-quality, culturally sensitive research.

Survey instruments developed for Triandis model studies require validity and reliability assessment. Concurrent validity with other existing scales is usually problematic. Correlations between the developed scales and existing, culture-neutral scales might offer little insight as to the developed scales' true value to measure a culture-specific variable. Content validity is supported by developing and piloting the instrument with the assistance of same-population focus groups or key informants. Alpha coefficients of adequate magnitude, when the instrument is subsequently used in a study sample, will add support for the reliability of developed scales for use in other groups within the same cultural population. Any significant change in the new population to be studied theoretically requires some adaptation of the survey scales to address the new cultural diversity.

CONCLUSION

Nursing research currently demands research that can guide nursing care of the diverse peoples who make up the population of the United States and the world. Will a sexually transmitted disease (STD) education program be successful in a culturally diverse population? How does comorbidity affect behavior in response to cardiac pain in elderly women? In what ways do limitations of access to care influence help-seeking behavior in working Americans? How can basic health information be disseminated among a largely illiterate homeless population?

The list of questions for nursing research would appear to be endless. Sensitive and sophisticated approaches to finding the answers to these questions are within our reach. To improve early case finding, effective symptom management, and optimal health for persons with diseases such as cancer or HIV, nurses need knowledge of specific approaches that will foster optimal health behaviors for each intervention group. Culturally sensitive research should be the standard for all nurse researchers, whether individual nurse scientists or research teams collaborating to create the needed expertise, involved with human subject research. The Triandis model offers a theoretical framework, suggestions for instrument development, and guidance for congruence in data analysis. Through the use of the Triandis model, the nurse researcher can target variables for future intervention studies to guide clinical practice. By using the model to incorporate culturally specific situational factors, guidelines for political action to address gaps in health care access might also be provided. The Triandis model offers an exceptionally promising theoretical framework to reexamine familiar health and illness problems with renewed sensitivity to cultural diversity.

REFERENCES

1. Spector RE. *Cultural Diversity in Health and Illness.* 3rd ed. Norwalk, Conn: Appleton & Lange; 1991.
2. Clinton JH. Ethnicity: the development of an empirical construct for cross cultural research. *West J Nurs Res.* 1982;4:281–300.
3. Lipson JG, Meleis AI. Issues in health care of Middle Eastern patients. *West J Med.* 1983;139(6):854–861.
4. Stevens PE, Hall JM. Stigma, health beliefs and experiences with health care in lesbian women. *Image: J Nurs Schol.* 1988;20(2):69–73.
5. Thompson JL. Exploring gender and culture with Khmer refugee women: reflections on participatory feminist research. *Adv Nurs Sci.* 1991;13(3):30–48.
6. Funkhouser SW, Moser DK. Is health care racist? *Adv Nurs Sci.* 1990;12(2):47–55.
7. Jemmott LS, Jemmott JB. Applying the theory of reasoned action to AIDS risk behavior: condom use among black women. *Nurs Res.* 1991;40(4):228–234.
8. Meleis AI, Lipson JG, Paul SM. Ethnicity and health among five Middle Eastern immigrant groups. *Nurs Res.* 1992;41(2):98–103.
9. Expert Panel on Culturally Competent Health Care. AAN expert panel report: culturally competent health care. *Nurs Outlook.* 1992;40:277–283.
10. Wallston BS, Wallston KA. Social psychological models of health behavior: an examination and integration. In: Baum A, Taylor SE, Singer JE, eds. *Handbook of Psychology and Health.* Vol 4. Hillsdale, NJ: Lawrence Erlbaum; 1984.
11. Godin G. Importance of the emotional aspect of attitude to predict intention. *Psychol Rep.* 1987;61:719–723.
12. Liska AE. A critical examination of the causal structure of the Fishbein/Ajzen attitude-behavior model. *Soc Sci Q.* 1984;47(1):61–74.
13. Miniard PW, Cohen JB. An examination of the Fishbein-Ajzen behavioral-intentions model's concepts and measures. *J Exper Soc Psychol.* 1981;17:309–339.
14. Sheppard BH, Hartwick J, Warshaw PR. The theory of reasoned action: a meta-analysis of past research with recommendations for modifications and future research. *J Consumer Res.* 1988;15:325–343.
15. Valois P, Desharnais R, Godin G. A comparison of the Fishbein and Ajzen and the Triandis attitudinal models for the prediction of exercise intention and behavior. *J Behav Med.* 1988;11(5):459–472.
16. Warshaw PR, Davis FD. Disentangling behavioral intention and behavioral expectation. *J Exper Soc Psychol.* 1985;21:213–228.
17. Bagozzi RP, Yi Y. The degree of intention formation as a moderator of the attitude-behavior relationship. *Soc Psychol Q.* 1989;52(4):266–279.

18. Bentler PM, Speckart G. Models of attitude-behavior relations. *Psychol Rev.* 1979;86(5):452–464.
19. Rosenstock IM. Why people use health services. *Milbank Mem Fund Q.* 1966;44(suppl):94–123.
20. Triandis HC. *Interpersonal Behavior.* Monterey, Calif: Brooks/Cole; 1977.
21. Triandis HC. Values, attitudes, and interpersonal behavior. In: Howe HE, ed. *Beliefs, Attitudes, and Values: Nebraska Symposium on Motivation.* Lincoln, Neb: University of Nebraska; 1980.
22. Lewin K. *A Dynamic Theory of Personality: Selected Papers.* New York, NY: McGraw Hill; 1935.
23. Triandis HC. *The Analysis of Subjective Culture.* New York, NY: John Wiley; 1972.
24. Triandis HC. *Variations in Black and White Perceptions of the Social Environment.* Champaign, Ill: University of Illinois; 1976.
25. Davidson AR, Jaccard JJ, Triandis HC, Morales ML, Dias-Guerrero R. Cross-cultural model testing: toward a solution of the etic-emic dilemma. *Int J Psychol.* 1976;11(1):1–13.
26. Davidson AR, Thomson E. Cross-cultural studies of attitudes and beliefs. In: Triandis H, Brislin RW, eds. *Handbook of Cross-Cultural Psychology.* Vol 5. Boston, Mass: Allyn & Bacon; 1980.
27. Montano DE. Predicting and understanding influenza vaccination behavior. *Med Care.* 1986;24(5):438–453.
28. Lauver D, Chang A. Testing theoretical explanations of intentions to seek care for a breast cancer symptom. *J Appl Soc Psychol.* 1991;21(17):1,440–1,458.
29. Butler PA. *Too Poor to be Sick: Access to Medical Care for the Uninsured.* Washington, DC: American Public Health Association; 1988.
30. Harrell SB. The meaning of prenatal care to African American women. Presented at the Sixth National Black Nurses Symposium; February, 1992; University of California, San Francisco, Calif.
31. Haynes MA. Making cancer prevention effective for African-Americans. *Stat Bull.* 1991;72(2):18–22.
32. Ajzen I, Fishbein M. *Understanding Attitudes and Predicting Social Behavior.* Englewood Cliffs, NJ: Prentice-Hall; 1980.
33. Fishbein M. A theory of reasoned action: some applications and implications. In: Howe HE, ed. *Beliefs, Attitudes, and Values: Nebraska Symposium on Motivation.* Lincoln, Neb: University of Nebraska; 1980.
34. Lierman LM, Kaspryzk D, Benoliel JQ. Understanding adherence to breast self-examination in older women. *West J Nurs Res.* 1991;13(1):46–66.
35. Montano DE, Taplin SH. A test of an expanded theory of reasoned action to predict mammography participation. *Soc Sci Med.* 1991;32(6):733–741.
36. Timko C. Seeking medical care for a breast cancer symptom: determinants of intentions to engage in prompt or delay behavior. *Health Psychol.* 1987;6(4):305–328.

Index